AN INTRODUCTION TO
THE MEDIEVAL BIBLE

The Middle Ages spanned the period between two watersheds in the history of the biblical text: Jerome's Latin translation circa 405 and Gutenberg's first printed version in 1455. The Bible was arguably the most influential book during this time, affecting spiritual and intellectual life, popular devotion, theology, political structures, art, and architecture. In an account that is sensitive to the religiously diverse world of the Middle Ages, Frans van Liere offers here an accessible introduction to the study of the Bible in this period. Discussion of the material evidence – the Bible as a book – complements an in-depth examination of concepts such as lay literacy and book culture. This introduction to the medieval Bible includes a thorough treatment of the principles of medieval hermeneutics, and a discussion of the formation of the Latin Bible text and its canon. It will be a useful starting point for all those engaged in medieval and biblical studies.

Frans van Liere studied theology and medieval studies at the University of Groningen, the Netherlands, and is Professor of History at Calvin College. His most recent publications include *Andrew of Saint Victor, Commentary on Samuel and Kings* (2009), and *Interpretation of Scripture: Theory* (Victorine Texts in Translation), vol. 3 (coedited with Franklin Harkins, 2012).

AN INTRODUCTION TO THE MEDIEVAL BIBLE

FRANS VAN LIERE
Calvin College

CAMBRIDGE
UNIVERSITY PRESS

CAMBRIDGE
UNIVERSITY PRESS

32 Avenue of the Americas, New York NY 10013-2473, USA

Cambridge University Press is part of the University of Cambridge.

It furthers the University's mission by disseminating knowledge in the pursuit of education, learning and research at the highest international levels of excellence.

www.cambridge.org
Information on this title: www.cambridge.org/9780521684606

© Frans van Liere 2014

This publication is in copyright. Subject to statutory exception and to the provisions of relevant collective licensing agreements, no reproduction of any part may take place without the written permission of Cambridge University Press.

First published 2014

A catalogue record for this publication is available from the British Library

Library of Congress Cataloguing in Publication data
Liere, Franciscus A. van (Franciscus Anastasius), 1964–
An introduction to the medieval Bible / Frans van Liere, Calvin College.
pages   cm. – (Introduction to religion)
Includes bibliographical references and index.
ISBN 978-0-521-86578-4 (hardback) – ISBN 978-0-521-68460-6 (pbk.)
1. Bible. Latin – History.   2. Bible. Latin – Criticism, interpretation, etc. – History – Middle Ages, 600–1500.   3. Literature, Medieval – History and criticism.   I. Title.
BS68.L54   2013
220.09′02–dc23   2013029649

ISBN 978-0-521-86578-4 Hardback
ISBN 978-0-521-68460-6 Paperback

Cambridge University Press has no responsibility for the persistence or accuracy of URLs for external or third-party internet websites referred to in this publication, and does not guarantee that any content on such websites is, or will remain, accurate or appropriate.

To the memory of my parents

Contents

vii

Preface

The influence of the Bible in the Middle Ages was enormous. Whether read in private devotions, prayed in communal liturgy, commented on in classroom lectures, expounded on in sermons, painted on church walls, or sculpted in cathedral portals, its influence shaped not only moral and spiritual life but also intellectual, aesthetic, and social life. One cannot understand the medieval world without appreciating the scope of medieval people's engagement with biblical stories, characters, and images. Students of medieval history and religion are the primary intended audience for this book. It aims to provide them with a basic understanding of the medieval Bible, the formation and transmission of its text, and its traditions of interpretation. Although there are many introductions and handbooks to the Bible, most of these follow the historico-critical method, a tradition of biblical interpretation that has its origin in the Enlightenment. This method builds on the assumption that in order to retrieve the meaning of a text, we need first to establish its "original" form, study this within its historical context, and analyze what the author tried to convey to his intended audience. Thus, textbook introductions to the Bible tend to pay ample attention to biblical archaeology and to the historical context of the authors, editors, and redactors of the Hebrew and Greek texts. They typically offer linguistic analysis of the text and perhaps an historical survey of its transmission, including the formation of the canon. But they usually stop there. If they do include a history of biblical scholarship and interpretation, this usually starts with the Renaissance and Reformation. The Middle Ages are thus obscured from view, although the rich body of medieval biblical illustrations is often freely exploited for its aesthetic value.

How deeply ingrained this tradition is in today's thinking was made clear to me by a student who once confessed, "I am not all that interested in how medieval people understood the Bible. What matters more to me is how God wants it to be understood." The tacit assumption was, of course, that medieval authors have nothing valuable to say about the latter. The idea that it is possible to read the Bible "just what it says,"[1] not influenced by any interpretive tradition, seems a fallacy, to say nothing of the equation of that interpretation with God's intended meaning. It is unfortunate banalization of the Protestant notion of the "sufficiency of Scripture," which holds that "whatsoever man ought to believe unto salvation is sufficiently taught" in Scripture.[2] In the sixteenth century, reformers such as Martin Luther challenged the authority of the Church to interpret the Bible, and claimed that it spoke to the believer without an intermediate authoritative tradition of interpretation. The Calvinist *Belgic Confession* likewise warns not to "consider custom, or the great multitude, or antiquity, or succession of times and persons, or councils, decrees and statutes, as of equal value with the truth of God."[3] Despite their huge debt to the achievement of medieval biblical scholarship, the Reformers regarded the contribution of these historical interpreters as irrelevant at best, and often pernicious. However, while affirming the Reformers' notion of the primacy of Scripture, one may still acknowledge that every historical period has its own traditions of interpretation that can offer some valuable insights into the deeper meanings of an ancient religious text. Luther himself tacitly acknowledged this when he made ample use of the works of the fourteenth-century Franciscan Nicholas of Lyra in his translation of the Bible into German.

Considering the neglect that medieval exegetes often suffered, especially within the Protestant tradition, I came to envision an additional audience for this book: biblical scholars and students who want to rediscover the rich tradition of medieval biblical interpretation as something still relevant to our understanding of the Bible today. This book was thus written from the conviction that the Bible is not just a historical text dating from before the first century C.E. but a dynamic tradition that gained its meaning within the life of Church and Synagogue over a period of several millennia.

This book started as an undergraduate course, taught at Calvin College, on the topic of "The Bible in the Middle Ages." The inspiration for this course came from one I had taken many years before, with my teacher and mentor, Prof. Dr. L. J. Engels, which came to shape my scholarly career. When I prepared to teach this course, however, I found that it was almost impossible to find a suitable textbook. The work that had most

---

[1] Kugel, *Traditions of the Bible*, xviii.
[2] *The Belgic Confession*, art. 7. In *Historical Creeds and Confessions*, 75.
[3] Ibid.

influenced my own study of this subject, Beryl Smalley's *The Study of the Bible in the Middle Ages*, was not only more than half a century old, but it was also written for an academic audience and thus not very accessible to undergraduates. Kate Brett, then managing editor of the religion division of Cambridge University Press, persuaded me to write such an introduction myself. More than seven years later, this suggestion has come to fruition.

The title of the book perhaps promises more than is offered here. This book mainly concentrates on the Latin Bible in the west during the Middle Ages. One chapter discusses bibles in the vernacular. In western Europe prior to the sixteenth century, these were most often translated directly from the Latin. It was regrettable but necessary to exclude the medieval Greek and Hebrew traditions. Jewish exegetical traditions are discussed here chiefly in relation to their influence on Christian traditions. Excellent introductions to the Hebrew Bible and Jewish exegetical traditions can be found in the essays by Barry Walfish and Jordan Penkover, in the *Jewish Study Bible*. Because this book was written for a general audience, I have limited footnotes to direct citations only. At the end of each chapter, a short list of chiefly English-language works aims to provide orientation for research in each particular field. The bibliography at the end of the book not only provides the full titles of all works cited in the footnotes but also acknowledges some of the scholarly works that were used but not cited.

The citations from non-English sources are generally my own translation, unless otherwise noted. Even where I have followed existing translations, however, I have sometimes taken the liberty of adapting them by comparing them to the original. Biblical quotations are generally taken from the New Revised Standard Version, or, where a closer proximity to the Latin version was required, the Douay-Rheims version. Throughout the book, I generally use the modern English names of biblical books (thus Chronicles instead of Paralipomenon, Samuel and Kings rather than Regum, and Revelation rather than Apocalypse), but Appendix B provides a concordance of variant names for Bible books. Most titles of Latin works are given in English, providing a first-time translation in parentheses or in the footnote. For works that are best known by their Latin names (such as the *Summa theologica* or the *Historia scholastica*), the Latin has been retained although an English translation is given. Medieval authors are referred to by their English names; thus, "Jerome" is used rather than "Hieronymus" and "Jacob of Varazzo" rather than "Jacobus de Voragine" or "Jacopo da Varazzo." In the bibliography and index, authors living before 1500 are generally listed by their first names rather than their nicknames, toponyms, or patronyms. If an exception is made, cross-references are provided. Bible verses, and especially Psalms, are cited according to their modern chapter and verse; where necessary, the Vulgate numbering is indicated with "Vulg." Appendix B provides a brief comparison between modern and Vulgate Psalm numbers.

I wish to thank the staff of the various libraries whose collections I was permitted to visit and use: Corpus Christi and Trinity College in Cambridge; Cambridge University Library; the Newberry Library in Chicago; the Biblioteca Medicea Laurenziana and Biblioteca Nazionale in Florence; the British Library in London; the Bodleian Library in Oxford; Salamanca University Library; the Vatican Library; the Waldo Library of Western Michigan University in Kalamazoo; and York Minster Library. For permission to use images from their collections, I wish to thank the staff of the Pierpont Morgan Library in New York, the Scheide Library in Princeton, Trinity College Library in Cambridge, the Bibliotheca Laurenziana, the British Library, the Metropolitan Museum in New York, and Hekman Library of Calvin College.

Special gratitude is due to those who read chapters and parts of this book, offered valuable feedback, and saved me from making embarrassing mistakes, especially Bert Roest, Laura Light, Celia Chazelle, Suzan Folkerts, Margriet Hoogvliet, Derek Krueger, Ittai Weinryb, Mayke de Jong, T. Michael Ladd, Yitzhak Hen, and the anonymous reviewer for Cambridge University Press. I especially wish to thank Ann Matter for her continuous support and encouragement of this project. The inspiration for many of the topics covered in this book came from the sessions of the Society for the Study of the Bible in the Middle Ages, in Kalamazoo and Leeds, and I wish to thank my colleagues for all that I learned at these sessions. My debt to them goes beyond footnotes. Colleagues in the History Department at Calvin College and the Institute for Advanced Study in Princeton provided a stimulating and supportive environment that allowed me to write this book. I am grateful to the students at Calvin College who have taken this course with me and who helped shape the contents of this book, and to Kate Brett and Anna Lowe, my editors at Cambridge University Press, for their patience and encouragement. The index was compiled by Lisa Eary, with help from Jenna Hunt. Further, I wish to thank the Board of Trustees of Calvin College, for granting a research fellowship and a sabbatical that allowed me to complete this work; the Calvin Center for Christian Scholarship for funding bibliographical research; and the Institute for Advanced Study, especially Dan Shapiro and Agnes Guld, for funding the research time there that made it possible to finish this book. My greatest debt is to my wife, Kate Elliot van Liere, who not only supported me morally and intellectually throughout the writing of this book but was also my most critical reader and the best editor for whom anyone could wish.

Princeton, Easter 2013
Frans van Liere

CHAPTER I

Introduction

For a long time, even in the scholarly world, the history of the Bible in the Middle Ages was thought to be a field that held little interest except for a small group of specialists. This began to change shortly after World War II, with three important, almost simultaneous publications: in 1946, Ceslas Spicq published his *Esquisse d'une histoire de l'exégèse latine au Moyen Âge* (*Sketch of a History of Latin Exegesis in the Middle Ages*), a concise survey of medieval biblical exegesis. Spicq's Esquisse was almost exclusively based on a survey of the texts he found in Jean-Paul Migne's *Patrologia Latina*, a comprehensive printed edition of Latin patristic and medieval church writers from Tertullian (second century C.E.) to Innocent III (1215). For the period after the latter, Spicq limited himself to the few authors whose work was edited, while providing a handlist of authors whose work was available in manuscript only. In 1952, Beryl Smalley published her *Study of the Bible in the Middle Ages*, an epoch-making work, which showed that serious textual biblical studies began not with the Enlightenment but much earlier, in the Carolingian period, and reached an intellectual peak in the twelfth century. In contrast to Spicq, Smalley's work ventured into the vast array of unprinted texts in medieval collections, uncovering sometimes surprising aspects of medieval biblical scholarship and putting half-forgotten authors, such as Andrew of Saint Victor, back into the limelight. Like Spicq, however, Smalley left the work of the fourteenth- and fifteenth-century exegetes largely unexplored. Between 1959 and 1964, Henri de Lubac published his magisterial four-volume *Exégèse médiévale. Les quatre sens de l'écriture* (*Medieval Exegesis. The Four Senses of Scripture*), in which he demonstrated that the rich spiritual tradition of medieval exegesis had relevance for twentieth-century theology. In fact, Lubac argued, modern theology might have omitted an essential Christian element by discarding the patristic and medieval traditions of interpretation and one-sidedly embracing the Enlightenment historical-critical method. Since then, medieval exegesis

I

has been a subject of serious scholarly attention and reappreciation. This reappreciation resulted in the publication of scholarly compendia: the second volume of the *Cambridge History of the Bible* (1969), the fourth volume of the French series *Bible de tous les temps* (*Bible of all Times*, 1984), the Italian *La Bibbia nel Medioevo* (*The Bible in the Middle Ages*, 1996), the massive multiauthor handbook *Hebrew Bible/Old Testament* (1996), and, most recently, the second volume of the *New Cambridge History of the Bible* (2011), which incorporated much of the scholarly progress made since the publication of the first Cambridge History.

SOME MISCONCEPTIONS

Much of this scholarship has not been readily available for undergraduate coursework, however. Partly, this may be due to departmental divisions: Bible and religion departments often pay little attention to the reception of the Bible whereas courses in history departments are wont to overlook the Bible as a subject for historical research. Interested students seeking to educate themselves via the Web often find themselves surrounded by religiously motivated misinformation. The topic of the medieval vernacular Bible is especially prone to anti-Catholic sentiment. Statements such as the following are still common in popular literature and on Web sites:

The Roman Catholic Church dominated religious life in Western Europe during the bulk of the medieval period, and it tightly controlled the availability of the Holy Bible. . . . The Papacy was officially opposed to the production and the translation of the Holy Bible in the vernacular languages, especially in the latter part of the medieval period.[1]

Access to the Bible was restricted to clerics, it is assumed here, because they were the only ones who could read Latin, or who could read at all. The laity was ignorant of the contents of the Bible and had to satisfy itself with the legends and stories told by the clergy until Luther first translated the Bible into the language of the people. Alongside the myth that the clergy monopolized the Bible, it is also still often taught that medieval exegesis contributed little to the serious study of scripture. Sixteenth-century reformers rejected the tradition of medieval exegesis and biblical scholarship, maintaining that its spiritual or allegorical interpretation helped

[1] Barry Val, "The Bible in the Middle Ages," online at suite101.com/article/the-bible-in-the-middle-ages-a112611.

to obscure the "true" meaning of the original text. In the words of John Selden, medieval biblical commentaries were "excellent instruments for the advancement of ignorance and laziness."[2] In this view, the "real" history of the Bible was that of the Greek and Hebrew text of that Bible and of its recovery in the Renaissance. Thus, the long millennium from circa 400 A.D., when the scriptures were translated into an imperfect Latin derivative of the "original" text, to circa 1500, when the first vernacular translations directly from the Greek and Hebrew began to appearing, was not deemed worthy of serious investigation.

This book aims to offer a more positive assessment of the medieval period of biblical studies. It concentrates on four main areas: first, the history of the Bible as a material object – whether a scroll, a codex, or a collection of such objects. The Middle Ages constituted an important period in the formation of the Bible as a book in a physical sense. The modern conception of the Bible, as a single volume of portable size containing all of the Old and New Testaments, is essentially a medieval invention. We will see that this changing physical shape of the Bible deeply influenced medieval notions about the biblical canon and scriptural authority. The second area is the history of the Bible as a written text, and its transmission by repeated copying, and the efforts medieval scholars made to establish a "correct" Latin Bible text to counteract the textual corruption that had resulted from this transmission. The third area is the history of the interpretation of this text, which often has been dismissed as derivative and irrelevant to modern theology. That it was neither will become clear in this volume. The final area discussed in this book is the diffusion of the biblical text and its influence on broader culture. Contrary to the popular myth, ordinary Christians did have access to the contents of the Bible, through numerous channels. Vernacular translations of the Bible did exist in the Middle Ages. However, reading Scripture in one's own language was far from the only way that medieval people came into contact with the contents of the Bible, for the medieval world was much more visual and oral in character than our own. Thus, the biblical dimensions of liturgy, sermons, literature, and visual art are also considered. Before beginning to examine each of these four areas, however, it will be helpful to define the term *Middle Ages* more precisely and to consider what makes this millennium-long period a distinctive one in the cultural history of Christian learning.

---

[2] Selden, *The Historie of Tithes*, ii. Selden was referring to medieval biblical commentaries known as Postills, which are discussed in Chapter 6.

THE MIDDLE AGES: SOME LANDMARKS

The Middle Ages are customarily understood to mean the millennium between the collapse of the Roman Empire (a gradual process which took place mainly over the course of the fifth century), and the fifteenth century, in which the intellectual movement of the Renaissance and profound demographic changes connected to the expansion of Europe combined to usher in the early modern age. In the history of the Bible, this period corresponds quite conveniently (and coincidentally) with two significant events: Jerome's completion of his final Latin translation of the Bible circa 405, and Gutenberg's production of the first printed bible in 1455. Both of these events were watersheds in the history of the biblical text, because for most of the interval between them, Jerome's Latin version of the Bible, which became known as the *Vulgata* or Vulgate, was the dominant biblical text. Although it existed for several centuries alongside other, older, translations, for most of the medieval millennium Jerome's Vulgate was, in a way, *the* medieval Bible, as the name "Vulgate" (meaning "the common one") suggests. Modern observers generally consider Gutenberg's achievement to have marked the beginning of a new era, but in the history of biblical scholarship, it makes more sense to see him as bringing the medieval period to its fruition; in making Jerome's Latin Bible available in large quantities, he accomplished what medieval scribes had been aiming to do for at least 150 years. This also had unforeseen consequences, however, that would usher in radical changes in the way scholars approached the Bible: by making the text of Jerome's Bible more widely available than ever before, printing spurred biblical scholarship on to a new level. Within a century of its publication, Gutenberg's printed version would come under criticism for its many faulty readings, which the unprecedented quantities of identical texts made more visible than they had been in the era of manuscripts. The first official critical revision of the Vulgate text was printed in 1590. At the same time, Renaissance and Reformation scholarship was putting increasing emphasis on the study of the Hebrew and Greek originals on which the Latin Bible was based. Vernacular translations of the Hebrew and Greek text began to appear, claiming equal authority with the Latin text, and eventually greater authority, since they were based on the supposed "original text," that is, the Hebrew and Greek, rather than the Latin Bible. Barely a century after Gutenberg's invention, the millennium-long dominance of the Latin Bible had come to an end.

The dominance of the Vulgate does not mean that the Middle Ages was a uniform period or that all medieval bibles were identical, however.

There was immense diversity in the physical appearance and contents of medieval bibles, and in the identity and aims of the people who produced, read, and interpreted them. As an introduction to this diversity, and to the some of the historical developments that account for it, let us consider here two different bibles that represent two very different historical moments between Jerome and Gutenberg. This also allows us to consider some of the important roles that bibles played in medieval culture, as bridges between different parts of Christendom, as markers of identity, as gifts, and as expressions of orthodoxy. And it will help us understand some of the changes that occurred in these respects, across the centuries that compose the medieval era.

The first example, the so-called Codex Amiatinus, represents the oldest surviving complete Latin Bible.[3] Complete bibles in one volume were a rarity in the Early Middle Ages. For example, most of the (often beautifully illuminated) "bibles" we so admire from this period, such as the Book of Kells, the Book of Durrow, or the Lindisfarne Gospels, are Gospel books, not complete bibles.[4] The Codex Amiatinus was produced in England around 700 C.E., at Wearmouth-Jarrow, a joint monastery that was one of the principal centers of learning in northern Europe. It was created as a means to confirm the links between the young English church and the church of Rome. Christianity had first been introduced into the British Isles in the fourth century, when the region was still under Roman rule, but successive waves of evangelization produced conflicting Christian traditions in England. From the fifth century on, England was ruled by Anglo-Saxon chieftains, who were pagans, but remnants of the Christian Church survived, especially among the British. In 596, Pope Gregory the Great (Gregory I) sent the monk Augustine to preach to the Anglo-Saxons and revitalize Christianity in England. Augustine and his monks were at first so daunted by the prospect of preaching the Gospel to a faraway people, whose tongue they did not even understand, that they grew discouraged before completing the journey and tried to return to Rome. But Gregory sent them on their way again, and they eventually established a mission in Kent, in the south of England, and the monk Augustine became the first archbishop of Canterbury. The Amiatinus was an important testimony to the special ties that the English church felt with its mother church in Rome.

---

[3] See Photos 1 and 2.
[4] The Lindisfarne Gospels can be viewed online at http://www.bl.uk/onlinegallery/sacredtexts/ ttpbooks.html and the Book of Kells at http://digitalcollections.tcd.ie/home/index.php.

Photo 1. Portrait of Ezra, seated in front of a classical *armarium* (book case), holding a Bible in nine volumes. The inscription reads "After the sacred books were burned in the hostile carnage, Ezra restored the work out of zeal for God." Codex Amiatinus 1, fol. 4r/5r. Photo (c) Biblioteca Medicea Laurenziana, Florence. By permission of the Ministerio per i Beni e le Attività Culturali. Further reproduction by any means is prohibited.

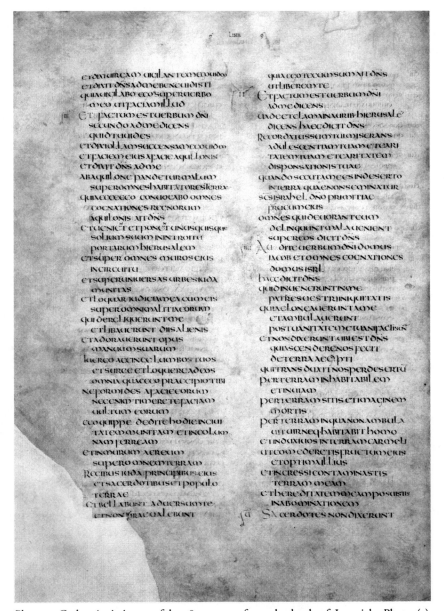

Photo 2. Codex Amiatinus 1, fol. 538v, a page from the book of Jeremiah. Photo (c) Biblioteca Medicea Laurenziana, Florence. By permission of the Ministerio per i Beni e le Attività Culturali. Further reproduction by any means is prohibited.

An important watershed for the Roman missions in England was the conversion of Edwin, the Anglo-Saxon king of Northumbria, in 627. Under his successors, several monasteries with ties to Augustine's Canterbury, alongside monasteries founded out of Iona, in Scotland, were established in the north of England. Wearmouth was one of these. Its first abbot was Benedict Biscop (d. 690), a Northumbrian nobleman who, after his conversion, maintained close ties to Rome. In the course of his life, he visited Rome no less than five times, each time bringing back with him stacks of books "on all subjects of divine learning," sacred images, and relics to supply the still young English church with needed spiritual treasures. On returning from his third journey to Rome, in 682, Abbot Benedict visited the court of King Egfrid, one of Edwin's successors, and showed him the bibles and relics he had brought with him from Rome. Egfrid, himself a recent convert, was well disposed toward the young church in his kingdom and granted Benedict permission to build a new monastery at Jarrow, close to Wearmouth. Benedict's companion on one of his earlier Rome journeys, Ceolfrid, became its first abbot, and after the death of Benedict, he became abbot of both monasteries. The two monasteries continued to cooperate closely. The scholar the Venerable Bede (ca. 673–735), Jarrow's most famous resident, who later recorded the lives of Benedict and Ceolfrid, described them as "a single monastery of the blessed apostles Peter and Paul, situated in two different places."[5]

Ceolfrid, no less eager than Benedict to promote learning at Jarrow and Wearmouth, doubled the size of the library of both monasteries. The double monastery housed not only a library but also a scriptorium, where monks labored in copying bibles. Ceolfrid had brought back a large one-volume copy of the Bible from his Roman journey. Under his direction, they copied three new bibles, modeled after this bible, which may have been among the first in the England to contain the complete "new translation" made by Jerome (ca. 341–420).[6] We do not quite know why Ceolfrid preferred the new translation. Was it more "Roman," or did he consider the text to be more reliable, or more readable? Or was Jerome's new translation already so widely used by the early eighth century that the decision to use it was not particularly innovative? Because of lack of evidence, answers to these questions are hard to come by. In any case, Ceolfrid's decision was one step in making Jerome's translation the dominant Bible text in western Europe.

---

[5] Bede, *Historia Abbatum*, 2: 15, ed. Plummer, 379.
[6] See also chapter 2, note 11.

The new bibles did not look at all like any of the books commonly produced in England at the time, such as the Book of Durrow. Their script and layout closely followed its sixth-century Italian late classical model to the extent that, until the nineteenth century, scholars mistook the Amiatinus for a bible of Italian provenance. Only fragments remain of the other bibles,[7] and the Codex Amiatinus today is the oldest extant complete copy of Jerome's Vulgate translation.

Ceolfrid must have been proud of his achievement. Two of the copies were for the use of the two monasteries, but the third he carried with him as a gift to Pope Gregory II, when toward the end of his life he set out to revisit the holy city. It was a precious gift; an estimated 500 sheep were needed to produce parchment for the Codex Amiatinus alone. This present to the pope was meant as a vivid proof of the energy of the young English church. By sending back to Rome a complete copy of the Bible, beautifully illuminated, and written in the best tradition of late antique paleography, the monks at Wearmouth-Jarrow were showing the pope the vitality of the recent mission and acknowledging the great debt that the English Church owed to the initiative of the bishops of Rome, the successors of the apostles Peter and Paul, the same to whom the monasteries of Wearmouth and Jarrow were dedicated.

Ceolfrid never made it all the way to Rome; he died on the way in Langres in France, "among people who did not speak his tongue."[8] The bible he carried with him was brought to Rome, however, and remained there until some time in the eighth century, when it became a gift again. The name of the original giver, "Ceolfrid abbot of the Angles," on the first folio was erased and replaced by "Peter, bishop of the Lombards," and the book was presented to the newly founded abbey of San Salvatore on Monte Amiata in Tuscany, where it stayed, until the eighteenth century. It was brought to Rome briefly in 1587, when it was used as a reference text for a newly authorized Latin Bible edition, the Sixto-Clementine edition of the Vulgate. In the eighteenth century, it was brought to the Biblioteca Laurenziana in Florence, where it remains today.

The second bible is a far less unique specimen than the Amiatinus. It is a northern French bible from the thirteenth century, probably produced in

---

[7] Today in the British Library, MS Add. 45,025 and MS Add. 37,777. It is very likely that both fragments are from the same codex (dubbed the "Ceolfrid Bible") whereas nothing remains of the third.

[8] Bede, *Historia Abbatum*, 2: 21, ed. Plummer, 386.

Paris around 1240 or 1250.[9] This bible is much smaller than the Amiatinus (142 × 94 mm against the Amiatinus's 505 × 340 mm), and the pages are made of extremely thin and fine vellum, with the text written in a minute hand. Like the Codex Amiatinus, it contains the entire text of the Bible in one volume, a phenomenon that, by the thirteenth century, had become much more common. Although the contents differed somewhat from that of the Amiatinus, it too contained the Vulgate translation of Jerome. By the time this bible was written, literacy and book possession had become much more common, and bibles were starting to be copied in great numbers. They were written by professional scribes and sold by lay booksellers. Because Paris was the most active center of production for these mass-market bibles, they are often called "Paris bibles." In modern European libraries, hundreds of similar bibles can be found. This bible was most likely never used by a monastic community, but was probably the individual possession of a university master, possibly a Franciscan or Dominican friar. Although we do not know who initially owned it, we know something about its later history, thanks to an inscription on its flyleaf, which reveals that in 1563, the Dominican Giovanni of Marssano gave it as a present to the bishop of Tortosa, Martín de Córdova y Mendoza. The occasion for the gift was the closing of the Council of Trent, the lengthy council in which the sixteenth-century Catholic Church discussed its response to the Protestant Reformation.

It was fitting that a thirteenth-century copy of the Vulgate Bible should serve as a gift from one delegate to another at Trent, where the question of biblical authority and the status of the Vulgate Bible were debated extensively. In 1545, a generation after Martin Luther's attack on the Catholic Church ushered in one of the most severe crises in the history of the western church, cardinals from all over Europe convened in a general council in the northern Italian city of Trent, to discuss the reforms necessary to see the Church through the crisis Luther had caused. The Bible was at the heart of the Reformation conflict. Luther had translated the Bible from the Hebrew and Greek into German and had declared that Church tradition and hierarchy should no longer be recognized as a source of authority in the Christian Church, but only Scripture (*sola scriptura*). By translating it into German, Luther had implicitly declared that its interpretation

---

[9] Until recently, this bible was in the private collections of Arthur Haddaway in Texas and the Boahlen Collection in Berne. See University of Texas, *Gothic and Renaissance Illuminated Manuscripts*, 14. It was offered for sale by the gallery Les Enluminures, Paris and Chicago, http://www.lesenluminures. com/, in 2007 and is currently in a private collection. All information presented here, including the ownership inscription, is derived from the Web site of Les Enluminures. See Photos 3 and 4.

Photo 3. The first page of a Paris bible, containing Jerome's preface to the Pentateuch. The miniature depicts a writing figure, possibly Jerome. Paris Bible, private collection, fol. 1r. Photo (c) Les enluminures, Chicago, New York, Paris.

was no longer a prerogative of the ordained priesthood, but of all believers. For the Catholic cardinals who opposed Luther's movement, it was now imperative to define the exact boundaries of biblical authority within the Church. This required determining not just who had interpretative authority, but also what "the Bible" meant. Was the authoritative Bible the Hebrew and Greek Bible? Or Jerome's Latin translation? And what books exactly belonged within it? And what guarantee was there that its text was without error? The Council of Trent dealt with this question in its fourth session, in 1546, defining the Scriptural canon and declaring that the Vulgate translation was the only Bible translation that should be assigned authority within the Catholic Church. But the bishops also recognized the need for a new, revised version of the Vulgate. The invention of printing a century before the Council of Trent had aided the proliferation of defective texts of the Latin Bible. Thus the council established a commission to correct and revise the Vulgate text, and resolved to issue the revised Bible in print.

The question of the authority and accuracy of the Vulgate text was clearly on the mind of Giovanni of Marssano when he inscribed the flyleaf of our thirteenth-century Paris bible for the bishop of Tortosa with these words:

When this Latin bible came into my hands, Your honorable Eminence, written so diligently and free from errors, so that no one would not admire the hand of the copyist, the small size of the volume, and the antiquity of the script, I did not esteem it unworthy to send it to you, especially in these very difficult and turbulent times, in which almost all printed bibles are full of up to six-hundred errors. You will have this book as a companion and friend, I pray, in the glorious labour, which you voluntarily take up every day for the sake of Religion and the Catholic Church during this sacred council, and as a very certain witness of my singular obedience and eternal goodwill towards you. Farewell.[10]

Marssano's dedication is ironic in several respects. Although he praised the volume as "free from errors," much of what the fathers at Trent recognized was wrong with the text of the Latin Bible in the sixteenth century could actually be traced back to the text that was diffused through these Paris bibles. Doubts about the Vulgate's quality and accuracy abounded, and the revisers of the Latin Bible felt the need to compare their text to that of the Codex Amiatinus to establish the "correct" text of the Latin Bible.

---

[10] Les Enluminures, Chicago, New York, and Paris, TM 213, today in a private collection. Online description at http://www.textmanuscripts.com/manuscript_description.php?id=2823&#, accessed 3/1/2013. See Photo 4.

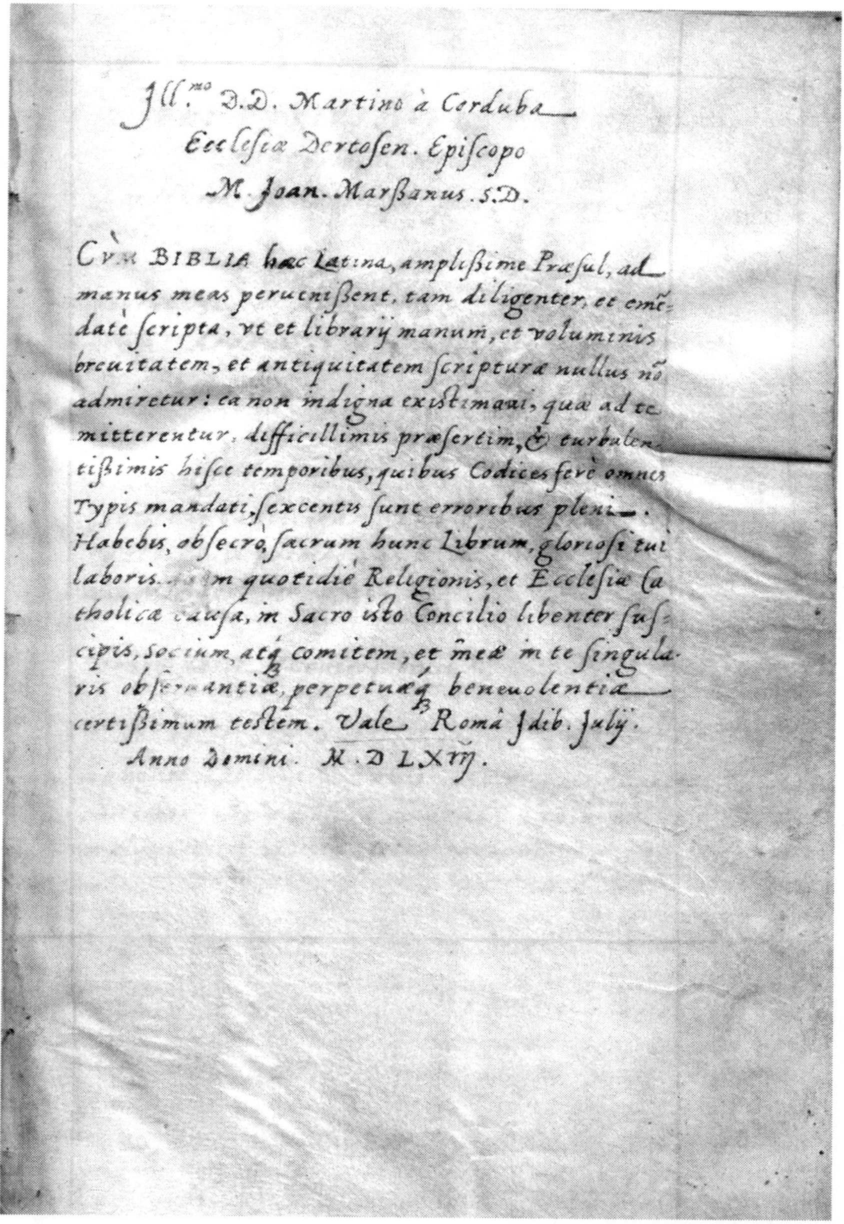
Ill.mo D.D. Martino à Corduba
Ecclesiæ Dertosen. Episcopo
M. Joan. Marssanus. S.D.

Cum BIBLIA hæc Latina, amplissime Præsul, ad manus meas peruenissent, tam diligenter, et emendate scripta, vt et librarij manum, et voluminis breuitatem, et antiquitatem scripturæ nullus non admiretur: ea non indigna existimaui, quæ ad te mitterentur, difficillimis præsertim, & turbulentissimis hisce temporibus, quibus Codices ferè omnes Typis mandati, sexcentis sunt erroribus pleni. Habebis, obsecro, sacrum hunc Librum, gloriosi tui laboris, quem quotidiè Religionis, et Ecclesiæ Catholicæ causa, in Sacro isto Concilio libenter suscipis, socium, atque comitem, et meæ in te singularis obseruantiæ, perpetuæque beneuolentiæ certissimum testem. Vale. Romæ Idib. Julij.
Anno Domini. M.D.LXIII.

Photo 4. Dedication to Martin of Cordoba by Giovanni Massani, 1563. Paris Bible, private collection, flyleaf. Photo (c) Les enluminures, Chicago, New York, Paris.

Even when they did so, however, it proved extremely difficult to determine which of the many textual differences between these two versions were more faithful to the original text. The officially approved version of the Vulgate eventually appeared in 1590 as the Sixtine edition, but it met with so much criticism that a complete revision was necessary after only two years. This was the so-called Sixto-Clementine edition of 1592. The establishment of a truly critical edition of the Latin Vulgate clearly went beyond the philological abilities of the sixteenth century; such an edition would not be attempted until the twentieth century and took several decades to complete.

Thus, strictly speaking, Giovanni of Marssano's assertion that his Paris bible was "free from errors" was patently false. But the Dominican was not a philologist, and for him, the antique bible surely represented something more than a correct text. It was a symbolic representation of the authenticity and integrity of the Bible as God's word. Marssano was suggesting, as most Catholic and Protestant Christians in his day would have agreed, that the beauty of this particular copy was symbolic of the Bible as a complete, singular, and immutable representation of the eternal Word of God, the one holy book. As we will see hereafter, this idea itself originated in the Middle Ages. Although the decree on scriptural authority by the Council of Trent underscored the profound differences between Catholic and Protestant concepts of Scripture, as shown later, both traditions had their roots in the theological and interpretative traditions of the Middle Ages.

At the same time, Marssano's desire for an uncorrupted "ancient" version of the biblical text reflects a widespread concern about the state of the Bible text in his own days. This was also one of the main concerns of medieval biblical scholars. Texts were hand copied, and medieval scholars knew very well that this process inevitably brought with it the risk of textual corruption. The call for the textual correction of the Bible, often accompanied by an expression of dismay over the current state of the Biblical text, did not originate in the Renaissance or in the Reformation, as we will see in the chapters that follow. In fact, Jerome's own fifth-century translation was born from such a desire to establish an uncorrupted, close-to-the-original text. Because the Bible was God's Word, keeping the biblical text faithful to that Word mandated the continuous critical revision of the text, in light of the older "established," or "original," traditions. The idea that the Middle Ages "was the period of the transmission of texts, not . . . of the critical revision of them,"[11] is patently false. Modern textual scholarship,

---

[11] Kenyon, *Recent Developments in the Textual Criticism of the Greek Bible*, 2.

which emerged in the Renaissance, had its roots in the traditions of biblical criticism of the Middle Ages. This recognition should also admonish us not to take the rhetoric about "corrupted" texts, which necessarily accompanied the continuous endeavor to correct these texts, at face value. Marssano's example shows that the Paris Bible, a text that was vilified as corrupted and modern in its own age, could be venerated as pure and hallowed two centuries later. By the same token, the Gutenberg Bible, maligned by Marssano, is the object of a similar veneration today.

THE SCOPE OF THIS VOLUME

The first three chapters of this book deal with the Bible in its physical form: the appearance, the contents (which biblical books were included), and the text (which versions or translations existed) of medieval bibles. The next three chapters primarily deal with how the Bible was read: its methods of interpretation and the social and educational contexts for this interpretation. The final chapters discuss the translation of the Bible into languages other than Latin, as well as its influence and dissemination in society.

We start with the physical history of the book. For most of the Middle Ages, the Bible was rarely ever one book; it was more a sacred library. Only toward the end of the Middle Ages did bibles begin looking more as we conceive them today: one book contained under one cover. In fact, one could argue that the idea of the Bible as one book, rather than a body of sacred writings, originated during the Middle Ages.

The next chapter introduces the formation of the biblical canon in the antique and medieval periods. To a certain degree, the discussion about what books were to be regarded as canonical was not entirely settled at the beginning of the medieval period. This explains why, at the end of the Middle Ages, two canons emerged: one including the so-called Apocrypha and another excluding them. In addition to the Old Testament Apocrypha (also called the deutero-canonical books), in the Middle Ages, there existed a large body of para-biblical and apocryphal literature (such as "Gospels" narrating the early childhood of Jesus or the life of Mary before she was married to Joseph) that influenced to a high degree how people interpreted the Bible. Early Christian apocryphal texts have generated considerable popular interest, often spurred on by best sellers such as Dan Brown's *Da Vinci Code*. Some have wanted to see in these apocryphal writings expression of an "alternative Christianity," which met with official disapproval and which was subsequently suppressed by the Church. It is too simple, however, to lump all non-canonical texts together as "lost," "concealed," or even "suppressed" sacred traditions, supposedly suppressed by "the Church" to keep them from "common people." Although some early Christian apocrypha certainly were condemned by the early Church, others were quite popular as devotional literature, and above any suspicion of heresy. Chapter 3 shows that the process of fixing the biblical canon was neither conspiratorial nor authoritarian. Although there was a broad consensus over the canonicity of a majority of the Bible books, there was still uncertainty on some books. When the debate was officially settled, in the sixteenth century, western Christianity eventually ended up with two sets of canonical scriptures. Today, Protestant churches follow a shorter canon, which they share with the Jewish tradition, whereas Catholic bibles usually include the so-called apocryphal, or deutero-canonical, books.

Chapter 4 examines how the text of the canonical Bible evolved during the Middle Ages. Handwritten and hand-copied, and continually refor-matted to meet the new demand of the time, the text of the medieval Bible was far from fixed. Different textual traditions fed into the medieval Bible – the Septuagint, the Hebrew Bible, and various Latin translations – and the text was continually in flux, not only because copyists made mistakes in their copying of the text but also because, on various occasions, the text was corrected and "improved," often in an attempt to make it more accurately reflect its "original" versions.

Chapter 5 discusses the method of interpretation, or hermeneutics, of Bible reading, which was often radically different from modern patterns of interpretation. Allegorical interpretation, or the tradition of spiritual reading, so utterly alien to the modern scientific mind, was common in the Middle Ages. No one today, for instance, would seek in Jesus' words about the two swords the disciples presented to him (Luke 22:38) the basis of a political theory about the division of power between pope and emperor; for medieval readers, however, the word *sword* brought the associated image of "power" to mind just as directly as it brings the more literal image of a weapon to the modern mind.

Chapter 6 considers this method of interpretation within its medieval educational context. Because the Bible was perhaps the most important school text of the medieval world, this chapter closely follows the history of the development of medieval education, with special attention to how the biblical text was taught and interpreted. Because there are good overviews of the history of exegesis available (see the Suggestions for Further Reading at the end of this chapter), I have refrained from making this chapter into an exhaustive overview of all medieval commentaries ever written and have focused instead on the social context that produced some of these commentaries and on the tools that were available for scholars to help them comprehend the biblical text.

The final three chapters consider the Bible as a "textual community." Who read medieval bibles, and what other ways were there to become acquainted with the Bible in a culture where many could not read? For the most part, medieval bibles were written and read in Latin. Contrary to popular belief, this did not mean that access was restricted to the clergy alone. For one thing, a number of vernacular Bible translations existed. Chapter 7 deals with the important subject of medieval translations of the Bible in the vernacular. Again, the aim is not to provide a full overview of medieval vernacular Bible translation in all possible languages or even a full list of all translations into the languages discussed here (the *New Cambridge History of the Bible* is a better resource for this) but to discuss some of the problems surrounding medieval vernacular bibles. Understanding who "read" the Bible requires reexamining some modern notions of literacy in the Middle Ages. And reading was not the only way to become familiar with the contents of a text; literacy did not always require the actual act of reading or writing, and it was not confined to the clergy. Biblical materials also circulated in texts that were not bibles in the strict sense. A spectator at a medieval mystery play or the listener to a medieval sermon, for instance, could acquire biblical literacy just as well as a reader of the written biblical text. Chapter 8, then, discusses the reading and preaching of the Bible in public worship and its place in private personal devotions. Chapter 9 looks at how the Bible was transmitted into the medieval imagination in figurative art and literature, from church decoration to theatrical productions. The topics of the vernacular Bible, medieval preaching, and medieval art have been the subject of much division between Protestants and Catholics. The latter have cited the ubiquity of biblical imagery and the rich tradition of medieval preaching as evidence to counter the Protestant claim that the Bible was not read during the Middle Ages;[12] however, they often ignored the Protestant claim that this Bible was "a Bible whose simple and immediate meaning is lost,"[13] because its presentation was dictated by a range of theological and exegetical assumptions that Protestants claimed were contrary to biblical teaching. Rather than taking a side in this debate, I hope that studying the rich and manifold biblical tradition of the

---

[12] Rost, *Die Bibel im Mittelalter*, 419–20.
[13] Martin, *Le métier de prédicateur en France*, 268 and 625. Cited in Wenzel, "The Use of the Bible in Preaching," 690.

medieval world will invite the reader to critically engage his or her own assumptions.

The brevity of this book dictates that the history of the Bible in the Middle Ages presented is selective. Many important aspects of this history cannot be discussed here. It should also be noted that this volume is concerned mainly with the history of the Latin Bible in the Christian tradition and sorely neglects the history of the Hebrew Bible and its interpretation in this same period, except for the few instances where the two intersected. It also focuses mainly on western Europe, to the neglect of Byzantium, the Slavic world, and the eastern Mediterranean. Students wanting a fuller and more comprehensive survey of this same material should turn to the second volume of the *New Cambridge History of the Bible* or similar introductory works.

RESOURCES FOR FURTHER STUDY

A general work of reference on the topic, the *Encyclopedia of the Bible and its Reception*, is currently being edited by Allison, Klauck, and others. A large bibliography of "studies concerning medieval and Franciscan exegesis and biblical studies" is available at http://users.bart.nl/~roestb/franciscan/exegesis.htm. A thematically organized, but out-of-date, bibliography is offered by Vernet, *La Bible au Moyen Age, Bibliographie* (1989). Both *Cambridge Histories* listed in the following are useful works of reference, but a reader wishing a more narrative introduction does well to start with De Hamel. Smalley's work is a classic but is intended for a scholarly audience. Boynton and Reilly's collection of essays works very well as a complement to the present volume.

SUGGESTIONS FOR FURTHER READING

La Bibbia nel Medioevo. Edited by Giuseppe Cremascoli and Claudio Leonardi. La Bibbia nella Storia, 17. Bologna: Edizioni Dehoniane, 1996.

The Cambridge History of the Bible. Vol. 2: The West from the Fathers to the Reformation. Edited by G. W. H. Lampe. Cambridge: Cambridge University Press, 1969.

De Hamel, Christopher F. R. *The Book. A History of the Bible.* London: Phaidon, 2001.

Hebrew Bible/Old Testament. The History of Its Interpretation. Vol 1: From the Beginning to the Middle Ages (until 1300). Part 2: The Middle Ages. Edited by Magne Sæbø, Chris Brekelmans, and Menahem Haran. Göttingen: Vandenhoeck & Ruprecht, 2000.

The New Cambridge History of the Bible. Vol. 2: From 600 to 1450. Edited by Richard Marsden and E. Ann Matter. Cambridge: Cambridge University Press, 2012.

The Practice of the Bible in the Western Middle Ages. Production, Reception, and Performance in Western Christianity. Edited by Susan Boynton and Diane J. Reilly. New York: Columbia University Press, 2011.

Smalley, Beryl. *The Study of the Bible in the Middle Ages.* Oxford: Blackwell Publishing, 1952. Third edition, 1983.

CHAPTER 2

The Bible as Book

In popular usage, the Bible is referred to as "the good book." But was the Bible always a book? Until the beginning of the Christian era, bibles were contained on scrolls or on collections of scrolls. For most of the Middle Ages, most bound "bibles" contained parts of the Bible rather than a complete set of both testaments. Not until the third decade of the thirteenth century did bibles start to resemble more or less what we expect to see in a bible today: a one-volume bound book (called a codex; see the following discussion in this chapter) in a portable format. The process of making a book was immensely laborious, and the materials (especially vellum) were prohibitively expensive. Western Europe became acquainted with the technique of making paper, which was much cheaper than vellum, in the twelfth century, but it did not become common until the fifteenth century. Books, and especially bibles (which were often more elaborately illuminated than other codices), were a precious resource, more than just a carrier of text. This chapter explores the history of the Bible as a physical artifact. It looks at the Bible as a book and at how it became a book in the modern sense. It also explores who made books, who owned them, how they were used, and who had access to them.

A tenth-century Anglo-Saxon riddle describes the elaborate process that went into the making of a bible. The riddle asks, "Who am I? First I was killed by an enemy, soaked in water and dried in the sun, where I lost all my hair. After that, I was stretched out and scraped with a knife blade and smoothed. Then I was folded, and a bird's feather traveled over my surface, back and forth, leaving black marks. Finally I was bound and covered with skin, gilded, and beautifully decorated." Lest we think this describes just any book, the riddle goes on to enumerate the spiritual merits of this object:

If the sons of men would make use of me, they would be safer and more sure of victory; their hearts would be bolder, their minds more at ease, their thoughts wiser; they would have more friends, companions and kinsmen (true and honorable, brave and kind) who would gladly increase their honour and prosperity, holding them fast in love's embraces. Ask what I am called, useful as I am to men; my name is famous, bringing grace to men, and itself holy.[1]

Thus, a bible was regarded as a valuable text in many senses. As the word of God, it brought news of salvation and grace to man. But its physical production was also a labor-intensive process that demanded utmost devotion and precious resources.

The bibles written at Jarrow under the direction of Abbot Ceolfrid, as described in Chapter 1, were costly to produce. Some 1,500 sheep went into the production of the three codices.[2] Thus, they were also testimony to the growing wealth of the double monastery of Wearmouth-Jarrow. Two codices were destined to serve a practical scholarly purpose: Ceolfrid placed the bibles in the monasteries "so that it would be easy for anyone who wished to read any chapter of either Testament to find what he wanted."[3] They may also have been used in the liturgy. The third, which became the Codex Amiatinus, also had important symbolic value; as a gift to the pope from this monastic community, it testified to Wearmouth-Jarrow's identity as a center of Christian learning and to its abbot's wish for the abbey to be recognized as a full-fledged member of the worldwide Christian scholarly community, headed by the bishop of Rome.

FROM SCROLL TO CODEX

Bibles were not always books. By "book" modern scholars mean a text consisting of separate pages bound together into a single volume. We also call these codices (the plural form of *codex*). Before codices, written texts were preserved in scrolls. These were usually made of papyrus (and occasionally of leather or parchment), glued together in long sheets that could be rolled up. The oldest known written witness to any part of the biblical text is the collection of sacred scriptures from the desert community of Qumran, in the Judean desert. These texts were found in 1948, and they probably represent what was left of the library of a Jewish religious community that lived there in the first century C.E., until its destruction by the Romans in 68 C.E. Most of the findings represent only small fragments

---

[1] *The Old English Riddles of the Exeter Book*, trans. Williamson, 82–83. Modern English translations in *The Exeter Book Riddles*, trans. Crossley-Holland, 29, and *Anglo-Saxon Riddles*, trans. Porter, 38.
[2] One leaf of the Amiatinus measures 337 mm × 483 mm, which is approximately one-half the size of a sheepshide (525 × 760 mm, according to Ganz, "Mass Production of Early Medieval Manuscripts," 55.) The Amiatinus had 1,029 leaves; this would require 515 sheep for this codex alone.
[3] Anonymous, *Vita Abbatum*, 20, ed. Plummer, 395.

of biblical books; the largest text, however, is a complete scroll of the book of Isaiah. The Qumran scrolls vary in date from the second century B.C.E. to the first century C.E. Most Jewish communities conceived of their sacred writings as a collection of scrolls, and as is still the tradition today, these scrolls were kept in a special chest or cupboard in the synagogue and were taken out and read in the liturgy. The earliest Christians presumably also used scrolls for their sacred writings. There are several references in the New Testament to scrolls as well: in the book of Revelation, for instance, the author mentions an angel handing him a scroll (Rev. 11:8–10). But for the most part, the early Christians seem to have preferred the codex format over the scroll.[4]

Codices were used before the coming of Christianity, but they were commonly used for taking notes and record keeping rather than for sacred or literary texts. A codex consisted of a series of folded leaves, bound together at the spine rather than glued together in long scrolls. The leaves of these codices at first would have been made of papyrus, the same material used for scrolls, but soon parchment or vellum (the thinly stretched and especially prepared skin of goats, sheep, or calves) came to be preferred.[5] The earliest manuscript witnesses of the New Testament consist of fragments of papyrus codices, dating from the second and third centuries C.E. They are, respectively, a fragment of the Gospel of John, now in the John Rylands Library in Manchester, the United Kingdom; fragments of the Gospels and the Pauline Epistles in the so-called Chester Beatty papyri, now partly in Dublin and partly at the University of Michigan; and the Bodmer papyri, containing Luke, John, Matthew, and fragments of the Catholic Epistles, now housed in a collection in Cologny in Switzerland.

By the fourth century, the scroll format as the main carrier for important and literary written texts seems to have gone out of fashion entirely, as it was supplanted by the parchment codex. This change coincided with the expansive growth of Christianity in the third century and its elevation to the official religion of the Roman Empire in the fourth century, and many scholars now believe that Christianity was an important factor in this change. After Christianity became the majority religion of the Roman Empire, the use of codices became ubiquitous, even for pagan literary works and Jewish biblical texts. Thus, although scrolls were still

---

4 This notion has, however, been challenged by Bagnall, *Early Christian Books in Egypt.*
5 Vellum strictly speaking is only calfskin; parchment is used as the more general term. Parchment was used for scrolls as well; the assumption that scrolls were made of papyrus and codices of parchment is an oversimplification: Roberts, *The Birth of the Codex,* 5–10.

the dominant medium during the poet Vergil's lifetime, the earliest surviving manuscripts of his work, the fifth-century Vergilius Vaticanus and the Vergilius Romanus, are both codices. The oldest complete copies of the Hebrew Bible are likewise written in codices, not scrolls. They are the Aleppo codex (now in Jerusalem) and the Codex Leningradensis (now in Saint Petersburg), both written in the early tenth century by members of the famous Ben Asher family, a dynasty of Jewish scribes who had settled in Tiberias on the Sea of Galilee.

Early Christians may have preferred codices because they were more portable. The argument has also been made that a codex was easier to consult and was more user-friendly (it did not have to be rerolled after use), but this remains subject to debate; some scholars have cast doubt on this explanation by showing that the scroll was easier to use than has been assumed. Others have argued that the durability of parchment may have played a role in the Christian preference for the codex. Parchment was also more widely available than papyrus, which was produced exclusively in Egypt. But this argument cannot entirely explain the preference for the codex either, because the earliest codices were just as often written on papyrus. Whatever the reasons for the change to the codex format, the transition from scroll to codex brought about changes in the conception of the biblical text. There was a certain limit to what could be comfortably contained in one scroll. Evidence of this can still be found in the division of some Old Testament books, such as Samuel and Kings, which had to be divided over two scrolls: 1 and 2 Samuel and 1 and 2 Kings. Codices were much more flexible in their format, and they could range in content from a single Gospel to the whole of the Old and New Testaments. When the emperor Diocletian (r. 284–305) persecuted the Christian church in 304 C.E, he also commanded Christian scriptures to be confiscated, and in the wake of these persecutions, a great many codices are reported to have been destroyed by the Roman authorities. Many of these were probably Gospel books of a small format, similar to the early Gospel codices mentioned earlier. When the Christian woman Irene was captured by the authorities and tried in Thessalonica, the officials found that she had "many parchments, books, tablets, small codices and pages," concealed in her house, in "cabinets and chests."[6]

After the emperor Constantine (r. 306–337) converted to Christianity and issued his Edict of Toleration in 313, bibles were no longer clandestine

---

[6] Gamble, *Books and Readers in the Early Church*, 148.

books. In 332, the emperor commanded Bishop Eusebius of Caesarea to oversee the production of bibles on a large scale:

It appeared proper to indicate to your Intelligence that you should order fifty volumes with ornamental leather bindings, easily legible and convenient for portable use, to be copied by skilled calligraphists well trained in the art, copies that is of Divine Scriptures, the provision and use of which you well know to be necessary for reading in church.[7]

Eusebius reports that "immediate action followed upon his word, as we sent him threes and fours in richly wrought bindings."[8] Eusebius does not specify whether these books contained the entire biblical text, although "the Divine Scriptures" might be taken to imply a complete text. The three oldest complete bible manuscripts that exist date from roughly the same period and have some features in common with the bibles Eusebius commissioned. They are the famous Codex Vaticanus (Vat. gr. 1209), dating from the fourth century, and the Codex Sinaiticus (BL Add. 43,725) and the Codex Alexandrinus (BL Royal 1.D.V–VIII), which date from the fourth and fifth century, respectively, and are both now in the British Library in London. All are complete texts of the Bible in Greek, written three or four columns to a page, which seems to correspond to Eusebius's mention of "threes and fours." But because these three codices are not exactly very "portable," and evidence seems to point to a different geographic origin as well, scholars have been reluctant to identify them with the books that Constantine ordered to be written.

The handwritten codex would remain the main carrier for texts in general, and more specifically biblical texts, until the invention of the printing press in the fifteenth century. Indeed, the codex remains the basic format for written texts today, although it remains to be seen whether it will be replaced in time by the digital text. The transition from manuscript writing to mechanical printing also ushered in the shift from parchment to paper as the primary writing material, because paper was both more convenient and less expensive to print on than vellum. Paper, first invented in China, was introduced to Europe through contact with the Muslim world in the late twelfth century, and by the fourteenth century it became quite common for less valuable books. Because it was made of rags, it at first was deemed inferior material.[9] It did not eclipse parchment before the advent of printing.

---

[7] Eusebius of Pamphilia, *Life of Constantine*, 4, 36, trans. Cameron and Hall, 166–67.
[8] Ibid.
[9] See Petrus Venerabilis, *Adversus Iudaeorum inveteratam duritiem*, ed. Friedman, CCCM 58, 130.

Despite the ubiquity of the book format, there was a considerable variety in the shape and content of bibles throughout the Middle Ages. Some bibles included the complete Old and New Testaments, but most included only parts of them. Early bibles, such as the previously mentioned Codex Vaticanus, Codex Sinaiticus, and Codex Alexandrinus, that contained the entire Bible were probably quite exceptional. More commonly, codices from this period, whether in Latin or Greek, contained only parts of the Bible, such as the Pentateuch, the Prophets, the four Gospels, or the Epistles. Some bibles included substantial commentaries (called "glosses"), the structure and purpose of which are explained later in this chapter as well as in Chapter 6. Some bibles were intended for use in the liturgy and were adapted especially for that purpose. Some were illustrated and illuminated, whereas others were plain books meant to be used rather than admired. This variety makes it impossible to speak of "the" medieval Bible without exploring the variety in its physical appearance.

PANDECTS AND MULTIVOLUME BIBLES

As a single-volume bible, the Codex Amiatinus was called a *pandect*, a Greek term meaning "cover all," derived from Byzantine legal texts and usually indicating a one-volume comprehensive legal code. The modern scholarly consensus is that pandects, or one-volume bibles, were rare in the Early Middle Ages and that it became more common only in the thirteenth century to have the entire Bible in one volume. Even after the thirteenth century, however, multivolume bibles were still very common, and some of the later medieval one-volume bibles on closer inspection appear to have been two-volume bibles that were bound together in a later stage.[10] On the other hand, the early Middle Ages knew plenty of pandects. Before 1200, several monasteries and cathedrals possessed large one-volume bibles, often used as lectern bibles for communal reading. As we have seen in the case of the Amiatinus, large one-volume medieval bibles in the early Middle Ages were produced throughout the Middle Ages. The Amiatinus was not the first pandect bible the monks of Wearmouth-Jarrow had seen; on one of his trips to Italy, Ceolfrid had brought back a pandect of the "old translation" (*uetusta translatio*), that is, the Latin Bible translation made from the Septuagint.[11] This book served as a template for the three new

---

[10] Newberry MS Case 203 is a good example.

[11] Scholarly consensus today holds that this was not the *Vetus Latina* but rather Jerome's revision of this same translation. See Marsden, *The Text of the Old Testament in Anglo-Saxon England*, 117. The book is mentioned by Cassiodorus, *Institutiones* I, 14, 3–4, ed. Mynors, 40.

bibles that were copied under Ceolfrid's direction, and they imitated it in layout, contents, and script.[12]

The pandect that Ceolfrid brought from Italy originated in the scriptorium of the Roman statesman-turned-monk Cassiodorus (d. 585). Cassiodorus had been a statesman in the service of the Ostrogothic kingdom of Italy, and later as ambassador at the court of the eastern Roman emperor in Constantinople. By the sixth century, the territories of the Roman empire in the west were no longer under Roman rule; they were ruled by a new elite who traditionally were considered barbarians in Roman society, such as the Ostrogoths, Visigoths, and Franks. Although these rulers were Christians, they were viewed with a certain suspicion by the Roman, and catholic, church elite. They had embraced a faith that was based on the heresy of Arius, which at one time had enjoyed a certain popularity in the eastern part of the Roman empire but which was condemned by the ecumenical councils of the catholic church in Nicaea in 325 and Constantinople in 381. Not until the sixth century did many of these kingdoms convert to catholicism. Theoderic's kingdom would see no such conversion, however. In the decades after Theoderic's death, the Ostrogothic kingdom collapsed in a protracted struggle with the Byzantine Empire. During this turmoil, Cassiodorus turned his family estate, Vivarium, in the south of Italy, into a monastery and a center for Christian learning and bible production. He wrote his *Institutions* as a guide for the monastic community. It contained an introduction to the biblical canon, a list of commentaries that were available for specific biblical books, as well as extensive instructions for the preservation and copying of biblical texts. It is an instructive text for the history of the Bible, and it shows us how Cassiodorus conceived of the Bible as a book. He commonly referred to his bible as a "sacra bibliotheca" (holy library), suggesting that he saw it as a collection of writings rather than one book. These collections of writings could be contained in one codex but just as easily in a number of separate codices. Modern scholars believe that the bible pandect brought to England by Ceolfrid may have been one that Cassiodorus had identified as the "codex grandior" (the larger book), and described as being written in the "clear script," probably referring to the Italian script that was common in those days, the same one that was used for the Amiatinus:

It has ninety-five gatherings of four folios each in which the translation of the Old Testament by the seventy interpreters is included in forty-four books; to this

---

[12] Meyvaert, "Bede, Cassiodorus, and the Codex Amiatinus". In what respect the "codex grandior" was a model for the Amiatinus (script, illustrations, or scriptural division) is unclear, however.

are added the twenty-six books of the New Testament and the total comes out as seventy books, symbolized perhaps by the number of the palm trees that the Hebrew people found at the resting place of Elim (Ex. 15: 27).[13]

The "codex grandior" was not the only bible the monastery of Vivarium possessed. Cassiodorus described two other bibles in his library, one a pandect Vulgate translation and one a complete bible of an unknown translation that filled nine separate codices. An image of such a bible is evoked on the first folios of the Codex Amiatinus, where a miniature depicts the scribe Ezra sitting in front of a late antique bookcase, an *armarium*, containing nine codices (see Photo 1). Ezra was the biblical sage who, according to legend, had restored the entire biblical text by divine inspiration after it was destroyed by the Babylonians in the siege of Jerusalem in 586 B.C.E. (4 Ezra 14: 19–48; see also the following discussion, Chapter 3). Scholars surmise that the image was in fact copied from an image in Cassiodorus's "codex grandior," the book carried to Jarrow, and that in the original the identity of the seated figure was probably not Ezra but Cassiodorus himself.[14] In any case, it gives us a vivid pictorial representation of how "the Bible" was often conceived: as a library rather than one single book. Nine volumes was only one of many possible divisions. An entry from the library catalogue of the monastery in Saint Riquier, dating from 831, shows the wide range of biblical formats: the library contained "a complete bible where 72 books are contained in one volume" as well as "a bible divided into 14 volumes."[15]

BIBLES FOR LITURGICAL USE

One of the main uses of bibles was for reading aloud in the worship of the church, either at Mass or during the times of prayer that are known as the "divine office." (This is explained more fully in Chapter 8.) Given the size of the books and the selectiveness of the readings, partial bibles were better suited for liturgical use than the larger pandects or even multivolume bibles. During Mass, a selection from the Epistles was read first by a deacon from a lectern in the front of the church. Later in the service, the Gospel book was carried in a small procession to the middle of the church, where the priest read from it. It made good sense to have separate books for these

---

[13] Cassiodorus, *Institutiones*, I, 14, 2, ed. Mynors, 40. English translation in Cassiodorus, *Institutions*, trans. Halporn and Vessey, 137. See also Meyvaert, "Bede, Cassiodorus, and the Codex Amiatinus."

[14] Meyvaert, "Bede, Cassiodorus, and the Codex Amiatinus"; and Chazelle, "Romanness in Early Medieval Culture."

[15] Ganz, "Carolingian Bibles," 326.

readings. Because the readings for Mass always included a reading from the Epistles and the Gospels, these books were the most frequently adapted for liturgical use. Other "bibles" for liturgical use included codices containing only the first five, six, seven, or even eight books of the Bible (named Pentateuch, Hexateuch, Heptateuch, or Octateuch, respectively), only the Prophets, or only the Wisdom books. Some liturgical sources even refer to a special "Book of Women," presumably containing Ruth, Esther, and Judith.[16]

The best example of partial bibles that were specifically designed for liturgical use is the bibles we know as Gospel books, or *Evangeliaria*. Not only these were beautifully illuminated, but because the book was to be carried in solemn procession to the place of reading in the church, the outside also was often richly decorated. Both the seventh-century Book of Durrow and the splendid eighth-century Book of Kells, for instance, were roughly contemporary with the Codex Amiatinus, but they were clearly intended for liturgical use rather than communal reading. They also reflect a much more intricately illuminated style than the deliberately classicizing Amiatinus. The Book of Kells, now in Trinity College Dublin, dates from around 800 C.E. and was housed for centuries in the monastery of Kells. Its origin is a matter of ongoing debate, especially between English and Irish scholars, with each group claiming the magnificent book as its national heritage. The "Golden" Gospel books produced in Germany during the Ottonian dynasty in the eleventh century at the abbey of Echternach are another example. These were lavish manuscripts, written entirely in gold. Some five copies survive of these; one was given by Emperor Conrad to the minster at Goslar, and another by his son, Emperor Henry III, to the cathedral of Speyer, showing that bibles such as these were not just books for liturgical use but also had value as prestigious gifts that strengthened the bond between rulers and the Church.

The readings at the Vigils (the nightly portion of the divine office) were done "continuously." This means that longer portions of scripture (sometimes a whole book or several books) were prescribed for the length of the liturgical season, and thus each day's reading resumed where it left off the previous day. (A more detailed account of the role of the Bible in the liturgy follows in Chapter 8.) By contrast, the readings prescribed for the Mass were shorter selections completed in a single reading and did not follow the sequence of the biblical book. Some bible manuscripts show that they were intended for liturgical use. The Golden Gospels had

---

[16] See Chapter 8, n4.

charts in the back that indicated what sections should be read on what days of the liturgical year. Other bibles had indications in the margin that showed where readings should begin or end and on what particular day they should be read. Even the more generic chapter headings at the beginning of biblical books (called *capitula, tituli,* or *breves*), a common feature of all biblical texts before ca. 1200 (explained more fully in Chapter 4), may have functioned to facilitate looking up the correct reading for certain days during the liturgical year.

Other books went a step further in meeting the liturgical needs of their users. What we call lectionaries are books that contain only the portions of the Bible read in the liturgy, arranged by the liturgical order in which they are read throughout the year rather than the order in which they appear in the Bible. Although a lectionary, strictly speaking, was not a bible, we can see that the line between bibles and liturgical books was sometimes a thin one.

PSALTERS

One of the most common types of partial bibles was the psalter. In fact, it was so common to have the Psalms in a separate psalter that some bible codices did not even include the Psalms.[17] The simple term *psalter* embraces a dazzling variety of books of different shapes, sizes, and destined for different uses. In the words of one scholar, "[n]o two identical Psalters survive from the medieval period."[18] Psalters contained Psalms (all 150 of them, or sometimes 151, as explained in Chapter 3) and canticles, that is, liturgical songs that were derived from other parts of the Bible. These canticles usually included the canticle of Isaiah (Isa. 12:1–6); Hizkiah (Isa. 38:10–20); Hannah (1 Kings 2:1–10); Miriam, the sister of Moses (Exod. 15:1–19); Habakkuk (Hab. 3:2–19); Moses (Deut. 32:1–43); the three men in the fiery furnace (Dan. 3:57–88); the hymn *Te Deum* ("We Praise Thee"); and the New Testament canticles of Zechariah (Luke 1:68–79), Mary (Luke 2:46–55), and Simeon (Luke 2:29–32). Some also contained the texts of the most common creeds of the medieval church – the Nicene Creed and the Athanasian Creed – and some included other liturgical prayers, such as the litany of the saints. Most psalters were liturgical books: the monastic tradition required the complete reading of all 150 Psalms in the course of one week in the divine office, the liturgy of daily prayers. (See Chapter 8.)

---

[17] Such is the case, for instance, in Newberry Case MS 203.
[18] Panayotova, "The Illustrated Psalter: Luxury and Practical Use," 253.

Psalms were often grouped according to their liturgical use: the most common division marked the beginnings of Psalms 27, 39, 53, 68, 80, 97, 101, and 109 (Vulg.)[19] with decorated initials. This division reflected the liturgical use of cathedrals and parish churches, whereas the monastic use grouped the Psalms in smaller units.

Psalters could also be personal prayer books. A good example is the "Golden Psalter," a small psalter made as a present from Charlemagne to Pope Hadrian I in 794. A very similar one was commissioned as a gift for Charlemagne's wife, Hildegard.[20] From the later Middle Ages, we have the example of the Luttrell Psalter, named after the wealthy fourteenth-century landowner who commissioned it. It is richly decorated and illustrated and is best known for its realistic marginal depictions of life in the late medieval English countryside.[21] In the later Middle Ages, the personal prayer books known as Books of Hours were modeled after the divine office and contained prayers and Psalms, arranged by their liturgical rather than their biblical order. (See also Chapter 8.) Psalters could even be used as literacy primers, much like a medieval *Dick and Jane*.[22] These psalters often included large-letter alphabets on their opening pages.

Theologically, the Psalms held a central place in the theology of the medieval church. The book of Psalms was often seen as a "miniature Bible" because it was believed to contain all the essential doctrines of the entire Bible, in prayer form. Some Psalms were seen as relating especially to the life of Jesus Christ (Psalms 21 and 108, for instance), whereas others were read as prayers of personal penitence (the so-called penitential Psalms, Psalms 6, 32, 38, 51, 102, 130, and 143). In some psalters, headings were added to the individual Psalms to emphasize their historical context, which set the tone for their interpretation (see also Chapter 4).

GLOSSED PSALTERS AND GLOSSED BIBLES

Although psalters never ceased to be prayer books, in the ninth and tenth centuries, they also became sophisticated books for biblical study. The Rule of Benedict, the monastic rule attributed to Benedict of Nursia, dating from ca. 540, advises monks to study Psalms between Matins (the

---

[19] The Vulgate numbering of Psalms was different than that of the Hebrew Bible: the numbering between Psalms 9 and 147 is off by one. See also Appendix B. Thus, the Psalm numbers here, according to modern Bibles, would be 28, 40, 54, 69, 81, 98, 102, and 110.

[20] McKitterick, *Charlemagne*, 334–35.

[21] It can be viewed online at http://www.bl.uk/onlinegallery/sacredtexts/ttpbooks.html. See also Backhouse, *Medieval Rural Life in the Luttrell Psalter*.

[22] A popular American series of basic readers in use from the 1930s to the 1970s.

first of the monks' eight daily prayer hours, performed in the middle of the night) and sunrise, and many of the extant psalters must have been used for this purpose in monastic communities. In his endeavor first to correct, and later to translate the entire Bible, Jerome had made three different translations of the books of Psalms (see Chapter 4), and two of these, the so-called Roman Psalter and Gallican Psalter, were used throughout Europe in the liturgy. Jerome's third translation, his so-called Hebrew Psalter, was considered a more literal translation from the Hebrew, and it was often used to aid the study of the biblical text. Some Carolingian (i.e., ninth-century) psalters displayed in parallel columns all three versions of Jerome's translations, as well as the Greek version, which was sometimes transliterated into Latin. The twelfth-century Eadwine Psalter, copied in Canterbury in the mid-twelfth century and now in Trinity College, Cambridge, was one example of such a learned psalter (See Photo 5). It contained the text of the Psalms and the Canticles, in its three versions: Gallican, Roman, and Hebrew, in parallel columns. The Hebrew and Roman versions had interlinear glosses (this term is explained in the next paragraph) that gave a complete translation into the vernacular, in Old English and Anglo-Norman, respectively, and the Gallican Psalter had the standard interpretive glosses of the *Glossa ordinaria* (the *Ordinary Gloss*, which by the twelfth century had become a common school study text; see Chapter 6) attached to it. This entire tripartite psalter was beautifully illustrated with an iconographical program copied from the Carolingian Utrecht Psalter, which in the eleventh and twelfth centuries was in the possession of Christ Church, Canterbury (see Chapter 9). It depicted the content of the Psalms with often very literal images so that the psalter could be said to illumine not only the mind but also the senses. Books such as these were intended for the intensive meditative study of the one book of the Bible that was seen to encompass the totality of scriptural doctrine.

Of course, the psalter was not the only subject of study. Most so-called glossed bibles were study bibles rather than liturgical bibles. Most commonly, "gloss" (from Greek *glossa*, "tongue") refers to a brief annotation or explanation written in the margins of the main bible text. As noted earlier, many Carolingian psalters came with commentaries, such as that of Cassiodorus, written in the margin. Likewise, in the early Middle Ages, there circulated copies of the Song of Songs, another well-studied text in monastic circles, that had a translation in one margin and commentaries in the other. Glosses were not just added in the margins; they could also be placed between the lines of the biblical text. In Anglo-Saxon England, for instance, interlinear glosses were often used to provide translations of

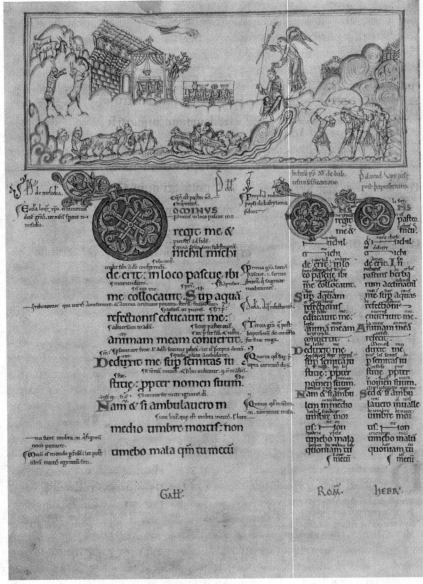

Photo 5. Psalm 23 (Vulg. 22) in the Eadwine Psalter, Trinity College Cambridge MS R.17.1, f.39v. The left column contains the Gallican Psalter text with interlinear and marginal glosses. The second column contains the Roman Psalter with Old English glosses, and the third Jerome's translation from the Hebrew, with glosses in Old French. Photo courtesy of the Master and Fellows of Trinity College, Cambridge.

uncommon words. The eight-century Vespasian Psalter was provided with an interlinear translation into Old English in the tenth century, and the Lindisfarne Gospels were similarly glossed sometime in the tenth century. In the twelfth century, the two features, marginal glosses and interlinear glosses, were combined to form a new type of bible: the glossed Bible book. While the marginal glosses contained longer excerpts of commentaries from the Church fathers, interlinear glosses contained shorter comments, often only a few words. The latter could vary in content from short word explanations to condensed versions of the longer marginal glosses. From the mid-twelfth century on, *libri glosati* ("glossed books") that is, individual Bible books (such as Genesis, Exodus, Samuel and Kings, or Psalms, and so on) with added interlinear and marginal glosses, became a very common phenomenon in medieval book collections. It was not until the thirteenth century that attempts were made to combine all these glossed books into one "glossed Bible."[23] The marginal and interlinear apparatus of these bibles eventually became so standardized that people came to speak of the "common gloss," in Latin *glossa ordinaria*. (The *Glossa ordinaria* as a work of exegesis is discussed in Chapter 6.)

EARLY MEDIEVAL CENTERS OF BIBLE PRODUCTION

When one thinks of medieval bible production, the image of monks penning beautifully illuminated volumes comes to mind. This image is historically somewhat one-sided, however. Commercial lay scribes were probably just as commonly engaged in the production of bibles as monks were; they may even have been the norm rather than the exception. We have very little evidence for the logistics of bible production in antiquity. As noted earlier, the emperor Constantine commissioned the production of "magnificent bibles" and charged Eusebius of Caesarea with the oversight of this project, but we do not know exactly where and how these manuscripts were produced. It is very likely, however, that they were made in small professional worships and scriptoria, like most other books at that time. A wealthy donor called Ambrose (not the famous church father of the same name) provided the means for Origen (ca. 184–ca. 254) to have his books produced in professional scriptorium. Eusebius offers us a lively description of Origen's copying shop. Many of the scribes were women:

more than seven shorthand writers were ready at hand, who relieved each other at fixed intervals, and as many copyists, as well as young women who were skilled

[23] A good example of an early pandect with (albeit incomplete) gloss is London, BL, MS Add. 15,253.

in fine writing, for all of whom Ambrose provided without stinting the necessary means.[24]

When Cassiodorus founded the monastery of Vivarium on his family estate in southern Italy, in the sixth century, he envisioned this monastery mainly as a center for the preservation and study of letters, and above all as a place where books would be copied. This marked an important change in the monastic attitude towards learning. Whereas his contemporary Benedict of Nursia had envisioned the monastery as a kind of school (a place for training in the virtues that were necessary for the religious life),[25] Vivarium, by contrast, was a primarily a school (a center for learning and book production), organized as a monastery.

From the time of Cassiodorus on, the copying of texts would be seen as an important part of the daily labour of monks, or indeed nuns. For the rest of the Middle Ages, monasteries would become places where bibles were kept, preserved, and copied. Many of the most beautiful and impressive Bibles that were produced in the Early Middle Ages, such as the Codex Amiatinus, stem from monasteries. Still, there is sufficient evidence, both from the Merovingian period (fifth through eighth century) and from the twelfth century, that lay scriptoria existed alongside these monastic scriptoria and that they, too, were important in the production of medieval bibles. In fact, after the thirteenth century, lay workshops became the dominant places where bibles were written, for a commercial fee of course. During the later Middle Ages, we can also see monasteries increasingly operating on the same basis as these commercial workshops: they copied books for paying patrons who more often than not were laypeople. They not only copied bibles but also prayer books, and, indeed, secular literary works.

A century after the Codex Amiatinus was produced, the court of Emperor Charlemagne (r. 768–814), who ruled over much of what today is France, Germany, and northern Italy, became the center of a veritable intellectual revival, based on a new appreciation for classical learning and classical texts. According to Charlemagne's biographer Einhard, he invited to his court the Anglo-Saxon cleric Alcuin from York, "the greatest scholar of the day," to become his personal tutor,[26] and the emperor personally stimulated the growth of monasteries and made great efforts to standardize

---

24 Eusebius of Pamphilia, *Church History* 6.23.2, trans. McGiffert, 271.
25 Benedict of Nursia, *Regula*, Prologue, ed. Neufville and trans. De Vogüé, SC 181, 422.
26 Einhard, *Vita Karoli*, 25, ed. Pertz, 25; and Einhard, *The Life of Charlemagne*, trans. Turner, 54.

the liturgy. Under his tutelage, northern France saw a rise in the production of manuscripts. The abbey of Saint Martin in Tours, where Alcuin had retired after his stay at the imperial court, became a major center for the copying of large bibles, although the average output of about two bibles annually sounds modest by modern standards. Some eighteen complete "Tour Bibles," many of them pandects, and several more fragments, survive; the first was probably made at the direction of Alcuin himself and presented to Charlemagne on the occasion of his coronation as "Emperor of the Romans" in 800 A.D. But it was especially after Alcuin's death in 804, during the abbacy of his successor, Fridugisius, that the abbey gained this reputation. It remained so until Viking attacks in the second half of the century devastated the abbey. Tours bibles (also called Turonian bibles, see Photo 6) were produced on commission; their neat layout and clear hand made them attractive volumes, worthy to be presented as gifts to bishops, monasteries, or even kings. But they were not just beautiful objects to be admired; Bibles such as these were ideal for communal reading or as templates for the production of further bibles. In one copy of a Tours Bible now in the British Library, the presence of musical notation above the text of the book of Lamentations indicates that this bible was read, and sung, during Church services.[27] Some 400 years later, the Franciscan Roger Bacon admired these bibles for their quality and praised them as better texts than the ones that were copied in his own time.[28]

Tours was not the only place where bibles were produced in the ninth century. In Orleans (or possibly Fleury), Bishop Theodulf (ca. 750/760–821) oversaw the production of bibles that stood out for the quality of their textual scholarship. Needless to say, great care went into the choice of exemplars for bible copying. But Theodulf went a step further and actively compared several versions in order to establish the best text possible. (See also Chapter 4.) Theodulf was a native of northern Spain, and he later became abbot of Fleury and bishop of Orleans. Like Alcuin, he was one of the trusted friends and theological advisors at the court of Charlemagne. His pandects were intended for reference and study or as exemplars for further copying, rather than for liturgical use. One copy of Theodulf's bible can be admired today in the Bibliothèque National in Paris, and another copy made under his supervision, which once belonged to the Abbey of Saint Hubert near Liège, today resides in the British Library.[29]

---

[27] London BL MS Harley 2805, fol. 170r ff.
[28] See also Photos 6 and 10, the Bible of Moutier-Grandval, London BL, MS Add. 10,546.
[29] Paris, BN MS. lat. 9380 most likely is Theodulf's own copy. For the Saint Hubert Bible, see Gibson, *The Bible in the Latin West*, plate 6.

Photo 6. Exodus, in the Moutier-Grandval Bible. London, British Library, MS Add. 10546, f.26r. Photo (c) The British Library Board.

The Theodulf bibles may not be as impressive in their number and size as the Tours Bibles, but they stand out as representatives of Carolingian biblical learning and textual scholarship.

BIBLE PRODUCTION IN THE LATER MIDDLE AGES

The eleventh and twelfth centuries seem to have been an especially productive period for the making of large one-volume display bibles, often beautifully ornamented and illuminated copies. Scholars have associated the production of these giant bibles with the Gregorian reform, an eleventh-century movement of Church reform that started in monasteries such as Cluny and Vallombrosa, and that through the influence of Pope Gregory VII (pope 1073–85) started to permeate the entire church hierarchy of western Christendom. This reform movement was born from the desire to free the Church from the influence of secular overlordship, which had become commonplace since Carolingian times, and to assign a greater leadership role to the clergy, not just in the administration of ecclesiastical lands but also in the moral and spiritual education of the laity. This need for reform was felt especially in the monasteries, many of which had come to be governed directly by their secular overlords and donors. The foundation charter of Cluny (910) itself was a testament to the attempt to set the monastery free from the influence of the noble donor; it emphasized the autonomy of the monks in all matters of policy and stressed the special relationship the monastery, dedicated to the Saints Peter and Paul, had with the bishopric of Rome, where the relics of these saints were kept.

In the eleventh century, a group of reform-minded monks got the chance to realize their ideals by reforming the Church from top to bottom, beginning with the Rome. In 1046, the Holy Roman emperor Henry III faced a crisis within the papacy. Three candidates called themselves pope, and even the most respectable of these owed his office to an act of shameless bribery. Henry decided to depose all three and nominated a reform-minded monk from Germany, Bruno, as the new pope, who took the name Leo IX (pope 1049–1054). Henry's move gave the reformers a powerful opportunity to take hold of the papacy. They sought to reform not only the clergy of Rome but the whole Church, from the upper to the lower clergy. To do this, they revived a dormant theory: that Rome was the head of the entire Church, to whom not only bishops but even princes owed subservience. This redefined the conception of authority and leadership in the Church. Leo IX convened and attended general councils in Germany, Italy, and

France to promote this program of reform, and assigned key positions in the Church's administration to reform-minded bishops, often clerics who shared his own monastic background. The papacy, in this period, was building up a network of bishops, abbots, and princes to support its political ideals. Bibles, especially beautifully illuminated and lavishly executed ones, would play an important role in building this network.

The monastic and Gregorian reform movement thus created a demand for new bibles, both for liturgical use in the new churches and monasteries founded in this period and as symbolic representations of the reformers' religious commitments. Lavish bibles could be presented as gifts to reform-minded bishops and abbeys and as tokens of orthodoxy and commitment to the religious ideal of Church reform and the apostolic authority of the Roman See, which, as the reformers claimed, was based on a biblical model. How the demand for these new bibles was satisfied can be seen in the production of one group of giant bibles produced in this period, the so-called Atlantic bibles. These were large pandects (with a page size similar to a modern newspaper), named after the mythical giant Atlas, who carried the entire world on his shoulders, and they were impressive by both their size and lavish illumination. For some time, scholars have associated these bibles with papal efforts to promote the Gregorian reform, and have assumed that they were commissioned by the pope and produced in Rome. More recently, however, detailed research by Lila Yawn-Bonghi has shown that the connection between these bibles and the reform ideals was much more a grass-roots movement.[30] Most of them were not produced in Rome but in Tuscany and in the area around Pisa, and many of them were commissioned by the laity and written and illustrated by lay craftsmen. Many of them were then subsequently given to monasteries as gifts and tokens of support; in return, these laypeople expected the spiritual support from these monasteries, in the form of intercessionary prayer. Thus, the reform movement was not merely a top-down process, but it also sparked a market mechanism that fed the demand for such giant bibles among the broader population. No doubt, monasteries with a saintly reputation were seen as more effective intercessors, and for this reason, the laity was eager to support them.

In the thirteenth century, the production of bibles became increasingly the business of professional book copyists, who aimed to make a living and a profit. The main catalyst for the explosion of commercial bookmaking

---

[30] Yawn-Bonghi, "The Italian Giant Bible."

was the new student market. The thirteenth century saw the first European universities flourish in cities such as Bologna, Paris, Oxford, Salamanca, and Cambridge. To meet the demands of these universities, which were in large part populated by Dominicans and Franciscans, professional scribes and booksellers began to produce bibles commercially. In this era, the study of biblical texts became the realm of ecclesiastics training in the universities for professional careers in the Church. The universities demanded a new type of bible: smaller copies, mainly for personal use and consultation, which were less expensive and more portable than the collectively owned and consulted volumes of the monasteries or cathedrals. Bibles were now more commonly contained in one volume.

Around 1230, these bibles were finally given a revolutionary new format, which came closer than any other medieval bibles to how we conceptualize a bible today: a portable and affordable one-volume. Thanks to the use of a parchment that was much thinner than usual, and a miniscule script, these scribes succeeded in fitting one entire Bible into a book of about 400–500 leaves, measuring seven by five inches at the most, whereas many were even smaller (see Photo 3). Sometimes these thirteenth-century "pocket bibles" are ambiguously called "Paris bibles," a confusing label because they were produced all over Europe, whereas the term *Paris bible* strictly speaking only applies to those produced in Paris (see Chapter 4). More than 1,000 of these bibles survive in library and private collections. The content of these bibles reflected the school curriculum of the medieval universities, with their emphasis on the study of historical chronology and philology as a basis for scriptural theology (see Chapter 5). They contained the entire text of the Bible, including the apocryphal books, in an order that followed closely the chronology of biblical history. (A comparison between the book order and content of the Amiatinus and the Paris Bible is provided on the tables in Appendix 1.) At the end of the text, these bibles almost always included a dictionary with the interpretation of Hebrew names.

These commercially produced texts owed their ubiquity to the free-market mechanisms of their day. The newly founded and quickly expanding mendicant orders (the Franciscans and the Dominicans) provided a huge demand for bibles. These mendicant orders were founded in the thirteenth century by Francis of Assisi (ca. 1180–1224) and Domingo de Guzmán (better known as Saint Dominic, 1170–1221), respectively. Members of these orders were supported by the charity of donors, often those of middle class in the rapidly expanding medieval cities. In contrast to the older monastic orders inspired by the Rule of Benedict, the new mendicant orders interpreted the apostolic life not primarily as dedication to communal poverty, prayer and contemplation but as a more active, individual following of Christ, with emphasis on personal poverty, preaching, and Christian mission. Whereas the Rule of Benedict emphasized "stability" and obliged monks to remain in one fixed location, the new orders saw the life of the itinerant preacher as the best way to follow Christ's command to "make all people into his disciples" (Matt. 28:19). With this missionizing effort, and the university training that was seen as a preparation for it, came a demand for portable bibles for the itinerant preacher to use on his journeys and the theology student to consult during his studies.

The late medieval commercialization of book production did not mean that monks were excluded from the copying of books after the thirteenth century. The tradition of the monastic scriptoria lasted until the coming of the printed book. Increasingly, however, because of the demand for such books from a growing lay market, we see religious houses in the later Middle Ages take up book and bible production as a commercial activity. Thus, for instance, in the later Middle Ages, houses of the Brethren of the Common Life became workshops where bibles and Books of Hours were copied at the request of lay patrons. The Brethren of the Common Life were a late medieval reform movement inspired by the work of the reform preacher Geert Groote (1340–1384). They chose a way of life between the cloister and the world, guided by the Augustinian Rule. For their sustenance, the brothers (and sisters) were engaging in simple and honest crafts, and the copying of books was one of them. The revenue of this labor was often the main source of income for these houses. This activity made them instrumental players in the book culture of the late medieval Low Countries. In 1435, for instance, the regents of the Saint Bavo church in Haarlem bought for the church a three-part bible, which was written by the women of the Saint Agnes convent in Delft. The dedication page of the bible states, "May they who read in it pray for them" (i.e., the regents).[31] This Saint Agnes convent was a house of Augustinian canonesses in the general chapter of Sion, associated with the movement of the Common Life. Thus, the image of the medieval monk, devotedly penning away at copying bible manuscripts, requires some modification. Scribes for late medieval bibles could be men or women, lay or monastic, and they could be motivated by market demands or by devotion to God, and sometimes both at the same time.

---

[31] Wüstefeld, *De boeken van de grote of Sint Bavokerk*, 50–51.

THE LAYOUT OF THE BIBLE TEXT

Paleography and Punctuation

The look of the pages of a medieval bible also varied over time. All the bibles described in the previous section had their own individual characteristics. The style of handwriting, the scripts in which they were written, their size and format, and their specific layout or illuminations can all serve as clues as to when and where they were written. Some of these elements have come to characterize an entire era. The particular script in which the Tours bibles were written, for instance, was the so-called Carolingian minuscule. (An example can be seen in Photo 6). It was a clear and distinctive script, free of most of the squiggles and look-alike letters that characterized some of the scripts of the day. Its development was specific to the Carolingian educational reform and was adopted for its readability and ease of use. When the first printers in the sixteenth century were looking for a good "classical" script to emulate in their printed texts, they chose this Carolingian minuscule. Even today, the modern font Times Roman shows its Carolingian ancestry.

Sometimes paleographic elements characteristic of a certain time and place were self-consciously carried over into different contexts. The Codex Amiatinus, for instance, was written in a deliberately Italian-looking script called uncial (meaning "inch-high"; see Photo 2), derived from its sixth-century Italian original, to emphasize the close connection between Jarrow and the Roman church. It is distinctly different from the handwriting in which several Gospel books from the Ireland and England were written, which is referred to as "insular." The choice of a script that was atypical for its own period often reflected a certain ideal that the scribes wanted to emulate. The Tours bibles, for instance, in addition to the main text written in Carolingian minuscule, used scripts that were typical of classical antiquity, such as the square capital or the rustic capital, for the chapter headings of their bibles. In this way, the scribes expressed their admiration for the classical ideal and added a sense of antiquity, and thus presumably authority, to their manuscripts.

The layout of medieval Bibles was determined not only by the variety of scripts or by size and physical format. The way in which the text was read also shaped their layout. Bibles were normally meant to be read aloud, but they could also be intended for private reading. Private reading in the Middle Ages was different from today. Silent reading, common today, was unusual, because many ancient and medieval texts did not employ the visual markers for the comprehension of the reader that we expect in modern texts, such as spaces between words, capitalization, and punctuation. Augustine, for instance, remarks on the curiosity that his friend and mentor, Ambrose of Milan, could read while his "eyes drew over the lines," but "his voice and tongue were silent."[32] The rules for punctuation were more often dictated by reading aloud than by silent reading. Many copies of the *Vetus Latina* and early copies of the Vulgate, for instance, lacked spacing between the words (a phenomenon called *scriptura continua*).[33] This meant that only experienced readers could read a text. To facilitate the reading of Scripture for the less educated, and to make sure that the meaning of a text was not lost, or worse, misconstrued, by an inexperienced reader, several systems were devised to aid the reader. Jerome, for instance, recommended dividing the text of his new translations of Isaiah and Ezekiel into phrases and fragments (*cola et commata*) to facilitate an easier reading of this difficult text.[34] The text of the Amiatinus maintains this division per *cola et commata* throughout.

Punctuation was not needed in texts that were divided by *cola et commata*, but it was quite useful where this system was absent. Cassiodorus tells us that he followed this system where Jerome had used it, but also recommended "that other books be supplied with punctuation marks," and he explicitly mentions placing colons, commas, and periods in his copy of the psalter, so as to "clarify its obscurities."[35] Punctuation was a novelty in his time. To supply it in the text often also meant choosing one possible interpretation of the text over another. Although this could clarify obscurities, as Cassiodorus said, sometimes it had the opposite effect. A false punctuation mark could lead to a false interpretation of the text, as in the sentence "Let's eat, Grandma!" where the removal of the comma has serious consequences. Medieval exegetes faced similar cases, and they sometimes commented on instances where the wrong punctuation forced a wrong interpretation. In 1 Samuel 3:3–5, for instance, the Vulgate text read "[Eli's] eyes had grown dim and he could not see before the lamp of the Lord went out." The twelfth-century exegete Andrew of Saint Victor, in his commentary on this verse, observed that this really seemed absurd:

---

[32] Augustine of Hippo, *Confessionum*, 6.3.3, ed. Verheijen and Skutella, CCSL 27, 75; and *St. Augustine's Confessions*, ed. Knöll and trans. Watts, 278. See also the discussion of this passage in Petrucci, *Writers and Readers in Medieval Italy*, 133–34.

[33] Examples in Gibson, *The Bible in the Latin West*, 1–2.

[34] Jerome, *Prologus in Isaiam* and *Prologus Hiezechielis Prophetae*, in *Biblia sacra*, ed. Weber, 1096 and 1266. The image of the Amiatinus, Photo 2, may illustrate this usage.

[35] Cassiodorus, *Institutiones*, I, 1, 9 and 15, 12, ed. Mynors, 8 and 48. Translation in Cassiodorus, *Institutions*, trans. Halporn and Vessey, 109 and 144.

"Nobody has such bad eyesight that he could not see a lamp burning at nighttime more easily than an extinguished one during the daytime."[36] His solution was a better punctuation of the text: "*His eyes*, that is Eli's, *had grown dim and he could not see*, add 'clearly'. That is the end of the verse. The next verse begins: *Before the lamp of the Lord had gone out . . .*"[37] Andrew based his punctuation on the text as he found it in the Hebrew Bible, and this in turn went back to the scribal traditions in eighth- to tenth-century Palestine, where a group of scribes known as the Masoretes had established a punctuation tradition that was based on the public reading of Scripture in the synagogues. They had devised a system of sectional breaks and of short and long pauses aimed to help the reader in recitation. Their tradition went back to older manuscripts of the Hebrew text, and there is no doubt that these older tradition also influenced the Greek translations and the Latin tradition derived from it, which were more often employing the *cola et commata* system. Needless to say, scribes who were naturally reluctant to make changes in the text often felt less inhibited in changing the punctuation.

Chapter and Verse

One of the most fundamental ways in which a modern reader navigates through a bible is by the division into chapters and verses. Modern readers of the Bible have become so familiar with the division into chapters and verse that it is hard to imagine them being different, or even absent, in early medieval bibles. A medieval monk would have been utterly baffled, for instance, at seeing a highway sign proclaiming, "John 3:16!" It was not until the thirteenth century, with the Paris bible, that a division into chapters close to the one known today became common. This new chapter division has sometimes been attributed to Stephen Langton, archbishop of Canterbury from 1207 to 1228, but it is likely that the system predates him and was invented sometime in the twelfth century, most likely in England.[38] Before that, several different division patterns were current; as we saw earlier, the tradition of the Hebrew Bible already had its system of sectional breaks that indicated some division into chapters. The chapters of early medieval bibles (especially the Gospels) were commonly shorter than those in modern bibles; the older chapter division probably corresponded

---

[36] Andrew of Saint Victor, *Expositio in I Regum* 3: 3–5, ed. Van Liere, CCCM 53A, 25; translation in Andrew of Saint Victor, *Commentary on Samuel and Kings*, trans. Van Liere, CCT 3, 58.

[37] Ibid.

[38] Saenger, "The Anglo-Hebraic Origins of the Modern Chapter Division of the Latin Bible."

to the sections read in the liturgy, and Gospel books normally included a list of chapter headings at the beginning. For example, the Gospel of Matthew had seventy-four, rather than twenty-eight, chapters in the Tours Bible. When the newer chapter numbering was introduced, some existing bibles were simply adapted by crossing out the older numbers and introducing the newer chapter numbers in the margins; this adaptation can be clearly seen in the margins of the Codex Amiatinus, for instance.

The new chapter division, which survives today, is not always ideal, and at times, it tends to confuse the modern reader. Because the division into chapters postdates the composition of the text, it also may reflect traditions of interpretation that arose long afterwards. Some of these traditions may seem counter-intuitive. Chapter 1 of Genesis, for instance, would more logically have ended at Genesis 2:3, rather than 1:31, because verse four, "This is the story of the making of heaven and earth when they were created," as we now know, introduces what is often referred to as the "second creation account." Medieval exegetes made no such distinction, however. Likewise, chapter 5 of the book of Deuteronomy should really begin at Deuteronomy 4:44, "This is the Law which Moses laid down for the Israelites," which seems to start the introduction to the Ten Commandments, which follow. The chapter numbering introduced in the twelfth century resembled its modern counterpart closely, but in some places, the numeration differs from that of modern bibles. Joel 4 does not exist in the Vulgate, for instance: chapter 4 is numbered 3, and Chapter 3 is 2:28–32. Differences in the chapter division of the book of Psalms led to two different Psalm numberings in the Hebrew tradition and the Greek/Latin tradition. The Hebrew numbering splits Psalm 9 into two Psalms and combines 146 and 147 into one; as a result, the Hebrew numbering for Psalms 9 through 146 differs from the Vulgate numbering by one. Thus, for example, the Psalm well known to modern Protestants (who use the Hebrew numeration) as Psalm 23 is Psalm 22 in the Vulgate numeration. (See also Appendix B.) The fact that Jerome seemed unaware of a different chapter division in the Hebrew text suggests that the variant Hebrew numbering for the Psalms postdates Jerome.

Although the division of the bible text into chapters became standard in the thirteenth century, these chapters did not yet have a division into verses. However, by the end of the thirteenth century, the Dominicans in Paris had devised a system of dividing each chapter into alphabetical partitions, which became quite widespread. It ranged from "a" through "g" for longer chapters and "a" through "d" for shorter chapters. Thus "xii a" would point to the first quarter of chapter 12, "xii b" to the second quarter, and so on. This system corresponded to the references in the Dominicans' concordances. The division into verses as we know it today would not occur until the sixteenth century. It was introduced by the Paris printer Etienne Robert in 1534. When the earliest Hebrew Bibles started to be printed, in the sixteenth century, their verse numbering was taken from the printed Latin Bible, and it replaced the older, traditional systems.

THE BIBLE IN MEDIEVAL LIBRARIES

Although surviving medieval bibles give us many clues as to how these books were produced, and quite a few clues as to how they were used or meant to be used, it is more difficult to discern how widespread the possession of bibles was in the Middle Ages. This final section explores in more detail what is known about this. Some evidence for access to and use of the medieval Bible can come from researching medieval book inventories, or book lists. The evidence is limited, however. There are hardly any book catalogues from before the eleventh century, for instance. The ones we do have tend to be institutional rather than individual, so we know very little about book possession by private persons until the later Middle Ages.

We must be careful not to overgeneralize based on the existing book lists, which may not be very representative. We are very well informed about the contents of the papal library in Avignon, for instance. A book inventory from the time of Boniface VIII, around 1300, lists a great number of bibles, many of them large and beautifully illuminated. But, obviously, a large collection such as this one can hardly be taken as a representative medieval private library, or even a parish church. It is hard to gauge how many parish churches actually possessed bibles. An inventory of all parish churches within the archdeanery of Norwich in 1368 shows that only 6 of all 358 churches inventoried possessed complete bibles, whereas 12 more owned a glossed Bible book or Gospel book; however, all but 30 owned a lectionary.[39] Nor do medieval book catalogues always yield valuable information about the books themselves. They are not really catalogues in the modern sense, but inventories. Their function was simply to assess a monastery's possessions, not to inform a user about what was in the library; this was the job of the librarian, and he often did not need a list for this purpose. Thus, these inventories often give a very vague description

---

[39] Watkin, *Archdeanery of Norwich: Inventory of Church Goods*, xxix, xxxv, and xlvii. I wish to thank John Shinners for drawing my attention to this source.

of the book ("a large bible," "a small bible," "a small bible bound in red leather") and quite an imprecise idea of the contents. (Was it a complete bible? A glossed one? What was its date?) As for the terminology used for the Bible in these book lists, we rarely find the word *Biblia* used to denote the Bible until after mid-twelfth century; people referred to their bibles as *bibliothecae* ("libraries") or to *libri glosati*, "glossed books." When citing the Bible, they used the term *scriptura* ("Scripture"), often in the plural ("the Scriptures").

Despite these limitations, medieval book lists can sometimes yield valuable information, especially when combined with carefully researched book history. Sometimes the books from book lists can be identified with books that are still extant in modern collections, and even in the absence of booklists, shelf marks can sometimes be used to reconstruct medieval libraries, as in the case of the Cistercian monastery of Buildwas, in Shropshire, which has been largely reconstructed from the surviving volumes that bear the owner's mark of this abbey. Buildwas possessed an exceptionally beautiful set of early glossed Bible books dating from the mid-twelfth century. The books of Exodus, Leviticus (two copies), Numbers, 1 through 4 Kings, the Psalter, Jeremiah, Isaiah, the Twelve Prophets, and the entire New Testament were all present in glossed form. They were brought to the abbey by a Parisian scholar, Robert Amiclas, who collected these volumes during his life as a teacher in Paris and left them to the abbey when he retired there towards the end of the twelfth century. Except for one, these volumes now all reside in the library of Trinity College, Cambridge.

Some general observations can be made based on medieval book lists. The first, hardly surprising, is that bibles were ubiquitous in medieval libraries and that they came in variety of sizes and formats. The consensus is that one-volume bibles were rare until the thirteenth century, but nevertheless a fair number of larger eleventh-century, Carolingian, or even pre-Carolingian pandect bibles survived in later medieval book collections. From the twelfth century onward, glossed bible books were the most common format for bibles in larger libraries. After the thirteenth century, we also find smaller one- or two-volume bibles. The cathedral library of Worcester, for instance, possessed some fine large pre-Carolingian Bible codices, including the sister codex to the Amiatinus. Only a few leaves now attest to what must have been a magnificent codex.[40] It took its place alongside an almost complete set of glossed Bible books and a thirteenth-century

---

[40] London, BL, MSS Add. 37,777 and 45,025; and Ker, *Medieval Libraries*, 105.

one-volume Bible.[41] These bibles were kept in the communal library for the private use of members of the monastic community. In the case of Worcester, a large number of the medieval manuscripts are still in the present collection of the cathedral library, which gives scholars a unique opportunity to study its collection in context.

At times, even otherwise uninformative book lists yield some indication as to how books were used, as in the case of the twelfth-century booklist from Reading Abbey. It was discovered in 1792 and probably dates to the 1180s. Now kept in the British Library, it contains the earliest surviving list of books from this abbey, listing several bible volumes, including four complete bibles, which it calls "bibliothecae." One was in four volumes, one in three volumes (a bible owned by "bishop R. of London"), and one was a small bible in two volumes that "G. the cantor had made to keep in the cloister." But the bulk of the bibles listed were glossed copies of individual books of the Bible, "as they are read in the schools."[42] The monks at Reading owned almost the entire biblical text with glosses, including Apocrypha such as Wisdom. Only lacking were Chronicles, Ezra-Nehemiah and Esther (of which no glossed copies existed yet), Job, Lamentations, and Ezekiel.

Most indications of the use of medieval bibles come from these books themselves. The church bible from Saint Martin's Church in York, for instance, bears clear marks of its use as a lectern bible. According to an inscription on the last leaf, it was given by William Richardson "to the Church of Saint Martin in Konynstreet, to be chained in the choir for eternity, Christmas, 1510." The chain was probably meant to prevent theft. Some of the marginalia indicate that a bible in such a public place was more than a book to be read from: it was also used to publish marriage vows (on fol. 150 we read, "Sir, if [sic] you are desired to publish the ban of matrimony between Paul Rushton in the parish of Saint Savior and Mary Clark of this Parish."), or it was an opportunity for vandals to immortalize themselves (on fol. 210 we read, "Francis Warnefors writ this in church on Jan. the 7th, Friday, 1743.")[43]

Of course, the usage of any particular medieval bible was likely to change from one century to the next. A wonderful example is a thirteenth-century bible now in the British Library in London (MS Add. 40,006). In its

---

[41] Glossed Bibles: Genesis, Leviticus, XII Proph., Isaiah, Jeremiah and Daniel, Psalter, Gospel of John, Letters of Paul, Catholic Epistles. Some of these are still in Worcester, some now in London (BL Royal MSS) and one is at the Bodleian in Oxford; The thirteenth-century bible is in the Bodleian Library in Oxford. Ker, *Medieval Libraries*, 207–10.

[42] London, BL MS Egerton 3031. Coates, *English Medieval Books*, 25.

[43] York Minster Library, MS XVI.D.13.

margin, we find the so-called *Correctorium Sorbonense*, marginal notes that contained alternative readings of the text taken from other manuscripts and learned commentaries (see Chapter 4). It was thus originally intended as a reference bible for scholars, not for everyday devotional or liturgical use. In the fifteenth century, this bible was given by a Margaret, duchess of Clarence, to the monastery of Syon, where it acquired the new purpose of being read in the liturgy. To adapt it to its new use, a lectionary was added at the beginning, and tabs were glued to enable finding the various biblical books more quickly. After the sixteenth century, with the dissolution of the monasteries under Henry VIII (r. 1509–1547), it changed owners again. According to a note on a flyleaf, it was bought from a certain John Askew, possibly a relation to the Protestant martyr Anne Askew, by Sir Arthur Darcy, lieutenant of the Tower of London (d. 1561), for the sum of six shillings. It became a family bible. Arthur Darcy used it to write down the births, baptisms, and marriages of his children, a practice still common today.

FROM WRITTEN CODEX TO PRINTED BOOK

After Johannes Gutenberg printed his first Latin bible in 1455, the way bibles were produced would change forever. Still, the invention of printing did not produce an instantaneous revolution in the availability and accessibility of the biblical text, as has sometimes been suggested. Although the invention of printing may have decreased the price of books and increased their production, it did not immediately put a bible in every home. The level of literacy and book possession was already fairly high in the Late Middle Ages. The invention of printing was one point on a gradual line of increasing book production and ownership, not a sudden revolution.

When we consider the form and format of the earliest printed books, the invention of printing may seem even less a revolutionary development. Early book printing aimed to mechanize the process of book production in order to make it less costly. The product, the book, was supposed to look like the manuscript it replaced. The visual similarity of the first Gutenberg Bible to a manuscript written around the same time in the same place, the so-called giant Bible of Mainz (currently in the Library of Congress), is striking.[44] Even the printed font was designed to mimic late Gothic

---

[44] One can compare the two on the website of the Library of Congress: http://www.myloc.gov/Exhibitions/Bibles/TheGiantBibleofMainz/ExhibitObjects/INT_BibleCollection.aspx.

handwriting. Most of the texts printed in the fifteenth century were not new texts, but medieval best sellers. The printing press simply provided a means to keep up with the high demand for such texts. One such text was the *Mammotrectus* by Marchesino of Reggio, a medieval "Bible for Dummies" handbook (more on this in Chapter 6). Although written in the late thirteenth century, its popularity peaked with the printing of the Latin Vulgate, presumably because of its use as a compendium volume to the printed Bible. Another was the *Glossa ordinaria* on the entire Bible, printed for the first time in Strassburg in 1485 in four volumes, in the form of a *Biblia cum glossa ordinaria* (*Bible with ordinary gloss*). This put the glossed Bible within the financial reach of even the smallest convent library.

There was, however, an important difference between this *Glossa ordinaria* and the twelfth-century glossed bibles, and a comparison between the twelfth-century books and their printed version illustrates how the process of printing could change the character of a book. The twelfth-century *Glossa ordinaria* usually appeared as a collection of individual glossed bible books, not as a complete bible. Each bible book was contained in its own volume, and, as we will see in Chapter 6, the gloss on each book had its own composition history and presumably a different authorship (although always anonymous). But, now, instead of individual *libri glosati* (glossed bible books), the printing presses were producing the entire Bible text together with the full *Glossa ordinaria*. Thus, for the first time, "the gloss" had become one book. It was, of course, a book without an author, because the authorship of the various glossed Bible books had become obscured over time. To make up for the lack of a known author, it was probably in the period of printing that the first attribution of the *Glossa ordinaria* to the ninth-century Walafrid Strabo started to surface, an attribution that was to survive for several centuries, although it was repudiated many times by twentieth-century scholars, most decisively by Beryl Smalley.[45] By the sixteenth century, printers were experimenting with ways to make this glossed Bible even more efficient and attractive; they started updating it by adding more texts in the margins; as of 1506, the Postilla of Nicholas of Lyra (d. 1349) was commonly printed alongside the *Glossa ordinaria*. Bibles in this format would be printed as late as 1617. This new format may have influenced the concept of the Hebrew Bible as well; the first Hebrew

---

[45] Froehlich, "The Fate of the Glossa Ordinaria in the Sixteenth Century"; Smalley, "Gilbertus Universalis, Bishop of London."

Bible was printed in 1494 by Moses ben Gerson Soncino in Brescia; a so-called rabbinic Bible, which had rabbinical commentaries in the margin in imitation of the Christian glossed Bible, appeared in 1518 by Felix of Prato, and again in 1524 by Daniel Bomberg in Venice.

In the long run, the printing press helped to fix the text of the Bible, a text that during the Middle Ages had been still in flux to a certain degree (see Chapter 4). It helped to fix the physical format of the Bible as a small portable volume, a format that had, as we saw, late medieval antecedents. By the later sixteenth century, the Bible was no longer regarded as a collection of sacred scriptures but as a book. From a sacred library, it had now become a holy book. Its form and contents now more uniform than ever, thanks to the mass production of the printing press. This process of consolidation and standardization was not the sudden and unprecedented consequence of mechanical printing, but heir to the changes brought by the scribes who produced the Carolingian pandects and by the medieval workshops that produced the thirteenth-century Paris bibles.

RESOURCES FOR FURTHER STUDY

Many resources can be found online, including numerous digitized manuscripts collections. The entire collection of the monastery of Saint Gall and many other Swiss libraries, for instance, can be consulted at http://www.e-codices.unifr.ch/en. The British Library also has digitized a number of great manuscripts, available at http://www.bl.uk/manuscripts, as has the Bibliothèque Nationale de France, at http://gallica.bnf.fr. One can also compare two versions of the Gutenberg Bible on the Web site of the British Library at http://www.bl.uk/treasures/gutenberg/homepage.html, and similarly, the Lindisfarne Gospels can be viewed online at http://www.bl.uk/onlinegallery/sacredtexts/ttpbooks.html. The Book of Kells is at Trinity College Dublin: http://digitalcollections.tcd.ie/home/index.php. Another Gutenberg Bible, the copy in Göttingen University Library, is at http://www.gutenbergdigital.de/. The contributions in the *New Cambridge History of the Bible*, as well as the books by Gibson and Gameson, listed in the following, are good starting points for those wishing to explore the history of the Bible as a book.

SUGGESTIONS FOR FURTHER READING

The Bible as Book. The Manuscript Tradition. Edited by John L. Sharpe and Kimberly Van Kampen. London/New Castle: British Library/Oak Knoll Press, 1998.

The Early Medieval Bible. Its Production, Decoration, and Use. Edited by Richard Gameson. Cambridge Studies in Palaeography and Codicology. Cambridge: Cambridge University Press, 1994.

Chartier, Roger. *The Order of Books. Readers, Authors, and Libraries in Europe between the Fourteenth and the Eighteenth Centuries.* Translated by Lydia Cochrane. Stanford, CA: Stanford University Press, 1994.

De Hamel, Christopher F. R. *Glossed Books of the Bible and the Origins of the Paris Booktrade.* Woodbridge: D. S. Brewer, 1984.

Gamble, Harry Y. *Books and Readers in the Early Church: A History of Early Christian Texts.* New Haven, CT: Yale University Press, 1995.

Gibson, Margaret T. *The Bible in the Latin West.* The Medieval Book, 5, 1. Notre Dame, IN: University of Notre Dame Press, 1993.

Gibson, Margaret T. "Carolingian Glossed Psalters." In *The Early Medieval Bible*, 78–100.

Ganz, David. "Carolingian Bibles." In *The New Cambridge History of the Bible.* 325–37.

Light, Laura. "The Thirteenth Century and the Paris Bible." In *The New Cambridge History of the Bible.* 380–91.

Marsden, Richard. "Anglo-Saxon Biblical Manuscripts." In *The Cambridge History of the Book in Britain.* Edited by Richard Gameson. 1: 406–35 Cambridge: Cambridge University Press, 2011.

McKitterick, Rosamond. "Nuns' Scriptoria in England and Francia in the Eighth Century." In *Books, Scribes, and Learning in the Frankish Kingdoms, 6th-9th Centuries.* Collected Studies Series, VII.1–35. Aldershot and Brookfield, VT.: Variorum, 1994.

Meyvaert, Paul. "Bede, Cassiodorus, and the Codex Amiatinus." *Speculum* 71 (1996): 827–83.

Panayotova, Stella. "The Illustrated Psalter: Luxury and Practical Use." In *The Practice of the Bible.* 247–71.

Parkes, Malcolm Beckwith. *Pause and Effect. Punctuation in the West.* Berkeley and Los Angeles: University of California Press, 1993.

Roberts, Colin Henderson. *The Birth of the Codex.* In collaboration with Theodore Cressy Skeat. London: Published for The British Academy by Oxford University Press, 1987. Originally published: 1983.

Rouse, Richard H., and Mary A. Rouse. *Manuscripts and Their Makers. Commercial Book Producers in Medieval Paris, 1200–1500.* Turnhout: Brepols, 2000.

Saenger, Paul. *Space between Words. The Origins of Silent Reading.* Stanford, CA: Stanford University Press, 1997.

Sheppard, Jennifer M. *The Buildwas Books: Book Production, Acquisition and Use at an English Cistercian Monastery, 1165-c.1400.* Oxford Bibliographical Society Publications, 3rd series, 2. Oxford: Oxford Bibliographical Society, Bodleian Library, 1997.

Smith, Lesley. *The Glossa Ordinaria: The Making of a Medieval Bible Commentary.* Commentaria. Sacred Texts and their Commentaries: Jewish, Christian, and Islamic, 3. Leiden: Brill, 2009.

Thomson, Rodney M. "Robert Amiclas: A Twelfth-Century Parisian Master and His Books." *Scriptorium* 49 (1995): 238–43.
Van Engen, John H. *Sisters and Brothers of the Common Life: The Devotio Moderna and the World of the Later Middle Ages.* The Middle Ages Series. Philadelphia: University of Pennsylvania Press, 2008.

CHAPTER 3

The Medieval Canon

A modern reader who opens a printed bible has a good idea of what to expect. The canon, that is, the list of books considered authoritative by the Christian Church, is fixed, and there is very little variation in the order of books within the Bible. Admittedly, there are some differences between Catholic and Protestant bibles: Catholic bibles have a longer canon, because they include the so-called apocryphal, or deutero-canonical, books. Some Anglican (Episcopalian) bibles, steering a middle way between the Catholic and Protestant traditions, contain these books in a separate section, wedged between the Old and New Testaments. Of course, a Hebrew Bible (called a *Tanakh*), or an English translation thereof, does not include the New Testament, and the reader might also note some differences in the book order between a *Tanakh* and a Christian Old Testament.

These differences, however, pale in comparison to the bewilderment that can confront a modern student who opens a medieval bible. For a start, some books may appear "out of order." In the New Testament, the book of Acts may not appear where one expects it. The Old Testament books show an even greater variety in order and organization. Books may have unfamiliar and varying names, or a different numbering. We commonly find the Old Testament Apocrypha in medieval Bibles (but not always), and in some bibles we find apocryphal books that are completely unfamiliar to any modern bible, such as 3 and 4 Ezra, the Letter of Paul to the Laodiceans, or even 3 Corinthians. Some books may appear to be invisible, such as Lamentations (often treated as part of the book of Jeremiah), and some biblical books have verses or entire chapters that cannot be found in modern bibles. For instance, some might contain a Psalm 151. And, finally, like their modern counterparts, medieval bibles contained a hefty portion of "extra-biblical text" in the form of prefaces, commentary, and chapter headings. These could also vary from one bible to the next. All this variety, of course, makes sense if one recognizes that bibles were not books but collections of sacred writings, and that many pandect bibles were copied

53

from multivolume collections. It is the intention of this chapter to bring some order in this bewildering variety and to explain some of the history behind it.

THE CONTENTS OF MEDIEVAL BIBLES

Medieval bibles, like most medieval books, did not usually have a table of contents. Even when they did, such as the Codex Amiatinus, they could be slightly misleading. The table of contents of the Codex Amiatinus states that there are seventy books in the Bible. Seventy is a symbolic and thus highly desirable number, and it could only be achieved by some creative counting of the biblical books. The two letters of Peter are taken as one, and the book of Lamentations was regarded as a part of Jeremiah. The table of contents reads as follows:

In this codex are contained the Old and New Testaments in seventy books: Genesis, Exodus, Leviticus, Numbers, Deuteronomy, Joshua, Judges, Ruth, Samuel, Kings, Paralipomenon (Chronicles), Psalms, Proverbs, Ecclesiastes, Song of Songs, Wisdom, Ecclesiasticus, Isaiah, Jeremiah, Ezekiel, Daniel, Hosea, Joel, Amos, Obadiah, Jonah, Micah, Nahum, Habakkuk, Zephaniah, Haggai, Zachariah, Malachi, Job, Tobias, Judith, Esther, Ezra, and the books of Maccabees. Matthew, Marc, Luke, John, Acts of the Apostles, the Letters of Paul: Romans, Corinthians two, Galatians, Ephesians, Philippians, Colossians, Thessalonians two, Timothy two, Titus, Philemon, Hebrews. The letters of James, Peter, three of John, Jude, the Apocalypse (Revelation).[1]

The actual content of the Amiatinus can be found in the second column of the tables in Appendix A. A comparison between the contents of the Codex Amiatinus and those of a thirteenth-century bible (column 3) is instructive. Like the Codex Amiatinus, a thirteenth-century bible typically began with the first five books commonly ascribed to Moses (the Pentateuch), followed by Joshua, Judges, and Ruth.[2] The place of the book of Ruth could vary in medieval Bibles, but this sequence of eight books was common enough that people came to speak of the Octateuch, the eight books. Next came a series of historical books, 1 and 2 Samuel and 1 and 2 Kings. In the medieval Latin tradition, these books were commonly referred to as 1 through 4 Kings ("Regum"), following a Greek tradition. Next came 1 and 2 Chronicles (also called "Verba Dierum," which is a Latin translation of its Hebrew title, or "Paralipomenon," which is its Greek title), to which

---

[1] Codex Amiatinus, fol. 4r.
[2] Berger, *Histoire de la Vulgate*, 335–36, nos. 93 and 132.

the thirteenth-century Bible had a short apocryphal addition, the so-called Prayer of Manasseh. The latter text was rarely found in bibles prior to the thirteenth century, and it derived from early medieval prayer books. Next in this series of historical books came Ezra and Nehemiah, also called 1 and 2 Ezra, followed by the apocryphal book of 3 Ezra. Most bibles, especially the later medieval ones, also included a fourth book of Ezra. Most of 3 Ezra and parts of 4 Ezra duplicated content from the books of Chronicles. The numeration of the books of Ezra could vary: if Nehemiah was called Nehemiah instead of 2 Ezra, this would make 3 Ezra into 2 Ezra, and 4 Ezra into 3 Ezra. Some bibles then divided 4 Ezra into two books, to again total four books of Ezra. But if Nehemiah was named 2 Ezra, then Ezra would be five books in total.[3] (Some modern Bible translations add to the confusion by calling the apocryphal books of 3 and 4 Ezra "1 and 2 Esdras," after its Greek title.) The sequence ended with Tobit (or Tobias), Judith, Esther, and Job. The first two of these books are considered apocryphal, as are some parts of Esther.

After these historical books came the book of Psalms, which could exist in two versions. While the Gallican Psalter (Jerome's revision of the Latin translation of the Greek Psalms translation) was more common, some bibles contained Jerome's translation of the Hebrew Psalter instead, and some bibles even had both side by side. Some contained an apocryphal Psalm 151.[4] After this came the five "Books of Solomon": Proverbs, Ecclesiastes, Song of Songs, Wisdom of Solomon, and Ecclesiasticus, also called the Wisdom of Jesus the Son of Sirach; the latter two are apocryphal. At the end of Ecclesiasticus, after a chapter titled "The Prayer of Jesus Sirach" (chap. 51), came an extra chapter, called the "Prayer of Solomon," which was a duplication of 1 Kings 8:22–30. Next came the books of the Prophets: the four major prophets, beginning with Isaiah and Jeremiah, the latter including Lamentations and the apocryphal Baruch. Chapter 6 of the book of Baruch was the so-called Epistle of Jeremiah, a brief satirical text on false gods. Some bibles placed this letter between Lamentations and Baruch. After Baruch came Ezekiel and Daniel (with three apocryphal additions to Daniel: the song of the three men in the fiery furnace, the story of Suzanna and the elders, and the story of Bel and the Dragon), and the twelve minor prophets. In the latter, the canticle of Habakkuk circulated, just as the Psalms did, in two translations: not only in the normal Vulgate

---

3 See Bogaert, "Les livres d'Esdras et leur numérotation."
4 This Psalm 151, a song David supposedly sang after the slaying of Goliath, can be found in the Septuagint and the Qumran Scrolls (11QPs[a]).

translation but also in the Old Latin translation, which was more common in the liturgy. The Paris bible Old Testament is concluded by 1 and 2 Maccabees. Some bibles even contained an apocryphal 3 and 4 Maccabees.

The thirteenth-century New Testament looked very much like the modern one, except that the book of Acts was sometimes placed between the Pauline Epistles and the Catholic Epistles (the letters of James, Peter, John, and Jude) or, more often, between the Epistles and the last book, Revelation. Some bibles included an extra letter of Saint Paul: the apocryphal letter to the Laodiceans. The late medieval bibles on which Gutenberg modeled his first printed bible in 1455 represented the medieval canon at its largest. But even within these bibles, there could be variety in the order of the books and even in the content of the canon itself. It is easy to see why the matter of the biblical canon, the question of what biblical texts were authoritative, became an issue of serious contention during the sixteenth-century Reformation.

The Council of Trent, in its decree on Sacred Scripture of 1546, declared that the following books were canonical:

The Old Testament: the five books of Moses, namely, Genesis, Exodus, Leviticus, Numbers, Deuteronomy; Josue, Judges, Ruth, the four books of Kings, two of Paralipomenon, the first and second of Esdras, the latter of which is called Nehemias, Tobias, Judith, Esther, Job, the Davidic Psalter of 151 Psalms, Proverbs, Ecclesiastes, The Canticle of Canticles, Wisdom, Ecclesiasticus, Isaias, Jeremias with Baruch,[5] Ezekiel, Daniel, the twelve minor Prophets, namely, Osee, Joel, Amos, Abdias, Jonas, Micheas, Nahum, Habacuc, Sophonias, Aggeus, Zacharias, Malachias, two books of Maccabees, the first and second.

The New Testament: the four Gospels, according to Matthew, Mark, Luke, and John; the Acts of the Apostles written by Luke the Evangelist; fourteen Epistles of Paul the Apostle, to the Romans, two to the Corinthians, to the Galatians, to the Ephesians, to the Philippians, to the Colossians, two to the Thessalonians, two to Timothy, to Titus, to Philemon, to the Hebrews; two of Peter the Apostle, three of John the Apostle, one of James Apostle,[6] one of Jude the Apostle, and the Apocalypse of John the Evangelist.[7]

The Protestant canon, as presented in the Calvinist *Belgic Confession* of 1561, excluded the Old Testament Apocrypha. In Appendix A, a comparative table shows the variations of the medieval canon.

---

[5] Lamentations is not mentioned here, but it is assumed to be part of Jeremiah.
[6] Usually placed before 1 Peter.
[7] *Conciliorum oecumenicorum generaliumque decreta*, ed. Ganzer et al., 15–16; *Canons and Decrees of the Council of Trent*, trans. Schroeder, 17–18 The English translation cited here retains the Latin form of most of the Bible books.

THE OLD TESTAMENT APOCRYPHA

The most prominent difference between the canon of most medieval bibles and that of a modern Protestant Bible is the inclusion of the Old Testament Apocrypha. (Since the late sixteenth century, the Catholic tradition has also used the term *deutero-canonical*, from a Greek word meaning "secondary," to describe these books.[8]) What exactly are these Apocrypha, and why are they found in some bibles and not in others? The word *apocryphal* comes from the Greek *apokruphos*, meaning "hidden" or "concealed." The term is somewhat unfortunate, because it gives the impression that these books are somehow clandestine or forbidden; in fact, however, it only means that these books were not given the same authority as the "canonical," that is, authoritative, books.

A story in the fourth book of Ezra (itself an apocryphal book) offers an account of how the Hebrew Bible was established. It tells the story of how the Jewish sage Ezra restored the Scriptures of the Hebrew Bible to writing after the destruction of Jerusalem and the First Temple by the Chaldeans in B.C.E. 586. All sacred books had been burned by the Chaldeans, but by divine inspiration, Ezra perceived their content – "all that hath been done in the world since the beginning, which was written in God's law" – memorized it, and committed it to writing. Ezra relates the following:

I took with me five men, as I had been told, and we went away to the field, and there we stayed. And the next day, I heard a voice calling me, which said: Ezra, open your mouth, and drink what I give you. So I opened my mouth, and was handed a cup full of what seemed water, except that its color was the color of fire. I took it and drank, and as soon as I had done so, my mind began to pour forth a flood of understanding, and wisdom grew greater and greater within me, for I retained my memory unimpaired. I opened my mouth to speak, and I continued to speak unceasingly. The Most High gave understanding to the five men, who took turns at writing down what was said, using characters which they had not known before. They remained at work through the forty days, writing all day, and taking food only at night. But as for me, I spoke all through the day; even at night I was not silent. In forty days, ninety-four books were written.[9] At the end of the forty days, the Most High spoke to me. 'Make public the books you wrote first', He said, 'to be read by good and bad alike. But the last seventy books are to be kept back and given to none but the wise among your people. They contain a stream of understanding, a fountain of wisdom, and a flood of knowledge.' And I did so. (4 Ezra 14:37–48)

---

[8] Apparently, the term was coined by Sixtus Senensis, *Bibliotheca sancta*, 34.
[9] Text corrupt: other manuscripts have 904, 204, or 970.

The story was generally accepted in the middle ages as an historical account of how the books of the Bible had survived after the Babylonian captivity.

Reality, of course, was more complicated. As was pointed out in Chapter 2, the "Bible" was originally not a book, but a collection of sacred texts. The Hebrew Bible was conceived as being divided into three groups of books, the five books of the Torah (Law), the Nevi'im (Prophets), and a miscellaneous group of writings known simply as the Ketuvim (Writings). The canon of the Hebrew Bible, as established in the first centuries of the common era, is displayed in the first column of the tables in Appendix A. Some of these texts were so ancient and venerable that no one questioned their canonicity. There was, for instance, virtually no discussion among Jews in the first centuries before the common era about whether the scrolls of the first five books of the Bible were authoritative. In fact, some groups such as the Samaritans, a sect from the north of Israel, and possibly the Sadducees, a group mentioned by Josephus and in the New Testament that was associated with the temple administration in Jerusalem, regarded *only* these texts as canonical. In the wider circles of Judaism, the canonicity of the Prophets was hardly a point of discussion either, even though the exact text of some of these prophetic books (such as Jeremiah) could vary. In the Hebrew canon, the prophets were divided into the "former" prophets – Joshua, Judges, Samuel, and Kings – and the "latter" prophets – Isaiah, Jeremiah, Ezekiel, and the twelve minor prophets. Unlike Christians, Jews did not regard Daniel as a prophetic book.

The last part of the Hebrew Bible, the body of texts known as the "writings," was still very much in flux by the time of the Roman conquest and destruction of the Second Temple of Jerusalem in the first century C.E. When the Jewish scriptures were translated into Greek, between the third century B.C.E. to the first century C.E., for the benefit of Greek-speaking Jews in the diaspora, many texts were translated that were not part of the canon as it was current among the Jews in Palestine (or perhaps even among the earliest Christians), although they may have been accepted by a wider circle within Judaism. What was the original language of these texts was not always clear. For some of these texts, such as 4 Ezra, 1 Maccabees, the additions to Daniel and Esther, the Letter of Jeremiah, and Judith, no Hebrew original has been preserved or has been discovered only recently (Ecclesiasticus, Psalm 151). Others, such as some of the additions to Esther and the books of Baruch, 2 through 4 Maccabees, and Wisdom, may even have been written in Greek originally. Jerome mentions in his prologues that he translated the books of Judith and Tobit from the Aramaic; only fragments of the book of Tobit in Hebrew and Aramaic exist today. Some of the writings circulated in different forms; Esther and Daniel, for instance, circulated in long and short versions, with the longer version being extant in Greek only.

For a long time, modern scholars believed that the canon of the Hebrew Bible was decreed by an official meeting of the "council of Jamnia" (modern Yabneh, close to Tel Aviv) around 90 C.E., but since the late 1970s, scholars agree that this council was probably legendary.[10] The canon of the Hebrew Bible is rather a reflection of a gradually evolving consensus among Palestinian Jewry, which, by the beginning of the second century, had become normative for all of Judaism and which eventually was reflected in the contents of the eighth- and ninth-century pandect codices of the Hebrew Bible, the Aleppo Codex and the Codex Leningradensis (today in Jerusalem and St. Petersburg, respectively). Thus, we know the outcome of the canon discussion, but the process of canon formation can only be pieced together through sparse references in ancient texts. The Gospels, for instance, refer to Sacred Scripture most often as "The Law and The Prophets" (Matt. 5:17, 7:12, 22:40 and Luke 16:16), and sometimes as "The Law of Moses, the Prophets and the Psalms" (Luke 24:44), and some scholars have taken this to be representative of the Palestinian Jewish idea of the canon. A list of the books of the Hebrew canon is also given in the Talmud, written between the third and fifth centuries C.E., which divides the canon into its three traditional parts: Law, Writings, and Prophets.[11]

For rabbinical Jews, the absence of Hebrew originals for most apocryphal texts was an important factor in deciding against their canonicity. Even some of the texts presently in the canon of the Hebrew Bible could evoke discussion: some references in the Mishnah (written around the second century C.E.) and Talmud show that there were some discussions on the canonicity of Song of Songs, Esther, and Ecclesiastes, and early Christian circles also questioned whether the book of Esther should be in the canon.[12] A text from the first century C.E., Josephus's *Against Apion*, speaks about a canon of twenty-two books, divided into "five books of Moses," Prophets in "thirteen volumes," and four volumes of "hymns to God and precepts for the conduct of human life."[13] Tantalizingly, we do not know what books

---

[10] Newman, "Council of Jamnia and the Old Testament canon"; and Aune, "On the Origins of the 'Council of Javneh' Myth."

[11] *Babylonian Talmud, Baba Bathra*, 14b–15a.

[12] *Mishnah, Yad.* 3.5, trans. Danby, 781–82; *Babylonian Talmud, Megillah* 7a and *Sanhedrin* 100a. Christian sources include Melito, cited in Eusebius of Pamphilia, *Church History* 4.26.4, trans. McGiffert, 206.

[13] Josephus, *Contra Apionem* 1.37–42, trans. Thackeray, 179.

exactly he included. Did he, for instance, include the Song of Songs and Esther? Twenty-two was also the number of books the Christian church father Jerome mentioned while describing the Hebrew Bible canon. In his prologue to the book of Kings (the so-called *Prologus galeatus*, the "helmeted prologue," so called because it was seen as a fitting defense of his new translation), he described the canon of the Hebrew Bible this way:

The first book is called [by the Jews] Bresith, which we call Genesis. The second is Hellesmoth, which is called Exodus. The third is Vaiecra, that is, Leviticus. The fourth is Vaiedabber, which we call Numbers. The fifth is Addaberim, which is Deuteronomy. These are the five books of Moses, which they properly call Torath, that is, the Law. They distinguish a second order, of the Prophets, and they start with the book of Jesus son of Nave, which is called by them Joshua Bennun. Next they add Sothim, that is the book of Judges. They count together with that the book of Ruth, because in it are narrated stories that happened in the days of the Judges. Third follows Samuel, which we call first and second Kings. The fourth is Malachim, that is, Kings, which is contained within [our] books of third and fourth Kings. It is much better to say Malachim, that is, Kings, rather than Malachoth, that is, Kingdoms,[14] since it does not describe the kingdoms of many peoples, but of one Israelite people which is contained in twelve tribes. The fifth is Isaiah, the sixth Jeremiah, the seventh Ezekiel, and the eighth the book of the Twelve Prophets, which with them is called Thareasra. The third order contains the "hagiographa," and the first starts with Job, the second David, which contains five divisions in one volume of Psalms. The third is Solomon, which has three books: Proverbs, which they call Parabolas, that is, Masloth, and Ecclestiastes, that is Accoeleth, and the Song of Songs, which they assign the title Sirassirim. The sixth is Daniel, the seventh Dabreiamin, which is *Verba Dierum*, which we can correctly call the "Chronicon" of the whole of divine history, which we entitle one and two Paralipomenon. The eighth is Ezra, which is also, just as it is by Greeks and Latin, divided into two books, and the ninth Esther.[15]

Thus, by taking 1 and 2 Samuel, 1 and 2 Kings, 1 and 2 Chronicles, the twelve Minor Prophets, and Ezra-Nehemiah together as one book, and counting all books of Solomon's authorship as one, counting Ruth as part of Judges, and Lamentations as part of Jeremiah, Jerome came to the number of twenty-two books. The number had a symbolic significance for him: twenty-two was also the number of the letters of the Hebrew alphabet. For this reason, Jerome's math may seem a bit contrived; Ruth

---

[14] As they are called in the Septuagint. See also Appendix B.
[15] Jerome, *Prologus in libro Regum, Biblia sacra*, ed. Weber, 364–65.

was not normally regarded as part of the former prophets, but as one of the Ketuvim. Jerome admits that some authors count Ruth and Lamentations among this latter group and concludes cheerfully that twenty-four also has great symbolic value: there were twenty-four elders adoring the lamb in the book of Revelation (Rev. 4:4).

However the books are counted, the most distinctive feature of Jerome's Old Testament canon was that it excluded the so-called apocryphal books. This made it narrower than that of most earlier Christians, who accepted the apocryphal books as part of the Old Testament. For reasons that are explained later, Jerome preferred the version of the Hebrew Scriptures, as it was eventually written down in manuscripts such as the Aleppo Codex and the Codex Leningradensis. The text of these bibles, known as the Masoretic text, is the basis of modern Hebrew Bible editions. The Ketuvim (Writings) eventually included in the canon of the Hebrew Bible were the Psalms, Proverbs, Job, Song of Songs, Ruth, Lamentations, Ecclesiastes, Esther and Daniel in their shorter versions, Ezra, Nehemiah, and 1 and 2 Chronicles.

Christians in the same period, however, generally accepted a wider canon of books of the Old Testament, which went back to the books found in most Greek translations of the Hebrew sacred scriptures. It included books such as Tobit, Judith, Wisdom, Ecclesiasticus, Baruch, and 1 and 2 Maccabees. For some canonical books, such as Daniel and Esther, the Greek translations contained chapters that were not found in the Hebrew Masoretic bibles. In his *Institutions*, Cassiodorus gives a canon list based on the writings of two fourth-century churchmen, Hilary of Poitiers and Epiphanius, bishop of Cyprus. Cassiodorus's list is probably more representative of what a Christian Old Testament looked like than Jerome's. It bears a close resemblance to other sixth-century canon lists, such as the so-called Decree of Gelasius.[16] (Pope Gelasius lived in the fifth century, and he is very unlikely the author of the decree.) It also looked remarkably like the contents of the Codex Amiatinus, and it is based on the Greek, rather than the Hebrew, canon tradition. For the Old Testament, Cassiodorus listed

Genesis, Exodus, Leviticus, Numbers, Deuteronomy, Joshua, Judges, Ruth, Kings in 4 books, Paralipomenon (in 2 books), The five books of Psalms, Five books of Solomon, that is: Proverbs, Wisdom, Ecclesiasticus, Ecclestiastes, Song of Songs. Prophets, that is: Isaiah, Jeremiah, Ezekiel, Daniel, Hosea, Amos, Micah, Joel,

---

[16] *Das Decretum Gelasianum*, ed. Von Dobschütz, 5–6. Several English translations can be found online, e.g., at http://www.tertullian.org/decretum_eng.htm.

Obadiah, Jonah, Nahum, Habakkuk, Zephaniah, Haggai, Zachariah, Malachi (who is also called the angel), Job, Tobit, Esther, Judith, two books of Esdras, two books of Maccabees.[17]

The Greek translations of the Old Testament are often collectively known as the Septuagint. The popularity of the Septuagint was boosted by a Jewish legend about its origin, which also accounts for its name. This legend was first related in an apocryphal source, the so-called Letter of Aristeas, but we also find it mentioned by Philo of Alexandria, a first-century Jewish-Hellenistic author. The legend tells how the librarian at Alexandria, Demetrius of Phalarum, brought to the attention of King Ptolemy II Philadelphus (ruled B.C.E. 283–246) that his famous library did not yet contain a copy of the Jewish law code, the Pentateuch. On hearing this, Ptolemy summoned from Jerusalem a group of seventy-two scholars (six from every tribe of Israel), who, after their arrival in Alexandria, set to work at producing a translation of the Pentateuch. Philo relates how they worked in complete isolation from each other, but the translations they produced miraculously agreed, a sign that their translation had been divinely inspired. After these seventy-two scholars, the text became the Septuagint, meaning "the seventy."[18] Interestingly, however, although the origin of the legend is certainly Jewish and probably served to promote the authority of one Greek translation of the Pentateuch over others, the legend eventually became a Christian argument for the superiority of the Greek biblical traditions over the Hebrew ones. Augustine, for instance, in his *On Christian Teaching*, admonished Christians to check their Latin translations against the Septuagint, because it should be regarded as inspired Scripture, for in this translation, he says, by the power of the Holy Spirit, "many men had spoken with a single voice."[19]

The actual history of the Septuagint's origins is somewhat more complex. Although the oldest parts of the Septuagint may indeed date from the third century B.C.E., as the legend suggests (the oldest surviving manuscript fragments date from the second century B.C.E.), the Septuagint probably found its historical origin not in the bibliophilic curiosity of a king, but rather in the need for a Greek translation of the Scriptures for the Jewish

---

[17] Cassiodorus, *Institutiones*, I, 14, 1, ed. Mynors, 39–40; and Cassiodorus, *Institutions*, trans. Halporn and Vessey, 137. Cf. *Codex Amiatinus*, fol. vii. This list is generally referred to as the "Septuagint" order.

[18] The name "Septuagint," first used in the second century C.E., did not become common until in the fifth century; before this, it was called the "common" version (Vulgata editio), just as the *Vetus Latina* was.

[19] Augustine of Hippo, *De doctrina christiana*, II.15.22, ed. Daur and Martin, CCSL 32, 47.

communities in the diaspora. Although the legend speaks only about the translation of the Pentateuch, the name Septuagint was soon used for the Greek translation of all diaspora biblical texts, even though the quality of some of the later parts of the translation clearly was not on the same level as the Pentateuch translation. Some parts offered a fairly accurate literal translation of their originals, but others, quite in accordance with the Hellenistic tradition of translating, were free translations and paraphrased, interpolated, or even summarized the content of the Hebrew text. Not all of them used the text of the Bible as it was current in Jerusalem: for some books, such as Kings, Jeremiah, and Ezekiel (not to mention Daniel and Esther), the Septuagint followed a Hebrew text that was significantly different from the later Masoretic text.

Thus, the divergence between the two oldest versions of the Hebrew scriptures, the Septuagint text and the later Masoretic text, was one of the main historical factors in the existence of the Old Testament Apocrypha, and it is important to keep in mind that, until the time of Jerome, the Christian canon tended to include, rather than exclude, the Old Testament Apocrypha because they were included in the Septuagint. In fact, the canonicity of these texts among Christians in the ancient world may even have been a factor in the rejection of these texts from the Jewish canon.

Some Apocrypha include historical accounts, such as the first and second book of Maccabees. These were the continuation of the history recounted in the books of Ezra and Nehemiah, telling the story of the revolt of the Jews against the Seleucids in B.C.E. 175–135. Other books, such as Tobit and Judith, can be more accurately characterized as historical fiction. Tobit tells the story of a pious Jew in the time of King Salmanasser of Assyria who has fallen on hard times. Through the intervention of an angel, Raphael, the man's fortunes are restored, mainly through the enterprising actions and the marriage of his son, Tobias. The book of Judith relates a Jewish victory against the Assyrians in the time of their king, Nebuchadnezzar, due to the heroic acts of one woman, Judith. This book especially could provoke some concern on the part of medieval authors because the historical content did not exactly fit in with the known facts of world history; Nebuchadnezzar was a king of Babylonia, not Assyria, for a start. The medieval exegete Hugh of Saint Victor, for instance, expressed such doubts. He eventually concluded that, even if the Apocrypha were not free of error, they were still useful for the edification of the faithful:

We certainly recognize that in these books there are many errors with regard to numbers due to scribal mistakes; nevertheless, the diligent reader should not be troubled by such things, for there is something that approaches truth even in those passages where we cannot completely comprehend the truth.[20]

Nevertheless, even if scholars and theologians did not treat these texts as having quite the same authority as the canonical writings, the texts were very popular because of their compelling stories. The stories of Tobit and Judith, together with the legends in the apocryphal additions to the book of Daniel, such as the story of Suzanna and the Elders or the story of Bel and the Dragon, were very frequently the subject of medieval and early modern works of art.

Some of the Apocrypha were prophetic texts, such as the book of Baruch, who was thought to have been the secretary of the prophet Jeremiah. This book was not contained in the Codex Amiatinus and the Alcuin bibles, but it could be found in the Theodulf bibles, which probably copied it from pre-Vulgate codices, translated from the Septuagint. It was common in later medieval bibles. The most popular and most widely used apocrypha in the Middle Ages were no doubt the collections of wisdom literature, such as the Wisdom of Solomon and the book of Ecclesiasticus, commonly present in Septuagint and Old Latin bibles. These books enjoyed great popularity in the Middle Ages because of their practical moral content. The book of 3 Ezra also offered some wisdom sayings, but for the rest, this book was largely a duplicate of materials also contained in the book of Chronicles. The books of 3 and 4 Maccabees, common in the Christian east, were very rare in the medieval western manuscript tradition. Finally, some of the apocryphal texts may have entered into the biblical canon through the liturgy, such as the prayer of Manasseh, one of the kings of Judah, who after a life of idolatry came to repentance and turned to God. It was a popular penitential text in the east, but relatively rare in western bibles and prayer books prior to the twelfth century.

PSEUDEPIGRAPHA

The time in which many of the apocryphal books mentioned earlier were written, roughly from the second century B.C.E. until the first century C.E., saw a lively production of religious texts. Originally, when they related to biblical materials and figures but were not included in the canon, all these texts were called "apocrypha" by the ancient and medieval Church. But after the Reformation, when the term *apocrypha* began to be used in a narrow sense for those books found in the Greek but not the Hebrew canon,

---

the term *pseudepigraphica* was coined for the larger corpus of apocryphal books that may have held authoritative status at some time, but eventually were not included in either canon.[21] Some of these pseudepigrapha are found today only in the canon of various branches of the eastern churches.

The word *pseudepigraphos* means "falsely ascribed" or "under a false title." Many of these texts claim to have been written by ancient biblical figures to enhance their authority, but, in reality, many of them date from the first century before or after the common era. The fourth book of Ezra, also known as the Apocalypse of Ezra, for instance, was purportedly written by the fifth-century sage Ezra, an important figure in post-exilic Judaism. There is no doubt that this ascription helped this book achieve great status in the medieval tradition; it even was included in the canon of most medieval Latin Bibles. The core of this work was Jewish, but the first three chapters and the last two chapters are generally considered to be of Christian origin. There also was a Book of Enoch, ascribed to the patriarch Enoch mentioned in Genesis, who "walked with God; then he was no more, because God took him" (Gen. 5:24). Many of these apocryphal books were presented as "testaments," such as the Testament of the Twelve Patriarchs, and some of them are best described as paraphrases of commentaries on canonical books, such as the book of Jubilees, the Life of Adam and Eve (also known as the Apocalypse of Moses), or the Lives of the Prophets. Some were collections of a more philosophical nature, such as 4 Maccabees, and some were liturgical texts, such as the Prayer of Manasseh or the Psalms of Solomon. The line between pseudepigraphical texts and apocryphal texts is sometimes hard to draw.

Although some of these pseudepigraphical texts were specific to certain sects and were virtually unknown until modern times (many of the texts contained in the Qumran scrolls fall into this category), many were popular in Jewish and Christian circles alike. Some of them may have been authoritative at one time, but lost that status in a later period. For instance, the book of Enoch is cited as an authoritative text in the New Testament Epistle of Jude (Jude 14–15). Some continued to be popular and influential in the Middle Ages. The pseudepigraphical Life of Adam and Eve, for instance, was widely read throughout the Middle Ages. It narrated the events in the lives of Adam and Eve after their expulsion from paradise. It relates how when Adam falls ill, Eve and her son Seth journey back to the gate of paradise to request some oil of the tree of life in order to cure

---

[21] The first to use the term in its modern sense is Johann Fabricius, in his *Codex pseudepigraphus Veteris Testamenti*, but it was coined by Jerome, *Prologus in Libros Solomonis*, in *Biblia sacra*, ed. Weber, 957.

him. They are turned back, however. Some Christian versions of the text here add a promise that in due time, Christ will come and lead Adam to the tree of mercy in paradise. Eventually, Seth writes down the story of the life of his parents on two stone tablets, to preserve it for posterity. This source found its way into exegetical handbooks such as Peter Comestor's twelfth-century *Historia scholastica* (*Scholastic History*, described in more detail in Chapter 6), in which it is used to provide some background to the events in the first chapters of Genesis.

The first part of the book of Enoch (also called the book of the Watchers) provides an extended commentary on Genesis 6, which relates how the "Sons of God," interpreted as the angels, saw that "the daughters of men were pleasing," had intercourse with them, and produced a race of giants. The book attributes much of the sinfulness of the human race to this transgression, and with its description of the fall of the angels, it provides popular supplements to the creation story. The story of the Fall of Angels was so widely known in the Middle Ages that some commentators even wondered why Moses did not start out the book of Genesis with it. It continued to be influential into the early modern period, as John Milton's *Paradise Lost* shows. Much of the rest of the book of Enoch (the book of Parables, and the Astronomical Book) contains extensive descriptions of the travels of Enoch through heaven and earth and his apocalyptic visions. The last part, the book of Dream Visions, is an allegorical account of the history of Israel. Thus, many pseudepigraphical books expanded on themes and stories found in the Old Testament or provided some kind of commentary on these stories. Another example is the book of Joseph and Senath, which narrates the courtship of Joseph with his Egyptian wife, the mother of Ephraim and Manasseh (mentioned in Gen. 41:50–52). A Latin version of this story was appended as a lengthy gloss to the manuscript of the Old English Heptateuch (see Chapter 7). All these texts were clearly held in some authority in the Middle Ages and were widely read, although never regarded as canonical. However, they had a huge influence on the interpretation of the canonical books of the Bible, and they were widely depicted in works of art as well (see Chapter 9).

THE NEW TESTAMENT CANON

The Bible of the earliest Christians was the Hebrew Scriptures, usually in their Septuagint translation. But by the end of the first century C.E., as the oral tradition about the life of Jesus started to fade, Christians began to develop their own scriptural tradition, consisting of Gospels (accounts of Jesus' life and collections of his sayings) and letters of instruction by various apostles, especially Paul. What authority these "new" texts held was not really clear until the end of the second century, when the Roman priest Marcion made one of the first attempts to establish a canon of sacred and authoritative scriptures for the Christian community. But Marcion was a contested figure, and some of his beliefs were not shared by all Christians. He believed that Jesus Christ was sent not by the ancient God of Israel but by a hitherto unknown god, whose law superseded the old one and who thus rendered the Jewish sacred Scriptures obsolete. Marcion held that the only authoritative texts for Christians should be an edited-down version of the Gospel of Luke and the Letters of Paul. From the latter he had expurgated any references to the God of the Old Testament. Many influential Christian church fathers disagreed with him, and although they berated the Jews for not believing in the divinity of Christ, they did confess that they believed in the same God as the Jews. They saw the Christian Church as a continuation of the ancient covenant that God had made with the people of Israel.

It was thus in reaction to Marcion that theologians such as Irenaeus of Lyon, by the end of the second century, first began to formulate a canon of New Testament Scriptures as authoritative for the Christian Church. They insisted that the Hebrew Scriptures (in their Greek translations), which they now called the Old Testament, were part of these Christian scriptures. At the same time, these early Church fathers tried to narrow down the list of sacred scriptures, by excluding from it the written witnesses about Christ that they considered heretical. Many of these contained esoteric teachings they called "gnostic." Their condemnation of these scriptures was very successful, because many of them were practically forgotten until the nineteenth or even twentieth century. These included writings such as the Gospel of Mary Magdalene. A large find of Gnostic Gospels in Nag Hammadi in Egypt in 1948 has substantially enhanced our understanding of this branch of early Christian Scriptures. Most of these were virtually unknown in the Middle Ages; others, such as the Gospel of Thomas, were known by title only, because these were copied from patristic lists of "heretical books."

Irenaeus' list of New Testament books contained most of what would become the New Testament canon, although he did not mention the canonical Epistles of James, Jude, 2 Peter, and 2 and 3 John, and did include an apocryphal book called the *Shepherd of Hermas*.[22] At the core of his New

---

[22] Irenaeus' list is cited in Eusebius of Pamphilia, *Church History*, 5.8.2–8, trans. McGiffert, 222–23.

Testament canon were the four canonical Gospels. There are indications that, even in Gnostic circles, these were held in high authority early on. One of the problems with these four different Gospels was that they partly overlapped but partly also diverged. Whereas the Gospel of Luke, for instance, tells the narrative of the birth of Christ with the now familiar scene of the shepherds in the field, Luke does not mention the visit of the three magi. We can find these in Matthew, however, who in turn omits the shepherds. Early on, Christians attempted to harmonize the four Gospels into one sequential narrative. One of these attempts was the so-called *Diatessaron* (meaning "across four") by Tatian, written at the end of the second century. Even though Tatian's Gospel harmonization would become a canonical text for the Syrian Church until the fifth century, most Christian Churches chose to adhere to the four Gospels as their canonical Scripture. Still, Tatian's compilation retained some of its popularity throughout the Middle Ages as a basis for devotional texts (the so-called Life of Christ tradition) and vernacular Gospel translations (see Chapter 7). A sixth-century Latin copy of the *Diatesseron*, the Codex Fuldensis, was based on Tatian's harmonization, but the translation was adapted to match the Vulgate, rather than the Old Latin; this manuscript is not only the earliest evidence of the use of Tatian in the west, but it may also be one of the oldest witnesses to the Vulgate text of the Gospels. This codex was the source, not only for a vernacular translation into Old Franconian but also for the Old Saxon biblical poem the *Heliand* (*The Savior*, see Chapter 7). To facilitate the harmonization of the canonical Gospels, Eusebius of Caesarea devised a system of parallel tables; many early medieval bibles and Gospel books contain a version of these Eusebian canon tables (see Chapter 4 and Photo 7).

Although a consensus on the New Testament canon was in place by the end of the third century, the discussion would not be completely over until the end of the fourth century. The status of some books was still debated, such as the Letter to the Hebrews (some western theologians, following Jerome, argued that it was not written by Paul, an argument that would be repeated by many medieval exegetes and is accepted today)[23] and the Apocalypse of John (not usually included in eastern canon lists). The main grounds for deciding on the canonicity of a book were apostolicity (whether it was purportedly written by one of the apostles), antiquity (whether it was ancient or recent), and, above all, whether it conformed to the basic creed of the early Churches. By the end of the fourth century, various

---

[23] Jerome, *Prologus in Epistulis Pauli*, in *Biblia sacra*, ed. Weber, 1748.

documents attest to a consensus on the New Testament canon. These do not reflect any "official decisions" of the Church as a body; instead, they suggest that, because there was a general agreement, no such decision was needed. In the east, one of the earliest documents attesting to the books in the New Testament canon is the Letter of Athanasius of Alexandria, dated 367. Athanasius still named two early patristic documents as part of the canon: the *Shepherd of Hermas* and the *Didache* (*Teachings of the Apostles*), an early catechetical text. The oldest surviving complete codex of the New Testament, the Codex Sinaiticus, also included these two texts. In the west, the Synod of Rome in 382 and the third Council of Carthage in 397 affirmed very much the same canon, while excluding the latter two texts.[24] Despite this consensus, medieval Latin bibles sometimes still included spurious Pauline Epistles such as Paul's letter to the Laodiceans. In the Eastern Orthodox or Coptic tradition, the *Didache* and the *Shepherd of Hermas*, in addition to early patristic texts such as the Clementine Epistles and the Epistle of Barnabas, were regarded as canonical.

NEW TESTAMENT APOCRYPHA

All the texts that were regarded as sacred in some early Christian circles but were eventually not included in the New Testament canon, whether by deliberate exclusion or otherwise, may be considered "New Testament apocrypha." This term is often subject to some misconceptions. A nineteenth-century English translation of these New Testament Apocrypha, for instance, was reprinted in 2005 under the title *The Lost Books of the Bible*. The promotional blurb claimed that "when the Bible was compiled in the end of the fourth century, these texts were not among those chosen. They were suppressed by the Church, and for over 1500 years were shrouded in secrecy."[25] Ironically, the texts contained in the book were not suppressed at any time and, contrary to the claim, were hugely popular and influential throughout the Middle Ages. To be sure, some spurious epistles of early Christian authors never really caught on as Sacred Scripture, and some Gnostic Gospels regarded as heretical by the early Church were probably "suppressed." But most New Testament apocrypha were thoroughly orthodox texts meant to offer edifying supplements to existing New Testament materials. Many of these texts remained popular

---

[24] *Enchiridion symbolorum*, ed. Denzinger, 71–72 and 74.
[25] Inside cover of the 2005 Dover reprint of *The Apocryphal New Testament*, trans. Jones and Wake, cited on its Amazon Web site: http://www.amazon.com/Books-Bible-Dover-Value-Editions/dp/0486443906/.

throughout the Middle Ages and profoundly influenced medieval culture. Some were written too late to be considered part of the canon, despite their ascription to some of the apostles, such as Thomas, James, or even Paul. Many were clearly dependent on the canonical Gospels and aimed to give additional narrative material that the believers felt was lacking in the Gospels.

A good example is the Gospel of Nicodemus, a Gospel narrative that concentrates on the passion of Christ. It begins with the trial of Jesus by Pontius Pilate, and most of the life of Christ, concentrating on his miracles, is narrated as a flashback by witnesses at the trial. After Christ's crucifixion and resurrection, the Gospel relates various disputes between the Jews and three secret disciples of Christ: Nicodemus, Joseph of Arimathea, and Gamaliel. This culminates in the testimony of two sons of Simeon, who rose from the dead at Christ's crucifixion and who give a vivid description of Christ breaking open the gates of hell and leading various Old Testament patriarchs out of hell into heaven. This apocryphal Gospel spread widely in the Middle Ages and was the principal source for dramatic depictions of the scenes preceding the resurrection of Christ, the so-called harrowing of hell. It also gave names to some otherwise anonymous figures in the Gospel, such as Longinus, the soldier who pierced Christ on the cross, and Veronica, the woman who was healed from a hemorrhage in Luke 8:44 and was thought to have wiped Christ's face on his way to the cross.

Other apocryphal gospels aimed to provide more narrative information about the events that came before the canonical Gospels, such as the proto-Gospel of James and the Gospel of the Birth of Mary, allegedly written by Matthew. The latter, often supplemented with materials from the Proto-Gospel of James, was widely read, copied, and incorporated into new proto-Gospels in the Middle Ages and eventually was included in Jacob of Varazzo's *Golden Legend*, a thirteenth-century devotional collection of saints' lives. The Gospel of the Birth of Mary relates how Mary's parents, Joachim and Anna, had been barren for a long time, and when an angel announces the birth to them both independently, the two rush to Jerusalem and meet at the Golden Gate, which the angel had announced as a sign for the miraculous conception of the Virgin Mary. Mary is born and is raised in the Temple of the Lord until she is to be betrothed to a man whose rod should flower and on whom the Spirit of the Lord rests. Of all the young men present, only Joseph's rod answers to that description. The Gospel ends with the betrothal, followed by the birth of Christ. The proto-Gospel of James reiterates much of the same material, but dwells longer on the events surrounding the birth of Christ. This proto-Gospel provided the many traditions and stories about the birth of Jesus that could not be found in the canonical Gospels. The Gospel of Luke does not mention that Jesus was born in a stable, for instance; the apocryphal proto-Gospels have Jesus born in either a cave or a stable. No canonical Gospel mentions the ox and the donkey that are ubiquitous in depictions of the nativity: they are mentioned in the proto-Gospel of Pseudo-Matthew, which cited the adoration by the two animals as a fulfillment of a prophecy of Isaiah (Isa. 1:3).[26]

Other apocryphal texts provide details about the childhood of Jesus, such as the Gospel of pseudo-Thomas (not to be confused with the Gnostic Gospel of Thomas). These childhood gospels also relate how, when Jesus entered Egypt on the flight into Egypt, his presence caused all idols to break into pieces. Jesus is depicted as a prodigious miracle worker who offers his father divine assistance in his woodworking projects and even brings toy clay birds to life. Some of the stories, especially those related in pseudo-Thomas, may alienate the modern reader, because they depict Jesus as a vengeful, all-powerful child who often uses his divine powers to avenge the injustices suffered at the hand of his (explicitly Jewish) playmates. Other apocryphal texts depict events that came after the canonical Gospels, such as the short *Transitus Mariae* (*Passage of Mary*), which tells of the death, assumption, and coronation of the Virgin Mary. Many of these apocryphal gospels circulated in the vernacular as well; the infancy Gospels seem to have been particularly popular in medieval Ireland. Also widespread were apocryphal acts of various apostles, such as the Acts of Peter, which tells of Peter's confrontation with Simon Magus and his martyrdom in Rome, or apocalyptic literature, such as the Apocalypse of Paul, which, with its vivid description of hell, was an important source for Dante's *Inferno*.

CANON AND AUTHORITY IN THE MIDDLE AGES

As we have seen, considerable variations were possible in the medieval canon, not only regarding what books were considered canonical but also regarding how these books were arranged and numbered. Jerome, for instance, argued that the Hebrew Bible contained twenty-two books, because the Hebrew alphabet contained twenty-two letters. The total of books in both testaments, for Jerome, came to forty-nine, which is seven times seven, a number that signifies completeness. Other authors, such as Augustine, counted the books in the canon differently and came closer to

---

[26] *Gospel of Ps.-Matthew*, 14, in *The Apocryphal New Testament*, ed. Elliott, 94.

a number of seventy-two for the total of books in the entire Bible, Old and New Testament. Augustine's canon list is cited, along with those of Jerome, and Hilary and Epiphanius, in the prefatory material of the Codex Amiatinus. It was derived from Augustine's book *On Christian Teaching*,[27] but the author of the preface to the Codex Amiatinus more likely found it cited in Cassiodorus' *Institutions*:

The entire holy scripture is divided thus: In the Old Testament: In history, twenty-two books. That is, of Moses five books, Joshua, Judges, Ruth, four books of Kings, two books of Paralipomenon, Job, Tobias, Esther, Judith, two books of Ezra, two books of Maccabees. In prophecy, twenty-two books, namely David's Psalms, three books of Solomon, two books of Jesus the son of Sirach; and the Prophets: Hosea, Joel, Amos, Obadiah, Jonah, Micah, Nahum, Habakkuk, Zephaniah, Zachariah, Haggai, Malachi, Isaiah, Jeremiah, Daniel, Ezekiel, sixteen books.

And in the New Testament: Four Gospels, according to Matthew, Mark, Luke, and John. Twenty-one letters of the Apostles; by Paul: Romans, Corinthians two, Galatians, Ephesians, Philippians, Thessalonians two, Colossians, Timothy two, Titus, Philemon, Hebrews; two of Peter; three of John, one of Jude, one of James. The Acts of the Apostles and the Apocalypse of John.[28]

This canon list adds up seventy-one books. Augustine argued that the unity of the whole canon would bring the number to seventy-two, which is the number of elders who had translated the Septuagint and is the number of disciples of Christ mentioned in Luke 10:1. The compilers of the preface of the Codex Amiatinus seem to have sympathized with the reader who might have been confounded by all the discrepancies between the various canon lists. Thus, after listing the three versions, the writer concluded that although these canon lists might seem contradictory, this "should not disturb the reader; the multiplicity of ways all leads into the same instruction of the heavenly Church."[29]

Whereas most of the New Testament Apocrypha throughout the Middle Ages were regarded as edifying but not authoritative, the status of the Old Testament Apocrypha was more ambiguous. Jerome intended his *Prologus galeatus* to make clear what books were not considered part of the canon:

This prologue to the Scripture can be regarded as a fitting "helmeted introduction" to all books that we have turned from Hebrew into Latin, so that we may know

---

[27] Augustine of Hippo, *De doctrina christiana*, II.8.13. ed. Daur and Martin, CCSL 32, 39; translation in *Saint Augustine, On Christian Teaching*, trans. Green.

[28] *Codex Amiatinus*, fol. viii, citing Cassiodorus, *Institutions*, trans. Halporn and Vessey, 136.

[29] *Codex Amiatinus*, fol. iv r.

that whatever is not included with them, should be put apart, among the apocryphal books.[30]

In a letter to the Roman noblewoman Leta, on the education of her daughter Paula, a nun, Jerome advised her to read the Scriptures diligently but warned her that

She should avoid all apocryphal books. And if she wants to read them not for the truth of doctrines, but out of reverence for its signs [i.e., for their allegorical meaning, see Chapter 5], she should know that they are not written by the ones with whose titles they are marked. There are many errors mixed in with them, and it requires great prudence to find some gold in the mud.[31]

In his preface to the so-called books of Solomon, he admonishes his readers about the books of Wisdom and Ecclesiasticus:

Just as the Church reads the books of Judith and Tobit and Maccabees, but has not accepted them among the canonical scriptures, thus also it should read these two works for the edification of the people, but not to confirm the authority of Church doctrine.[32]

Of course, Jerome could not (and probably did not intend to) stop their circulation; they were too much part of the Christian scriptural tradition. Because they were commonly included in the Old Latin Bible translations (see Chapter 4), they often were copied and transmitted together with Jerome's new translation, as we have seen in the case of the Codex Amiatinus. Only the bibles copied in Orleans under Theodulf's direction made a clear distinction between canonical and apocryphal texts, by including them in a separate section between the Old and New Testaments.[33] In practice, the Old Testament Apocrypha were treated as authoritative texts. Still, due in part to Jerome's assertions, doubts lingered, and discussions about the canon would continue to reverberate throughout the Middle Ages.

To gain an idea of how later medieval theologians and exegetes viewed the biblical canon, it can be instructive to look at the work of Hugh of Saint Victor (ca. 1096–1141), a Parisian scholar who wrote a small introduction to the entire Bible, called *On Sacred Scripture and Its Authors*. For Hugh,

---

[30] Jerome, *Prologus in libris Regum*, in *Biblia sacra*, ed. Weber, 365 The word *helmeted* probably refers to the helmet as a defensive devise against heterodoxy.

[31] Jerome, *Epistola* 108, PL 22, 877.

[32] Jerome, *Prologus in libris Solomonis*, in *Biblia sacra*, ed. Weber, 957.

[33] Thus, London MS Add. 24,142, fol. 164r, which contains these books in a fourth section, after the Law, Prophets, and Writings, as "those books who are in the Old Testament, outside the canon of the Hebrews."

all canonical books of the Bible were divinely inspired, free of error, and absolutely true:

> Only that scripture is rightly called "sacred" that is inspired by the Spirit of God and that, administered by those who have spoken by the Spirit of God, make the human person holy – reforming him according to the likeness of God, instructing him to know God, and exhorting him to love Him. Whatever is taught in it is truth; whatever is prescribed in it is goodness; whatever is promised in it is happiness. For God is truth without falsehood, goodness without malice, happiness without misery.[34]

In considering what books were considered canonical, for the Old Testament, Hugh mainly followed the canon list provided by Jerome in the *Prologus galeatus* cited earlier. But he added that

> Besides these, there are some other books that are certainly read – such as the Wisdom of Solomon, the book of Jesus the son of Sirach, the book of Judith, and Tobit, and the books of the Maccabees – but are not included in the canon.[35]

The main reason to declare these books "apocryphal" is that they were not written by the persons whose names they bear. Thus, Hugh defines "apocryphal" as what we would call pseudepigraphical:

> They are called apocryphal, that is, "concealed" and "secret," because they have come into question. Their origin is obscure, and the holy Fathers do not tell us by whom they were written. There is some truth in them, but because of their many errors they nevertheless have no canonical authority. It is rightly concluded that they were not written by those to whom they are attributed, for many were published by heretics under the names of the prophets and the more recent ones under the names of the Apostles. After due consideration, all of these works have been removed from [those works possessing] divine authority and they have been called apocryphal.[36]

Hugh has to admit that this definition does not always hold water. Some perfectly canonical books have an uncertain authorship, he says, such as the book of Job. By contrast, the authors of some apocryphal books are perfectly well known, such as the book Ecclesiasticus, which, according to

---

[34] Hugh of Saint Victor, *On Sacred Scripture* 1, in *Interpretation of Scripture: Theory*, 213.

[35] Hugh of Saint Victor, *On Sacred Scripture* 6, in *Interpretation of Scripture: Theory*, 219.

[36] Hugh of Saint Victor, *On Sacred Scripture* 11, in *Interpretation of Scripture: Theory*, 222; cf. Hugh, *Didascalicon de Studio Legendi*, IV.7, ed. Buttimer, 77–78.

its own prologue, was written by Jesus Sirach. Thus, Hugh modifies his definition:

The word "apocryphal," that is, a doubtful and hidden book, is used in two ways: either because its author is uncertain, or because it has not been accepted and confirmed by the general assent of the faithful Synagogue or Church, even though there is nothing reproachable in it.[37]

Thus, ultimately, it was the authority of the Church or Synagogue, not authorship, that decided what books were apocryphal or not.

Although God was seen as the ultimate "author" of Scripture, the books had their human authors, too. They were commonly referred to by medieval authors as the "scriptors," as writers rather than authors. For medieval Christian scholars, there was no doubt that Moses had written the Pentateuch; Joshua, the book of Joshua; and Samuel, the book of Judges and part of Samuel. The rest of Samuel and the Psalms were written by David (whereas Ezra was thought to have written the *tituli*, or headings, of the Psalms), and the books of Kings were collected by Jeremiah from the writings of various prophets. All prophets wrote the books bearing their names. Hugh also says that Solomon wrote the books that were traditionally ascribed to him, that is, Proverbs, Ecclesiastes, and Song of Songs. The book of Wisdom was apocryphal: it allegedly was written by Solomon, but in fact, it "reeked of Greek eloquence."[38] Ezra wrote the books of Ezra and Esther, and Nehemiah the book that bears his own name. Ezra was also considered the author of the books of Chronicles. The authorship for the New Testament writings was hardly ever in doubt: all were regarded as being written by the people whose name they carried. Only for the letter to the Hebrews, as we saw, did some doubt linger as to its canonicity, because Jerome had already cited some doubts about its authorship in his preface to the Letters of Paul: "Some are of the opinion that the Letter that is written to the Hebrews is not by Paul, for the reason that it is not entitled with his name, and because of the distance in word and style."[39] Jerome himself, incidentally, disagreed with this opinion. The differences in style could be accounted for by the fact that Paul initially wrote this letter in Hebrew, he said.

Hugh's discussion on the canon of the New Testament, however, seems to stretch the definition of "canonical" to embrace all works that were

---

[37] Hugh of Saint Victor, *On Sacred Scripture* 12, in *Interpretation of Scripture: Theory*, 223.
[38] Hugh of Saint Victor, *On Sacred Scripture* 7, in *Interpretation of Scripture: Theory*, 220.
[39] Jerome, *Prologus in Epistulis Pauli*, in *Biblia sacra*, ed. Weber, 1748.

"authoritative" and "approved by the common consensus of the Church." In one of his earlier writings, the *Didascalicon*, a work intended to be a guide to the study of the arts and Scriptures, Hugh described the canon of the New Testament as including the "decretals, which we call canons, that is, rules. Then come the writings of the holy Fathers and the Doctors of the Church: Jerome, Augustine, Gregory, Ambrose, Isidore, Origen, Bede, and many other orthodox writers whose works are so vast that they cannot be counted."[40] There has been some discussion among modern scholars about whether Hugh really intended to include the decretals and church fathers here within the canon of Scripture.[41] In any case, Hugh's suggestion must have struck even his contemporaries as innovative and radical. For instance, a later contemporary of Hugh, a fellow canon at the abbey of Saint Victor, Robert of Melun, says in his *Sentences*,

Some people divide the New Testament into three parts: [1] the Gospels; [2] the Canonical Epistles, the epistles of Paul, the Acts of the Apostles, and the Apocalypse of John; and [3] the writings of the Fathers, that is, of Jerome and Augustine and the other commentators on the Old and New Testaments. Others, however, do not want the writings of the Fathers to be part of the New Testament. The Gospels, they say, are the first part, and the Canonical Epistles and the epistles of Paul are the second part. They declare that the third part is the Acts of the Apostles and the Apocalypse of John. For they want the New Testament to consist of these books alone, because in them there is nothing that can be corrected or changed or deemed false.[42]

Perhaps realizing the oddity of his earlier statement (no one would argue that the writings of the church fathers were without error, because Augustine himself had written a book called *Retractationes* [*Retractions*], in which he admitted and corrected many of his own errors), Hugh modified it somewhat in his work *On Sacred Scripture*, to disavow the idea that the writings of the Church fathers had the same authority as Sacred Scripture. The writings of the Church fathers, Hugh says, are to be treated with the same respect as the Old Testament Apocrypha: they may not be without error, but they still are held to be authoritative within the Christian tradition:

These writings of the Fathers are not included in the text of the Sacred Scriptures, just as in the Old Testament there are some books, as we said, that are not

---

[40] Hugh of Saint Victor, *Didascalicon*. 4.2, in *Interpretation of Scripture: Theory*, 135.
[41] Berndt, "Gehören die Kirchenväter zur Heiligen Schrift? Zur Kanontheorie des Hugo von St Viktor."
[42] Robert of Melun, *Sentences* I.1.12, in *Interpretation of Scripture: Theory*, 466.

included in the canon but are still read, such as the Wisdom of Solomon and others.[43]

The long list of New Testament Apocrypha that Hugh cites in his *Didascalicon* probably does not contain any books that he knew firsthand: they are cited from the pseudo-Gelasian Decree, a sixth-century canon list.[44]

The question of whether the Apocrypha were part of Sacred Scripture was never definitively settled until the sixteenth century. When this discussion was settled, Christian paths diverged. Protestants chose to exclude from the canon of Sacred Scripture certain books that Catholics said should be considered part of it. Sixteenth-century reformers such as Martin Luther followed Jerome's Hebrew canon of Scripture rather than Augustine's. Often, theological content influenced the reformers' views on the authority of the canonical books; many of the apocryphal books were used to bolster support for ecclesiastical practices and beliefs of which the Reformers disapproved. The book of Maccabees, for instance, seemed to lend support to the idea of offering prayers for the dead (2 Macc. 12:42) and the book of Baruch supported the idea of the intercession of the saints (Bar. 3:4). The book of Ecclesiasticus (Ecclus. 15:14) provided a proof text for the idea of free will, against divine predestination. The Catholic Church's official reaction to the Protestant Reformation was proclaimed at the Council of Trent, which met in three lengthy sessions beginning in 1545. Its third decree, *On Sacred Scripture*, issued in 1546, confirmed the wider canon (that of Augustine) as true and inspired Scripture while at the same time purging some of the content of the thirteenth-century bibles. For instance, 4 Ezra, 3 and 4 Maccabees, and Laodiceans were rejected.[45] Baruch, probably for its association with Jeremiah, stayed.

Thus, strictly speaking, the biblical canon was not completely "closed" in the Middle Ages. The canonical books were, of course, held in high authority, and the same authority was generally ascribed to the deuterocanonical books; the reservations that Jerome had expressed regarding these books were often repeated, but in practice were not heeded, in the Middle Ages. The medieval canon is perhaps best imagined as a set of concentric circles. In the center were the books that were "definitely in." They were surrounded by a number of books that were "perhaps not in:" the apocryphal books that were normally included but not regarded with the

---

[43] Ibid., in *Interpretation of Scripture: Theory*, 467.

[44] The fifth book of the *Decretum Pseudo-Gelasinum*, ed. Von Dobschütz. English translation at www.tertullian.org/decretum_eng.htm.

[45] *Conciliorum oecumenicorum generaliumque decreta*, ed. Ganzer et al., 15–16.

same authority as the rest. There were also some books that were "perhaps in:" apocrypha that occurred only rarely in medieval bibles, such as the Epistle to the Laodicensians and 4 Ezra; we find them in some medieval canon lists, but not in all. Finally, there were the books that were "definitely not in," such as the Gospel of Nicodemus. Although these latter books were never really regarded as canonical, some continued to have considerable influence on the interpretation of the canonical books. One of the aspects that often surprises modern students is the absence of Church regulation on this matter. There was a broad consensus, but an absence of definitive rules. In the Middle Ages, when every copy of a book was unique, it was next to impossible to regulate the exact contents of every copy of the Bible. This changed with the invention of printing. It is therefore no coincidence that the canon of Scripture became permanently fixed by an ecclesiastical decision only after the Middle Ages ended.

RESOURCES FOR FURTHER STUDY

The best introduction to the biblical canon is by McDonald, *The Biblical Canon*. Regrettably, most studies on the canon and the Apocrypha do not cover the Middle Ages. Scholarly study of the Apocrypha should start with the *Clavis apocryphorum Veteris Testamenti*, edited by Haelewyck and the *Clavis apocryphorum Novi Testamenti*, edited by Geerard. A useful Internet portal is http://www-user.uni-bremen.de/~wie/bibel.html. A large collection of biblical translations, apocrypha, and pseudepigrapha can be found in the *Christian Classics Ethereal Library*, http://www.ccel.org/, and the *Internet Sacred Text Archive*, http://www.sacred-texts.com/.

SUGGESTIONS FOR FURTHER READING

The Canon Debate: On the Origins and Formation of the Bible. Edited by Lee Martin McDonald and James A. Sanders. Peabody, MA: Hendrickson, 2002.

Filson, Floyd V. *Which Books Belong in the Bible? A Study of the Canon*. Philadelphia: Westminster Press, 1956.

Jobes, Karen H., and Silva Moisés. *Invitation to the Septuagint*. Grand Rapids, MI: Baker Academic, 2000.

McDonald, Lee Martin. *The Biblical Canon. Its Origin, Transmission, and Authority*. 2nd ed. Peabody, MA: Hendrickson, 2007.

Metzger, Bruce M. *The Canon of the New Testament. Its Origin, Development and Significance*. Oxford: Oxford University Press, 1987.

———. *The Text of the New Testament. Its Transmission, Corruption, and Restoration*. 3rd enlarged ed. Oxford: Oxford University Press, 1992.

Von Campenhausen, Hans. *Die Entstehung der christlichen Bibel.* Beiträge zur historischen Theologie, 39. Tübingen: J. C. B. Mohr (Paul Siebeck), 1968.

Würthwein, Ernst. *The Text of the Old Testament.* Translated by Erroll F. Rhodes. 2nd ed. Grand Rapids, MI: Wm. B. Eerdmans Publishing Co., 1995.

CHAPTER 4

The Text of the Medieval Bible

When Jerome was asked by Pope Damasus in 382 C.E. to produce a reliable version of the Latin Gospels and Psalter, he did not interpret this as a request to produce a new translation from the Greek and Hebrew originals. A Latin translation, or, rather, translations (for there were several versions), which later came to be known as the *Vetus Latina* (the "Old Latin [Bible]"), already existed. Instead, Jerome set out to create a corrected text of this existing Latin Bible, by comparing it to the Greek. Born in 347 in Stridon, in modern-day Slovenia, Jerome was a student of classical rhetoric in Rome. After his conversion to Christianity, he studied for some time in the east, eventually to return to Rome in 382, where he enjoyed the patronage of Pope Damasus. In 385, after falling out with the Roman clergy and the death of Damasus, he took up residence in the Palestine, where he learned Hebrew and redefined himself as a biblical scholar. It was here that he decided to extend his correction project to the entire biblical text. But by 390, he decided that for some Bible books, he might as well start from scratch and translate directly from the original Hebrew. By the time he had finished the project in 404, he had translated most books of the Bible, and this translation formed the basis of the Latin Bible that would be used for most of the Middle Ages.

Two observations must be made here to understand the history of the medieval Vulgate. First, what today is known as "Jerome's translation" or "Jerome's Vulgate" is only partly Jerome's work. Some parts of the old translation he deemed in need of only minor revision, and some Bible books he never translated. Thus, even complete Latin Vulgate bibles are always necessarily a combination of Old Latin and Jerome's texts. Second, Jerome's new translation did not immediately carry the day. For several centuries, it existed alongside the Old Latin versions. The two translations may even have mutually influenced each other, with scribes copying elements from both versions. We call this process of cross-influence between two versions "contamination" and its result a "mixed text." It is easy to see how it could have occurred: a scribe working to copy a new, unfamiliar Bible translation could easily have changed some words or phrases into ones with which he was more familiar. Sometimes, scribes were more conscious of the differences between the two translations and tried to harmonize them. A tenth-century Vulgate text from León, Spain, for instance, contains Old Latin readings written in the margin.[1]

When Gutenberg produced the first printed Bible in 1455, the Vulgate text that he used was the result of centuries of scribal activity. Every time a bible was copied by hand, changes were introduced into the text, whether intentionally or unintentionally, and thus, textual corruption could creep in. No two handwritten copies of a Bible were entirely alike; multiple versions circulated and were copied in different scriptoria around Europe. Often simple chance dictated which version became more widely copied than others. Sometimes, however, conscientious efforts were made to correct the text, and produce a "clean" copy that then could serve as the basis for subsequent copies. We call such an exemplar and the texts copied from it a "recension." In all this, however, we have to keep in mind that bibles were thought of as collections of writings rather than as single books. Thus, in one and the same pandect, the text of the Pentateuch could be copied from a different codex than the text of the Gospels. This makes it very difficult to make general statements about the history of the Bible text, because it may differ for individual books.

This chapter discusses some of the important junctures in the history of the Vulgate, its creation and background, the reasons for the contamination and corruption, and the different recensions. It also shows how the textual variety was sometimes unsettling to medieval authors. They sought to establish a better text, one that they felt was the correct one and was closer to the "original." Of course, the latter notion is prone to ambiguity, and potentially theological controversy. Was this "original" represented in the Hebrew version, or in the Latin? If Jerome was such a holy man, was his translation to be considered inspired by God? In the time of the sixteenth-century Reformation, questions such as these would severely divide the Church. But they also helped to establish the beginnings of scholarly textual criticism, which was one of the great accomplishments of the medieval study of the Bible.

---

[1] Léon, S. Isidoro, Codex Gothicus Legionensis. See Würthwein, *The Text of the Old Testament*, 93.

THE VETUS LATINA

It was not until the eighth or ninth century that Jerome's translation became the most widely used Latin Bible of western Christendom, and it was not until the sixteenth century that his translation came to be referred to as the "Vulgate." When Jerome himself spoke about the "Vulgatae editiones" (common editions), he used the term to refer to the Septuagint and its Latin translations, which we now know as the *Vetus Latina*. Jerome's new translation eventually became so widespread that the Old Latin versions gradually stopped being copied. As a result, manuscript copies of the Old Latin Bible are rare, and no complete copy containing the entire Bible exists. There are a number of Gospel books and psalters, and some fragments of the Pentateuch and the Prophets. Thankfully, however, the text can be partially reconstructed from Bible citations in the works of Church fathers such as Augustine and Ambrose of Milan, which are very frequent and cover large parts of the entire Bible. The first to attempt such a reconstruction was the eighteenth-century Benedictine monk Pierre Sabatier. Today, his work is continued at the Benedictine Abbey of Beuron in Germany.[2]

As a translation, the *Vetus Latina* has received a bad name; it is said to often render the Greek into Latin word by word, without paying much attention to the literary qualities of its Latin. It retains Hebraisms that already sounded strange in Greek.[3] Its translators were not particularly concerned to produce a text in literary Latin. On the contrary, because of the association of literary Latin with pagan antiquity, they tried to create a new type of Latin that was deliberately different from classical Latin and bore a more distinctive Christian mark. The translators also used a large amount of neologisms that were derived from the Greek, such as *baptizare*, "to baptize"; *paradisus*, "Paradise"; and *ecclesia*, "church or congregation." They thus gave Christian Latin a distinctive flavor, different from classical Latin. Like some of the famous Bible translations of the early modern age, those of Martin Luther and King James, the *Vetus Latina* had a lasting influence on the language in which it was written.

Part of the bad name the *Vetus Latina* has received comes from the negative assessment by the church fathers. In particular, Augustine and Jerome, in their letters, frequently complain about the deplorable state of the text of their Latin bible translations, and they stress the need for correction. Jerome complained about the *Vetus Latina* that there were as

---

[2] Würthwein, *The Text of the Old Testament*, 91–94. See also the resources at www.vetuslatina.org, including a list of manuscripts.

[3] Examples in Stummer, *Einführung in die Lateinische Bibel*, 64–74.

many versions as there were codices, "and each and everyone at will adds to it or leaves out as seems right to him, and there is no way that what is in disagreement can be true."[4] Similarly, Augustine complained that there was hardly a text of the Gospels "in which there was no mistake."[5] Such diversity, as noted earlier, was inevitable in an age of manuscript copying. But in this case, the textual variation was probably less the result of a corruption by copying than a reflection of the *Vetus Latina*'s origins. There was not one single translation at its origin, but a collection of locally made translations. The *Vetus Latina* is thus not properly the name of one translation but of a family of translations. Modern scholars distinguish between at least two regional variant texts, one called the "Afra," which was current among early Christian writers such as Cyprian and Tertullian, and one that seems to have been much more widely spread, referred to as the "Itala." The various local translations may have been subsequently altered to make them correspond more closely to each other, or they may have been corrected by comparing them to the text of the Septuagint. This "correction" probably caused greater diversity rather than uniformity, as was intended, because the Septuagint itself had been revised on several occasions and circulated in different versions. Some scholars have even suggested the possibility that some versions of the *Vetus Latina* were altered by comparing them to the Hebrew text.[6] For all these reasons, textual critics refer to the *Vetus Latina* text as a "contaminated tradition."

JEROME'S FIRST BIBLE REVISION

Jerome and Augustine both agreed that the Latin Bible was in need of correction, although they eventually came to disagree on the solution to this problem. Augustine held the Septuagint to be divinely inspired and thought that all Latin texts should be tested against the Greek.[7] When he undertook to follow Pope Damasus's request in 382, Jerome initially set out to do exactly this. He produced a critical revision of the text of the Gospels, and corrected the existing Latin text of the Psalter twice, in slightly varying versions. The earlier (the so-called Gallican Psalter) became widely used in much of Europe, whereas the later one (the Roman Psalter) was used mainly in Italy. Working from the text of the Septuagint as found in Origen's *Hexapla* (discussed later in this chapter), he also revised the text of

---

[4] Jerome, *Prologus in libro Iosue*, in *Biblia sacra*, ed. Weber, 285.
[5] Augustine of Hippo, *Epistola* 71, PL 33: 241.
[6] Blondheim, *Les parlers judéo-romans et la Vetus latina*.
[7] Augustine of Hippo, *De doctrina christiana* 2.15.22, ed. Daur and Martin, CCSL 32, 47.

the Old Testament, starting with the books of Solomon, Chronicles, and Job. Within this translation, he took care to distinguish, by a system of diacritical signs (obelisks, †, and asterisks, *), what parts could be found in the Greek only and what parts in the Hebrew only, a system already used by Origen. No manuscripts evidence of this work remains; most of it was apparently already lost during Jerome's own lifetime. Augustine initially praised him for his excellent work.[8] But the more Jerome worked on the Old Testament, the more convinced he became that he should work from the Hebrew, not the Greek.

"COMMON EDITIONS" OR HEBRAICA VERITAS?

As we have seen in Chapter 3, the Septuagint translation differed in many respects from the text canonized by the Palestinian Jewry in the decades after the Fall of Jerusalem in 70 C.E., the so-called proto-Masoretic text. Because of this divergence, many Greek-speaking Jewish communities had become unhappy with the Septuagint, and had produced some alternative Greek translations that more accurately reflected the proto-Masoretic text. Of one these was the translation of Aquila of Sinope, a convert to Judaism. He followed the Hebrew original as closely as possible. Other alternative translations, such as those of Symmachus and of Theodotion, originated in Jewish-Christian circles. The text of the Septuagint itself was also continually improved; some later textual revisions, such as one by Lucian, tried to make the Septuagint conform more to the proto-Masoretic text. Thus, by the end of the second century C.E., a number of Greek translations of the Hebrew Bible were circulating. Conveniently, they were all contained in one book: the *Hexapla* (sixfold), devised by the Alexandrine church father Origen sometime in the mid-third century. It was a manuscript of the biblical text that presented the Hebrew text in parallel columns alongside a transliteration of the Hebrew text into Greek letters and the translations of the Septuagint, Aquila, Symmachus, Theodotion, and a fifth Greek recension, known appropriately as the *Quinta* (fifth), created to facilitate a comparison among the many different Greek versions. It was an important philological tool for Jerome in his efforts to correct the text of the *Vetus Latina*.

The more Jerome worked to revise the Old Latin, the more he became convinced that the Septuagint was a corrupted version of a text that had

---

[8] Augustine of Hippo, *Epistola* 82.34 and 28.2, PL 33, 200 and 112.

been perfectly preserved in the Hebrew Bible. In his view, the latter was closer to God's word as it was really intended; he called the Hebrew version the *Hebraica Veritas*, the "Hebrew Truth." For Jerome, the multiple versions of the Septuagint contrasted starkly with the very uniform tradition of the Hebrew Bible. Jerome came to see in the proto-Masoretic text of the Hebrew Bible a stable, uncorrupted text, which had been faithfully preserved throughout the centuries, as opposed to the Septuagint, which he thought had corrupted the textual tradition through translation. Reading the writings of the Roman Jewish historian Josephus, whose work was very popular among Christian authors, strengthened him in this view. In his apologetic work *Against Apion*, Josephus had stated that, through the centuries, "no one had ventured to add, alter, or remove a syllable" of the Hebrew Bible.[9]

Jerome also came to question the legend of the miraculous origin of the Septuagint. "It is one thing to be a prophet, another to be a translator," he says in his Letter to Desiderius, which became the Preface to the Pentateuch.[10] The translators of the Septuagint, in his view, were just translators, not divinely inspired prophets. They were inaccurate translators to boot. Jerome pointed out that they changed the content of the text they were translating. He also claimed (with less foundation) that Ptolemy, at whose request the translation was made, was a Platonist monotheist and that in order not to offend his monotheist paganism, all overt references to the Trinity that could be found in the text had been translated in a veiled way or had simply been left out. As a result, he said, the translation does not represent a reliable witness to the Christian truth, whereas the Hebrew text does.

Furthermore, Jerome began to doubt the status of the Septuagint as an authoritative text, partly because it did not seem to correspond to what he found in the New Testament. He pointed out that the apostles in the Gospels quote the Hebrew Bible, and never the Septuagint. He gave a number of Old Testament quotes that he said could be found in "our books" of the Greek Old Testament. All these quotes contained clear Christological references, such as Hosea 11:1, "Out of Egypt I have called my Son," and Zechariah 12:10, "They will look upon me whom they have pierced." All these references, however, could be found in the Hebrew text without any difficulty, Jerome said; hence, he concluded, we have to

---

[9] Josephus, *Contra Apionem* 1.37–42, trans. Thackeray, 179.
[10] Jerome, *Prologus in Pentateucho*, in *Biblia sacra*, ed. Weber, 3.

"return to the Hebrews," that is, the Hebrew codices, which both the Lord and the apostles used.[11]

Today we know that these arguments of Jerome's are not accurate. The argument about the influence of Ptolemy rests on assumptions that are, at best, historically unlikely. As for the other argument, the apostles' supposed preference for the *Hebraica*, we know that the authors of the Gospels actually did cite the Greek versions rather than the Hebrew ones. Finally, Jerome failed to recognize that the uniformity he found in the Hebrew text was not, in fact, the reflection of a text that had preserved the original intact and unchanged but, rather, was the result of centuries of textual comparison, emendation, and standardization. In some cases, the Septuagint may actually have been a better witness to the long-lost original than the Hebrew texts were, because it may have preserved some traditions that were lost, or changed, in the Hebrew tradition.

The Hebrew text of the Bible, of course, had its own transmission history. The proto-Masoretic text of the Old Testament as Jerome encountered it was essentially the same text that was current among pious Jews in Palestine in the first century C.E., even though the earliest extant manuscripts date from the ninth and tenth centuries C.E. It contained more than just the plain Hebrew text; the text was accompanied by the annotations of scribes who aimed to preserve the traditional pronunciation and the proper liturgical performance of the text. These scribes were called the "masoretes," from Hebrew *masorah*, "tradition." The Hebrew script contained only consonants, and thus, there was always room for uncertainty and ambiguity in the reading of some words. To avoid this, scribes, first in Babylonia and later in Tiberias, had devised a system of annotation, either interspaced with the Hebrew letters or in the margin of the text, to record the proper reading of the text. It explains, for instance, how the *Vetus Latina* in Amos 4:13b ("He reveals to Man what he thinks") could be read by Jerome, "he reveals to Man his Christ"; the Hebrew words *mah shecho*, without vowels, could easily be read as *mashiacho* ("his anointed one/Christ").

Jerome's decision to use this text for his Latin translation initiated a strong conviction among medieval Christian scholars that this Hebrew Bible presented the *Hebraica Veritas*, the most original and uncorrupted text of the Old Testament. But by choosing the proto-Masoretic text, Jerome was not necessarily choosing the most "correct" version of the Old Testament. Some books from the proto-Masoretic tradition did represent a less corrupted text than did the Septuagint, as did, for instance, the five

---

[11] Jerome, *Prologus in libro Paralipomenon*, in *Biblia sacra*, ed. Weber, 547.

books of the Pentateuch. For other books, however, such as Samuel and Kings, the proto-Masoretic manuscripts contained a sometimes corrupted text. The attempts of later generations to harmonize the *Vetus Latina* versions with the Vulgate ensured that these passages would continue to interest medieval exegetes concerned with the literal sense of Scripture. Jerome, of course, was unaware of these philological considerations. For him, one of the things that mattered most was to have a translation that was reliable and accurate, and that, in his view, could withstand the scorn the Jews, who loved to point out the deficiencies in the current Latin translations.[12]

JEROME'S NEW TRANSLATION

Sometime around 390, Jerome set out to produce a fresh translation of the Hebrew Bible, working directly from the proto-Masoretic text. Whatever the extent of Jerome's mastery of the Hebrew language may have been (still a subject of discussion among scholars),[13] for a great part his work built on the work that earlier scholars had done to reconcile the many Greek versions that existed with the Hebrew version, especially Origen's *Hexapla* and Aquila's translation. He was helped by several Jewish friends, one of whom supplied him with Hebrew scrolls.[14] The first books that he completed, by 394, were Samuel and Kings, the Prophets and Daniel, Job, Ezra, and Chronicles. The three books of Solomon (Proverbs, Ecclesiastes, and Song of Songs) he boasted to have translated in a time span of only three days, in 398.[15] The Octateuch, however, took much longer, and the entire translation was not completed until 405.

The apocryphal books of Ecclesiasticus, Wisdom, 1 and 2 Maccabees, and Baruch (with its appendix, the letter of Jeremiah) Jerome never translated. Nor did he touch 3 and 4 Ezra. In his view, all these books contained fables, and any books not contained in the Hebrew canon should be "completely cast out."[16] (See Chapter 3.) He did complete new versions of the four Gospels, but these were more revisions of the *Vetus Latina* text than fresh translations from the Greek. The rest of the New Testament he never translated. The Vulgate text of the Pauline Epistles probably originated in

---

[12] Jerome, *Prologus in Isaia*, in *Biblia sacra*, ed. Weber, 1096.
[13] Burstein, "La compétence de Jérôme en hébreu"; and Adkin, "A Note on Jerome's Knowledge of Hebrew."
[14] Jerome, *Epistola 36*, PL 22, 452.
[15] Jerome, *Prologus in libris Solomonis*, in *Biblia sacra*, ed. Weber, 957.
[16] Jerome, *Prologus in libro Ezra*, in *Biblia sacra*, ed. Weber, 638.

Rome, sometime in the fifth century, in circles closely connected to the Irish monk Pelagius, whom Augustine regarded as a heretic on the issue of human merit and God's grace. Ironically, these issues formed a very prominent theme in Paul's theology.

When parts of Jerome's new translation began to circulate, his fellow church father Augustine had serious reservations. Augustine was not so much concerned about criticism from Jews; one of his main concerns was the unity between Greek-speaking and Latin-speaking Christians. He also thought that the Greek (Septuagint) text had a higher status than the Hebrew. He wrote to Jerome in a letter:

I would rather see you translate those Greek canonical Scriptures that are given the name Septuagint. If your translation is going to be regularly read in several churches, it will be a great obstacle that the Latin churches differ from the Greek ones, especially also because a faith-denier will be more easily be convinced if a Greek book is brought forth, because it is a more noteworthy language.[17]

Augustine even cited an example of a case where the reading of Jerome's new translation had caused people to riot:

A certain brother of ours, a bishop, when he decided to read from your new translation in the church over which he presided, touched on something in the prophet Jonah (Jon. 4:6) that was translated by you quite differently from what was engrained in the feelings and memory of all, and recited by all throughout the ages. There ensued such a tumult among the people – especially among the Greeks, who argued and called it a great scandal – that this bishop was required to call for the advice of the Jews. They responded, either from ignorance or malice, that it said exactly in the Hebrew codices what was also in the Greek and [older] Latin ones.[18]

Jerome's explanation that the word *ciceion* (Hebrew *kykayon*, a word with an uncertain meaning – some modern translations render it as "castor-oil plant"), which in the Septuagint was translated *cucurbita* (cucumber), was better translated as *hedera* (vine), did not do much to abate Augustine's reservations.[19] Other examples of divergence between the Vulgate and the *Vetus Latina* had even more far-reaching exegetical consequences. Perhaps the most infamous example is Exodus 34:29 ("And when Moses came down from the mount Sinai . . . , he did not know that the skin of his face was radiant"), in which Jerome translated the Hebrew word *qeren* as *cornuta*

---

[17] Augustine, *Epistola* 71: 4–5, PL 33, 242.
[18] Ibidem.
[19] Jerome, *Epistola* 112: 21, PL 22, 930.

(horned) rather than as "radiant," as in the Septuagint. The result was centuries of depictions of Moses with horns, including Michelangelo's famous statue of Moses in Rome's San Pietro in Vinculis. Yet Jerome's translation was not the result of a simple mistake: the two words in Hebrew come from the same root. Even later Jewish exegetes explained that Moses was described as "horned" because rays of light have the appearance of horns.[20] Some of Jerome's translation choices were motivated by Christological concerns. Such was the case in his translation of Habakkuk 3:18 ("I will exult in God my saviour"), in which the word *yish`y* was rendered by Jerome as *Jesus*, as opposed to *savior*, as in the Septuagint. The Hebrew name Joshua/Jesus means "savior," but Jerome's translation is a stretch. In general, however, Jerome's translation was much better than the rather archaic-sounding *Vetus Latina*. It was more congruent with the rhythm of the Latin language, and (perhaps thanks to Jerome's classical training), it was stylistically altogether more pleasing.

THE ESTABLISHMENT OF A TEXTUS RECEPTUS

For all its virtues, Jerome's Vulgate did not immediately replace the *Vetus Latina*. In fact, it took several centuries for Jerome's Vulgate to catch on. Some of Jerome's new translations never became commonplace. For instance, his last translation of the Psalter (known as the "Hebrew" Psalter because he translated it directly from the Hebrew) was never used in the liturgy. Although we find it in some medieval bibles, such as Theodulf's, or some thirteenth-century English bibles, his earlier translation, the so-called Gallican Psalter, which could be found in Alcuin's Bible, remained more widely used. When Jerome's translation finally did start to spread, both it and the older translations circulated side by side until at least the eighth century. When new copies were made, readings from the *Vetus Latina* were sometimes introduced into the text of the Vulgate; the result was sometimes a contamination between the two traditions. "Mixed" versions were common until the ninth century.

In the course of the Middle Ages, starting as early as Alcuin, there were several attempts to purify the Vulgate text from common errors, and to establish some unity amid the variation that existed even in the text of Jerome's "new translation." This is an important aspect of the textual transmission of texts that are as widespread as the Bible: as time passes, not only do variation and mistakes creep into the text, but the opposite

---

[20] Rashi, commentary on Ex. 34: 29. Online at *The Complete Jewish Bible with Rashi*, trans. Rosenberg.

also happens: through a process of emendation and correction, a version of the text is eventually established that is acknowledged as the commonly used version of that text. Scholars call this the *textus receptus* (received text). Centuries of transmission of the Latin Bible established such a *textus receptus*; needless to say, such a text does not always necessarily represent the version that the author (in this case, Jerome) wrote.

The more times a text was copied, the more the number of variants would increase. When the eyes of a scribe turned from the original to the copy he was producing, he could misremember words, skip lines, or simply misread words in the original text. Medieval texts commonly used abbreviations for certain words, and these abbreviation could easily be misread, especially if the words were closely related or even synonyms. For instance, the abbreviation for the word for *deus* (god), d̄s, looked very much like the one for *dominus* (lord), d̄ns. Another very common mistake was to resume copying at a different instance of the word or phrase where one had just left off, thus eliminating, or repeating, several lines of text. Other mistakes could originate with the custom of scribes dictating the words to themselves as they copied the text. This way, words that sounded the same could be easily replaced by their homophones. In Genesis 1:1, for instance, "He divided the light and the darkness," the last two words in Latin are *ac tenebras* ("and darkness"). However, several codices read *hac tenebras*, "this darkness," reflecting the fact that the *H* was not commonly pronounced in Latin, just as in French or Italian today. A subsequent scribe, taking the copy as his original, would faithfully incorporate these mistakes into his own copy. Sometimes scribes altered the text deliberately, for theological or other reasons. One of the most significant additions to the Latin text of the Vulgate, for instance, included the so-called Johannine comma, 1 John 5:7–8: "There are three witnesses in heaven: the Father, the Word, and the Spirit, and these three are one." Long cited as the only verse that mentions the Trinity in the New Testament, the verse is in fact an extraneous addition that is not original to the Vulgate text. It appeared first in the fourth century and became commonplace in the Vulgate after the sixth century. The Codex Fuldensis, a sixth-century Vulgate manuscript, contains not only the comma but also a prologue, spuriously attributed to Jerome, which points out the omission by "unfaithful translators."[21] It is historically more likely, however, that the prologue was composed to justify the addition of this theologically significant text; Jerome himself never mentions the comma in any of his other works.

---

[21] *Codex Fuldensis*, ed. Ranke, 399.

Scribes not only made mistakes; they corrected them, both their own mistakes and those of previous scribes, as well. When a passage was obviously corrupt, a scribe could make a sophisticated guess at what the text was supposed to say and write that instead. This, of course, carried a certain risk: if the text was hard to understand, scribes might assume that the text was corrupt and change it into something that was easier to understand. The mistake, however, would be harder for later readers to detect, because it was no longer obviously wrong. Because medieval scribes had a certain reluctance to alter the text of the Bible on their own (after all, it was considered God's word), a more common way to correct a text was by comparison with another manuscript. As we have seen earlier, however, the risk here was that of contamination between the two versions that were compared to each other. By the standards of modern textual scholarship, these individual efforts by medieval copyists to correct mistakes and to ensure textual uniformity were sporadic and inadequate, but they do demonstrate that medieval scholars were well aware of the problems of textual corruption and of the desirability of establishing a uniform text.

BIBLE REFORM IN THE EARLY MIDDLE AGES

One place where Jerome's translation seems to have been popular, at least among the orthodox clergy, by the sixth century was Italy. Cassiodorus (d. 585) owned at least one copy in his monastery in Vivarium. When the Ostrogothic king Theoderic, an Arian Christian and considered a heretic by the Roman clergy, in the first quarter of the sixth century commissioned a luxury Gospel Book, he had a copy made of the *Vetus Latina* text,[22] but when Pope Gregory the Great set out to deliver a set of sermons on the books of Job (his so-called *Moralia in Job*), he explicitly mentioned that he would follow Jerome's text.[23] This same Pope Gregory in 595 or 596 sent the monk Augustine to England to convert the Anglo-Saxons who had settled in Kent (see Chapter 1). The flow of books from Italy to the newly established monastic centers in England made it an important center of learning and Bible production. At the time, *Vetus Latina* texts circulated side by side with the new translation, and mixed versions (such as the Book of Durrow, or the Book of Kells) were common. We do not know how widespread copies of the *Vetus Latina* were in Anglo-Saxon England, because the Vulgate's later popularity ensured that copies of the

---

[22] Verona, Biblioteca capitolare, MS 6. See also Chapter 7.
[23] Gregory, *Sancti Gregorii Magni Moralia in Iob*, Praef. 5, ed. Adriaen, CCSL 143, 7.

Vulgate were more likely to survive. Still, it is likely that the Anglo-Saxon church played an important role in making Jerome's version the more generally accepted Bible translation. Bede, for instance, referred to the Vulgate bible as "nostra edito" (our version) *versus* the "antiqua translatio" (old translation).[24]

The really decisive turn toward the Vulgate was made in Gaul, which by the end of the eighth century was united with Germany and northern Italy into one empire ruled by the Carolingian dynasty. Its authority extended over the Church as well. The Carolingian rulers made ambitious efforts to stimulate the growth of learning and literacy in their empire and to instill a sense of unity and uniformity in Christian worship. Their efforts resulted in a flourishing of arts and letters that modern scholars have dubbed the "Carolingian Renaissance." But the unity of the empire sometimes stood in sharp contrast with the diversity of local ecclesiastical traditions, and this diversity was especially noticeable in the Bible text in use in the liturgy. As we saw earlier, mixed versions were still common, and more variance in the text was introduced simply by scribal error. Charlemagne (r. 768–814) and his successors sought to remedy these problems. He was especially concerned with establishing proper liturgical rites, which required correct Gospel books, psalters, and missals. Charlemagne enjoined the clergy in his *General Admonition* of 789:

Maintain schools to teach youngsters to read. Psalms, notes [music notation?], song, time-reckoning and grammar, and all catholic books, [should] all be well corrected, throughout all individual monasteries and bishoprics. For often it happens that people have the admirable desire to pray to God, but they address him in an inappropriate way, because their books are uncorrected. Do not allow your youngsters to make mistakes, either in reading or in writing, and if it is necessary to write a Gospel book, psalter, or missal, have mature men write those with all diligence.[25]

Thus, proper worship, for Charlemagne, required the provision of reliable copies of the Bible. Having mistakes in the text, or using a text that could produce incorrect interpretations, was spiritually dangerous. Throughout his empire, Charlemagne supported the monasteries, with their scriptoria and schools, with the understanding that they would take special care to preserve the sacred traditions of correcting and copying the Bible. In a letter

---

[24] Bede, *Libri quatuor in principium Genesis* I, 2, 8, ed. Jones, CCSL 118A, 46.
[25] *Admonitio generalis*, no. 22, in *Capitularia regum Francorum*, ed. Boretius, MGH, Leges, 2, 60.

addressed to Abbot Baugulf of Fulda but intended for wider circulation, written around 790, Charlemagne admonished the monks that

if there is less care in writing, there is also much less wisdom for understanding the Holy Scriptures than there ought to be. And we all know well that, although errors of speech are dangerous, errors of understanding are far more dangerous. Therefore, we exhort you not only not to neglect the study of letters, but to teach them earnestly, with an attitude that is most humble and pleasing to God, so that you may more easily and more correctly penetrate the mysteries of the divine Scriptures.[26]

Charlemagne's admonition was followed in many parts of his empire, but the efforts of two men to establish a correct text of the Vulgate stand out in particular: Theodulf of Orleans (ca. 750/760–821) and Alcuin of York (ca. 760–804).

Theodulf

Theodulf of Orleans was born of a Visigothic family in Spain and became a courtier of Charlemagne, who made him abbot of Fleury and bishop of Orleans in northern France. He probably divided his time between these places and Charlemagne's court until he was forced from the court in 817 following a political scandal at the time of Charlemagne's successor, Louis the Pious. Accused of siding with the king's rebellious cousin, Bernard of Septimania, Theodulf was exiled to Angers. He is known not only for his polemical penmanship but also for his biblical scholarship. The influence of Theodulf's bibles seems to have been limited, however. Today, only half a dozen copies of Theodulf's Bible are extant. But his philological method was exemplary. In a way that resembles our modern footnote system, some codices conscientiously listed alternate readings in the margins of the text, marked with letters that indicated the origin of the variant: $\bar{a}$ for the Alcuin text, $\bar{s}$ for Spanish manuscripts, and *al.* for others (*alia*).

Theodulf's aim was clearly to establish a text "according to the Hebrew Truth." The text of the Psalms in Theodulf's bibles was, for instance, the translations that Jerome had made directly from the Hebrew. He also corrected Jerome's text by comparing it to the Hebrew. It is unlikely that he knew Hebrew himself, but he enlisted the help of a Jewish convert to

---

[26] Charlemagne, *Epistola De litteris colendis*, no. 29, in *Capitularia regum Francorum*, ed. Boretius, MGH, Leges, 2, 79. English translation at the Medieval Sourcebook, http://www.fordham.edu/halsall/source/carol-baugulf.asp.

overcome this difficulty. The modern scholar Avrom Saltman was able to identify this Jewish convert with the author of a spurious commentary on Samuel and Kings, which, in the Middle Ages, was often mistaken for a work by Jerome, because of the frequency of Hebrew sources it cited.[27] Theodulf's efforts did not really produce one standard Bible text, however. He worked from a variety of originals that he compared to each other in order to establish the best text, and his improved text remained a work in progress. Many of his bibles show the influence of the Spanish Vulgate tradition; later examples show that Theodulf also had access to Alcuin's Bible text. It is thus hard to speak of a "Theodulfian recension."[28]

Alcuin

More influential than Theodulf's efforts in the long term was the text produced at Tours, where Alcuin was abbot (see Chapter 2). Alcuin, unlike Theodulf, did produce a uniform text of the Vulgate that was copied in many subsequent manuscripts. From his correspondence, we know that, by 800, Alcuin was working on the correction of a bible at the behest of Charlemagne.[29] Some scholars have assumed that because Alcuin came from Northumbria, he was familiar with the textual tradition of the Amiatinus. However, no such link can be established.[30] The codices used to establish the Alcuin Bible's text were mostly local, northern French, not English in origin. Manuscripts of the *Vetus Latina*, which until that time was still commonly used in the liturgy, were assiduously avoided in establishing the new text, however. Most of the textual correction and production of Bible manuscripts actually took place after Alcuin's death (in 804).

Unlike Theodulf's Bible recension, which sought to establish a critically corrected bible text, but which did not circulate very widely, Alcuin's Bible represented only a modest revision of earlier texts. Most of the improvements were fairly basic; they consisted in weeding out obvious scribal errors through comparison with other, locally available codices.

---

[27] Pseudo-Jerome, *Quaestiones on the Book of Samuel*, ed. Saltman, 15–17.

[28] Early example: Bible from Saint Hubert, London, BL, MS Add. 24,142. Also, Stuttgart, Württembergische Landesbibliothek, HB.II.16. Later examples such as the Bible from Saint Germain-des-Prés, Paris, Bibliothèque Nationale, MS lat. 11,937, show influence of the use of Alcuin's Bible text.

[29] Alcuin's letter to Gisela and Rodtrude and other examples are cited in Fischer, *Lateinische Bibelhandschriften*, 106.

[30] Berger, *Histoire de la Vulgate*, and Quentin, *Mémoire sur l'établissement du texte de la Vulgate* argued for the English origin of Alcuin's text. The claim was rejected by Fischer, *Lateinische Bibelhandschriften*, 130–32.

Alcuin also modified orthography and corrected grammatical mistakes. The main reason for the success of Alcuin's text, then, was not its textual superiority but the sheer quantity of copies produced. The number of bibles produced at Tours made this text the basis for many subsequent copies, to the extent that some modern scholars have suggested that Alcuin's Bible was the officially propagated, corrected text of the Carolingian Empire. This assumes more top-down direction than really occurred. Although with little doubt Charlemagne's *General Admonition* provided the impetus for Alcuin and Theodulf's work, their texts were not promoted as official bible texts. Their efforts to establish a reliable text based on Jerome's Bible were only two among many of such attempts. As we will see, the practice did not end in the ninth century. Eventually, various local traditions blended to form the *textus receptus* of the medieval Vulgate.[31]

"RECENSIONS" OF THE TWELFTH AND THIRTEENTH CENTURIES

The Carolingian renaissance was not the last instance when medieval scholars attempted to improve the Bible text through the process of correction. The production of biblical texts in this period was not a mere copying of texts, but there is plenty of evidence that scribes (or the overseers of the scribal activity) took an active part in evaluating and improving the text, often by comparing various codices. The medieval chronicler Sigebert of Gembloux, for instance, describes how Abbot Olbert of Gembloux (d. 1048) had one copy of the entire Holy Scripture made into a pandect, after he had allegedly gathered no fewer than 100 copies of sacred books.[32] That number is no doubt hyperbolic, but it shows that the correction of the Bible text by comparison to other codices must have become common practice in medieval scriptoria. Similarly, the archbishop of Canterbury, Lanfrank of Bec (d. 1089), according to his biographer,

because Scripture was corrupted by the fault of many scribes, took care to correct all the books of the Old and New Testament, as well as the writings of the Fathers, according to the orthodox faith. And thus he emended with great exactitude many writings we now use day and night in the service of the Church, and he not only did this himself, but also had it done by his students.[33]

---

[31] Fischer, *Lateinische Bibelhandschriften*, 133 and 202–03. A good example is the Bible of Moutier-Grandval, London, BL, MS Add. 10,546, Photo 7.

[32] Sigebert of Gembloux, *Gesta abbatium Gemblacensium*, PL 160, 625B.

[33] Milo Crispin, *Vita Lanfranci*, PL 150, 55BC.

Lanfrank's editorial activity did not leave a clear mark on the history of the Vulgate text, and there is no "Lanfrankian recension" in the sense that we can speak of the "Alcuinan recension." We should, therefore, not see these tenth- to twelfth-century examples of emendatory activity as endeavors to establish a new critical edition or recension of the Vulgate text, but rather as efforts by medieval scribes to compare different texts and to weed out singular readings for the use of their particular order, monastery, or cathedral. For the modern scholar, this process of contamination created a philological nightmare, making it virtually impossible to establish which codices were copied from which, and thus to distinguish the original readings from later variants. But this was the process that eventually produced the *textus receptus* of the scholastic Vulgate.

In addition to the two examples cited earlier, various monastic communities in the eleventh and twelfth centuries produced "clean" texts of the Bible for use in their own monastic communities. The most impressive attempt at biblical criticism was made in the twelfth century under the direction of Stephen Harding, the abbot of Cîteaux, the motherhouse of the Cistercian Order, in eastern France, for use in the Cistercian community. Harding was abbot from 1109 until 1134. In his *Admonition (Monitum)*, attached to one of the volumes of this Bible, he describes how he collected several volumes of the biblical text from various churches, in order "to follow the most truthful text." He was dismayed at the diversity of the readings he found in these bibles, especially at the interpolations in the book of Samuel that he found in some Latin bibles but not in others. Stephen set out to correct the text, sometimes relying on the supposed antiquity of the manuscripts he used and sometimes on the help of Jews who were "experts in their own Scriptures."[34] But, in general, most of the texts circulating in Europe at this time were in some way or other descended from, or were related through, a process of comparison and correction to the Alcuin text. It was a descendant of this text that was glossed (i.e., commented on) in the cathedral schools of twelfth-century northern France. The text of these glossed bibles became, in turn, the basis for the first professionally copied and mass-produced bibles in the thirteenth century.

One of the most influential recensions of the Late Middle Ages was the one that radiated out from Paris, in the thirteenth century. The thirteenth-century bibles produced in Paris had a small portable format, with a specific order of books, specific prologues, and the dictionary of Hebrew names at the end. We should not assume that all bibles with this physical appearance

---

[34] Stephen of Cîteaux, *Censura de aliquot locis bibliorum*, PL 166, 1373–1376.

were produced in Paris or contained the same version of the Bible text, however. The chapter divisions, and the choice of materials to accompany the biblical text, could be easily added onto any text a scribe was copying. One manuscript, found today in York Minster Library, which looks in every way like a thirteenth-century Paris bible, is in fact copied from a ninth-century codex and has a text that is quite different from most of the other known thirteenth-century pocket bibles.[35] However, most of the bibles copied in Paris in this format contained a common text, which was the text they found in the bibles they copied. It was not that different from that of the common twelfth-century glossed Bible, widely available to scribes at the time.

For a long time, scholars assumed that this text was an "official" recension of the University of Paris, which was established by the end of the twelfth century, and soon became one of the most important centers of biblical scholarship in northern Europe. This university had its own system for producing and distributing books for the use of its students and teachers. In this so-called *pecia* system, one stationary copy of a book was deposited at a bookseller (*stationarius*), where scribes could retrieve it one quire at a time to make their own copies. A *pecia* was a section of a book; the book was taken apart into sections so that several copyists could work at the same book at the same time. The copies made from these *stationarii* were usually subject to correction, and thus, modern scholars have supposed that the university could oversee the distribution of a corrected, "official" Bible text. But recently, this idea has been challenged.[36] Although the pecia system was certainly used for some books, hardly any evidence has been found that any of the Paris bibles were actually copied according to this system. Some late-thirteenth-century bibles were, no doubt, intended to be used as reference texts, most notably the Bible of Saint Jacques, which was the bible for the use of the Dominican order in Paris. This bible was just one representative of the text that circulated in Paris at the time; it was not in any way an "official" university text, even less a corrected recension, of the Vulgate. The wide diffusion of these Paris bibles ensured that this text became the most widely spread by the later Middle Ages. This same recension Gutenberg printed, and it was essentially the basis for the Sixto-Clementine edition as well. The ubiquity of this recension owed everything

---

[35] York Minster, MS XVI.N.6. See also Glunz, *History of the Vulgate*, 267–68. In another York Minster manuscript, MS XVI.Q.3, we can see how this copying must have worked: the older chapter number are stricken out and new chapter numbers are supplied. Fol. 117 contains some instructions for the scribe on what text to insert while copying.

[36] Light, "French Bibles c. 1200–30."

to the demand for a small portable bible among the Paris students who were trained for the office of preacher, and the ability of the professional Paris scribes to produce such a bible in great quantities (see Chapter 2).

MEDIEVAL TEXTUAL CRITICISM

This lack of a critical recension and official oversight irked some thirteenth-century scholars. Among them was the Oxford Franciscan Roger Bacon (d. 1294), one of the most astute textual critics of the time. He deplored that the copying of this text was not done by expert clerics, but by laypersons, commercial book copiers. Because the Paris Bibles were not the result of an official recension, the quality of the text was deplorable, compared to earlier versions (which he called the "codices antiqui," ancient codices.) The frustration of medieval Bible scholars such as Bacon with the Paris text may have spurred textual biblical scholarship to a new level. Textual criticism was not a new phenomenon in the thirteenth century. As we have seen, Cassiodorus in the sixth century and Theodulf in the ninth century had employed methods of simple textual criticism to improve their Bible texts. The practice of biblical textual criticism also received an important stimulus in the twelfth century with the work of Cistercians such as Stephan Harding (mentioned earlier) and Nicholas Maniacoria (fl. ca. 1145). The latter was a Cistercian monk at the abbey of S. Anastasio alle Tre Fontane in Rome, who in 1140 wrote a critical treatise on the correction of the text of the Psalms. In his dedicatory letter to his abbot, he claimed to have only a minimal knowledge of Hebrew:

I have determined to note carefully all the places that are corrupted, either by the carelessness of scribes, or by whatever other presumption, and to detect, insofar as I could, the reasons for their particular corruption, availing myself of whatever help I could get, and especially of the fount of Hebrew wisdom, even though I have tasted of it only a moderate amount, as you know.[37]

This was false modesty: what makes Maniacoria's treatise stand out from the other textual revisions of his time is his expert knowledge of Hebrew and the sophistication of his emendatory activity.

One of the most accomplished textual critics of the twelfth century, and, indeed, the one who would have the most influence on the correction of the Vulgate text in the thirteenth century, was Andrew of Saint Victor (d. 1175), a canon at the abbey of Saint Victor in Paris. Andrew wrote commentaries

---

[37] Peri, "'Correctores immo corruptores', un saggio di critica testuale," 88.

on most books of the Old Testament, and many of his comments address the possible corruption of the Vulgate text. As a way of detecting and correcting errors in the text, he frequently referred to the Hebrew text of the Old Testament, which he presumably knew through oral contacts with Jews in Paris. His commentaries were a trove of valuable information for later scholars who set out to produce a Latin Bible text that was more in line with the Hebrew "original." Thus, scholars such as Andrew, Harding, and Maniacoria set a new standard of textual scholarship, which became the basis of the textual scholarship that was practiced, for instance, by the Dominicans at the convent of Saint Jacques in Paris in the thirteenth century.

All these medieval scholars tried to correct their bible texts in order to establish a text that was more "true;" Andrew of Saint Victor, for instance, deplored the "mendacitas" (mendacity) of some codices. But they went beyond the principle of correcting the Bible in "according to the orthodox faith" that was employed by Lanfranc of Bec. The methods and practices of these medieval textual critics sometimes sound surprisingly modern and belie the assumption that the medieval period only corrupted the bible text without attempting to improve it. Even though their standards of textual scholarship may not be as sophisticated as later ones, medieval scholars nevertheless developed a number of principles to detect and correct mistakes, of which the two most important were relying on older codices and checking with the Hebrew original.

When medieval scholars suspected textual corruption, they often consulted other, older codices, in the conviction that these presented the better readings. Cassiodorus had already recommended the practice of collecting "ancient codices" to correct his Bible text. Roger Bacon even gave his reader some advice on how to recognize older codices: he noted that bibles without a gloss but with canon tables were the older ones.[38] Guillelmus Brito, a thirteenth-century biblical critic, claimed to have examined codices written before the time of Charlemagne and stated that the agreement of various codices against one was an indication that the latter codex might be corrupt. Roger Bacon employed the same basic principles. With the possible exception of Stephen Harding,[39] medieval textual scholars had not yet developed the insight, fundamental to textual scholarship today, that the oldest reading was not necessarily the more correct one (a good recent copy

---

[38] Light, "Roger Bacon and the Origin of the Paris Bible," 489 and 496; and Bacon, *Opus Minus*, ed. Brewer, 331.
[39] Cauwe, "Le Bible d'Étienne Harding," 442.

is better than an ancient bad one) or that a numerical majority did not necessarily prove a more correct reading. (If ten corrupt codices all gave the same reading of a passage, and one single codex gave a variant reading, the single reading may be the correct one, because the ten others could all be copied from a single corrupt original. The frequent proliferation of misinformation on the Internet, often copied from a single erroneous source, makes this phenomenon well known to modern readers.) But what was new was the insight, shared by modern biblical scholars, that textual criticism could be used to remove human error from the text. Some of the insights that these medieval scholars developed are, indeed, still in use by modern textual critics. Medieval textual critics often relied on internal evidence to decide on the correctness of a certain reading. They weighed the likelihood that a scribe had made an error: Andrew of Saint Victor, for instance, observed that scribes often make mistakes in the copying of Roman numerals.[40] Most commonly, however, they weighed variant readings by their theological veracity. This could, of course, lead to the rejection of more problematic but correct readings in favor of corrupted readings that were easier to understand or that presented fewer theological problems, as we saw earlier in the case of the Johannine comma. In all these cases in which the text needed correction, of course, medieval scholars insisted that it was not the Bible that erred, but the scribes who had corrupted the text of the Bible.[41]

One of the main tools of the medieval textual critic was recourse to the Hebrew text of the Old Testament. Medieval textual critics often took as their reference point the *Hebraica Veritas*, the text of the Hebrew Bible, just as Jerome had done, and used it not only to clarify unclear passages but also to weigh variant readings in the Vulgate text. Jerome had admonished his readers: "Whenever I seem to you to err in my translation, ask the Hebrews."[42] This sentence would become an influential motivator for Christian Hebrew scholarship in the centuries to come. However, since Jerome, few Christian scholars had actually endeavored to learn Hebrew, and Jerome's commentaries themselves were often their best source for knowledge about the Hebrew text of the Old Testament. But there were exceptions, especially after the twelfth century. Some medieval textual critics, such as Andrew of Saint Victor, worked together with Jews to

[40] Andrew of Saint Victor, *De concordia annorum regum Israel et Iuda*, ed. Van Liere, CCCM 53A, 140.
[41] Peter Comestor, *Historia scholastica*, PL 198, 1625D.
[42] Jerome, *Prologus in Pentateucho*, in *Biblia sacra*, ed. Weber, 4.

understand the Hebrew text or had contacts at a local synagogue where they consulted with Jews on the interpretation of the Bible. Some may have even learned to read some Hebrew themselves with the help of local Jews. For instance, the twelfth-century cleric Herbert of Bosham, secretary to the exiled archbishop Thomas a Becket, wrote a commentary on Jerome's translation of the Hebrew Psalter, in which he consulted Jewish commentaries on the Psalms, written in Hebrew, and more than a century later, the Franciscan Nicholas of Lyra made intensive use of the commentaries of the eleventh-century exegete Solomon ben Isaac, that is, Rashi (1040–1106). When conversion from Judaism to Christianity became more commonplace, after the thirteenth century, converted Jews, such as the biblical scholar and polemicist Raymond Martin, who wrote a critical appendix to Nicholas of Lyra's commentaries, could also become authorities on textual scholarship.

One of the sources on which these medieval Jewish exegetes drew included the Aramaic translation from the Old Testament, known as the *Targumim* (sing. *Targum*). These translations dated from the first centuries of the common era, and Jewish communities often read them alongside the Hebrew Bible. Two of them, namely, the Targum Onkelos on the Torah (Pentateuch) and the Targum Jonathan ben Uzziel on the Nevi'im (former and latter Prophets), gained special status, because they were mentioned in the Talmud. Medieval Jewish exegetes, such as Rashi, made frequent use of them in their commentaries. These Aramaic (or, as medieval commentators called them, Chaldaic) translations were, however, more than just translations. They often paraphrased the text or added interpretive glosses to it, and as a result, they were hailed as authoritative sources for the interpretation of the biblical text. Medieval Christian Hebraists used them, too. Nicholas of Lyra and Raymond Martin, for instance, knew the Targum and cited it frequently.

Building on this tradition of textual criticism, the Franciscans and Dominicans in Paris set out to correct the text of the Vulgate and produced a critical apparatus that listed all known corruptions of the text with their improved readings, called a *correctorium*. We know of five *correctoria* that were produced at the mendicant schools in Paris; they usually took the form of lists of suggested improvements on the text, in biblical verse order, or of a Bible text with diacritical signs indicating which readings were in accordance with the Hebrew, and which words had alternative readings. One such *correctorium* was produced by Guillelmus Brito, mentioned earlier, relying largely on authorities such as Jerome and Andrew of Saint Victor. For some more critical spirits, such as Roger Bacon, this reliance on the work of others was problematic. Instead, Bacon urged scholars to consult the actual Hebrew and Greek originals:

we should go back to the original Hebrew text, and if Andrew is right, we should believe the Hebrew, not him. But we do have to commend him greatly for pointing us to many dubious spots in our translation . . . , and he refers us to the Hebrew, so that we may search for explanations with greater certainly at the roots.[43]

Interestingly, and perhaps somewhat paradoxically, the effect of all this medieval textual criticism on the quality of the bibles that were circulating was limited. Medieval critics did not have the means to ascertain with any certainty which readings were true and which were false. Thus, most medieval textual critics were content to show the diversity of the textual tradition rather than deciding on one reading. They left the final choice up to the reader. Medieval exegetes rarely strove to produce a new Bible text, but rather aimed to explain the text as it was, with its diversity of textual traditions. Thus, the main purpose of the *correctoria* was glossing rather than altering the text, and Christian Hebraism did not necessarily lead to the establishment of an improved Bible text. Another reason that the influence of medieval textual criticism was limited was that with a few exceptions, most of the later medieval Bibles were produced commercially, rather than by scholars. The main consumers of the *correctoria* were exegetes, not scribes. The former, by the thirteenth century, were often learned scholars at the universities, whereas the latter were lay craftspeople. Medieval textual criticism remained largely a learned debate, without much direct implication for most of the actual texts produced. Of course, all this was to change in the sixteenth century, with the work of humanist textual critics such as Desiderius Erasmus.

THE VULGATE AFTER THE REFORMATION

Before the sixteenth century, the text of the Vulgate was very much regarded in western Christendom as the one normative and authoritative text. But with the advent of Renaissance humanist scholarship, the idea had grown that this Latin Bible was but one translation among many; for the true text of the Bible, one had to go back to the Hebrew or Greek original. As we saw, the notion that the study of Hebrew was necessary for the correction of the Old Testament text of the Vulgate was not a new idea. In 1488, the Hebrew Masoretic text of the Bible was printed for the first time. The study of Greek

---

[43] Roger Bacon, *Compendium philosophiae*, ed. Brewer, 482–83.

seems to have lagged behind the study of Hebrew during the Middle Ages. But in the late fifteenth and early sixteenth centuries, it caught up with the work of scholars such as Lorenzo Valla and Desiderius Erasmus. One of the problems was the lack of a good edition of the Greek New Testament; the more the Greek text was studied, the more the differences with the Latin became apparent. Whereas the scholars employed in the project of the edition of the Complutensian Polyglot Bible (a multivolume edition of the Bible in Greek, Latin, Hebrew, and Aramaic, undertaken at the University of Alcalá under the direction of Cardinal Cisneros) seemed intent on correcting the text of the Greek New Testament by comparing it with the text of the Vulgate, Erasmus did exactly the opposite: he produced a new, corrected Latin translation, based on his edition of the Greek text, which in turn was based on a study of the Greek manuscripts. Thus, Erasmus's scholarship turned the tables on the authority of the Vulgate. "Back to the original," whether Greek or Hebrew, became the guiding principle of Renaissance Bible studies. In 1519, these efforts led Erasmus to publish the first scholarly edition of the *textus receptus* of the New Testament in Greek. For Renaissance philologists, these Hebrew and Greek editions, rather than the Vulgate tradition, represented the "true" Bible text. At the same time, the Protestant Reformation advocated the use of the vernacular Bible, in place of (and not alongside, as happened in the Middle Ages, as we will see in Chapter 7) the Latin Bible. The era in which the Latin Vulgate dominated the scene was over.

Still, some scholars, most notably those working on the Complutensian Polyglot, continued to advocate for the use of the Vulgate as an authoritative text and divinely inspired translation, albeit one that was in need of critical revision. One of the aims of the Alcalá project was exactly such a critical revision. In 1546, the Council of Trent sided with this opinion, declaring that

the old Latin Vulgate, which, in use for so many hundred years, has been approved by the Church, be in public lectures, disputations, sermons and expositions held as authentic [i.e., authoritative], and that no one dare or presume under any pretext whatsoever to reject it.[44]

At the same time, as we saw in the introduction to this book, they advocated for a newly corrected Vulgate text, which eventually led to the 1592 Sixto-Clementine edition. It was a new recension of the *textus receptus* of the

---

[44] *Canons and Decrees of the Council of Trent*, trans. Schroeder, 18; Latin text in *Conciliorum oecumenicorum generaliumque decreta*, ed. Ganzer *et al.*, 16.

Vulgate; for the first time, this was a recension established and propagated by the central authority of the Catholic Church.

In the twentieth century, critical editions of the Latin Vulgate began to appear. For modern medievalists, the value of such critical editions is especially in the critical apparatus. It is sometimes less important to know what Jerome might actually have written than to know what his text had come to look like in the eighth or thirteenth century. Insofar as the Sixto-Clementine Bible of 1592 is a more accurate version of the medieval *textus receptus*, it represents the text of the late medieval Latin Bible better than many modern editions.

OUTSIDE THE BIBLICAL TEXT

The Bible text is not the only text that was transmitted by the process of copying. As we saw in Chapter 2, the punctuation, and chapter and verse division, that we take for granted in modern books often have a history that is quite independent of the actual text. Bibles also contained what are called paratextual elements, that is, materials intended to facilitate the reading and comprehension of the text. These include tables of contents, prefaces, and introductions to the biblical text, section and chapter headings (called rubrics), chronological tables, and dictionaries. All these elements were not part of the Bible per se, but they often were transmitted as part of its textual tradition, and they are important clues to the textual history of the bible, as well as the history of its interpretation. They were also more likely to be changed and adapted to the demands of the time. Although some of the materials may be found even in modern bibles (such as headers for pericopes or prefaces to Bible books), some may be unfamiliar to modern readers.

Hebrew Bibles copied during the Middle Ages, for instance, commonly had a marginal apparatus called the *masorah* (which means "tradition"). Its aim was twofold: the correct pronunciation of the text and its correct transmission. Because Hebrew was a consonantal script, written without vowels (or, strictly speaking, with very few vowels, because some consonants could take on vowel quality), the vocalization of the text could be subject to some ambiguity. In the first centuries of the common era, generations of scribes (called *masoretes*) had developed a system of dots and dashes that were added to the script and that represented the correct vowels in order ensure its proper pronunciation. For some words, they noted the so-called *ketib* and *qere* forms, which were forms of words that should be substituted for the words that were actually written. The most obvious example is the replacement of the written word *YHWH*, that name of God that should not be pronounced, by *'adonai*, "the Lord." Some of the most significant differences between the translation of the Septuagint and the Hebrew Bible may trace back to these matters of vocalization; the Septuagint may express the pronunciation tradition of a word that predates that of the *masorah*. An example can be found in 1 Samuel 11:5 ("Saul came after the cattle"), in which the Hebrew *bqr* was read by the Septuagint translators as *boqer*, "in the morning," whereas the Masoretic vocalization has *baqar*, "after the cattle." Of course, when Christian Hebraists in the Middle Ages consulted Jews to help them correct the Latin text, it is not always clear whether the system of vocalization as Jerome encountered was the same as the system of vocalization current among medieval Jews; this could, in turn, lead to a corruption of the Latin text.

The main function of the *masorah* was not just to ensure the correct pronunciation; they also added pauses and breaks to the texts, and as we saw in Chapter 2, these may have eventually influenced the chapter division in the Latin Old Testament. But an important function was also to ensure the correct transmission of the text. The margins contained a system of notes that helped the scribe check whether he had transcribed the text correctly. We call these stichometric notes, and they contain a final count of the total verses and words in one specific bible book. Stichometric notes can be found not just in Hebrew Bibles. We find them frequently in Latin bibles as well: a twelfth-century bible today in York Minster Library, for instance, has stichometric notes at the end of most bible books. At the end of Psalms, for instance, we read, "Here ends the book of Psalms. In the Name of the Lord. It has five-thousand verses."[45]

The most common type of paratextual element found in both medieval and modern Bibles are chapter headings, or (as they appear in modern Bibles) section headings. Chapter headings were a common feature of early medieval Bibles, whereas they all but disappeared in the thirteenth century. We should keep in mind, of course, that for some bible books (especially the Gospels) in early medieval bibles, the chapters were considerably shorter than they are now. In early medieval bibles, these chapter headings were called "breves" or "tituli," and a list of all these breves usually preceded the text of each Bible book; they were closely related to the selections that were read during the liturgy. In addition, some books, such as Song of Songs and Psalms, had special explanatory headings called rubrics. The word *rubrication* derives from the Latin *rubrum*, meaning "red," because

---

[45] York Minster Library MS XVI.Q.3.

these additions were usually written in red ink to distinguish them from the actual text.

These rubrications were usually interpretive. The Song of Songs in a modern Bible, for instance, often has an indication of the speaker in the margin, because the text is conceived as a dialogue between two lovers. These indicators are, however, not original to the Hebrew text, and they are very much a matter of interpretation. Medieval bibles had a similar system, reflecting later interpretations. For the Song of Songs, for instance, some sections were headed, "The voice of Christ addressing the Church," or vice versa, showing that the text was intended to be read as an allegory of the love between Christ and the Church. The book of Psalms had similar rubrications. Some of these were very old, and they were already contained in the Hebrew text of the Psalm. Psalm 50/51:1, for instance, reads, "For David, when Nathan the Prophets came to him, because he had been with Bathsheba." But some rubrications were decidedly more recent and were intended to give readers suggestions as to their interpretation. One rubrication for Psalm 1, in an Oxford manuscript, for instance, read, "The first Psalm shows that Christ is the Tree of Life."[46]

One paratextual element frequently found in early medieval bibles were the so-called canon tables. These tables, devised by Eusebius in the fourth century, were a standard addition to Gospel books written before the year 1000. They offered a quick comparison across the texts of the four Gospels and showed a listing of all passages that could be found in all four Gospels; followed by passages common to Matthew, Mark, and Luke; the passages common to Matthew, Luke, and John next; and so on, until all possible combinations were covered. The tables contained numerical codes that corresponded to numbers in the margin of the Gospels texts, facilitating a quick lookup of the parallel passage in any of the other Gospels. An example of these canon tables can be found in the beginning of the Lindisfarne Gospels, as Photo 7 shows.

Medieval bibles contained prefaces, either to individual bible books or to larger parts of the Bible, which were often excerpted from the letters of Jerome. Just like the prefaces to biblical books in modern bible translations, these prefaces contained historical information about the author of the biblical books, their intended audience, Jerome's translation, earlier versions and translations, and the canonicity of some books. Thus, they served as important tools for medieval exegetes in the interpretation of these books. Some of these prefaces were almost as old as the text of the Vulgate itself and were frequently recopied over many centuries, but some were

[46] Oxford Bodleian Library, MS Auct. D.4.10, fol. 253r.

Photo 7. The canon tables of the Lindisfarne Gospels, showing the correspondence between the four Gospels. London, British Library, MS Cotton Nero D. IV, f.10. Photo (c) The British Library Board.

specific to the various recensions of the Bible. The Tours and Theodulf Bibles, for instance, had their own specific sets of prefaces. The Paris Bible standardized the prefatory material for all biblical books. Many of these prefaces for the latter were newly created, although they stemmed largely from Jerome's letters. Together with some of the traditional prefaces, this material became such a standard part of the thirteenth-century Bible that many readers came to think of it as part of the biblical text itself.[47]

RESOURCES FOR FURTHER STUDY

The authoritative edition of the Septuagint is by Ralphs (Stuttgart: Deutsche Bibelstiftung, 1979); a new edition is in preparation by the Academy of Sciences in Göttingen, Germany. An edition of the *Vetus Latina* is being prepared at the Benedictine Abbey of Beuron (Germany), which also has its own Website: http://www.vetuslatina.org/. The scholarly edition of the Vulgate was done by the Monks of the Abbey of Saint Jerome in Rome. More affordable and available, however, is the edition by Weber, Fischer, and others (1969), which was based on the Roman edition (only partly completed at the time), and on Wordsworth's 1889 New Testament Vulgate edition. The edition called *Nova Vulgata* is not useful for medievalists. The Douay-Rheims translation offers a translation of the Latin Vulgate text (online at http://www.drbo.org/), while a translation of the Septuagint is available by Pietersma and Wright. A public domain translation of 1851 can be found at http://www.ccel.org/bible/brenton/. The software program *Bible Works* allows the comparison and study of multiple Bible versions (http://www.bibleworks.com/). A translation of Jerome's biblical prologues can be found at http://www.bombaxo.com/prologues.html. Some of the best introductions to the material in this chapter are, regrettably, in French (Bogaert), Italian (Cimosa), and German (Stummer), but the contributions in the *New Cambridge History of the Bible* (vol. 1 and 2) and *Hebrew Bible/Old Testament* also provide an excellent start. Older accounts, by Berger, Quentin, and Glunz, may still be useful but have been challenged on many accounts.

SUGGESTIONS FOR FURTHER READING

Bentley, Jerry H. *Humanists and Holy Writ: New Testament Scholarship in the Renaissance*. Princeton: Princeton University Press, 1983.

---

[47] Light, "Roger Bacon and the Origin of the Paris Bible," 499.

Berger, Samuel. *Histoire de la Vulgate pendant les premiers siècles du moyen âge.* Paris: Hachette, 1893. Reprint Hildesheim and New York: Georg Olms Verlag, 1976.

Bogaert, Pierre-Marie. "La Bible latine des origines au moyen âge. Aperçu historique, état des questions." *Revue théologique de Louvain* 19 (1988): 137–59, 276–314.

Cimosa, Mario, and Carlo Buzzetti. *Guida allo studio della Bibbia Latina, dalla Vetus Latina, alla Vulgata, alla Nova Vulgata.* Sussidi Patristici, 14. Roma: Istituto Patristico "Augustinianum", 2008.

Fischer, Bonifatius. *Lateinische Bibelhandschriften im frühen Mittelalter.* Vetus Latina: Die Reste der altlateinischen Bibel. Aus der Geschichte der lateinischen Bibel, 11. Freiburg im Breisgau: Herder, 1985.

Forme e modelli della tradizione manoscritta della Bibbia. Edited by Paolo Cherubini. Littera Antiqua, 13. Città del Vaticano: Scuola vaticana di paleografia, diplomatica e archivistica, 2005.

Glunz, Hans Hermann. *History of the Vulgate in England from Alcuin to Roger Bacon, Being an Inquiry into the Text of some English Manuscripts of the Vulgate Gospels.* Cambridge: Cambridge University Press, 1933.

Light, Laura. "French Bibles c. 1200–30: A New Look at the Origins of the Paris Bible." In *The Early Medieval Bible.* 155–76.

———. "The Bible and the Individual." In *The Practice of the Bible.* 228–246.

———. "The Thirteenth Century and the Paris Bible." In *The New Cambridge History of the Bible.* 380–91.

Marsden, Richard. *The Text of the Old Testament in Anglo-Saxon England.* Cambridge Studies in Anglo-Saxon England, 15. Cambridge: Cambridge University Press, 1995.

Quentin, Henri. *Mémoire sur l'établissement du texte de la Vulgate. 1ère partie: Octateuque.* Collectanea Biblica Latina, 6. Roma: Desclée & Cie., 1922.

Schulz-Flügel, Eva. "The Latin Old Testament Tradition." In *Hebrew Bible / Old Testament.* 642–62.

Stummer, Friedrich. *Einführung in die Lateinische Bibel. Ein Handbuch für Vorlesungen und Selbstunterricht.* Paderborn, 1928.

Tov, Emanuel. *Textual Criticism of the Hebrew Bible.* 2nd rev. ed. Minneapolis: Augsburg Fortress Publishers, 2001.

Van Liere, Frans A. "The Latin Bible, c. 900 to the Council of Trent, 1546." In *The New Cambridge History of the Bible.* 93–109.

Würthwein, Ernst. *The Text of the Old Testament.* 2nd ed. Translated by Erroll F. Rhodes. Grand Rapids, MI: Wm. B. Eerdmans Publishing Co., 1995.

CHAPTER 5

Medieval Hermeneutics

The word *hermeneutics* is derived from the Greek *hermeneuein*, "to interpret." It denotes the art of finding meaning in a text. In the case of such an authoritative text as the Bible, this is more problematic than it seems. On the surface, the Bible can seem to make statements about God that are contrary to reason or even contradicting each other. For example, if God is omniscient, and has ordained all things before all times, how can this same God change his mind and admit to a mistake, saying, "I regret that I made Saul king," (1 Sam. 15:11)? Or how could Adam have lived to be 930 years old (Gen. 5:5) after eating of the forbidden tree in paradise, if God had said "the day that you eat of it, you shall die" (Gen. 2:17)?

Other texts in Scripture pose even greater challenges, because they seem very specific to an historical context that is utterly alien to the reader. David Steinmetz gives an example from Psalm 137, which bemoans the Jews' captivity in Babylon, expresses a longing for Jerusalem, curses the Edomites, and pronounces a blessing on him who "take your little ones and dash them against the rock." (Ps. 137:9). A French priest in the twelfth century, Steinmetz points out, had never been to either Babylon or Jerusalem, had no quarrel with the Edomites, and was expressly forbidden by Jesus to avenge himself on his enemies. Hence, "unless Psalm 137 has more than one possible meaning, it cannot be used as a prayer by the Church, and must be rejected as a lament belonging exclusively to the piety of ancient Israel."[1]

The solution for many modern readers is to see the Bible in the first place as the product of an historical human author. Modern exegetes are trained in the tradition of historico-critical criticism, which saw the Bible as a compilation of texts that were composed at different times, with different worldviews and even different ideas about God. To be sure, it could be inspired by God, but this inspiration was filtered through the voice of

---

[1] Steinmetz, "The Superiority of Pre-Critical Exegesis," 28.

its human author, and thus, its meaning could only be established by examining its historical context. In this view, Scripture was seen as a set of texts that intended to appeal to the emotions of the reader and to provoke him or her to greater devotion toward God. As such, these texts might still be inspired by God, but they were subjective, rather than objective. This idea was first expressed in the Dutch Enlightenment by the skeptical Jewish philosopher Baruch de Spinoza; thus,

Scripture does not explain things by their secondary causes, but only narrates them in the order and the style which has most power to move men, and especially uneducated men, to devotion; and therefore it speaks inaccurately of God and of events, seeing that its object is not to convince the reason, but to attract and lay hold of the imagination.[2]

The attitude of medieval exegetes could hardly have been more different. For medieval authors, the one thing that set the sacred scriptures apart from all other scriptures was that they all originated from one ultimate author, God. The Bible was not just a story about God, but also a story by God. He was its author (its human authors were seen as merely "scribes"), and thus, everything that the text related was absolutely true, because God did not speak falsehood.

In the first quarter of the twelfth century, the Parisian scholar Hugh of Saint Victor wrote an introduction to the Bible, *On Sacred Scripture and Its Authors*, in which he instructed his students about the way to interpret Scripture. Hugh defined the subject matter of the Bible as follows:

There are two works of God, and they encompass everything that was made. The first is the work of creation, by which those things that did not exist were made. The second is the work of restoration, by which those things that had perished were restored. The work of creation is the making of this world with all its elements. The work of restoration is the incarnation of the Word with all its mysteries (*sacramentis*), both those that came before the incarnation from the beginning of the world and those that followed it until the end of the world. . . . In light of these two works, then, consider the subject matter of Sacred Scripture, so that you can distinguish these writings from others with regard to both what they treat and how they treat it, that is, their subject matter and their mode. For all other writings have as their subject matter the works of creation, whereas it is clear that only Sacred Scripture deals with the works of restoration.[3]

According to Hugh, all writings of this world (including the Bible) deal with the created world, but only the Bible speaks about God's restoration

---

[2] Spinoza, *Works*, trans. Elwes, 91. Cited in Frei, *The Eclipse of Biblical Narrative*, 43.
[3] Hugh of Saint Victor, *On Sacred Scripture* 2, in *Interpretation of Scripture: Theory*, 214.

of this creation after it had fallen into sin and damnation. If the Bible is not absolutely true and reliable on this subject, then humankind cannot be saved from its fallen state. For medieval authors, the Bible was not just a text that tried to persuade; it was a text that was always and absolutely true and written in the best interest of humankind. In Hugh's words,

Those writings, then, in which there is no truth without the contagion of error and by which the soul is not restored to the true knowledge or love of God are never worthy to be called "sacred." Only that scripture is rightly called "sacred" that is inspired by the Spirit of God and that, administered by those who have spoken by the Spirit of God, make the human person holy – reforming him according to the likeness of God, instructing him to know God, and exhorting him to love Him. Whatever is taught in it is truth; whatever is prescribed in it is goodness; whatever is promised in it is happiness. For God is truth without falsehood, goodness without malice, happiness without misery.[4]

If the Bible were a book unlike any other, it also needed to be interpreted in a unique way. If there seemed to be a contradiction in it, the fault was the reader's, not the text's. Of course, Hugh's assumption could only be maintained if the Bible did not always mean what it appeared to say. For him, it was clear that certain passages in the Bible could not be taken literally. In case of the Genesis 2:17, cited earlier, "day" in the Bible did not always mean a day: in at least one instance it meant a thousand years, as Psalm 90:4 says, "a thousand years in your sight are like yesterday when it is past."[5] Texts that were less obviously metaphors could be read on two levels as well: one literal and one metaphorical. Psalm 137, for instance, was in one sense a prayer uttered by the people of Israel at the time of the Babylonian captivity, but it could also have a deeper meaning: Babylon signified this earthly life, Jerusalem was heaven, the Edomites were evil demons, and its children were one's personal vices that needed to be crushed and destroyed. Texts such as these might be strange and contradictory in their literal sense; in their metaphorical sense, however, they were perfectly congruent with the principles of the Christian faith.

Thus, to understand what the Bible truly said, one needed to read beyond its primary, obvious sense. In the words of the twelfth-century theologian Honorius Augustodunensis, "the doctrine of eternal life lies hidden in the Scriptures."[6] In order to unlock these hidden mysteries, one needed to read the entire Bible as one extended metaphor, a Great Code, which

---

[4] Hugh of Saint Victor, *On Sacred Scripture* 1, in *Interpretation of Scripture: Theory*, 213.
[5] These and more examples are discussed in Kugel, *How to Read the Bible*.
[6] Honorius Augustodunensis, *In Canticum Canticorum*, PL 172, 359.

was mystically referring to a higher truth. Medieval authors commonly referred to this principle of interpretation by citing the apostle Paul: "The letter kills, but the Spirit gives life." (2 Cor. 3:6). This chapter explores some assumptions that medieval authors adopted when interpreting the text. Although some of these changed over time, the idea that the Bible was absolutely true, and needed to be read according to its own hermeneutical rules, was not really challenged until the time of Enlightenment philosophers such as Spinoza.

AN EXAMPLE OF ALLEGORICAL EXEGESIS: HAIMO ON JONAH

To see how medieval readers interpreted the biblical text, and what hermeneutical principles governed their exegesis, we may consider the following example, taken from the commentary of the ninth-century monk Haimo of Auxerre on the book of Jonah. Not much is known about Haimo. In fact, because medieval biblical commentaries were often transmitted in manuscripts with no author's name attached, for many years, the bulk of Haimo's work was misattributed or the author was misidentified as his contemporary Haimo of Halberstadt. Today, scholars have identified Haimo as the author of commentaries on Genesis, Deuteronomy, the Song of Songs, and most of the prophetic books, as well as the Gospels, the Pauline Epistles, and the Apocalypse.

The story of Jonah tells us about a reluctant prophet, who is commanded to announce God's wrath to the city of Nineveh. At first, he tries to flee, by taking a ship in the opposite direction, but God sends a storm, the sailors throw Jonah overboard, and he is swallowed by a large fish, which brings him back the shore. God commands Jonah a second time to go to Nineveh, and this time Jonah obeys. After his preaching, the Ninevites repent, and God decides to spare the city, much to the chagrin of Jonah, who resents God's grace towards them. In his commentary, Haimo does not deny that the text has a historical, literal meaning. At the beginning of his commentary, Haimo provides some detail on who Jonah was, when he lived, and where he was buried, and he spends some time wondering what happened to the Ninevites after their conversion. (Because of its great sinfulness, the city was destroyed afterward, according to Tobit 14:6. So, if the city of Nineveh converted to the Lord by the preaching of Jonah, after a while, they must have reverted to their old ways.) But at the same time, for Haimo, the text in its entirety contained a deeper, hidden meaning: the mystery of salvation through Jesus Christ. In this medieval Christian exegesis, known as typology, events and figures in the Old Testament were a kind of blueprint (called a "type") for God's plan of salvation as it would be fulfilled in Christ. Thus, Jonah was read here as a "type," or prefiguration, of Christ. For Haimo, all the historical events in the book of Jonah eventually refer to this deeper meaning.

Jonah's first verse reads, "Now the word of the Lord came to Jonah son of Amittai, saying 'Arise, and go to Nineveh, that great city, and preach in it, for the wickedness thereof is come up before me'" (Jon. 1:1). Haimo comments that

Jonah, which means "dove," signifies the simple and gentle Christ, on whom the Holy Spirit appeared as a dove. Jonah also means "the grieving one," because he (Christ) wept over the destruction of Jerusalem. That Jonah signifies Christ, the Lord himself attests in the Gospel, saying, "For as Jonah was in the whale's belly three days and three nights, so shall the Son of Man be in the heart of the earth three days and three nights" (Matt. 12:40). He is the *Son of Amittai*, that is, of God, because God is truth.[7] He is sent to Nineveh, which means "beautiful," which signifies the world, because we have never seen anything more beautiful with our earthly eyes.[8]

In Haimo's interpretation, the story of Jonah was really an extended metaphor for the work of Jesus Christ. Just as Jonah was sent to move the Ninevites to repentance, thus Christ was sent to this world. Jonah spent three days in the belly of the fish, just as Christ was buried for three days prior to his resurrection. Jonah was, of course, not exactly Christ-like in the literal sense. He tried to escape God's command by fleeing on a ship in the opposite direction, to a city, Tarshish. But this fact, too, had a deeper, spiritual meaning for Haimo, which to modern readers seems counterintuitive:

Our Jonah, that is, Christ, fled to Tarshish, for he relinquished his fatherland, that is, heaven, and, after he took on flesh, came to the sea of this world, and he so loved the people whose flesh he took on that he did not refuse to suffer, so that the synagogue [that is, the Jews] would not perish after Nineveh, that is, the Gentiles, was saved.[9]

The storm, which forced the sailors to throw Jonah overboard, was interpreted mystically by Haimo, as the "ire of the Jews who hoped for his death, crying out 'crucify him, crucify him.'"

---

7 In the preceding verse, Haimo had explained how *Amittai* means "truth."
8 Haimo of Auxerre, *Enarratio in Jonam*, PL 118, 128D–129A. English translation in Haimo of Auxerre, *Commentary on the Book of Jonah*, 7.
9 Haimo of Auxerre, *Enarratio in Jonam*, PL 118, 129C.

Again, the literal Jonah was no model prophet. He eventually does go to Nineveh to preach repentance, but after God spares the city, he sits sulking on a hill outside the city and resents God's grace. The sun beats on his head, and he is hot and uncomfortable. God decides to teach him a lesson: he sends a miraculous plant (either a vine or a cucumber plant; see Chapter 4) that provides shade for Jonah. But early the next morning, a worm attacks the plant, and it withers. If Jonah cares so much about a plant that he did not even grow, God tells Jonah, would not God care much more about the city of Nineveh, "in which there are a hundred and twenty thousand people,... to say nothing of all the animals?" (Jon. 4:11). Even where Jonah in the story's literal sense comes off as disobedient and querulous, in the allegorical sense these events still apply to Christ: Jonah sitting on the hill represents Christ judging the living and the dead at the end of times. The miraculous plant signifies the Jews, who wither after Christ's resurrection, which happened early on the morning of the first day of the week (e.g., Matt. 28:1). Even the number of Ninevites has spiritual significance:

We should not skip over the fact that in Nineveh more than 120,000 people are said to have lived; this number contains within itself a great mystery. For if you start with one, and you add natural numbers to it up to fifteen, you get one-hundred and twenty. Add two to one, and you have three; add three, and you have six; add four, and you have ten. If that is done up to fifteen, according to the series of natural numbers, there will be one-hundred and twenty. On this many people the Holy Spirit descended on the day of Pentecost. The number fifteen consists of seven and eight, for seven and eight is fifteen. Just as many steps were there in the temple of the Lord, and the same number of Psalms have the title "a gradual canticle" (Ps. 119–133). Just as many days did Paul stay with the apostles and is said to have discussed the Gospel with them (Gal. 1:18). Thus such a number rightly prefigures the multitude of the Church....[10]

The allegory of Jonah as Christ, and Nineveh as the world he was sent to save, was maintained fairly consistently throughout Haimo's commentary. Thus, the story was read as an allegory for events that were described in the New Testament: the death and resurrection of Christ (Jonah in the fish referred to Christ in the tomb), God's rejection of the Jews as the chosen people and acceptance of the Gentiles (the rejection of Jonah as prophet and the mercy of God on the Gentile city of Nineveh), and the foundation of the early Christian Church (the conversion of the Ninevites). Thus, Haimo made his reading of the book of Jonah a prolonged meditation on the mystery of redemption through Christ, in which the anti-Judaic theme

---

[10] Haimo of Auxerre, *Enarratio in Jonam*, PL 118, 142CD.

of the rejection of the "old Israel," Judaism, and the creation a "new Israel," the Christian Church, played a central role.

Haimo was not particularly original in his approach to the book of Jonah. Much of his exegesis was derived from Jerome. Haimo's interpretations may seem arbitrary to the modern reader, and they certainly do not always seem to do justice to the literal sense of the story. Although Jonah is the villain of the story, Haimo's allegorization seems to turn this upside-down. But Haimo's allegorizations are not without their own logic. Haimo often found his clue for an allegorical interpretation in the etymology of the Hebrew names in Scripture, many of which were suggested in a dictionary compiled by Jerome.[11] These names were thought to contain hints at their mystical meaning. Jonah, for instance, meant "dove," and he was the "son of Amittai," that is "truth." A dove appeared over Christ when he was baptized, and Christ was the son of God, who is Truth. Thus, Haimo was able to link Jonah to Christ through the signification of his name. Nineveh, translated as "beauty," thus signified the beauty of this world. Numerology provided an entry into allegory as well. The number 120,000 was an indication that Nineveh signified the Church out of the Gentiles. The idea that Jonah in the fish was a "sign" for the death and resurrection of Christ could be found in the New Testament (Matt. 12:40). Thus, Haimo's exegesis very much followed suggestions that had been presented to him by the New Testament and patristic tradition.

THE ORIGINS OF ALLEGORY

Before Christianity made its appearance, allegorical reading had long been a tradition in Hellenistic rhetorical education. It was a way of dealing with ancient texts that seemed strange, even objectionable, in their literal sense. The classical epics of Homer or Hesiod, for instance, often presented the Greek gods in a crude anthropomorphic fashion (describing the gods as having human traits, such as anger, jealousy, or lust) or even in immoral ways (Zeus committing adultery, for instance). Under the influence of Neoplatonism, by the third century C.E., gods were thought of as purely spiritual beings, connected to the highest moral good. For the reader in the Hellenistic schools, the highly regarded classical epics could not possibly mean what they said; their stories were now commonly read as really referring to deeper, philosophical realities. The Stoic philosopher Zeno, for instance, used Hesiod's account of the theogony (the struggle between

---

[11] Jerome, *Liber Hebraicorum nominum*, PL 23, 771–858.

the Gods that eventually gave birth to the universe) to demonstrate the principles of Stoic cosmology. Even the Hebrew Bible was read in this way by Jewish Hellenistic philosophers such as Philo of Alexandria (d. ca. 50 C.E.).

There are several indications that the "spiritual" reading of Old Testament texts was also common practice among the earliest Christians. It was a way to give meaning to ancient texts and make them come alive for the listener, a function that was inherent to the use of sacred texts in religious communities, Jewish and Christian alike. This way of reading the sacred texts is referred to as "paraenetic" exegesis, from the Greek word *paraenesis*, "evocation."[12] The typology on which Haimo built his commentary, of Jonah as Christ, was derived from the New Testament, as we saw above. Similarly, the brazen serpent of Moses was interpreted as a sign of Christ's crucifixion (John 3:14; Num. 21:4–9). The New Testament is rife with allusions that interpret the book of Psalms as referring to Jesus Christ. The "cornerstone" mentioned in Psalm 118, for instance, was seen in 1 Peter 2:7 as a veiled reference to Christ, and according to Matthew 22:44, Jesus interpreted Psalm 110:1 ("The Lord said to my Lord: "Sit at my right hand until I make your your enemies your footstool.") as a reference to himself. In Paul's letter to the Galatians, the figures of Hagar and Sarah were seen as allegories for the Jews and the Christians (Gal. 4:21ff.). Isaiah 53 and Psalm 22 were read as extended references to the suffering of Christ; for Christians, the story of Jesus' suffering "explained" the text of Isaiah and Psalms.

Early Christians had many reasons to read the Bible in this way. In the first place, it invoked the presence of Christ through the reading of the Scriptures, which for the earliest Christians meant the Old Testament. Although the Old Testament did not mention Christ directly, Christians read it as a prediction of his coming. But even after Christians developed their own canon of sacred writings in the Gospels, the allegorical reading of Scripture helped the early Christians to establish some arguments in the two polemics that were dominating the early Christian Church: one against Judaism and the other against heretics.

First, early Christians wished to define their faith as different from mainstream Judaism, whose Scriptures they shared in the form of the Old Testament. Many of their allegorical readings thus had a distinctly anti-Judaic edge, reflecting the ambivalent attitude of Christians toward the Scriptures of Judaism. On the one hand, ancient and medieval Christians

---

[12] Young, *Biblical Exegesis.*

were convinced of the *Hebraica Veritas*, the idea that God had revealed himself through these Jewish scriptures. (See Chapter 4.) On the other hand, they needed to explain why they were different from the Jews. To this end, they developed the conviction that at the moment of Jesus' crucifixion, the Jews themselves had collectively rejected God's offer of salvation and thus had alienated themselves from God's kingdom. In Haimo's commentary, for instance, Jonah, although a type for Christ, could also stand collectively for the Jewish people, who were "disinherited," as it were, as soon as the good news of God's salvation was brought to the Gentiles of Nineveh. It is very unlikely that Haimo in his lifetime actually saw a living Jew, but the polemic against a rejected Judaism confirmed for Christians their belief that theirs was the chosen religion.

At the same time, the Jews were not always held personally culpable for their rejection of Christ. The church father Augustine, for instance, held that God had blinded the Jews, and intended them by their very blindedness to be a living witness to the truth of Christianity. Augustine saw the Jews as incapable of grasping this spiritual sense of Scripture; in his view, they followed the letter of Scripture only and accepted merely the signs, rather than the hidden truths signified by them. Like the donkey in the sacrifice of Isaac (Gen. 22), they carried all that was necessary for the mystery of salvation, but they themselves did not comprehend that mystery.

However, some Christians in the early Church went much further in their rejection of Judaism, its Scriptures, and its god. They argued that the God of the Old Testament (and thus, the Jews) was in fact an evil demon posing as the supreme god, but whose scheme had been unmasked by the revelation of Jesus. In their view, Jesus had revealed to them a higher, hitherto unknown God, different from the God of the Jews. To them, the Scriptures that told the story of the "old" God no longer had spiritual relevance. Many early Christian writers, such as Tertullian and Irenaeus of Lyon, rejected this idea, which they called "gnosticism." They maintained the legitimacy of the Old Testament as divine revelation, and they confirmed that the God of the Old Testament was also the divine father of Jesus Christ, while at the same time maintaining a critical distance from the Jews. They saw the Church as the New Israel, the legitimate continuation of the Old Israel, whose followers, the Jews, had fallen out of God's grace. This idea of continuity also provided these Christian apologists with a legitimation of Christianity as an "ancient" religion, a notion that helped them raise their credentials with the Roman officials, for whom novel religions were suspect.

TYPOLOGY AND ALLEGORY

Haimo's exegesis of the book of Jonah illustrates one of the basic hermeneutical assumptions of the early medieval commentary tradition: that the message of New Testament salvation (the passion and resurrection of Christ, the foundation of the Christian Church, and the completion of God's salvation in the heavenly Jerusalem) was already prefigured in the Old Testament. Or, as the church father Augustine expressed it, "[i]n the Old Testament, the New lies hidden, and in the New, the Old is opened."[13] Thus, Abraham and Isaac's sacrifice (Gen. 22:1–19) signified the sacrifice of Christ on the cross; Melkisedek's greeting of Abraham with bread and wine (Gen. 14:18–20) foreshadowed the Last Supper; Moses raising the brazen serpent referred to Christ's crucifixion, and Jonah's adventure with the fish pointed toward Christ's death and resurrection. The figures in the Old Testament that were to be fulfilled in Christ were called "types." Medieval theologians often refer to the types as being the "shadows" of the events that are fulfilled in the New Testament, or they speak of events that took place "under the veil," whereas the New Testament displays these events unveiled. Typological exegesis not only informed medieval Bible commentaries; we often find it expressed in visual forms of exegesis, which are further discussed in Chapter 9.

Following the French Catholic scholar and cardinal Jean Daniélou, modern scholars have often wanted to see this "typology" as distinct from what they call allegory by emphasizing that typology always did justice to the historical realities of both New and Old Testaments, whereas allegory, in their view, was arbitrary. (Some of this seeming arbitrariness we have already observed in Haimo's Jonah commentary.) Other scholars, however, have argued that the concern about the historical validity of both type and anti-type reflects a modern, and not a medieval concern, and they have pointed out that the term "typology" is a nineteenth-century neologism.[14] Although medieval authors did use the words *type, similitude,* or *figure* for the Old Testament foreshadowing, more often they used the terms *allegory, mystical sense, spiritual sense,* or even, in Jerome's case, *tropology* (a word generally used by medieval authors to mean the moral sense of Scripture) to denote the deeper meaning that was different from their literal or historical interpretation. Isidore of Seville, author of a seventh-century etymological dictionary called *Etymologies (Etymologiae),* associated the word

---

[13] Augustine of Hippo, *Quaestionum in Heptateuchum libri VII,* 2:73, ed. Fraipont, 106.

[14] Daniélou, *Sacramentum futuri;* Daniélou, *Essai sur le mystère de l'histoire;* Louth, *Discerning the Mystery,* 118; Young, "Typology."

allegory with the Greek *allos*, "other." Citing Isidore, Hugh of Saint Victor (d. 1141) defined allegory as follows: "Allegory occurs when what is signified by the letter signifies something else, either in the past, present, or future. Allegory is, as it were, "other-speech" because one thing is said and another is meant."[15]

Augustine was perhaps the first Christian theologian to reflect systematically on just how this "other-speech" worked and to distinguish between the use of metaphor as literary device and the use of allegory. In his *On Christian Teaching*, he shows how words can refer to objects in a literal way. As an example, Augustine says, the word *ox* refers to the animal of that name. But some objects can also refer to other things, in a metaphorical way; for instance, *ox* may be a metaphor for the worker in the Gospel, as is the case in 1 Corinthians 9:9. All this is part of the literal sense of Scripture. But whereas words are signs for things, things can also be signs for other things, and this is called allegory. God speaks to us not only directly, through his words, but also through the things that are signified by the words. This applies not only to the "facts" of biblical history, but to the entire world around us: through all the works of Creation, God was thought to be speaking to humans in an allegorical way. Medieval authors referred to this as the "Book of Nature," in contrast to the "Book of Scripture." If we want to establish the exact meaning of Scripture, Augustine says, we must first carefully examine the text and do away with ambiguities. But, eventually, the signs instituted by God in the history of the Old Testament have meaning on a higher level, which we can grasp only by faith. The historical signs are but the husk; inside, there is the grain, which feeds the faithful.[16] The following is a schematic overview:

words—sign for → things   (literal/historical exegesis)

things—sign for → spitiual things   (allegorical exegesis)

THE MULTIPLE SENSES OF SCRIPTURE

Thus, underlying medieval biblical commentary was the notion that Scripture had more than one meaning: there was a literal or historical sense and a mystical or spiritual sense. The literal sense could alternately refer not only to the historical reference of the text (the "fact") but also to the primary meaning of words. Overt metaphors and figures of speech, such as exaggeration, were part of this literal meaning. The mystical sense was the

[15] Hugh of Saint Victor, *On Sacred Scripture* 3, in *Interpretation of Scripture: Theory*, 215.
[16] Augustine of Hippo, *De doctrina christiana*, III.7.11. ed. Daur and Martin, CCSL 32, 84.

allegorical or typological reading. In addition, the text could also be read as conveying a simple moral lesson; this was called the "moral," or sometimes "tropological," sense. The simple moral message of the Jonah story, for instance, was that one should not spurn God's commands; by disobeying God and fleeing to Tarshish, Jonah almost came to a bad end. However, once he sensed God's wrath in the storm at sea, Jonah willingly confessed his sin, and thus was spared a worse fate.[17] This literal and moral meaning of the text coexisted with the typological and spiritual meaning that identified Jonah with Christ. Medieval authors usually distinguished a number of spiritual senses. The twelfth-century abbot Joachim of Fiore, for instance, distinguished five senses of Scripture – historical, moral, metaphysical, contemplative, and mystical – and the ninth-century scholar Angelomus of Luxeuil (d. 895) distinguished no fewer than seven senses – historical, allegorical, mixed, trinitarian, parabolical, adventist, and moral – although in practice he used only the literal and allegorical senses in his commentary.[18] Most common was the notion that the allegorical or spiritual sense could be divided into two distinct senses: it could refer either to the New Testament or to eschatology (the so-called four last things – death, judgment, heaven, and hell). Or, as Thomas Aquinas distinguished the two, the spiritual sense could either refer to the Church militant, on earth, or to the Church triumphant, in heaven: "The Old Testament is an image (*figura*) for the New; the Old and New both are figures for heavenly things."[19] Although the first of these senses was commonly called the allegorical sense, the latter was sometimes referred to as the anagogical sense. Some authors, such as Hugh of Saint Victor, considered anagogy as a kind of allegory, but most medieval authors saw anagogy as a distinct category and came to a total of four senses. By the thirteenth century the idea that there were four senses of Scripture had become commonplace. The Dominican Aage of Denmark (d. 1282), or, as he was called in Latin, Augustine of Dacia, summed it up in the oft-quoted jingle:

Littera gesta docet, quod credas allegoria;
moralia quid agas, quid speres [or: quo tendas] anagogia.[20]

[The letter (i.e., literal sense of the text) teaches the facts; allegory what you should believe. / The moral sense what you should do, and anagogy what you should hope for (or: what you should strive for).]

---

[17] Haimo of Auxerre, *Enarratio in Jonam*, PL 118, 129.
[18] Spicq, *Esquisse*, 103 and 24.
[19] Thomas Aquinas, *Quodlibet* VII, q. 6, art. 2, co., in Thomas Aquinas, *Opera omnia*, ed. Busa, 3: 479.
[20] Augustine of Denmark, "Augustinus de Dacia. Rotulus Pugillaris," 252.

The city of Jerusalem thus could be interpreted on four levels, according to one of the monastic fathers, John Cassian:

One and the same Jerusalem can be taken in four senses: historically as the city of the Jews; allegorically as the Church of Christ, anagogically as the heavenly city of God "which is the mother of us all," tropologically, as the soul of man, which is frequently subject to praise or blame from the Lord under this title (Ps. 147:12).[21]

Not all verses of Scripture necessarily contain all three or four meanings at the same time, as Hugh of Saint Victor pointed out. Citing Isidore of Seville, Hugh used the metaphor of a zither to show that one does not need to touch all parts of the instrument in order to make music:

While in many cases we can rightfully assign all three senses to a verse, we have to consider whether it is difficult if not impossible everywhere. In the same way, on a zither and similar musical instruments, not all the parts that are touched produce music, but only the strings. But the rest of the zither has been made in such a way that it is connected to and joined together with those parts that the musician touches to produce a sweet melody. Likewise, some things have been set forth in Sacred Scripture that can only be understood spiritually, some serve only the dignity of morality, and some have been said only according to the simple historical sense. But there are some that can be aptly understood according to history, allegory, and tropology.[22]

What level of interpretation was appropriate for what situation depended in part on the psychology of the reader. According to Augustine, for instance, whether a word is more useful in its literal or mystical sense depends on the spiritual development of the reader. God has adapted Scripture to the different spiritual levels of the reader. This means that Scripture is always full of meaning, on a variety of levels, literal, moral, and spiritual. Still, Augustine warns his reader that some passages in Scripture clearly only have spiritual meaning; in fact, many things taken in their literal sense alone may seem strange, absurd, or even offensive. Anything in Scripture that offends against the love of God and neighbor should not be taken literally, he says. For instance, when Scripture says, "Unless you eat the flesh of the Son of Man and drink his blood, you will not have life in you" (John 6:54), we should not take this as an injunction to cannibalism. In considering what constitutes good morals and what does not, we should also apply some historical context, Augustine says. For example,

[21] John Cassian, *Conferences*, 2.14.8, trans. Gibson, 438. Online at Christian Etherial Classics Library, http://www.ccel.org/ccel/cassian/conferences.iii.v.viii.html
[22] Hugh of Saint Victor, *On Sacred Scripture* 4, in *Interpretation of Scripture: Theory*, 215–16. Citing Isidore, *Quaestiones in Vetus Testamentum*, Praef. 4, PL 83, 208–209.

whereas today, polygamy might be considered sinful, in the time of the Old Testament, it was perfectly accepted "in the interest of perpetuating the race."[23]

JEWISH TRADITION: THE DERASH

As was said previously, reading the Bible in the Jewish tradition was not all that dissimilar to the Christian tradition, in that it was read in a "paraenetic" way, in order to make the text relevant to everyday life. This interpretive reading of Scripture was called "*derash*", from *darash*, "to seek" or "to ask." This *derash* could either provide legal guidelines on matters of ritual conduct (which was called halachic commentary), or it offered homiletic commentary, that is, exegesis that was meant to be used for exhortative preaching and moral edification (called haggadic commentary). In the first centuries of the common era, Judaism developed a concept of "oral Torah," which involved the notion that God had revealed himself on Mount Sinai not just in the written Law but also in an oral tradition of interpretation of this written Law. This oral Torah was regarded as just as authoritative as the written Law itself; its tradition was carried on by sages, called *tanna'im*, who were regarded with almost as much reverence as a Torah scroll itself. Although originally conceived of as a purely oral tradition, this tradition eventually found a written version in the Mishnah (the writing that is at the core of the Talmud) and Tosefta (a legal compilation that was regarded as a supplement to the Mishnah).

The primary concern of this tradition was the question of how to adapt the Torah as a rule for everyday life, and much of it had a legal (halachic) character. But some biblical interpretations were more exegetical and homiletic in character; these interpretations often included folkloristic and anecdotal elements or moral exhortation. They were called haggadah and were not considered legally binding. The earliest collections of homiletic interpretation of Scripture, called midrashim, contain plenty of haggadic materials. The best example of these collections of midrashim is the Midrash Rabbah, the collective name for a number of commentaries on biblical books, such as the Genesis Rabbah, Leviticus Rabbah, and so on.

Some of the midrashim used exegetical techniques that were not all that different from allegory. The Song of Songs, for instance, was commonly interpreted as a poem not about earthly love but about the love of God

---

[23] Augustine of Hippo, *De doctrina christiana*, III.12.20, ed. Daur and Martin, CCSL 32, 90.

for his people Israel. In interpretation of the book of Genesis, the figure of Isaac stood for the people of Israel, whereas his disinherited brother Esau (also called Edom) was interpreted as the people of Rome, who were more generally associated with Christendom. But more often, the midrashim used the unique technique of "filling in the gaps" in the text, by relating the text to an extratextual narrative. When the text was unclear, contained words that did not seem to make immediate sense in their overt meaning, or seemed to skip a step in the narrative, it provided an opportunity for an anecdote that was supposed to explain the deeper meaning of the text. Thus, those elements in the text that did not make sense within their own context (often because the style was archaic or repetitive or because the context was no longer understood or no longer relevant to the lives of the listeners) were thought to refer to a meaning beyond the text. Many examples of this *derash* exegesis were magisterially retold at the beginning of the twentieth century by Louis Ginzberg in *The Legends of the Jews*. In Genesis 22, for instance, God calls on Abraham to sacrifice Isaac, his only son, with these words: "Take your son, your only son Isaac, whom you love, and go to the land of Moriah" (Gen. 22:2). To make sense of this apparent repetition, Jewish exegetes constructed the following imaginary dialogue between God and Abraham, to show both Abraham's obedience to God, while at the same time emphasizing his love for his child:

[God] said to Abraham: "Take now thy son." Abraham: "I have two sons, and I do not know which of them Thou commandest me to take." God: "Thine only son." Abraham: "The one is the only son of his mother, and the other one is the only son of his mother." God: "Whom thou lovest." Abraham: "I love this one and I love that one." God: "Even Isaac."[24]

In another example, the question why, in Genesis 2:21, God created Eve out of Adam's rib, and not any other body part, is transformed into a moral lesson on female behavior:

When God was at the point of making Eve, He said: "I will not make her from the head of man, lest she carry her head high in arrogant pride; not from the eye, lest she be wanton-eyed; not from the ear, lest she be an eavesdropper; not from the neck, lest she be insolent; not from the mouth, lest she be a tattler; not from the heart, lest she be inclined to envy; not from the hand, lest she be a meddler; not from the foot, lest she be a gadabout. I will form her from a chaste portion of

---

[24] Ginzberg, *The Legends of the Jews*, vol. 1, 274.

the body," and to every limb and organ as he formed it, God said, "be chaste, be chaste!"[25]

As we will see later, in the twelfth century, Christian scholars started to value the Jewish tradition for its contribution to the interpretation of the literal sense of the Bible. Ironically, in doing so, they often took the pseudo-historical *derash* materials at face value as historical reality, and regarded the Jewish tradition as having preserved some specific insight into the historical context of the biblical text. In his commentary on 1 Samuel 15:3, God's command to Saul to destroy Amalek, including "man and women, babe and suckling, ox and sheep, camel and donkey," the French Christian exegete Andrew of Saint Victor (d. 1175) cites a midrash one can also find in Rashi to explain why God's violence even extended to innocent animals:

There are some who say that the Lord ordered them to kill the cattle of the tribe of Amalek as well, lest the Amalekites should change themselves into cattle by sorcery, in which they were very experienced, and thus evade the massacre.[26]

Clearly, Andrew took this *derash* exegesis at historical face value.

THE LETTER AS THE FOUNDATION

The allegorical approach championed by Augustine set the tone for the exposition of Scripture within Christendom for centuries to come. For the medieval reader, especially the monastic reader, God had given the texts of Scripture to Christians to meditate on, to read them over and over, both in the liturgy and for personal devotion. This way of prayerful reading is often referred to as the *lectio divina*. In this meditative reading, medieval Christians encountered a multiplicity of meanings and multilayered signs, all leading them to a deeper understanding of God's salvation. Monks, according to Bernard of Clairvaux, were like ruminators; they chewed and chewed on Sacred Scripture to find spiritual nourishment in it.[27] Scripture was also sometimes likened to a forest: as many as there were trees in the forest, there were allegorical meanings within Scripture.[28] But the dangers of an excessively free rumination on Scripture were all too clear as well: without the guidance of authoritative interpretation, some readers might

[25] Ginzberg, *The Legends of the Jews*, vol. 1, 66 Both examples are derived from Genesis Rabbah. Ginzberg's book gives an excellent sampling of *derash* exegesis, arranged by biblical narrative.
[26] Andrew of Saint Victor, *Commentary on Samuel and Kings*, trans. Van Liere, 91.
[27] Bernard of Clairvaux, *Sermons on the Song of Songs*, I, 7.5, ed. Verdeyen and Frasseta, SC 414, 1: 164.
[28] These and more similes can be found in Bori, *L'interpretation infinie*, and D'Esneval, "Les quatre sens de l'écriture."

find interpretations that led them away from, rather than toward, sound Christian doctrine. This is why medieval authors usually stayed within the boundaries of tradition by following closely the teachings of the Church fathers, who they believed were inspired by the Holy Spirit.

The development of the cathedral schools and, eventually, the universities in the twelfth century highlighted the need to define the relationship between the spiritual and literal sense more clearly, however. For schoolmen who sought not to edify their own faith but to dazzle an audience with sophisticated allegories, the danger of sophistry was real, and unguided sophistry could easily lead to heresy. One attempt to recapture the spirit of Augustinian hermeneutics was made in the school of Saint Victor in the twelfth century by Hugh of Saint Victor. The school at this abbey, just outside Paris, was one of the many schools that made Paris into the foremost center of learning in Europe. It was started in 1108 by William of Champaux, who, before his conversion to the monastic life, had been teaching at the cathedral school of Notre Dame in Paris. By the mid-twelfth century, the abbey had gained a reputation for solid Christian teaching, with an emphasis on biblical studies and history. Much of this was Hugh's doing. His views on the pursuit of biblical learning are contained in his guide to the study of the Arts, the *Didascalicon*, and in his treatise *On Sacred Scripture and Its Authors*. Hugh of Saint Victor's learning program was directed toward the personal spiritual growth of the students rather than their purely intellectual instruction. For him, the ultimate goal of study was to restore Man from his fallen state, by redeeming him from his ignorance and inordinate desires. Preachers who employed allegory while spurning the literal sense were prone to both. Hugh warned:

I wonder how some people dare to present themselves as scholars of allegory when they do not even know the first meaning of the letter. They say: "We read Scripture, but we do not read the letter. We do not care about the letter, for we teach allegory." How can you read Scripture and not read the letter? If we take away the letter, what is Scripture?[29]

In Hugh's view, one needed not only to know the allegorical sense of a passage; one must also understand the foundation on which it rested. This required an understanding of the literal sense, which is what the words meant in their primary meaning. Following Augustine, for Hugh, the words themselves did not lead directly to spiritual truth, but the objects or events that these words referred to did. The proper understanding of

---

[29] Hugh of Saint Victor, *On Sacred Scripture* 5, in *Interpretation of Scripture: Theory*, 216.

Scripture must then start with the literal sense, and a proper understanding of the historical facts that the letter of Scripture recounted. God speaks to his people in two ways, Hugh says. First, he speaks through the Book of Nature, in which the entire created world can be seen as an extended metaphor for God's salvation. The second way is through the Book of Scripture, which is the perfectly true record of God's deeds in history. The words of the Bible refer to the reality of this world. In turn, the reality of this world points spiritually towards the mysteries of salvation, or "sacraments," as Hugh calls them. One cannot skip a step and proceed immediately from word to spiritual truths: one needed first to comprehend the bare meaning of the words before any allegorization should be attempted:

If you leap before you can run, you will fall flat on your face. He who proceeds in the right order, proceeds rightly. First make sure to learn the primary meaning of those things that God's word presents to you to be read [ultimately] according to their mystical signification, so that, when you know the initial meaning of their outward appearance, you can later meditate on them and gather from them through similitudes what you need for building up your faith or for instructing good morals.[30]

Hugh emphasized a stringent program of reading and memorization of the Sacred Scriptures, starting with their literal meaning, and continuing with their spiritual signification, as a preparation for right moral action and mystical contemplation. Hugh saw the letter as a foundation on which one could erect a building of faith. For this building, Hugh used an extended metaphor of Noah's ark. Erecting this "ark" was a kind of mental exercise, aimed at building up one's faith.[31] The keel of the ark was the temporal framework of salvation history: Creation, Fall, Redemption, and Completion, as related in the history of the Old and New Testaments. At its center was the salvation of Mankind in Christ's passion; all the doctrines of the Christian faith were to be spiritually built on this historical framework. Eventually, the structure was painted on the outside. This paint was the moral sense of Scripture, Hugh said, which educated humanity into Christian living, the outward completion of the structure of faith.

HISTORICAL EXEGESIS

Hugh of Saint Victor's emphasis on the literal sense led medieval authors to reconsider the role of history in biblical interpretation. God's work

---

[30] Ibid., *Interpretation of Scripture: Theory*, 217.
[31] The ark is described in Hugh of Saint Victor, *Selected Spiritual Writings*, 45–153.

of restoration, Hugh said, was the primary subject matter of Scripture according to its literal sense, and that referred to the history of this world. A right understanding of the Bible showed that this history was not a succession of random events but God's structured plan for the salvation of this world.

This notion not only led to an increased interest in biblical chronology in the twelfth century, but it also spurred an interest in the periodization of history. Some authors even saw this as a way to interpret the signs of their own time in the light of biblical prophecy. Following Augustine, Hugh divided history into two "states" (*status*), according to the Old and New Testaments, three periods (*tempora*), and six "ages" (*aetates*), respectively:

we must know that this whole order and extent of time can be divided into two states (the old and the new), three time periods (that of the natural law, of the written law, and of grace), and six ages (the first from Adam to Noah, the second from Noah to Abraham, the third from Abraham to David, the fourth from David to the Babylonian captivity, the fifth from the Babylonian captivity to the coming of Christ, [and the sixth from the coming of Christ to the end of the world]).[32]

These six ages mystically corresponded not only to the ages of Man, infancy, childhood, youth, adolescence, maturity, and old age, but also to the six days of Creation, to form a symmetry between God's two works, creation and restoration. After this last age would come a seventh day and an eternal Sabbath, with the second coming of Christ, which also would complete the two states and three time periods. Another popular periodization, common in historiography, was the division of history into four empires. This scheme was proposed in the work of the late antique Christian historiographer Paul Orosius (ca. 417) and was based on the vision of the composite statue in Daniel 2 and the four beasts in Daniel 7. The last and final empire was the Roman Empire, whose rule was considered to last until the present age.

Whereas Hugh had defined world history as God's work of restoration, other authors after him made a connection between the periodization of that history and the three persons of the Trinity. Hugh's contemporary Rupert of Deutz (d. 1129), abbot first of the abbey of Saint Lawrence near Liège, and later of Deutz near Cologne, for instance, wrote a universal world history on the basis of Scripture, titled *On the Holy Trinity and Its Works* (*De Sancta Trinitate et operibus eius*). In it, he distinguished three periods: the period of the Father (the work of creation, lasting until the

---

[32] Hugh of Saint Victor, *On Sacred Scripture* 17, in *Interpretation of Scripture: Theory*, 229.

Fall), the period of the Son (from the Fall until the passion of Christ), and the period of the Holy Spirit (from the resurrection of Christ until the end of times). Rupert confirmed the idea of the unity of all the Sacred Scriptures: they were all written by the Spirit, all formed part of the one divine plan of salvation, and all were centered around Christ's work of redemption.

This trinitarian division of history was further developed in the work of Joachim of Fiore (ca. 1135–1202), abbot of the monastery of Saint John in Flore, Calabria, which later became associated with the Cistercian order. But rather than seeing the work of the Holy Spirit as something in the past, Joachim argued that the best part was yet to come. The world was not just "growing old" (a popular adage among the spiritual writers of his time); based on his trinitarian interpretation of history, Joachim predicted that in his very own time, a spiritual renewal would take place, ushering in a spiritual age, which would last until its final fulfillment with Christ's second coming. In his main works, *The Ten-Chord Psalter* (*Psalterium decem chordarum*) and *The Concordance of the Old and New Testament* (*Concordantia veteris et novi testamenti*), Joachim offered a typological interpretation of world history and argued that historical patterns that were apparent in the Old Testament were to be repeated twice on a higher spiritual level, once in the time of the New Testament and another time in a spiritual age that was yet to come.

Like Rupert before him, Joachim distinguished three "states" (*status*) in world history: the period of the Father, of the Son, and of the Holy Spirit. Each of these three states corresponded with the domination of one "order" (*ordo*), a group of people who assumed spiritual leadership in this period. Like trees, these "orders" could have their roots in earlier periods, but they would come to full fruition in the time of their appointed "state" and would decline in the next one. In the "state" of the Father, which lasted from the beginning of creation to the time of Christ, the dominant "order" was the laity, starting with Adam and coming to full fruition with Abraham. The state of the Son started in the reign of King Uzziah (or Azariah, 2 Kings 14-15), came to full fruition in the time of Christ, and lasted until Joachim's own time; it was the period dominated by the order of priesthood. For Joachim, the status that was about to begin was that of the Holy Spirit, and the dominant order was that of the monks; it had started with Elijah in the Old Testament and Saint Benedict, but was to start its full fruition not until shortly after Joachim's own time. Joachim argued that the events of each period corresponded to each other typologically, an idea he called "concordance" (*concordantia*). Thus, Abraham corresponded to Zachariah, Sarah to Elizabeth, Jacob to Christ, the twelve sons of Jacob to the Twelve Apostles. This idea of concordance, together with his exegesis of Revelation, led Joachim to predict the signs for the coming spiritual age, where the priesthood would be in decline, and God would communicate directly with his believers through the Holy Spirit.

Needless to say, Joachim's work was not very favorably received by the Church hierarchy; it was condemned after Joachim's death, at the Fourth Lateran Council in 1215. However, his ideas were eagerly received by prophetic movements in the thirteenth and fourteenth centuries, especially within the Franciscan Order. Joachim, in his Revelation commentary, had predicted the coming of an "angelic messenger" who would harbinger the third, spiritual, age; many Franciscans identified this messenger with Francis of Assisi. When some Franciscans found themselves in conflict with the pope in the fourteenth century, they embraced Joachim's idea of a more "spiritual" Church not ruled by the clergy.

THE LITERAL SENSE AND THE PESHAT TRADITION

Hugh's directive to study the literal sense before anything else also led to a more developed hermeneutics of the literal sense. This development within Christian exegesis was paralleled by a similar interest within Jewish exegesis. Jewish exegetes in the eleventh and twelfth centuries had developed a new kind of exegetical technique, and they called it the *peshat*, the "simple sense" of Scripture. As we saw earlier, the late antique and early medieval Jewish commentaries on the Bible, the midrashim, were often associative and allegorical in character. This associative kind of exegesis was called *derash*. In the eleventh and twelfth centuries, however, Jewish exegesis in northern France took a distinctive turn away from *derash* and, starting with the commentaries of Rabbi Solomon (b. Isaac of Troyes, nicknamed Rashi, 1040–1106), and especially his grandson, Samuel ben Meir (Rashbam, ca. 1085–ca. 1174) increasingly emphasized the simple, that is, more literal and direct, meaning of Scripture, called the *peshat*. This exegetical technique aimed to exclude any external traditions of interpretation that could not be found strictly within the text itself. It strove to explain the text primarily by grammatical analysis and by finding parallel usage of the same words or expressions elsewhere in Scripture. Rashi also offered translations of scriptural expressions into the vernacular to clarify the meaning of individual words. These vernacular glosses are called *la'azim*; they are a valuable source for the knowledge of old French in this period. Scholars assume that

Rashi could draw for these on contemporary Hebrew-French dictionaries, or possibly interlinear translations of the Hebrew text.[33]

One example of the *peshat* method may be cited here, Rashi's commentary on Genesis 1:1. Rashi here argues that the sentence "In the beginning, God created heavens and earth" really should be translated as "In the beginning of God's creating heaven and earth." The verse does not want to tell us that God created the heavens and earth before he created anything else, Rashi says, because Scripture would have used a different expression in Hebrew:

If you wish to explain it according to its simple meaning, explain it thus: "At the beginning (*bereshit*) of the creation of heaven and earth, the earth was astonishing with emptiness, and darkness ... and God said, 'Let there be light.'" Scripture did not come to teach the sequence of the Creation, to say that these came first, for if it came to teach this, it should have written: "At first (*berishonah*) He created the heavens and the earth."[34]

Besides, Rashi argues, the Hebrew words for beginning, *ra'shit*, is commonly used in the *status constructus*, a Hebrew grammatical construction that connects a word to a subsequent one to indicate a possessive relation. He cites several examples:

There is no *ra'shit* ("beginning") in Scripture that is not connected to the following word, like, "In the beginning of the reign of Jehoiakim" (Jer. 27:1); "The beginning of his reign" (Gen 10:10); "The first of your corn." (Deut. 18:4) ... And similar to this is, "At the beginning of the Lord's speaking to Hosea," (Hos. 1:2), that is, at the beginning of the speaking of the Holy One, Blessed be He, to Hosea, "the Lord said to Hosea, etc."[35]

One could assume, of course, that there was an ellipsis, that is, a deliberate omission in the text, and read, "In the beginning [of creation] God created ... ," but the historical context of the verse makes that impossible: it is evident that other things were created before heavens and earth, Rashi says:

Now if you say that [Scripture intended] to teach that these (i.e., heaven and earth) were created first, and that its meaning is: In the beginning of all, He created these, and that there are elliptical verses that omit one word ... , then be astounded at yourself, for the water preceded, as it is written: "and the spirit of God hovered over

---

[33] Banitt, "The La'azim of Rashi and the French Biblical Glossaries."

[34] Rashi, commentary on Gen. 1: 1. *Mikra'ot gedolot. Genesis*, trans. Rosenberg. Also in *The Complete Jewish Bible with Rashi Commentary*, trans. Rosenberg, which is published online http://www.chabad.org/library/bible_cdo/aid/8165/showrashi/true.

[35] Ibid.

the face of the water," and Scripture did not yet disclose when the creation of water took place! From this you learn that the water preceded the earth. Moreover, the heavens were created from fire and water. Perforce, you must admit that Scripture did not teach us anything about the sequence of the earlier and the later [acts of creation].[36]

Rashi offers this linguistic and contextual analysis not simply to enable a more plausible or naturalistic account of the sequence of creation, however, but for quite a different purpose: to allow for the possibility that God first created the *Torah* before he created anything else. The latter is, of course, a midrashic exegesis, and in Rashi's commentaries, *peshat* and *derash* were not always strictly separated. Similarly, in Christian commentaries, a detailed literal explanation often functioned as a pathway to one particular allegorical exegesis, even if the latter was not always explicitly stated. Indeed, the *peshat* tradition may even have started as a polemic against the Christian allegorical interpretation of the Old Testament, which, as we saw, was often anti-Judaic in character. But its methodology, that of close reading and explaining the text by relating it to its context, proved successful in Christian circles as well.

One student of Hugh of Saint Victor who heeded his call to study the literal sense of Scripture was his fellow canon Andrew of Saint Victor, who wrote commentaries on a number of books of the Old Testament. Andrew often found himself consulting his Jewish contemporaries who were considered experts in this field. Like the commentaries of the northern French Jewish exegetes he consulted (probably through personal communication with the Jews in Paris, and possibly in England, where Andrew later became an abbot), Andrew's commentaries offer a text-centered technique of close reading, in which he carefully attempted to put the text in its historical and textual context. Andrew's "new departure in the search for the literal sense," in which he was indebted to Hugh, to quote William McKane, was the "awareness that [the books of the Old Testament] are historical documents which have a time, a place and a setting, which were written by human authors and whose primary sense must be sought by bringing all these factors into play."[37]

Thus, by the mid-twelfth century, Jews and Christians, when explaining the literal sense of Scripture, were working with a very similar methodology. Not all Christian exegetes were comfortable, however, with this Jewish influence on Christian biblical studies. They were worried that this

---

[36] Ibid. Modifications to the translation are mine.
[37] McKane, *Selected Christian Hebraists*, 49–50.

influence would lead to what they called "judaizing." What was, for instance, the true meaning of prophetic texts that the Christian church had always read as prophecies about Christ, such as Isaiah 7:14 ("Behold a virgin shall conceive"), Isaiah 11:1–11 ("A shoot shall come forth from the stump of Jesse"), and Isaiah 53 (the so-called song of the suffering servant)? If these texts referred to Christ, was that according to the literal sense or the mystical sense? Questions such as these would come to redefine the scope of biblical hermeneutics in the later twelfth century.

THE EXTENDED LITERAL SENSE

In his commentary on Isaiah, written around 1150, Andrew commented on Isaiah 7:14: "[a] virgin is with child, and will give birth to a son, whom she will call Emmanuel," which, Isaiah said, would be a sign that the liberation of Jerusalem from the hands of two kings who were besieging it, Rezin and Pekah, was at hand. Of course, in the Christian tradition, starting with Matthew 1:23, this verse has been interpreted as a foretelling of the birth of Christ, who was born of the Virgin Mary. Andrew, however, had cited the doubt that Jewish exegetes of his own time raised about this interpretation. How could the birth of Christ, 600 years later, serve as a sign to King Ahaz, the person addressed in this passage, that he would be freed from the hands of his enemies? A sign, the Jews pointed out, usually comes before, not after, the signified thing; if this prophecy were indeed referring to the birth of Christ, the sign of liberation would come 600 years after the actual liberation of Jerusalem from these two kings, a notion that was, of course, absurd. According to the Jews, as cited by Andrew, the sign Isaiah predicts refers to the young wife of the prophet who will conceive a son. *Alma*, translated here as virgin, simply means "young woman," not technically a virgin, Andrew points out. In its "simple" literal sense, the prophecy meant that by the time this son was about two or three years old (which is probably what the prophet meant when he said, in verse 15, "by the time he knows how to refuse evil and choose the good"), the siege of Jerusalem would be over. Although he does not mention it, there was no doubt for Andrew that this verse referred to the mystery of Christ's birth in its *spiritual* sense, but that could, of course, be grasped only with the eye of faith. Jews were by definition blind to this. Therefore, Andrew says, he will refrain from answering the Jews' objections:

These are the insults that the Jews throw at us, calling us the corrupters and violent distorters of sacred writings. It is not necessary for us to answer them since others have done so before us. They who have [already] answered them may see if these answers are sufficient.[38]

One of the other canons at the abbey of Saint Victor, Richard of Saint Victor (d. 1173), Andrew's slightly younger contemporary, was furious with Andrew's reticence. How could Andrew cite the opinions of the Jews as if they were his own, without any refutation? Richard sought to set the record straight in his own polemical treatise, titled *On Emmanuel (De Emmanuele)*. For Richard, the primary meaning of Isaiah's words was the foretelling of Christ. This was the subject matter that the authors of the Old Testament, inspired by God, had intended to communicate. To suggest that Isaiah had wanted to say anything else here amounted to blasphemy and denial of the Virgin Birth. Richard explained that prophets, through the grace of God, could indeed foresee things that would happen far away in the future and had expressed these truths in the Old Testament. He maintained that the biblical text spoke of Christ *in its literal sense*, because the authors of the text intended it to speak of Christ when they wrote it. If the Jews do not accept this as prophecy, Richard said, we should try to convince them of the Christian truth, rather than use them as guides for the primary sense of Scripture.[39]

Richard's argument testifies to the growing awareness that an appeal to the literal sense carried more weight than an argument from allegory, because it could be perceived by reason; the allegorical or mystical sense could be grasped by faith only, which carries no weight for those outside that faith. Richard's argumentation thus marks a subtle shift in biblical hermeneutics. Like Hugh, he emphasized the importance of the literal sense, but his notion of the literal sense was wider than that of Hugh: it comprised what later would be called the "parabolic" or "prophetic" literal sense.[40] Richard's argument, however, would become more dominant in the milieu of the twelfth- and thirteenth-century schools and universities. In the encounter with other religions, such as Islam and Judaism, and especially in the encounter with the philosophy of pagan philosophers such as Aristotle, the defense of Christianity by logical argument became important in a way that it had not been in the previous centuries.

---

[38] Andrew's exegesis of this passage is quoted in Richard's refutation of it, Richard of Saint Victor, *De emmanuele*, PL 196, 603D.

[39] Richard of Saint Victor, *De emmanuele*, PL 196; 601 ff. See also Van Liere, "Andrew of Saint Victor and His Franciscan Critics."

[40] Thomas Aquinas, *Summa theologica*, Ia, q. 1 art. 10 ad 3, in Thomas Aquinas, *Opera omnia*, ed. Busa, 2: 187.

We can see Richard's hermeneutics more fully developed in the writings of the scholastic theologian and Dominican Thomas Aquinas (d. 1274), who discussed the senses of Scripture a century after Richard of Saint Victor in his *Summa theologica* (*Theological Sum*), as well as in his *Quodlibetal Questions*.[41] For the most part, Thomas agreed with Hugh, and with Augustine before him, that there were multiple senses of Scripture, based on the notion that not only words, but also things, can carry meaning. Thomas Aquinas added to this, however, that all the essential lessons of the faith were contained in the literal sense of Scripture:

There can be no confusion in Sacred Scripture, since all senses [of Scripture] are founded on one, namely the literal sense. A rational argument can only be based on the latter one, but not on those senses that are called allegorical. . . . But there is nothing lost in Sacred Scripture, for there is nothing contained under the spiritual sense necessary for the faith that Scripture does not also treat plainly elsewhere in its literal sense.[42]

This meant that readers did not need to fear the arbitrariness that seemed inherent in allegorical exposition. In his *Quodlibetal Questions*, Thomas had offered a similar reassurance:

There is nothing that is related in any passage within Sacred Scripture in a hidden way that is not also said openly elsewhere. Thus any spiritual explanation of Scripture needs to have its rest on some literal exegesis of sacred Scripture, and thus all occasion for error is avoided.[43]

For the scholastic theologians such as Thomas Aquinas, all essential lessons of Scripture could be derived from its literal sense, and thus could be understood by common reason. In this way, the literal sense had achieved a primacy that it had not possessed for the Church fathers. But in order to maintain this primacy, the domain of the literal sense had to be extended to include some aspects that modern readers would perhaps see as allegory. The key to understanding this extended literal sense was the idea of authorial intention. The literal sense of scripture was determined by what the author intended to say. This increased attention to authorial intention gave

---

[41] Thomas Aquinas, *Summa theologica*, Ia, q. 1, art 10, in Thomas Aquinas, *Opera omnia*, ed. Busa, 2: 186, and *Quaestiones quodlibeta* VII, q. 6, art. 2 and 3, in Thomas Aquinas, *Opera omnia*, ed. Busa, 3: 479.

[42] Thomas Aquinas, *Summa theologica*, Ia, q. 1, art. 10 ra 1, in Thomas Aquinas, *Opera omnia*, ed. Busa, 2: 186–87.

[43] Thomas Aquinas, *Quaestiones quodlibeta* 7, q. 6, art. 1 ra3, in Thomas Aquinas, *Opera omnia*, ed. Busa, 3: 479.

a new importance to the human authors of Scripture, and led the scholastic exegetes to reflect on what it meant that these authors were acting as prophets. Thomas distinguished between the human author of Scripture, which he called the "instrumental author," and the "real" author, God or the Holy Spirit. Because the latter was omniscient, it was not inconceivable that the human author, by inspiration, could have expressed ideas that could not be comprehended under normal circumstance, or refer to events that were far off in the future – as when the prophet Isaiah deliberately intended to foretell the coming of Christ.

The new emphasis on the literal sense also meant that the "four senses" of Scripture were now prioritized in a new way. The idea of the four senses did not go out of fashion, but allegory gradually became subsidiary to literal sense. Allegory came to be considered useful for ornament, for meditation, or for spicing up a sermon. It was for edification, not persuasion. The literal sense was now promoted from being merely an initial stage in understanding Scripture to being the most essential way to understand it. This gave both reason and the literal sense a higher status than traditionally accorded to them. In his handbook *Didascalicon*, Hugh had distinguished three successive stages of reading, in which an analysis of the text (*littera*) was followed by an explication of the overt meaning of the text, the *sensus*; after this, the theological meaning, the *sententia*, was established. For Hugh, it went without saying that this *sententia* was a higher, spiritual kind of understanding, which could be attained only if one had reached a certain spiritual maturity. In the words of Honorius Augustudonensis, cited previously, it was a mystery to be unlocked. For Thomas, by contrast, this *sententia* belonged to the literal sense of Scripture (which included metaphors and prophecy), and could be attained by logical analysis and the force of human reason. God does speak in a mysterious way through Scripture, leaving plenty of room for allegory, but only after he has instructed us through the voice of reason.

THE DOUBLE LITERAL SENSE AND THE UNEQUIVOCAL SENSE OF SCRIPTURE

Scholastic theologians after Thomas Aquinas defined this extended literal sense more precisely. They distinguished between two literal senses: the literal sense proper and a "parabolic," or "prophetic," literal sense. The Franciscan fourteenth-century theologian Nicholas of Lyra (d. 1349), for instance, referred to this as the "double literal sense." For Nicholas of Lyra, a prophecy could be true in a direct literal sense, while at the same time it could be a metaphor and apply to Christ. The latter, a prophecy inspired by the Holy Spirit, was what the author intended to say and thus was part of its literal sense. Nicholas used a real-life simile to express this idea: the sign of a wine vessel above the door of an inn, he said, is a thing in itself: a painted piece of wood. But that is not its primary *meaning*; what it intends to tell us is that we can find a good glass of wine inside the inn.[44] Thus, it was quite possible that the primary reference of a prophecy was actual things and events in the prophet's lifetime. However, the deeper meaning was really what the prophets intended to convey, by speaking in similitudes. The Song of Songs, for instance, uses the imagery of corporeal love to express the love between Christ and the Church; there is no doubt, however, that the latter was what Solomon had intended to express in this book, and therefore, this was the actual literal meaning of this book.

One of the results of this use of the "extended literal sense" was that the sense of historical development that Hugh had brought to the text was sometimes lost. The danger was that the Bible was seen as a textbook of doctrinal statements, packaged in metaphorical language that only needed to be decoded in its proper way. Some exegetes, however, retained a sense of historical development in their hermeneutical theories. For the late thirteenth-century Franciscan commentator Peter John Olivi, for instance, prophesies could very well refer to events in the prophets' own lifetime and could be fulfilled partially before the coming of Christ. But eventually, all these prophesies would be fulfilled in Christ. Because their divine revelation lifted them above the vicissitudes of temporal history, prophets could acquire a visionary grasp of history, which allowed them to see all historical events, even the ones ahead of them, as signs referring to Christ. Olivi uses the simile of a pyramid to make this point: just as an eye on the top of a pyramid sees all the lines of the pyramid simultaneously from the point where they all converge, the prophets are elevated above temporal history and see the lines of all history coming together into the point where all history culminated, the revelation of Christ.[45]

However, by the late fourteenth century in Oxford, a heated debate was raging exactly over this double literal sense. Some of the scholastic philosophers there were arguing that Scripture, in its primary literal sense, sometimes could be false and contrary to the rules of logic. For instance, in John 10:9, Christ says, "I am the door." How can this be true in its literal sense, scholastic philosophers asked, when it is clear that he was a

44 Nicholas of Lyra, *Biblia sacra cum ... Nicolai Lyrani Postilla*, vol. 2, 555.
45 Olivi, *Postilla in Isaiam*, 1, in *Olivi on the Bible*, ed. Flood and Gál, 254–55.

human being? They were vehemently opposed by the English theologian John Wycliffe, who was later regarded by some as the "morning star of the Reformation" for his defense of biblical truth and his idea that Scripture is its own interpreter.[46] In his *On the Truth of Holy Scripture* (*De veritate sacrae Scripturae*), Wycliff pointed out to his adversaries that in the example cited, Christ here clearly intended to speak in a metaphor; thus, the metaphorical sense is its primary literal meaning. In other instances, the philosophers pointed out that Christ contradicted himself in Scripture, or even spoke lies. For instance, in John 7:8–10, Christ first asserts to his disciples that he would not go to Jerusalem, because his time had not yet come. Yet after his disciples were gone, he followed them in secret. Wycliff replied that Christ was not lying: the intention of his words was that he would not go to Jerusalem openly, as he would later do in order to be crucified.[47]

For Wycliff, all of Scripture had a literal sense, which was true and error free. If we see error in Scripture, he said, it is human interpretation and our unfamiliarity with the mode of speaking of Scripture that causes that error rather than Scripture. It was also possible that the text was somehow corrupt, but this should not detract from the idea that Scripture was inerrant, because Scripture, as first conceived by God and revealed to the writers of the sacred texts, was originally without fault. If the meaning we derive from Scripture is obviously false, then that is not its true literal meaning, Wycliff insisted. All seeming contradictions and difficulties would not occur, if we read Scripture not according to our own sense of logic, but according to the logic of Scripture itself. Rather than trying to test Scripture by the rules of philosophy, we should adapt ourselves to the language and the logic of Scripture. In order to see this logic, we must read Scripture with the eyes of faith; if we do this, it will become clear that Scripture contains no contradictions, is entirely consistent and true to itself, and is a rule for Christian life and society.

Wycliffe's ideas were firmly grounded in medieval theology. In some ways, however, Wycliff's hermeneutics clearly marked a transition from medieval hermeneutics to the early modern period of the Reformation. He maintained, for instance, that, if there is any doubt about the meaning of Scripture, one should not resort to the church fathers, church tradition, or the *Glossa ordinaria* to explain it, but to Scripture itself. And allegorizing

---

[46] The first one to use this epithet may have been Livesey, *The Life of John Wiclif, Morning Star of the Reformation*.
[47] John Wyclif, *On the Truth of Holy Scripture*, trans. Levy, 45–55.

was only a valid way of explaining Scripture where the Bible itself intended to present an allegory. He discredited the Church's tradition of allegorizing as random and arbitrary. Needless to say, Wycliffe's ideas on this were not shared by all late medieval theologians. The chancellor of Paris University, for instance, Jean Gerson, while sharing many of Wycliffe's ideas on the one "true," or "unequivocal," sense of Scripture, maintained that Church teaching was the only authoritative way to determine what exactly this true meaning was; the two could not possibly contradict each other. Gerson's arguments were mainly directed against a student of Wycliffe, Jan Hus, who was condemned and burned for heresy at the council of Basel in 1415. A century later, Martin Luther's ideas would echo much of what Wycliffe had said.

RESOURCES FOR FURTHER STUDY

Much of the literature on this topic is in French. For those who do not read French, Fr. De Lubac's *Medieval Exegesis* is now available in English translation. Kugel offers an excellent introduction to premodern biblical interpretation, and Young more specifically to early Christian biblical interpretation. The work by Minnis offers an introduction to the literary, rather than theological, interpretation of texts in the Middle Ages. A variety of source texts in translation is available as well. Both Haimo of Auxerre, *Commentary on the Book of Jonah*, and John Wyclif, *On the Truth of Holy Scripture*, are edited in the TEAMS Commentary Series, which offers more sources in translation for the history of medieval commentary and medieval hermeneutics. *Interpretation of Scripture: Theory*, edited by Harkins and Van Liere, is an especially valuable collection of source texts in translation. See also the resources mentioned in Chapter 6.

SUGGESTIONS FOR FURTHER READING

Archambault, Paul. "The Ages of Man and the Ages of the World: A Study of Two Traditions." *Revue des études augustiniennes* 11 (1966): 193–228.

Bori, Pier Cesare. *L'interpretation infinie. L'herméneutique chrétienne ancienne et ses transformations*. Translated by F. Vial. Passages. Paris: Éditions du Cerf, 1991.

Chenu, Marie-Dominique. "Les deux âges de l'allegorisme scripturaire au moyen âge." *Recherches de théologie ancienne et médiévale* 18 (1951): 19–28.

Cohen, Jeremy. *Living Letters of the Law: Ideas of the Jew in Medieval Christianity*. The Mark S. Taper Foundation Imprint in Jewish Studies. Berkeley and Los Angeles: University of California Press, 1999.

De Lubac, Henri. *Exégèse médiévale. Les quatre sens de l'Écriture.* Théologie. 41, 42. Paris: Aubier, 1959–64. English translation: *Medieval exegesis.* Translated by Mark Sebanc. Grand Rapids, MI: Eerdmans; Edinburgh: T&T Clark, 1998.

Dahan, Gilbert. *Lire la Bible au moyen âge: Essais d'herméneutique médiévale.* Titre courant, 38. Genève: Droz, 2009.

————. *L'exégèse chrétienne de la Bible en occident médiéval, XIIe-XIVe siècle,* Patrimoines. Christianisme. Paris: Éditions du Cerf, 1999.

Evans, Gillian R. *The Language and Logic of the Bible. The Earlier Middle Ages.* Cambridge: Cambridge University Press, 1984.

Goez, Werner. *Translatio imperii; ein Beitrag zur Geschichte des Geschichtsdenkens und der politischen Theorien im Mittelalter und in der frühen Neuzeit.* Tübingen: Mohr, 1958.

Häring, Nikolaus M. "Commentary and Hermeneutics." In *Renaissance and Renewal in the Twelfth Century,* edited by Robert L. Benson and Giles Constable, 173–200. Cambridge, MA: Harvard University Press, 1982.

Kugel, James L. *How to Read the Bible: A Guide to Scripture, Then and Now.* New York: Free Press, 2007.

Louth, Andrew. *Discerning the Mystery: An Essay on the Nature of Theology.* Oxford: Clarendon Press, 1983.

Medieval Literary Theory and Criticism, c.1000–c.1375. The Commentary Tradition. Edited by Alastair J. Minnis and A.B. Scott. Oxford: Oxford University Press, 1988.

Minnis, Alastair J. *Medieval Theory of Authorship. Scholastic Literary Attitudes in the Later Middle Ages.* The Middle Ages Series. Philadelphia: University of Pennsylvania Press, 1984.

Neusner, Jacob. *Introduction to Rabbinic Literature.* The Anchor Bible Reference Library. New York: Doubleday, 1994.

Reeves, Marjorie. *Joachim of Fiore and the Prophetic Future: A Medieval Study in Historical Thinking.* London: S.P.C.K., 1976.

Steinmetz, David C. "The Superiority of Pre-Critical Exegesis." *Theology Today* 37 (1980): 27–38.

Synan, Edward A. "The Four 'Senses' and Four Exegetes." In *With Reverence for the Word. Medieval Scriptural Exegesis in Judaism, Christianity, and Islam,* edited by Jane Dammen McAuliffe, Barry D. Walfish, and Joseph W. Goering, 225–36. Oxford: Oxford University Press, 2003.

Young, Frances M. *Biblical Exegesis and the Formation of Christian Culture.* Cambridge: Cambridge University Press, 1997.

CHAPTER 6

The Commentary Tradition

Christian communities throughout the Middle Ages used the Bible as a tool for the education and edification of both the clergy and the laity. No other book in the Middle Ages invited commentary as the Bible did, and the sheer bulk of the material that has been preserved is impressive. Commentaries alone do not do justice to the wide range of scholarly writing that the Bible inspired. Lexicons, chronologies, concordances, versifications, and abridgments all attest to the primacy of the Bible as the medieval study book. Not all of this material is available today in print; much of it exists in manuscript only. Most of it is also forgotten or ignored by modern biblical interpreters, which is unfortunate. In modern Jewish circles, it is not uncommon to consult Rashi, a medieval interpreter, on matters of scriptural interpretation; by contrast, no equivalent for Rashi exists in the Christian tradition. The inaccessibility of the texts is partly to blame for this; of the medieval commentaries that are available in print, relatively few have been translated into modern languages. Another reason is that, as we have seen in the previous chapters, modern hermeneutical assumptions have shifted away from the questions that medieval commentaries asked of the text. Their reasoning seems hard to follow and often appears repetitive and unoriginal. The influence of patristic commentary on the medieval tradition is immense, to the extent that some scholars have dismissed the medieval exegetical tradition as purely derivative.[1] As we will see later, however, this assessment does not do justice to the medieval commentary tradition. Although not everyone may agree that these medieval commentaries are relevant for modern theologians and preachers, read in their proper context, they can nevertheless give fascinating insights into a variety of aspects of medieval life, not just theology and biblical interpretation. The tradition of biblical interpretation touches on topics as diverse as science, education, psychology, and politics.

---

[1] Spicq, *Esquisse*, 10.

141

THE ANTECEDENTS: PATRISTIC BIBLICAL INTERPRETATION

The medieval commentary tradition, especially down to the twelfth century, relied heavily on its patristic antecedents. One of the earliest centers for Christian biblical exegesis was the Egyptian city of Alexandria, a flourishing center of learning already in Hellenistic times, and home to the finest library of the classical world. By the third century, the city was especially known for exegetes such as Clement of Alexandria (ca. 150–215) and Origen (ca. 182–254). The latter was the author of the *Hexapla*, the textual comparison between various Greek Old Testament translations mentioned in Chapter 4, and he wrote sermons and commentaries on almost the entire Bible. Many of these were translated into Latin by Rufinus of Aquileia (ca. 340–410). Origen strongly advocated the primacy of the spiritual over the literal sense, and hence, the allegorizing commentary tradition is sometimes referred to as Alexandrian, as distinct from Antiochene, exegesis, which emphasized a more literal and historical reading. The latter found its representatives in the fourth-century church fathers John Chrysostom (347–407) and Theodore of Mopsuestia (350–428), who both originated from the city of Antioch in Asia Minor (present-day Turkey).

The Greek tradition, with the exception of Origen, was less well known in the west, mainly because of the lack of Latin translations. Many Greek sources, such as Cyril of Alexandria (378–444), were virtually unknown entities until Thomas Aquinas used them in his continuous gloss on the Gospels, known as the *Catena aurea* (*Golden Chain*).[2] The commentaries of John Chrysostom were better known among western exegetes from the twelfth century on. We should keep in mind, however, that the most widely used work that medieval authors attributed to Chrysostom, the *Unfinished Work on Matthew* (*Opus imperfectum in Matthaeum*), was composed prior to the sixth century by an Arian author.

In the Latin western tradition, two towering figures exerted the greatest influence on the medieval commentary tradition: Augustine and Jerome. Augustine, the early fifth-century bishop of Hippo, wrote commentaries on Genesis (two, in fact), Psalms, John, and the Pauline Epistles, in addition to various minor exegetical treatises and numerous sermons. He was best known, of course, for his massive theological treatise, *The City of God* (*De civitate Dei*). Jerome stood out for the depth and breadth of his exegetical

---

[2] The English translation of the *Catena Aurea* on Matthew by Newman is available in the Christian Classics Ethereal Library, http://www.ccel.org/ccel/aquinas/catena1.i.html.

commentaries, many of which were written concurrently with his Bible revisions and translations. The two men often corresponded on the topic of biblical translation and interpretation.

Jerome was hugely influenced by the work of Origen, which is apparent in his commentaries on the Pauline Epistles. An even more important influence on Jerome's thought, however, was Hebrew biblical exegesis, which informed not only his bible translations but also some of his finest commentaries. Jerome became acquainted with Hebrew biblical scholarship while he lived in Palestine as a monk. His *Hebrew Questions on Genesis* (*Quaestiones hebraicae in Genesin*) makes ample use of Jewish exegetical traditions and served as an important source of Hebrew philology for biblical exegetes throughout the Middle Ages. His commentaries on the Prophets presented the text of these books in two translations, one from the Hebrew and one from the Greek. The first of these translations was followed by a philological and linguistic analysis of the text, according to its literal sense, while the second (the translation of the Septuagint text) was followed by a more Christological interpretation, which Jerome called the "tropological sense" (see also the previous chapter). The latter often presented a polemic against those Christians who expected the coming of a 1,000-year reign of Christ before the last Judgment; Jerome considered this interpretation of the text to be "judaizing," and he argued that most of the prophecies in these books could be applied to events during the life of Christ on earth instead. In addition to his commentaries, Jerome's dictionary of Hebrew names and his writing on the geography of the Holy Land became standard works of reference for generations of medieval scholars.

DIGESTING THE PATRISTIC HERITAGE

In the Roman Empire, literacy was the gateway to careers in public service. But classical, and therefore pagan, learning was sometimes thought to be at odds with Christianity. The early monastic communities, which had started to form within Christendom in the second or third century C.E., did not value learning per se. On the contrary, it was often considered one of the aspects of worldly behavior that the monks desired to leave behind when they entered the religious life. By the fifth century, however, monastic attitudes toward learning began to change, largely under Jerome's influence. Jerome saw biblical reading and biblical study as a way to dedicate oneself to religious living. By combining his scholarship with a life of ascetic dedication, he promoted the idea that the study of Scripture was a monastic vocation. Following Jerome's example, monks (and nuns) began to define their search for God not as a flight from the world into the wilderness but as a turning toward the study of Scripture. The result was a transformation of the Late Antique conception of the monastery from an ascetic refuge, a place in the "wilderness" away from the world, to a school and a scriptorium, a place where biblical texts were read, studied, preserved, and reproduced. Although one should not underestimate the role that bishops, and even secular rulers, played in the commissioning and writing of biblical commentary, the monastery would remain a place for biblical study for many centuries to come.

One of the most formidable challenges that faced early medieval biblical scholars was to transform the rich patristic heritage into a readily accessible corpus of biblical commentary. They did this by producing compilations or florilegia. Modern scholars have sometimes referred to this type of commentary as a catena, a "chain" of patristic citations and commentary, arranged in the order of the biblical text. The genre was flourishing in the Greek east, although there is very little evidence that Greek commentaries were widely known in the west. Medieval authors themselves did not use the term *catena*. Instead, describing themselves as "collecting flowers," "bringing forth wine from a cellar," or gathering pearls "from the treasury of the fathers,"[3] they referred to their own commentaries as "commentaria" or "expositiones." In a world in which books were scarce, the value of these florilegic commentaries could be immense, both for private study and for the use of the preacher.

Isidore of Seville

In 587, the Spanish Visigothic king Reccared converted to the orthodox faith, and under royal patronage, the newly united Spanish church flourished. The cooperation between kings and bishops was instrumental in this flourishing. Among the latter was the longtime archbishop of Seville, Isidore (ca. 560–636). Isidore was known and appreciated for his authorship of the *Etymologies*, which has been characterized as the first medieval encyclopedia. It was a huge treasury of classical and late classical lore and knowledge, which would be intensely used by medieval exegetes in centuries to come. Isidore was also the author of an influential compilation of allegories on the Old and New Testament, which, in his own words,

---

[3] Thus, Isidore, *Quaestiones in Vetus Testamentus*, praef. 5, PL 83, 209A; Alcuin of York, *Epistola* 196, ed. Dümmler, MGH Epistolae, 4, 324; and Alcuin of York, *Epistola* 213, ed. Dümmler, MGH Epistolae, 4, 357.

he handpicked out of the works of various patristic authors, "Origen, Victorinus [of Pettau], Ambrose, Jerome, Augustine, Fulgentius [of Ruspe], Cassian, and the contemporary man of such distinguished eloquence, Gregory [the Great]."[4] Thus, Isidore's commentary, known as the *Questions on the Old Testament*, was really one of the first so-called florilegia, aiming to offer quick access for those who thought that ploughing through the works of all these church fathers was impossible:

Aided by divine grace, we strive to touch on some of the things that are said or happened in a figurative sense, which are full of mystical sacraments; and, bringing together the opinions of ancient churchmen, just as if we hand-picked flowers out of diverse meadows, gathering a few out of many, putting several of them side by side, and even arranging a few of them, we offer them not only to studious readers but even to squeamish ones who are bored by too much wordiness.[5]

In addition to these exegetical *Questions*, covering the historical books of the Old Testament, Isidore produced a list of short allegorical sketches on biblical figures, organized in chronological order, the *Allegories on the Old Testament (Allegoriae in Vetus Testamentum)*. Eve, taken from the ribs of Adam, prefigures the Church; Cain and Abel stand for the people who killed Christ, and Christ, respectively; Noah is Christ and his ark the Church – and so on. These allegories were probably intended as a reference work for the use of preachers.

Bede

In England, one of the most prolific authors of this period, and probably one of the most learned men of his time, was the Venerable Bede (ca. 673–735), whom we already encountered in the first chapters of this book. A native of Northumbria who lived his entire adult life in the monastery of Jarrow, Bede wrote numerous biblical commentaries, as well as works that explain biblical chronology, computation, and world history. Bede's exegetical productivity shows that around the turn of the eighth century, Northumbria had become a major center of learning. Judging from the sources to which Bede had access, Jarrow must have been home to a well-equipped library of patristic and biblical books.[6] It even included a copy of Josephus's *Antiquities (Antiquitates)*, a re-narration of the biblical history

---

[4] Isidore of Seville, *Quaestiones in Vetus Testamentum*, praef. 5, PL 83, 209A.
[5] Ibid., praef. 2, PL 83, 207BC.
[6] Lapidge, *The Anglo-Saxon Library*, 36. In an appendix, Lapidge gives an overview of works cited by Anglo-Saxon authors.

written by a first-century Jewish author. Bede praised Josephus's insight into the historical sense of Scripture, saying that "no one can easily be found to be more learned about these things, after God's word itself."[7] Bede's appreciation would find many medieval followers, and Josephus came to be widely regarded in medieval Europe as one of the most important sources for the literal sense of Scripture.

For the use of his fellow monks and other clerics Bede wrote allegorical commentaries on Samuel and Kings, Ezra and Nehemiah, Tobit, Proverbs, and Song of Songs, and most of the New Testament, but also on select passages from the Bible, such as the first chapters of Genesis, the description of the tabernacle in Exodus, the temple in Kings, and the canticle of Habakkuk (Hab. 3). Bede's commentaries were not mere digests. Even though Bede aimed to follow in these commentaries the exegesis of the fathers, at times he felt compelled to add interpretations of his own, carefully noting in the margins what came from where. In his dedicatory letter to his friend, Bishop Acca of Hexham, Bede writes,

Encouraged by the urging not only of you, Acca, my dearly beloved bishop, but also of many other brothers, we took care, inasmuch as the Lord grants us the ability to write, to gather on the Gospel of Mark especially those comments that we found in the writings of the venerable fathers, gathered from here and there. But we also inserted a few of our own, where it seemed appropriate, imitating their efforts, and I humbly beseech the reader, if he finds our work worthy of transcription, to retain in writing the notation of their names, which are placed above in the margin, just as presently is done in the commentary on the Gospel of Luke, which with God's help we composed many years ago.[8]

Regrettably, not all subsequent copyists followed Bede's careful instructions, and many of the notations indicating the sources of the commentary have been lost.

THE CAROLINGIAN COMMENTATORS

Less than a century after Bede's death, in 793, the monastery of Jarrow became a target of repeated raids by Viking plunderers and fell into decline. However, in the same period the Continent witnessed a flourishing of scholarly and literary activity, as we have seen in Chapter 2. Biblical studies were very much part of this. The late-ninth-century biographer of Charlemagne, the monk Notker of Saint Gall, tells us that when Alcuin of York "heard

---

[7] Bede, *In primam partem Samuhelis*, 2, praef., ed. Hurst, CCSL 119, 69.
[8] Bede, *In Lucae evangelium*, praef., ed. Hurst, CCSL 120, 432.

how eagerly Charles, the most devout of rulers, received wise men, he boarded a ship and came to him." Alcuin, Notker said, "was more skilled in all the breath of writings than other men of modern times, being a pupil of Bede, the most learned interpreter of the Scriptures since St Gregory."[9] Notker, who wrote almost a century after Alcuin, may have oversimplified the circumstances of Alcuin's move to the continent, but it is clear that Alcuin, some time in the early 780s, was welcomed and appreciated at Charlemagne's court for his qualities as biblical exegete.

Alcuin wrote his commentary on the Gospel of John at the request of two religious women, Gisela and Rodtrude, a sister and a daughter of Charlemagne, respectively, who were both nuns. The two admitted that reading Augustine was a challenge for them, and this is why they asked Alcuin for a selective digest:

We do have the explanations of that most famous doctor Augustine in his sermons on the same Gospel, but they are in some places too obscure and adorned with too much rhetorical flourish to be grasped by our very limited comprehension. It would be better for us to drink from the sweet waters of the brook with your devout help than to commit our ship to the depths of boisterous rivers.[10]

The style of the letter belies their humble self-assessment. Alcuin answered with a similar self-deprecating modesty:

As much as I praise your zealous devotion for sacred wisdom, I lament my own inexperience of the same; I know myself to fall much short of your praiseworthy devotion. And I wish I had in me as much ability to write as you have desire to read.[11]

Alcuin set out to write a commentary on John for the two women, in which he wanted to "scour the flowery meadows of many fathers," and use the works not only of Augustine but also those of Ambrose, Gregory the Great, and Bede, and "many other holy fathers, in as far as I could find them,"

using their ideas and words, rather than acting on my own presumption, to satisfy the reader's curiosity, working with a cautious pen, and with God's grace helping me not to write anything against the ideas of the Fathers.[12]

Alcuin was not the only biblical scholar in Charlemagne's service, and the close association of court and church in the Frankish empire continued

---

[9] Notker of Saint Gall, *Charlemagne*, trans. Thorpe, 56.
[10] Alcuin, *Epistolae* 196, ed. Dümmler, MGH Epistolae, 4, 324.
[11] Alcuin, *Epistolae* 213, ed. Dümmler, MGH Epistolae, 4, 354.
[12] Ibid., 357.

under Charlemagne's successors. The Carolingian court formed an important catalyst for the writing of biblical commentary. Several commentaries were written in the ninth century by abbots and bishops from the emperor's entourage, often commissioned by or presented to lay rulers and other figures closely associated with the court, some of them women, as we saw earlier. The abbot of Fulda, Hrabanus Maurus, one of the most prolific biblical commentators of his time, wrote his commentary on Samuel and Kings at the request of the abbot Hilduin of Saint Denis, "archchaplain of the sacred palace," and presented it in person "in our monastery" to Louis the Pious, the son and successor of Charlemagne.[13] His commentary on Chronicles was dedicated to this same Louis, and his commentary on Esther and Judith to Louis's wife, the empress Judith.

The aim of most Carolingian commentators was primarily educational. Like Isidore and Bede before them, they wanted to make the patristic heritage accessible by harmonizing the diverse commentaries, sermons, homilies, treatises, histories, and handbooks, and transform them into consistent, running commentaries on almost the entire Bible. These commentaries are seldom highly original works of exegesis, and many modern scholars have dismissed these commentaries as merely "derivative," a "tireless repetition of [their] predecessors."[14] But this judgment misses the essential achievement of the Carolingian commentary tradition. The selection bears the signature of the commentator. By selecting, paraphrasing, and rearranging the old materials, these scholars were creating a new type of commentary, and they were extending their skill to books that the fathers had neglected. Hrabanus was the first one to comment on the books of Deuteronomy, Judith, Esther, Wisdom, and Chronicles, for instance. He described his cautious method in the preface to his commentary on Chronicles:

What could I, as a learned teacher, try to find out or explain from among all the mysteries [of these books]? But following the footsteps of the fathers, I set in order what I found explained by them, and what I could investigate by myself, in accordance with their [opinion], and with God's grace agreeing, and carefully collected it into one work.[15]

Like Bede before him, Hrabanus took care to mark his sources with large capital letters in the margin, A for Augustine, G for Gregory, and so on. His own opinions he indicated with a large M, for Maurus, "as his teacher

---

[13] Hrabanus Maurus, *Epistola* 18, ed. Dümmler, MGH Epistolae, 5, 423.

[14] Spicq, *Esquisse*, 59, and Smalley, *Study of the Bible*, 37–38.

[15] Hrabanus Maurus, *Epistola* 18, ed. Dümmler, MGH Epistolae, 5, 423.

Alcuin, of blessed memory, had taught him."[16] In addition to solidly ortho-dox authors such as Augustine, Jerome, Gregory, Bede, Isidore, Hrabanus made use of Josephus, as well as "a certain Hebrew of modern times, well-versed in the Law, who cites Hebrew traditions in many places."[17] Knowing that this use of Jewish sources was perhaps somewhat contested, he assured the reader that he cited them not as definitive authorities, "but simply to find out what he has written, leaving its approval to the judgement of the reader."[18] As pointed out in Chapter 5, it is very likely that this Hebrew source that Hrabanus used was the same (converted) Jew who assisted Theodulf in his correction of the Bible text (mentioned in Chapter 4).

Of a similar stature to Hrabanus' oeuvre is the work of Haimo of Auxerre, which was already mentioned in Chapter 5. Founded in the ninth century by an Irish monk, Muretach, Auxerre grew into a center of biblical study under Haimo and his colleague Remi of Auxerre. Just as Hrabanus's commentaries on most historical books of the Bible would form the basis for the later *Glossa ordinaria*, Haimo's commentaries did the same for the Prophets.

QUESTIONS AND RIDDLES

At the same time Isidore and Bede wrote their predominantly allegorical commentaries, many biblical commentaries composed in the seventh and eighth centuries were distinctly more "Antiochene" in character, that is, primarily concerned with basic textual understanding and historical anal-ysis. Although many scholars have characterized these commentaries as "insular" or "Irish" in origin, it is important to note that most of them were probably composed on the Continent, albeit in monasteries that had close ties with Irish monasticism, such as Saint Gall, Werden, Bobbio, and Reichenau. In the seventh and eighth centuries, monks from Ireland held to the ideal of what they called green martyrdom, or peregrination for the sake of Christ, as opposed to the red martyrdom, which denoted the mar-tyrdom of the persecuted early Christians, and white martyrdom, which denoted the monastic life. These monks traveled from the British Isles to the Continent, where they founded new monasteries and revitalized old ones. Their settlement often brought about a revival of Latin learning and literacy. Most of the texts they produced are typical school texts, and many

---

[16] Hrabanus Maurus, *Epistola* 14, ed. Dümmler, MGH Epistolae, 5, 402.
[17] Ibid. See also *Epistola* 18, ed. Dümmler, MGH Epistolae, 5, 423.
[18] Ibid.

of them are anonymous, although some of them were falsely attributed to Bede or Isidore of Seville in a later period.

Although many of these texts can be characterized as "glosses" (see the following section), the more substantial commentaries were structured as a series of questions and answers. A representative one of these, probably dating from the middle of the eighth century, was an anonymous text titled *A Few Questions on Problems in the Canonical Books*. It cites Isidore's *Etymologies*, on occasion the *Questions on the Old Testament*, and patristic sources: not only Augustine, Ambrose, Jerome, and Origen, but also Eucherius of Lyon. Unlike the "digest" commentaries of Bede and the Carolingian authors, it made hardly any attempt to identify its sources, referring simply to "some" and "others." The text is mainly concerned with the literal meaning of the text and very rarely presents "moral" or "spiritual" explanations. The former could lead to intense quasi-historical or theological speculation, however. While commenting on Genesis 3, the anonymous author wonders why the speaker in the text is speaking in the first-person plural:

"Behold Adam is become as one of us." (Gen. 3:22). To whom does he say this word, and who heard it? In internal reasonings, by way of the Word, co-eternal with him, he says, "one of us," of the Trinity. Just as "they will be like gods, knowing good and evil" [means knowing these things] just as we do. Or "one of us" could mean similar to the demons that have come forth from us. Or "one of us" could mean, he has exalted him whom he has made, for he shall be "as one of us," by taking on flesh, in Christ.

And sometimes the author speculated about questions about which the text was silent:

What age was Adam when he sinned? Some say twelve years old, for at that age, malice enters into a human being. Or: he was created at the age of thirty, and he sinned at that age. But some say that he was in paradise for fourteen years, to test his patience, and in those fourteen years he begat sons without sin, and in those years the sun shone at night. But more likely we trust that he was made, sinned, and was thrown out all on one day: the sixth day of the week and the fifteenth of the month, just like the day, the Friday, that Christ died to save what had perished. Again, others say that Adam remained in paradise for forty-two and a half days, and that he ate [of the apple] after the third hour, and was driven out of paradise on the ninth hour.[19]

---

[19] *The Reference Bible*, ed. MacGinty, CCCM 173, 89–90.

The question–answer style that is prevalent in this commentary indicates that this text had a didactic purpose. Some of the earlier Carolingian commentaries, such as Alcuin's commentary on Genesis and Wigbod's commentary on the Octateuch (the first eight books of the Bible), also followed this Anglo-Irish question-and-answer format.

Other early medieval monastic texts even reformatted the exegetical questions as a series of riddles. Riddles were a popular way to transmit knowledge and wisdom lore in this period. These exegetical collections were intended to amuse as well as teach. This type of riddle existed not only in Latin; we also find them in the vernacular.[20] An Old English collection survives in the same manuscript that also contains the only extant copy of the Old English poem *Beowulf.* It was a riddle contest, in which the pagan god Saturn tests the wise king Solomon on a variety of mainly biblical and apocryphal trivia, such as "Tell me how many years Adam lived in this world. I tell you, he lived nine-hundred and thirty years in toil and in misery and then he went to hell and there he suffered grim torments for five-thousand two hundred and twenty-eight years." Others sound more like classical riddles, rather than trivia: "What is the heaviest thing to bear?" The answer: "A man's sin and God's anger."[21] Whereas Frederick Tupper, the early twentieth-century editor of the riddles of the Exeter Book, still saw these collections as "odd ends from Holy Writ, eked out by monkish additions to scriptural lore,"[22] today we may appreciate that most of this "monkish" lore derived from apocryphal, patristic, and even rabbinic sources.

GLOSSES

The other format frequently used in these early medieval "insular" commentaries was the gloss. The term *gloss* denotes both a short explanatory note to a text, and a commentary added in the margin or between the lines of a text. Glossing was a reading exercise: glosses were intended to explicate the text, give grammatical or stylistic analysis, offer a translation, or supply further commentary and references to authors and other texts, in the course

---

[20] An example can be found in St Gall MS 913, fol. 148ff. Available online at http://www.e-codices. unifr.ch/en/preview/csg/0913. Some of these texts were dispersed under the name of Isidore of Seville, *De veteri et novo testamento quaestiones*, PL 83, 200–08, or pseudo-Bede; Bayless, "The *Collectanea* and Medieval Dialogues and Riddles."

[21] *The Prose Solomon and Saturn*, ed. Cross and Hill, 27 and 33; translations on 72 and 114.

[22] *The Riddles of the Exeter Book*, ed. Tupper, xxi.

of reading. Collections of these glosses could exist either as additions to the biblical text written on the same page (either in the margins or between the lines, as an "interlinear gloss"), or gathered independently of the text, as "glossae collectae" ("gathered glosses").

Some of these early medieval gloss collections can be traced back to the scholarly activity of the Greek archbishop Theodore (d. 690) and his companion Hadrian, whose arrival in Canterbury in the seventh century initiated a rich tradition of learning in England. Some of the glosses cite these scholars by name: "Hadrian says . . . " or "Theodore says . . . " Although most of these were simple word explanations, many of them were characterized by their curiosity about the historical circumstances of the biblical narrative, and they all show a keen interest in biblical realia. In one gloss, for instance, the Latin word *locusta* ("locust," the food of John the Baptist, in Mark 1:6) was explained as a kind of lobster, because locusts were virtually unknown in northern Europe. Another gloss on Genesis 3:7 explains the odd Graecism *perizomata* ("they sewed together fig-leaves and made themselves *perizomata*"), as "girdles" (*cinctoria*). It continues: "like a sort of sheep-skin garment, that is, *bracas* (breeches)."[23] Theodore brought a considerable tradition of Greek learning to his new archiepiscopal see: the commentaries of John Chrysostom and Theodore of Mopsuestia, two of the foremost representatives of the Antiochene tradition of biblical exegesis, were cited frequently in these glosses. The work of these authors was hardly known in the west until the late twelfth century.

Some of the glosses in these commentaries were purely linguistic and gave word explanations, often in the vernacular. Linguistic vernacular glossing of the Bible was to remain common in England until well into the eleventh century, when Old English word glosses were often added to older Bibles. Thus, the Vespasian Psalter was glossed in the ninth century, and the Lindisfarne Gospels in the tenth. The practice was prevalent on the continent as well, and some of the oldest documents in Old High German come from these collections of biblical word explanations, some organized in their biblical order, and some in alphabetical order. In this way, biblical study led to the medieval tradition of vernacular lexicography.

The Glossa Ordinaria

Glossing continued in the eleventh and twelfth centuries at the schools that had formed around the cathedrals of many northern French cities,

---

[23] Bischoff and Lapidge, *Biblical Commentaries*, 408 and 311.

which, after the Viking invasions of the tenth century, had finally started to recover and even flourish. The most monumental and lasting achievement of these twelfth-century cathedral schools was no doubt the redaction and compilation of patristic and Carolingian exegesis into glosses on most Bible books. These glossed books combined two formats: the interlinear short glosses, which were common in the insular bible commentary tradition, and the longer digest commentary, which was commonly practiced in the Carolingian tradition. The latter, longer comments were adapted to fit in the margin surrounding the Bible text, whereas the shorter glosses, offering more limited comments (and sometimes even abridgments of the marginal glosses), were placed between the lines of the Bible text (see Photo 8). There does not seem to have been a rule, other than length, for what gloss belonged in the margin, and what in between the lines; in different manuscripts, a specific gloss could be found in either place. As in footnotes today, an intricate system of asterisks and other signs made clear what gloss belonged to what Bible verse.

By the end of the twelfth century, these glosses had become such a common feature of the Bible text that most scholars referred to them as "*the* gloss" (*Glosa*, or *Glossa*), and they came to be regarded as the standard commentary to the entire biblical text. Modern scholars refer to these glosses as the *Glossa ordinaria* on the Bible, but one should keep in mind that this *Glossa ordinaria* was not originally conceived, or indeed produced, as one work. Individual Bible books (such as Genesis, Exodus, Samuel and Kings, Psalms, and so on) were glossed at different dates, by different authors, and probably in different places as well, and they circulated as individual books. Most of these glossed books were not novel in their content because they largely drew on patristic traditions, filtered through the Carolingian commentaries mentioned above. The first to gloss books in this way was Anselm of Laon (d. 1117), who by the beginning of the twelfth century had already built a reputation for biblical exegesis that attracted great scholars such as Peter Abelard. The latter, however, who was accustomed to the more intellectually stimulating practice of dialectical disputation (see the following), was greatly disappointed by Anselm's skills. In his autobiography, the *Story of his Misfortunes* (*Historia calamitatum*), Abelard reported,

I therefore approached this old man, who owed his reputation more to long practice than to intelligence or memory. Anyone who knocked at his door to seek an answer to some question went away more uncertain then he came. Anselm could win the admiration of an audience, but he was useless when put to the question. He had a remarkable command of words but their meaning was worthless and devoid of

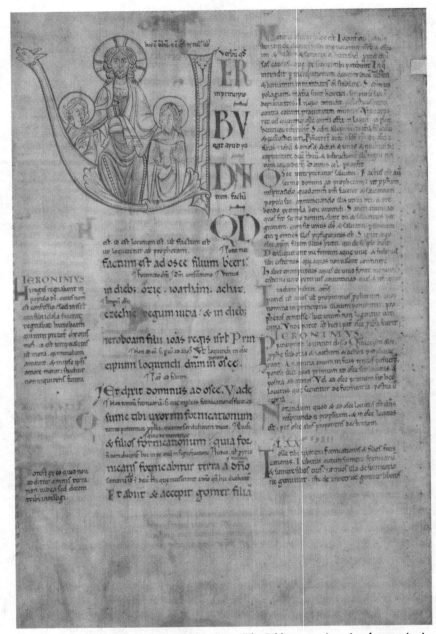

Photo 8. A twelfth-century glossed Bible: Hosea. The Bible text, written in a large script in the middle column, is interspersed with interlinear glosses and flanked by marginal glosses. Pierpont Morgan Library, MS. M.962, f. 2r. Photo (c) Morgan Library and Museum, and Courtesy of the Index of Christian Art.

all sense. The fire he kindled filled his house with smoke but did not light it up; he was a tree in full leaf which could be seen from afar, but on a closer and more careful inspection proved to be quite barren.[24]

Anselm was assisted by his brother Ralph of Laon (d. 1133), who continued to work on glossing biblical books after the former's death. Anselm and Ralph were probably the authors of the gloss on the Gospels and on the Epistle to the Romans. The glosses on the Pauline Epistles bear a close resemblance to those written by Lanfrank, the abbot of Bec Abbey in Normandy, and some scholars surmise that the masters at Laon were students of Lanfrank. Another master of the Gloss came from nearby Auxerre. Gilbert of Auxerre (d. 1134), also nicknamed Gilbert "the Universal," was the likely author of the Gloss on Lamentations, the Twelve Prophets, and possibly Samuel and Kings. Gilbert's dependence on Haimo of Auxerre suggests that Auxerre must have continued to be a center for biblical studies since Carolingian times.

The early history of the Gloss is sometimes obscure, and the glossing of the Bible was not a very systematic or planned process. There were no less than three successive redactions of the Gloss on Psalms, for instance, by Anselm of Laon, Gilbert of Poitiers (d. 1154), and Peter Lombard (d. 1160), respectively. Some biblical books received their gloss fairly late (such as Maccabees), whereas others were never glossed (such as Baruch and 2 and 4 Ezra). For some books, such as Revelation, several different glosses were in circulation.[25] But an important phase in the production of these glossed bibles came in the 1140s and 1150s in Paris. The collegiate abbey of Saint Victor became a major center for the copying of these glossed Bibles, and exegetes there, such as Andrew of Saint Victor (whose influence will be discussed later), made regular use of them in the writing of their own commentaries.[26] By the fourteenth century, the *Glossa ordinaria* had become such a standard schoolbook that students at the University of Paris were required to bring their glossed bible with them to every class.[27]

The technique of glossing was not limited to the *Glossa ordinaria*, however, and not all glosses were attached to a full Bible text. Abelard himself

---

[24] The story of Abelard's adventure at Laon can be found in Peter Abelard, *The Letters of Abelard and Heloise*, trans. Radice, 7.

[25] Smith, *The* Glossa ordinaria: *The Making of a Medieval Bible Commentary*, 26. Scholars should thus use caution when using the early modern printed *Glossa ordinaria* as representative of the glossed bible books of the twelfth century. A critical edition of the entire Gloss is foreseen in the CCCM.

[26] Van Liere, "Andrew of St Victor and the Gloss on Samuel and Kings."

[27] *Chartularium Universitatis Parisiensis*, 1189, ed. Denifle and Chatelain, 2, 698, cited in Froehlich, "Christian Interpretation of the Old Testament in the High Middle Ages," 518.

provides an example of how glossing had become a common school practice. After his initial disappointment with his teacher Anselm of Laon, Abelard boasted to Anselm's students that he could do better in explaining the Bible than his teacher, without relying on any patristic authorities. Anselm's students challenged him to do so, and according to Abelard's own somewhat boastful report, he held a lecture on the book of Ezekiel the next morning. By his own account, Abelard's lecture was a resounding success:

All those who came approved, so that they commended the lecture warmly, and urged me to comment on the text on the same lines as my lecture. The news brought people who had missed my first lecture flocking to the second and the third ones, all alike most eager to make copies of the glosses which I had begun with on the first day.[28]

Although it almost certainly exaggerates his own pedagogical brilliance, Abelard's report exemplifies the practice of teaching the Bible in the schools. His explanatory lecture resulted in a set of what scholars of the time called "running glosses" or "notes." Brief citations of the Bible text indicated what part of the verse was being commented on, whereas the commentary itself consisted of the teacher's lecture notes. The *Glossa ordinaria* was often the starting point of these lectures.

CHRONOLOGY AND BIBLICAL HISTORY

Biblical exegesis did not only find expression in the writing of commentaries and glosses, however. Medieval historiography was also very dependent on the interpretation of the Bible; in fact, one could see in it a form of biblical exegesis. As we have seen in Chapter 5, medieval biblical hermeneutics often dictated the understanding of the meta-historical narrative. But biblical exegesis also informed the writing of history on a more detailed scale. To combine the two into one, however, could sometimes pose challenges for medieval historiography and exegesis alike. These challenges give rise to a rich tradition of computistical and chronological treatises throughout the Middle Ages. For a start, biblical exegesis was essential for calculating the date of Easter, and, by extension, for establishing an accurate chronological calendar. For those living in the age of atomic clocks, it can be difficult to appreciate the formidable challenges that time reckoning posed for the medieval student of exegesis, astronomy, and mathematics. By the end of

---

[28] Peter Abelard, *The Letters of Abelard and Heloise*, trans. Radice, 8.

the seventh century, there were two conflicting traditions in the English church on how to calculate the date of Easter. It was seen as essential for the unity of the Church that all Christians should celebrate Easter on the same date. That date was hard to pin down on the common Roman (solar) calendar, however. The date for Christ's resurrection was closely related to that of the Jewish Passover, which was celebrated according to a lunar (or, more accurately, a soli-lunar) calendar. Although the conflict in the English church was eventually solved at the Synod of Whitby in 664, problems with the calendar persisted. Full moons did not always occur on the days that they were predicted (with the result that the Easter date was off, because it depended on the first full moon in spring), and the text of the Gospels could not be reconciled with the astronomical data in order to establish the exact date of Jesus' crucifixion. The date that Bede calculated, for instance, March 25, 34 C.E. did not fall on a Friday but a Thursday that year. These problems challenged not only Bede's exegetical skills; thirteenth-century scholars such as the Franciscan Roger Bacon (see also Chapter 4) would combine Arab astronomical and mathematical science with Hebrew sources to try to tackle some of these exegetical *insolubilia*. They also advocated calendar reform, but that was not accomplished until the sixteenth century.

Scriptural exegesis, in combination with astronomical data, could also be used to construct a chronology of world history, which was essential for reconciling classical with biblical history. In his Easter tables, the fifth-century monk Dionysius Exiguus had dated the birth of Christ to I C.E. (the "Annus Domini", or year of the Lord), and from Bede onward, it became increasingly common to date events according to this so-called Christian era (although it may have been inaccurate for Christ's actual birth). In the fourth century, Eusebius of Caesarea had constructed a world chronology, translated into Latin by Jerome, which put the date of Creation at 5,199 years before the birth of Christ, based on dates found in the Septuagint. However, the numbers in the Septuagint differed considerably from those in the Hebrew Bible. In his *Reckoning of Time*, Bede proposed a new chronology of world history, based on the Hebrew Bible (in Jerome's translation). He said,

So that no one takes offense that I have followed the Hebrew Truth rather than the Septuagint in the order of events of the world, I have inserted the latter also wherever it seemed to disagree, so that whoever reads it, can observe both at once, and choose whichever he would rather follow. But for me, the opinion stands firm, which I think should be disputed by no wise man, as the same very reverend translator of the Hebrew Truth (Jerome) says to his critics: "I do not condemn or fault the Septuagint, but I prefer the Apostles greatly over it!"[29]

Bede calculated the date of Creation at 3,952 years before the birth of Christ. But although his work on this matter was hugely influential throughout the Middle Ages, it was by no means the final word. The Bible, for instance, did not offer a continuous chronology between the time of the Old and New Testament. At times, even chronological statements within the same biblical book (such as the indication of the ruling years of the kings of Israel and Judah, in the book of Kings) appeared to contradict each other. In the mid-twelfth century, the biblical scholar Andrew of Saint Victor attempted to solve some of these contradictions by consulting contemporary Jews on the exact text of the book of Kings. He concluded that much of the contradiction was due to textual corruption. His fellow monk Richard of Saint Victor, however, did not think that there was any contradiction at all. He also doubted that the Jews should have the last word on the matter:

I consulted the writings of the Jews, by way of the Jews, and have learned to combine their writings with ours into one opinion. It is clear to me that in these things there is no contradiction at all, even though even for them [i.e., the Jews] so far the truth remains hidden. May it be far from me to believe that in Sacred Scripture the truth is somehow so far hidden that it can in no way be recovered![30]

Richard's solution was simple: the Kings of Israel and Judah must have crowned their own sons as co-regnants during their own lifetimes, just as the kings of France often did. Not everyone accepted Richard's solution, however, and biblical chronology continued to be a lively topic of debate for medieval exegetes well until the early modern period, when luminaries such as Joseph Justus Scaliger (1540–1609) and Archbishop James Ussher (1581–1656) continued to tackle the same problems.

THE SCHOOL OF SAINT VICTOR AND ITS INFLUENCE

Richard and Andrew were both students of Hugh of Saint Victor, whose work has already been discussed in Chapter 5. By the mid-twelfth century, the abbey of Saint Victor, where all these men lived and taught, had gained a reputation as a center for biblical studies and history. Hugh emphasized a stringent program of reading and memorization of the Sacred

---

[29] Bede, *De temporum ratione*, praef., ed. Jones, CCSL 123B, 263–64, English translation in Bede, *The Reckoning of Time*, trans. Wallis.

[30] Richard of Saint Victor, *De concordantia temporum*, PL 196, 241B. Translation forthcoming in *Interpretation of Scripture: Practice*.

Scriptures, starting with their literal meaning and continuing with their spiritual signification, as a preparation for right moral action and mystical contemplation. For this literal understanding of history, a good grasp of historical chronology and history was mandatory. Hugh's motto was "Learn everything, and later you will see that nothing is superfluous. A meager knowledge is not a pleasant thing."[31] For Hugh, the study of Scripture should begin with the memorization of the exact events and order of the biblical narrative. In his *Chronicon, or On the Three Main Circumstances of Historical Facts*, Hugh offered his students a comprehensive chronology of world history, as a framework for further memorization:

First, our task is to commit history to memory, as the foundation of all doctrine. Because, as we said, memory rejoices over brevity, but the facts of history are almost infinite, we have to construct a brief summary out of all of them, as a foundation of the foundation, that is, the first foundation, which the mind can easily understand and retain in its memory.[32]

Hugh's recommendation was followed by long lists of world empires, rulers, patriarchs and priests, and popes, all arranged in parallel columns, meant to be memorized by Hugh's students. Hugh's understanding of history was closely related to his Augustinian hermeneutics. As we saw in Chapter 5, for him, history was not just a series of past events. It was the record of God's actions in the past, and, by understanding them spiritually, one could gain insight into God's work of salvation.

That Hugh's *Chronicon* was common material for all students at Saint Victor is attested by the presence of very similar lists among the works of both Richard and Andrew of Saint Victor. In addition to his world chronology, Hugh wrote exegetical notes ("notulae," or glosses) to the historical books of the Old Testament, in which he explained these books according to their literal sense. This example of a purely literal commentary would be followed in more detail by his student Andrew, who elevated the art of historical commentary to a new level. Hugh's influence reached further than just chronology and biblical commentary, however. The authors of large world chronicles that covered everything from the time of Adam to the present, such as Helinand of Froidmont (ca. 1160–ca. 1237), and later Vincent of Beauvais (ca. 1190–1264), gratefully used these literal-historical commentaries of the Victorine exegetes as sources.

---

[31] Hugh of Saint Victor, *Didascalicon*, 6.3, in *Interpretation of Scripture: Theory*, 166.
[32] Hugh of Saint Victor, "De Tribus Maximis Circumstantiis Gestorum," 491. English translation in Carruthers, *The Book of Memory: A Study of Memory in Medieval Culture*, 339–44.

Hugh's emphasis on the importance of the literal sense was also followed in the schools of medieval Paris. Students could sometimes get lost in reading the plain story line of the Bible, because they had to read large quantities of allegorical glosses, whereas literal explanations could be sparse. To meet this challenge, Peter Comestor (d. 1179), a canon of Paris cathedral with close ties to the abbey of Saint Victor, wrote a running commentary on the entire historical sequence of Scripture, explaining it entirely in the historical sense. He wrote this work, the *Historia scholastica*, sometime before 1173. In his letter of dedication to his powerful friend William, the bishop of Sens, also known as William Whitehands, Peter explained his intentions:

The reason for the work at hand is the immediate request of my friends. When they read through the history of sacred scripture in sequence, interspersed with glosses, too short and without explanation, they asked me to undertake this work, so that they could consult it in order to find the truth of history. In this work, the Spirit is directing the pen, so that we do not shun the sayings of the Fathers, even though novelty may be more favorable and pleasing to the ear. Thus, starting with the description of the universe by Moses, I have followed the stream of history, up to the ascension of our Savior, leaving the sea of spiritual understanding (*mysteriorum*) to more experienced men, and in these one is allowed to follow the old and not consider the new.[33] I have also inserted certain events from the stories of the Gentiles, to complete the chronology, just as a river does not pass by a sunken whirlpool, but joins up with it and thus goes on with renewed strength.[34]

The *Historia scholastica* became a standard textbook for the teaching of Sacred Scripture in the schools almost immediately after it was written, and it was to remain that for the rest of the Middle Ages. Comestor relied on the *Glossa ordinaria*, Josephus's *Antiquities*, and the commentaries of Hugh and Andrew of Saint Victor to create a doctrinally sound, running literal commentary on the historical books of the Bible, which were seen as mandatory reading for student starting out in the study of divinity. Thus, Comestor achieved what Hugh of Saint Victor had envisioned as the soundest method for theological study: establishing biblical history as the basis for biblical reading.

MONASTIC COLLATIONES IN THE TWELFTH CENTURY

For Hugh of Saint Victor, the study of the historical sense of Scripture did not run counter to its mystical reading. It was, rather, the necessary

---

[33] Jerome, *Prologus in libris Solomonis*, in *Biblia sacra*, ed. Weber, 957. Following the suggestion of the Vulgate's aparatus, I read "condere" rather than "cudere."

[34] Peter Comestor, *Historia scholastica*, prol., ed. Sylwan, CCCM 191, 3.

preparation for the practice of reflective reading, the *lectio divina*, which was commonplace in monastic communities. This *lectio divina* was a prayerful, slow reading of Scripture, which, through the practice of spiritual interpretation and meditation, would allow one to contemplate God's mysteries. These meditative readings were presented to the community in communal reflections, called *collationes*, held during the evening hours. These *collationes* combined learning with devotion and resulted in production of some massive mystical commentaries in the twelfth century by monastic authors such as Guibert of Nogent, who wrote a commentary on the Twelve Prophets; Peter of Celle and Adam of Dryburgh, who wrote commentaries on the Tabernacle of Moses; and Richard of Saint Victor (d. 1173), who commented on, among others, the Vision of Ezekiel, Revelation, and the Song of Songs.

The last of these was especially popular. In fact, in the twelfth century, together with the Hexaemeron, the Psalms, and Romans, the Song of Songs ranked among the most frequently commented-on books of the Bible. It was also considered one of the most difficult books to interpret, because its intimate and often sensuous poetry could potentially confuse the (monastic) reader. As we have seen in Chapter 5, the Song was usually read as a story of divine, rather than human, love. Of all books of Solomon, it was regarded as a book only for those experienced in the spiritual life; beginners were advised to start with the book of Proverbs, which gave practical guidance to the moral life and to proceed with Ecclesiastes, which taught the vanity of all earthly existence, before reading the Song of Songs, which spoke about the contemplative life.[35] Until the twelfth century, most commentators on the Song of Songs, such as Honorius Augustudonensis, followed the interpretive tradition of Origen, who read the poem as a song about the triumphant love of Christ for his "bride," the Church. In the twelfth century, however, this interpretation shifted, to take on a more personal dimension. Increasingly, monastic authors such as Bernard of Clairvaux (who wrote an impressive eighty-six sermons on the first three books of the Song of Songs – see Chapter 8) interpreted this poem as an allegory of the love between God and the human soul. Many monastic writers expressed similar interpretations in their commentaries, especially within Bernard's own Cistercian Order, such as his close friends and companions William of Saint Thierry and Geoffrey of Auxerre. Many of these commentaries read, in fact, like series of sermons, indicating their origin as learned and spiritually edifying talks for the monastic community.

---

[35] Richard of Saint Victor, *Explicatio in Canticum Canticorum*, PL 196, 409. Also, Gilbert Foliot, *Expositio in Canticum Canticorum*, PL 202, 1150AB.

Not all commentaries were intended for a male audience. Wolbero, the twelfth-century abbot of Saint Pantaleon in Cologne (d. 1167), addresses his commentary to a community of Benedictine nuns on Nonnenwerth, the island in the Rhine south of Bonn. Well aware of the potentially sensuous content of the Song of Songs, Wolbero warns the nuns,

we have to pay attention to the fact that nothing in this book should be understood in a literal and carnal sense, but that everything refers to the spiritual sense, for "the letter kills, but the spirit gives life" (2 Cor. 3:6).[36]

Perhaps self-conscious about addressing a female audience, he cites Saint Gregory's commentary on the Song of Songs, as he continues:

Here are mentioned words of bodily love: kisses, breasts, cheeks, and thighs, so that the soul, by discussing these intimate matters, is warmed out of its numbness, and, by means of this lower form of love, is stirred up to love that which is above. We should neither be irritated by the sacred description, nor spurn it, but instead take note of the mercy of God, in this matter and beyond, for he inclines himself to the weakness of our words in order to lift us up to the embrace of sacred love.[37]

These mystical commentaries are often rich sources for medieval psychology, since the biblical text invited medieval monks to find an imagery that helped them describe the interior development of the faithful soul seeking God.

SCHOLASTIC COMMENTARY

For Hugh of Saint Victor, true wisdom – not worldly wisdom, but the wisdom from above – should be sought by humble memorization, followed by quiet contemplation. Hugh's model of learning was a courageous attempt to hold together two poles that in the subsequent decades would grow increasingly apart: the older more contemplative learning of the monasteries (the *lectio divina*) and the newer scholastic learning of the emerging schools and universities. In Peter Abelard, we find a representative of the latter. In his work *Sic et Non* (*Yes and No*), written around 1121, Abelard showed that for every authoritative statement that could be found in the Bible or the church fathers in favor of an argument, it was possible to

---

[36] Wolbero of St Pantaleon, *Commentaria in Canticum Canticorum*, PL 195, 1005B.
[37] Wolbero of St Pantaleon, *Commentaria in Canticum Canticorum*, PL 195, 1012CD, citing Gregory the Great's commentary on the Song of Songs.

find a statement that said exactly the opposite. Only through the process of dialectic questioning, relying on one's reason, could one establish the truth. A similar approach should also be used in explaining the biblical text, he argued. Abelard's notes on Ezekiel (see the previous discussion) are regrettably lost, but later in life, he wrote commentaries on Romans and on the first chapters of Genesis.

The Schools in the Later Twelfth Century

Although they shared Abelard's predilection for the dialectic method, many scholars in the later twelfth-century schools had a more practical purpose in mind than philosophical probing. They aimed their scholarship toward theological instruction and pastoral training for clerics. The ecclesiastical reform movement, which deeply influenced and altered ideas about the role and function of the Church in society from the eleventh century onward (see Chapter 4), had stressed the pastoral responsibilities of the clergy, especially preaching and confession, and as a result, cathedral schools, and later the nascent universities, were offering a more practical training for those embarking on ecclesiastical careers.

Scholars in this period, such as Peter the Chanter (d. 1197), Robert of Melun (d. 1167), and Peter Lombard (d. 1160), were active not only as exegetes but also as clerics and bishops. They saw the reading of the Bible at the basis of their theological studies, but, unlike Hugh, their ultimate aim was not to develop the contemplative mind but to apply this biblical knowledge to theology and moral instruction. They had little use for Hugh's admonition to "learn everything." In fact, in his *Abbreviated Word*, a preachers' handbook and moral compendium, Peter the Chanter took a stab at some of the learning then current at the school of Saint Victor:

In our reading we are devoured by superfluities, such as the exact location of places, the number of years and periods, genealogies, the mechanical dispositions in building, such as the disposition of the tabernacle, the temple, even the imaginary temple.[38] Holy Scripture is not given to us to search for idle and superfluous things in it, but to search for faith and moral lessons, for guidance and answers to the infinite troubles that arise in the church.[39]

---

[38] That is, the temple vision of Ezekiel. Both Andrew and Richard had written commentaries on the tabernacle and the temple, as well as the chronology of the reigning years of the kings of Israel and Judah. Richard also wrote a commentary on the temple of Ezekiel. Hugh and Richard both wrote detailed biblical chronologies.

[39] Peter the Chanter, *Verbum adbreviatum*, 1, 2, ed. Boutry, CCCM 196, 15.

Peter borrowed Hugh's building metaphor (see Chapter 5), but instead of applying it to the literal, allegorical, and moral senses of Scripture, he applied it to his ideal school curriculum:

The study of Scripture consists of three things: reading, disputation, and preaching. Prolixity is the mother of oblivion and the stepmother of memory in each of these. Reading is like the foundation, and the substrate of those that follow, for the other uses are placed upon it. Disputation is like the wall in this study and this building, for nothing can be clearly understood and faithfully preached, unless it is first broken by the teeth of disputation. But preaching, to which the former two are subservient, is like the roof, protecting the faithful against the heat and the storm of vice. Thus, after reading Scripture and investigating difficult passages through disputation (and not before), we should preach, so that thus one curtain may draw another.[40]

Thus, scriptural exegesis was now seen as a prelude to scholastic disputation, and both trained a scholar to be an effective preacher.

The most basic of these three exercises, reading (*lectio*), increasingly came to mean going through the entire text according to its literal sense, with the help of a handbook, such as the Gloss or Peter Comestor's *Historia Scholastica*. In the first decades of the thirteenth century, when schools grew into universities, this "cursory" (*cursorie*) reading of the Bible, meaning "all the way through, from beginning to end," was the standard practice for first-year students in theology. One who had accomplished this was called a *cursor biblicus*. The second step, disputations, or *quaestiones*, as they were called, could, of course, follow the order of the biblical text, but more often, they were thematically organized. Robert of Melun, for instance, a student both of Hugh of Saint Victor and of Peter Abelard, wrote his *Questions on the Letters of Paul* (*Quaestiones de epistolis Pauli*) as a commentary in the form of a series of scholastic disputations, organized by the sequence of the Bible text. But he also wrote a series of disputations arranged in a more thematic order, the *Sentences* (*Sententiae*). In them, he discussed, in order, the authority of Scripture, the persons of the Trinity, sin and redemption, the sacraments, virtues and vices, and the Last Judgment. Another such collection of sentences, arranged according to systematic theology, were written by Peter Lombard. Peter, who took his name from his native Lombardy in northern Italy, became attached to the abbey of Saint Victor in the 1130s, and eventually became master of the school of Notre Dame in Paris. He is also the author of the last redaction of the *Glossa ordinaria* on the Psalms. In the thirteenth century, his *Sentences* became

---

[40] Ibid., ed. Boutry, CCCM 196, 9. "One curtain": cf. Ex. 26: 5 and *Thesaurus proverbiorum*, 12: 285.

the main textbook for teaching systematic theology and was subject to commentary almost as frequently as the Bible. Whereas the Bible was used as lecture material for the beginning students, the more advanced lectures in theology came to be based on the *Sentences*.

Thus, by the end of the twelfth century, theology had become a discipline that no longer depended on the study of the Bible alone. This did not mean that the Bible was no longer an important textbook. The men emerging from these late twelfth-century schools were Church leaders, driven by the idea that the study of Scripture, through glossing, disputing, and preaching, should have a direct impact in the life of the Church, in the realm of ethics and morals. A measure of the success of this message can be seen in the popularity of the new religious orders, the Franciscans and Dominicans, at the beginning of the thirteenth century (see also Chapter 8). They saw their way of life as one that was uniquely based on a literal following of Jesus in the way the Gospel intended it.

The Universities in the Thirteenth and Fourteenth Centuries

By the end of the twelfth century, the many schools that had made Paris a vibrant center of learning were incorporated into the *Universitas Parisiensis* (University of Paris), whereas wealthy burghers, such as Robert de Sorbonne, endowed new colleges within the university where students and masters alike could pursue learning. Similar foundations followed in England, Spain, and Italy. Before too long, the theological schools at these universities were dominated by the presence of the Franciscans and the Dominicans, and both were a major influence on the biblical scholarship of their day.

The main convent of the Dominicans in Paris, Saint Jacques (Saint James), became a major center for the study of the Bible; it was well known for its achievements in biblical criticism (see Chapter 4), and the first biblical concordances were also written here (see the following). Reading and commenting on the Bible was an integral part of the training of these Dominican friars. The result of this emphasis on Bible study was the production of massive biblical commentaries, called *lecturae* (lectures) or *postillae* (postills). The origin of the latter word is uncertain; the Latin words *post illa* mean "after these things." Perhaps the term refers to the biblical commentary that follows the reading of a biblical verse, or it could refer to the commentary that was read in addition to the glosses, which by now had become standard literature in the medieval schools. At the Dominican convent of Saint Jacques, the most prominent biblical commentator was no doubt Hugh of Saint Cher (d. 1263). He served as the prior of this convent in the 1230s, before becoming provincial for the Dominican Order in France, and later cardinal. Hugh's commentary was clearly intended for the use of the preacher, as is attested by the inclusion of so-called *distinctiones* (see the following discussion) in his commentary.

Among the Franciscans biblical scholarship also flourished, with the work of postillators such as Peter John Olivi (ca. 1249–1298). But the most influential Franciscan commentator was no doubt Nicholas of Lyra (ca. 1270–1349). Nicholas was born in Lire, Normandy, and he entered the Franciscan order at the age of thirty. In the first decade of the 1300s, he became biblical lecturer and, later, provincial of the Franciscan order and Magister in theology at the University of Paris. He died there, presumably a victim of the great bubonic plague, in 1349. His *Postilla literalis* (*Literal Postill*), written some time between 1322 and 1331, discusses the literal sense of Scripture only. Lyra did write a *Postilla moralis* (*Moral Postill*), but it is modest in size compared to the former. Nicholas's *Postilla litteralis* is known for its high standard of Hebrew scholarship, and in the sixteenth century, it was often printed together with the *Glossa ordinaria*, and thus remained an influential exegetical work well into the Reformation era. Nicholas made frequent use of the commentaries of Rashi (see Chapter 5), or "Master Solomon," as Nicholas calls him. It is not clear where Nicholas learned Hebrew. At one time, it was assumed that he must have been a convert from Judaism, but this is no longer widely believed. Several manuscripts, such as bilingual Bibles and glossed Hebrew psalters, attest that Nicholas may not have been the only thirteenth-century friar to learn Hebrew.[41] Although he appreciated the textual insight that the Jewish commentators gave him, Nicholas did not refrain from correcting them on several points. Above all, he faulted the Jews for not interpreting their own Scriptures correctly, because, in his view, they clearly foretold the coming of Jesus as the Messiah.

Nicholas's and Hugh's *postillae* both reflected the scholastic practice of reading the Bible *cursorie* in the first years of theology study. They covered the entire text of the Bible, and they combined the exegetical technique of the *lectio* (interspersing the biblical text with running glosses) with that of the *disputatio* (the treatment of more difficult passages, or "dubia," in the form of a scholastic *quaestio*). As we saw above, the *quaestio* was one of the

---

[41] Spicq, *Esquisse*, 191. See also Olszowy-Schlanger, "The Knowledge and Practice of Hebrew Grammar."

main scholastic exercises in use at the universities. Their commentaries also show the influence of Aristotle's philosophy, which by this time had become a standard part of the university curriculum, on biblical interpretation. We notice this influence in the commentary prefaces to individual bible books, for instance. From the twelfth century, bible commentaries were usually prefaced by a short *accessus* (prologue), which briefly discussed things such as the author, matter, intention, and the title of the book. It was common practice to introduce texts this way in the study of classics and law. By the thirteenth century, these *accessus* mostly discussed the four Aristotelian *causae* (causes) of the work. In his preface to Mark, for instance, Hugh of Saint Cher discusses the "formal cause" (that is, the layout and division of the book), the "efficient cause" (the author Mark, or the grace of God speaking through him), the "material cause" (Jesus and his ministry), and the "final cause": "These are written, that you may believe that Jesus is the Christ, the Son of God." (John 20:31).[42]

Another influence of Aristotelian techniques of textual analysis can be found in the importance of textual division as a way of approaching each bible book. Nicholas of Lyra's *Postilla* on Samuel and Kings offers a good example of this. Before starting out in the first chapter, the first verse of 1 Samuel, Nicholas discusses the division of the entire book of Samuel and Kings. The books of *Reges* (the Latin term for Samuel and Kings), Nicholas tells us, are in fact two separate entities: the books of Samuel and the books of Kings (*Malachim*). These books deal with the reign of the people of Israel by the kings, first as a united entity (in 1 and 2 Samuel), later as a divided entity (1 and 2 Kings). The books of Samuel are divided into two: the first part (1 Samuel) deals with the reign by a king who is elected by popular acclamation (Saul); the second (2 Samuel) deals with the reign of the kings of God's choosing, who rule by paternal succession (David and Solomon). The first book of Samuel first describes the decline of the preceding form of government, that of the judges (chapter 1–9), before describing the emergence of the reign by kings (chapter 10 through the end). Of the life of the last judge ruling over Israel, Samuel, we are first informed about his birth and, later, about the moral decline of his sons. The first part, Samuel's birth, is subdivided into three parts: the petition of his mother for a child, God's answer to her prayer, and finally the gratitude Hannah expresses in her prayer. It is only after dividing the material into ever smaller parts that Nicholas starts his running commentary on a verse-by-verse basis, with 1 Samuel 1:1, providing short glosses on the text.

---

[42] Hugh of Saint Cher, *Hugonis de Sancto Charo Opera omnia*, vol. 6, 90.

The flow of the running commentary was interrupted by short *quaestiones*, wherever specific problems arose that seemed to have larger theological or ethical implications. Usually Nicholas introduces these problems with expressions such as "Here arises a question" or "Some may wonder at this point." In 1 Samuel 17, for instance, the description of the fight between David and Goliath, gives Nicholas occasion to discuss the question on whether dueling is permissible, a hotly debated issue at a time when the Church was trying very hard to ban tournaments as a form of public entertainment. On one hand, Nicholas says, it seems as if the Bible here is tacitly approving of the duel between David and Goliath; on the other, dueling leads to the killing of innocent people, which is illicit. Nicholas concludes that in this particular case, the duel was justified, since David was fighting a just fight in the name of God (1 Sam. 17:45). Duels in the second case are not permitted, however, because they run against the divine command "Thou shalt not kill." Nicholas finds himself here in hot water, however, because he has to admit that even saintly kings such as Charlemagne and Louis IX at times permitted dueling. He concludes that under certain circumstances, rulers are permitted to allow such duels, to avoid a greater evil, just as "prostitution is allowed in cities, so that not all are disturbed by lust."[43] Thus, aside from textual analysis and literal commentary, these *postillae* were using the Bible as a source of answers to questions of everyday moral and doctrinal importance. This direct application of the Bible to contemporary social problems, which became even more widespread in the fifteenth century and indeed survives in many Christian communities today, was very different from the mystical expositions of the monastic commentary tradition of the early and high middle ages.

DIDACTIC WORKS OF THE LATER MIDDLE AGES

The thirteenth and fourteenth centuries saw an unprecedented production of biblical commentaries, since the Bible was at the basis of an entire system of higher education. The masters who worked in Paris, Oxford, and Cambridge stood at the top of a pyramid. But below them was a growing network of universities and local schools that trained friars for clerical tasks and, above all, for preaching. Learning the Bible during these first years of study obviously required more than just the biblical text, or sophisticated commentary. Not only did students use the *Glossa ordinaria*

---

43 Nicholas of Lyra, *Biblia sacra cum . . . Nicolai Lyrani Postilla*, vol. 2, 427–28.

and Peter Comestor's *Historia scholastica* to master the text; starting in the twelfth century, a number of exegetical and lexicographical works were also developed that could be considered the basic tools of biblical pedagogy for the beginning student. (Lexicographical tools intended for the use of preachers are discussed further in Chapter 8.)

Several books circulated that were intended to aid the beginning biblical scholar in understanding its primary, literal meaning, and to help him memorize the entire biblical history. One example of such a text is the *Historical Compendium to the Geneaology of Christ* (*Compendium historiae in genealogia Christi*). This work is sometimes attributed to Peter Comestor because it was often used as illustrative material to the *Historia scholastica*, but it was more likely written by Peter of Poitiers (1130–1205), chancellor of Notre Dame Cathedral. In the words of the medieval chronicler Alberic of Troisfontaines, "helping out poor clerics, he came up with the idea of depicting trees of the Old Testament histories, on sheets of parchment."[44] The *Historical Compendium* offered a brief version of biblical history, presented as a family tree of Christ's ancestry, complete with diagrams and explanatory notes. It was often included with the prefatory material in medieval Bibles.[45]

More extensive was the summary of the entire Bible offered by the Franciscan author Peter Aureoli. His *Compendium on the Literal Sense of Scripture*, written around 1319, divided the Bible into eight parts, namely political (Pentateuch), historical (Joshua through Maccabees), hymnodical (Psalms, Song of Songs, and Lamentations), disputative (Job, Ecclesiasticus), ethical (Proverbs, Wisdom, Ecclesiasticus), prophetic (the major and minor prophets), testimonial (the Gospels), and epistolary (Acts, all the Epistles, and Revelation). The part covering the last book of the Bible, Revelation, takes up almost a quarter of the entire work, because Peter used it to give an overview of world history, reading the visions contained in this book as prophesies predicting the events from the time of the New Testament until his own time.[46] The writing of compendia such as these, either on the literal or the moral sense of Scripture, proliferated during the later Middle Ages.

Poetry was also often used to teach the Bible. Some poems were simply mnemotechnical verses for remembering the Bible's contents. One

[44] Alberic of Troisfontaines, *Chronica*, ed. Pertz, MGH, Scriptores, 23, 866. Cited in Hilpert, "Geistliche Bildung und Laienbildung," 327, n1.
[45] Hilpert, "Geistliche Bildung und Laienbildung". Bibles that contain the genealogy are, for instance, London BL, MS Royal 1.B.X, and Oxford, Bodleian, MS Auct. D.4.10.
[46] Petrus Aureoli, *Compendium sensus litteralis totius divinae Scripturae*, ed. Seeboeck.

such poem was the *Summarium Biblicum* (*Biblical summary*) attributed to Alexander de Villa Dei. The first line of this text looked like this:

Sex ^opera dierum^ prohibet ^lignum^ peccant ^adam et eva^ abel ^occiditur^ enoch ^transfertur^ archa fit ^noe^ intrant ^archam 47^

[Six ^days' work^ prohibits ^the tree^ they sin ^adam and eve^ abel ^is killed^ enoch ^taken up^ ark made ^by noah^ they enter ^the ark^]

The poem was written in hexameters, a classical six-foot poetic meter. Each word, or group of words, referred to one individual Bible chapter. At first sight, the line produced nonsense, albeit in stylish poetic meter: "Síx prohíbits they sín Abel Énoch árk made they énter," Superscriptions above each word, however, elaborated on the single words, and the short phrase provided a brief summary of the entire chapter. The first seven chapters of Genesis were summarized thus in one line: Gen. 1: The work of six days. Gen. 2: God prohibits the tree. Gen. 3: Adam and Eve sin. Gen. 4: Abel is killed. Gen. 5: Enoch is taken up. Gen. 6: Noah makes the ark. Gen. 7: They enter the ark. Because there are more than 1,200 chapters in the Bible, the entire poem took up some ten pages in its first printed edition in 1660.

Other poetic works aimed more at exegetical instruction. An example is the verse summary of the entire Bible, titled *Aurora* (*Dawn*), written by a canon of Rheims cathedral, Petrus Riga (1140–1209). This massive poem (some 15,000 lines) was widely popular in the Middle Ages. It was often used to teach poetry, as a Christian alternative to the Classical pagan epics of Homer and Vergil. The title, *Aurora*, Petrus said, referred to the dawn of the new covenant chasing away the shadows and darkness of the Old Testament. Petrus did more than just versify the biblical content; he strove to

pull out from it some allegories, as a nut from its shell, grain from the chaff, honey from wax, fire from smoke, kernels from barley, wine from must. I did my best to show you how all its consonant parts fit together; Christ's pearls with Moses's steel, the flowers of the Church with the grass of the synagogue, the gold of Christians with the iron of the Jews, the new law and the old, like millstones grinding against each other, and cogwheels fitting together.[48]

---

47 Cited from MS Vatican Library, MS lat. 1027, fol. 6r. An early modern edition, available on Google books, can be found in *Biblia maxima*, ed. De La Haye, 1–10.
48 Petrus Riga, *Aurora*, ed. Beichner, vol. 1: 7.

Riga was offering here in poetic form what Comestor had intended to provide with his *Historia scholastica*: a schoolman's exegetical digest to the entire Bible. It is no coincidence that Comestor was one of Petrus's chief sources. Whereas the earliest redaction of the *Aurora* extended to the historical books of the Bible, later redactions also included versifications of the Song of Songs, Daniel, Job, and the apocryphal books, and a later author, Giles of Paris (d. 1224), augmented the poem even further.

Even more fundamental than the historical reading of Scripture was the need for its grammatical understanding. Grammar was the first of the liberal arts taught in the schools, and it was the basis for any textual comprehension. Alexander Neckam (1157–1217) was a prolific biblical commentator and preacher, with a strong interest in the teaching of grammar. Like many English schoolmen of his time, he had received his education in Paris, before he became abbot of Cirencester. In his *Corrogationes Promethei* (the exact relevance of the title, the *Gatherings of Prometheus*, is not entirely clear), he applied his grammatical interests to biblical exegesis. It is divided into two parts: the first part is a treatise on grammar, and the second consists of running grammatical glosses on the entire biblical text. These glosses give meanings of words, their pronunciation, declension, and etymology, often citing literary examples of similar word use, and at times giving a translation *gallice*, that is, in French. Alexander's commentary on Genesis begins with this characteristic series of explanatory aids:

After this [introduction to grammar] we will, if we may, say something about some words from the individual books of the Bible ("*bibliothecae*"), so we may at times comment on their accents, sometimes on their meaning. We will only rarely make mention of proper names, because they are so variable. The first word is found in Genesis, where we read "Abyss" ("the deep," Gen. 1:2). This "abyss" means a profound depth, as in "a-byss" (without *byss*), that is, without radiance.[49] Where the water is deep, it does not emit any radiance. This [radiance] is called "byssus." Hence Hildebert says: "His cross the altar, his sepulchre the chalice, the stone with which it was closed / the paten. The radiant linen (*byssus*) takes the place of the shroud."[50]

Citing literary examples to illustrate the use of certain words was common school practice in the Middle Ages. Although Neckam's commentary on the New Testament is less grammatical and more exegetical and theological in character, it is evident that his main objective was the very

[49] Byssus is a type of white linen.
[50] Meyer, "Notice sur les 'Corrogationes Promethei' d'Alexandre Neckam," 669. Citing Hildebert of Lavardin, *De mysterio missae*, PL 171, 1194.

basic understanding of Scripture at the lexicographical and grammatical level.

Neckam was not the only writer to address these concerns. Fewer than 100 years later, a Franciscan *lector* in northern Italy wrote a very similar work. Marchesino of Reggio wrote the *Mammotrectus* (the title means, roughly, "Nourished by a Wet-Nurse") sometime in the 1280s, and it became one of the best sellers of the late medieval and early modern period. It offers a brief recapitulation of the pronunciation, declension and conjugation, and sometimes the etymology of most words in the Bible. Marchesinus did not stop there: he did the same for the text of the liturgy and the Sunday homilies, and even the Franciscan Rule. With the help of the *Mammotrectus*, even a priest who did not know sufficient Latin would be able to make his way through a Latin service without looking too ignorant. Marchesinus explained this intention in the preface to his work:

Impatient with my own inexperience and weary of the ignorance of poor clerics who are promoted to the office of preacher, I have decided to read the Bible from cover to cover and diligently to study all the other materials that are read aloud in church – should God grant me the time – and to point out to the poor reader the meaning, pronunciation, and gender of all the difficult parts, as far as my limited intelligence allows me to compile these things from the works of others, so that sense of the etymology may edify the intellect and the proper sound of the words may please the ears.[51]

With the advent of printing in the late fifteenth century and the consequent proliferation of printed Bibles, Marchesinus's work reached the peak of its popularity. Serving as an indispensable foolproof handbook, the *Mammotrectus* helped to ensure that the Latin Bible, now more widely available than ever, was no longer the prerogative of the learned elite only.

THE END OF COMMENTARY?

Some modern scholars have wanted to see the late Middle Ages as a period of decline of biblical exegesis, a period of "stunted growth."[52] The sheer output of exegetical materials of the late medieval universities and *studia*, both at the beginner's and the advanced level dramatically belies this view. The Bible was at the center of medieval education, at every level. It was the most commented, glossed, and paraphrased text by the Late Middle

---

[51] Marchesinus of Reggio, *Mammotrectus*, prol., ed. with trans. in Van Liere, "Tools for Fools: Marchesinus of Reggio and his Mammotrectus".
[52] Smalley, "The Bible in the Medieval Schools," 219.

Ages. Almost every medieval library could boast a copy of the *Aurora* and the *Mammotrectus*. Schoolmen at every level of schooling were producing biblical commentaries, often in the form of sermons collections, on almost all biblical books.

With the invention of printing, in the 1450s, tools for the interpretation of the Bible and commentaries proliferated. Texts such as the *Mammotrectus* enjoyed a renewed popularity when printed bibles started to circulate. The *Glossa ordinaria* was first printed in the 1480s by Adolph Rusch, containing the entire glossed Bible in four volumes, and later editions soon followed. Many of the *postillas* were now printed for the first time, too. Nicholas of Lyra's *Postilla* was printed together with the *Glossa ordinaria* in 1506, and the combination of the two texts in one book proved to be immensely successful. The combined commentaries continued to be printed alongside the text of the Bible until 1634. More sermons and commentaries were written in the period from 1400 to 1500 than ever before. Because of their sheer volume and quantity, most of them sit in libraries and archives, and still await their first edition. This bulk of material reflects the skyrocketing growth of biblical literacy since the thirteenth century. Compared to the Early Middle Ages, when biblical exegesis was a privilege of the few cloistered religious, the rich heritage of medieval biblical interpretation was now accessible to Christians of all levels of education.

By the sixteenth century, however, the very tradition of biblical commentary came under severe criticism. Some scholars were concerned that the sheer quantity of the commentary tradition was drowning out the understanding of the biblical text itself. For all its popularity, the *Mammotrectus* provoked the anger and scorn of men such as Erasmus and Luther, who saw in it a clear sign of the ignorance of the clergy of their time.[53] The irritation with the prolixity of glosses and commentaries that the Reformers expressed was not a new thing; as we saw earlier, Robert of Melun, Peter Comestor and Peter the Chanter had already expressed frustration with this. But in the sixteenth century, the very presence of glosses in Bible became a subject of intense contention. Although the more traditional churchmen insisted that the Bible should never be read without proper commentary (especially not by the laity, as we will see in the next chapter), many humanist scholars (especially those sympathetic to the Reformation) saw them as a patchwork that obscured the true meaning of the text. Luther's close friend Philip Melanchton saw the "frigid petty glosses" as "hindrances to the

---

[53] Erasmus, "Letter to Maarten Dorp," in *The Correspondence of Erasmus*, trans. Baskerville and ed. Mynors, Thomson, and Ferguson, 121–22.

intelligence," and William Tyndale accused the Church of having "nailed a veil of false glosses on Moses' face, to corrupt the true understanding of his Law."[54] Many of these Reformers were advocating a fresh start by pushing aside the tradition that had come before them. It seems that this push was successful. Today, the medieval Christian commentary tradition seems not so much scorned as simply forgotten. At the same time, we have to acknowledge that Reformers did not just reject the medieval commentary tradition; they engaged with it, used it, and, in a sense, added to it. Biblical scholars far into the sixteenth century were using the same textbooks as their predecessors in the fifteenth century; they were using the same techniques of biblical interpretation, and often were writing Bible commentaries that differed only on few points from the interpretations of their medieval predecessors. A common proverb, dating back to the late sixteenth century acknowledged this fact: "Si Lyra non lyrasset, Lutherus non cantasset": "Had not Lyra strummed his lyre, Luther would not have sung his song."[55]

RESOURCES FOR FURTHER STUDY

Smalley's study is an indispensable classic, but for the beginning student, Reventlow may be a more accessible work of reference. Stegmüller's *Repertorium Biblicum Medii Aevi* offers a valuable tool to find editions and manuscripts of medieval biblical commentaries. It is now searchable online, at the University of Trier: http://www.repbib.uni-trier.de/cgi-bin/rebihome.tcl. Some medieval commentaries and *postillae* are available in early modern editions that can be viewed on-line. Migne's *Patrologia Latina* and the *Corpus Christianorum*, which contain the editions of numerous Bible commentaries, are both available on CD-ROM and through a Web interface. A portal site that lists links to freely available editions of medieval bible commentaries, in French, is www.glossae.net. Until a critical edition is available, the best edition of the *Glossa ordinaria* remains the reprint of Adolph Rusch's 1485 edition, by Froehlich and Gibson. Several early modern editions of the Glossa ordinaria with the *Postilla* of Nicholas of Lyra exist, and some can be viewed online, such as the 1603 *Bibliorum sacrorum cum glossa ordinaria*: http://openlibrary.org/books/OL7062373M/Bibliorum_sacrorum_cum_glossa_ordinaria.

---

[54] Both cited in McClymond, "Through a Gloss Darkly," 483.
[55] The verse first seems to have surfaced in Reisch, *Margarita philosophica*. Cited in Nestle, "Lesefrüchte," 668–70.

Rashi's commentaries are online in English translation at http://www.chabad.org/library/bible_cdo/aid/63255/jewish/The-Bible-with-Rashi.htm.

A bibliography of medieval commentaries in English translation is provided by Jonathan Hall, at the University of Virginia: https://sites.google.com/site/miscelleneatheologica/home/transbib. In addition, the TEAMS Commentary series (Kalamazoo: Medieval Institute Publications) publishes medieval commentaries in English translation.

SUGGESTIONS FOR FURTHER READING

Bischoff, Bernhard. "Wendepunkte in der Geschichte der lateinischen Exegese im Mittelalter." *Sacris erudiri* 6 (1954): 189–281. Also in *Mittelalterliche Studien* 1 (1966): 205–73.

Brown, Peter. *The Rise of Western Christendom: Triumph and Diversity, A.D. 200–1000*. The Making of Europe. 2nd ed. Oxford: Blackwell Publishers, 2003.

Dahan, Gilbert. *L'exégèse chrétienne de la Bible en occident médiéval, XIIe–XIVe siècle*, Patrimoines. Christianisme. Paris: Éditions du Cerf, 1999.

Froehlich, Karlfried. "Christian Interpretation of the Old Testament in the High Middle Ages." In *Hebrew Bible / Old Testament*. 496–558.

Kamin, Sarah. *Jews and Christians Interpret the Bible*. Jerusalem: Magnes Press, 1991.

Klepper, Deeana Copeland. *The Insight of Unbelievers: Nicholas of Lyra and Christian Reading of Jewish Text in the Later Middle Ages*. Philadelphia: University of Pennsylvania Press, 2007.

Matter, E. Ann. *The Voice of My Beloved: The Song of Songs in Western Medieval Christianity*. Philadelphia: University of Pennsylvania Press, 1990.

Neue Richtungen in der hoch- und spätmittelalterlichen Bibelexegese. Edited by Robert E. Lerner and Elisabeth Müller-Luckner. Schriften des Historischen Kollegs, Kolloquien 32. München: R. Oldenbourg Verlag, 1996.

Nicholas of Lyra. The Senses of Scripture. Edited by Philip D. W. Krey and Lesley Smith. Studies in the History of Christian Thought, 90. Leiden: E. J. Brill, 2000.

Nothaft, C. Philipp E. *Dating the Passion: The Life of Jesus and the Emergence of Scientific Chronology (200–1600)*. Time, astronomy, and calendars, vol. 1. Leiden: E. J. Brill, 2012.

O Cróinín, Dáibhí. "Bischoff's Wendepunkte Fifty Years On." *Revue Bénédictine* 110 (2000): 204–37.

Ocker, Christopher. *Biblical Poetics before Humanism and Reformation*. Cambridge: Cambridge University Press, 2002.

Reventlow, Henning. *History of Biblical Interpretation. Volume 2: From Late Antiquity to the End of the Middle Ages*. Translated by James O. Duke. SBL – Resources for Biblical Study, 61. Atlanta: Society of Biblical Literature, 2009.

Riché, Pierre. *Education and Culture in the Barbarian West: From the Sixth through the Eighth Century*. Translated by John J. Contreni. Columbia: University of South Carolina Press, 1976.

Smalley, Beryl. *The Study of the Bible in the Middle Ages*. Oxford: Blackwell Publishing, 1952. Third edition, 1983.

Smith, Lesley. *The Glossa ordinaria: The Making of a Medieval Bible Commentary*. Commentaria. Sacred Texts and their Commentaries: Jewish, Christian, and Islamic, 3. Leiden: Brill, 2009.

Spicq, Ceslas. *Esquisse d'une histoire de l'exégèse latine au Moyen Âge*. Bibliothèque thomiste, 26. Paris: J. Vrin, 1944.

Williams, Megan Hale. *The Monk and the Book. Jerome and the Making of Christian Scholarship*. Chicago: The University of Chicago Press, 2006.

CHAPTER 7

The Vernacular Bible

Few debates on the Bible in the Middle Ages are as neatly divided along confessional lines as that on the medieval vernacular Bible. It is a common misconception, especially in Protestant circles, that people (or, at least, the "common" people) in the Middle Ages did not read the Bible. Biblical literacy was restricted, so it is believed, to the very small intellectual elite of monks and priests, who did everything they could to safeguard this monopoly. Even authors of otherwise solid scholarly works could solemnly declare that "[e]cclesiastical policy was accustomed to withholding Scripture from those ignorant in Latin."[1] This perception probably originates in the Protestant Church histories of the sixteenth century, such as Foxe's *Book of Martyrs*, which recounted many tales of hapless Christians, burned at the stake for the mere possession of a bible in English. Foxe's book was published in for the first time in 1563, when England's Protestants were still emerging from a period of persecution at the hands of the Catholic Queen Mary I (d. 1558) and were witnessing the continuing persecution of fellow Protestants in many parts of Continental Europe. Needless to say, this perspective deeply colored English Protestant views of church history. Anticlericalism and religious partisanship, however, should not inform a modern analysis of the relationship of the laity and the Bible in this period.

Catholic scholars, in contrast, have pointed out that the idea of this clerical monopoly on biblical literacy cannot be maintained.[2] They point to an overwhelming amount of evidence to show that biblical texts, and texts based on biblical material, circulated widely in the vernacular in the Middle Ages. The idea that the medieval Church thought that the Word of God should be kept out of the hands of the laity, is, of course, in

---

[1] Shepherd, "English Versions of the Scriptures before Wyclif," 377.
[2] Rost, *Die Bibel im Mittelalter*, 79.

177

contradiction with what the Church confessed to be its main aim: the spread of the Gospel and the encouragement of lay piety. Biblical literacy was not only widespread among the laity in the later Middle Ages, but it was even actively encouraged by the Church. Most scholars today, Catholics and non-Catholics alike, agree with the latter point of view. As Andrew Gow argued in 2005, it is time to challenge the "Protestant paradigm" that Luther's Reformation provoked a sudden surge in lay Bible reading and to acknowledge that, on the contrary, the flourishing culture of lay biblical literacy in the vernacular helped create the milieu that made Luther's achievement possible.[3] To be sure, the Protestant Reformation did achieve a change in the way the Bible was read and the way it functioned within Christian spirituality, but this change was largely due to a long medieval tradition of lay access to biblical texts.

Nonetheless, even if biblical literacy in lay circles was common, it is true that the issue of biblical translation was contested in the Middle Ages. As we will see later, some clerics still were hesitant to translate the Bible directly into the vernacular for use by the laity; these hesitations only would grow after the twelfth century, when the possession and reading of the Bible in the vernacular was increasingly associated with heresy and dissent. Although the "Protestant paradigm" targeted by Gow is indeed problematic, there was still a lively discussion in the Middle Ages on the question of whether Bible translations in the vernacular were legitimate and, if they were, what authority these translations held. For the most part, medieval Bible translations were not accorded the same degree of authority as the Latin Vulgate. *The* authoritative Bible remained the Vulgate text. The principal use of vernacular texts was to help the laity or those unschooled, or poorly schooled, in Latin to understand the literal and historical meaning of the Latin text and teach biblical literacy. In the long period we call the Middle Ages, a wide range of genres and texts was encompassed by what scholars today call "vernacular bible translations," and these could be intended for a wide variety of audiences. But, overall, the primacy of the Latin text was not in doubt.

Exploring the question whether common people in the Middle Ages read the Bible in their own language will require examining a series of component questions in more detail. What do we mean by "reading," who exactly were the "common people" (the laity or the lower classes?), and what do we mean by "their own language"? The question about lay biblical literacy is, of course, closely connected to the larger question of lay literacy

---

[3] Gow, "Challenging the Protestant Paradigm."

during the Middle Ages. Obviously, the answers will not be the same for the Early Middle Ages as for the Late Middle Ages.

Full literacy in the Early Middle Ages, meaning the ability to read and to write in Latin, was mainly confined to a narrow group in society, the clergy, or ever more narrowly, the monks. But *mainly* does not mean "exclusively." Many people, clergy and laity alike, may have been able to read but not write, and even those who could not were not entirely cut off from the written word, because they could have others read it to them. Recent research has added many shades of gray to a black-and-white image. There was both more illiteracy among the clergy, and more literacy among the laity, than is often supposed. Some vernacular translations made in the early Middle Ages, such as Williram's Song of Songs (ca. 1085), were clearly intended primarily for monks. At the same time, literacy, even in Latin, and book possession among the nobility and higher classes in early medieval society were more common than is often assumed. In ninth-century France, the noblewomen Dhuoda wrote a handbook of advice in Latin for her son, from whom she was separated by a series of unfortunate political events. Dhuoda expressed the hope that her son William would spend as much time reading it as children did playing dice or women looking into their mirrors. She expressed confidence that in time he would acquire "many more books" besides the one she had written.[4] Even if William had not been able to read Latin – and he probably did – he could have "read" the book by having it read aloud to him.

Literacy in the Early Middle Ages did not always require active command of the pen. Many people read who could not write for themselves. We are not sure whether Dhuoda actually wrote her book herself or whether she dictated it to a scribe. A similar case is the emperor Charlemagne. His biographer Einhard tells us that "he tried to write, and he used to keep tablets and blanks in bed under his pillows, to practice writing letters when he had some free time; however, as he did not have much success since the labour was too much, and it was started too late."[5] But that did not make him illiterate; indeed, Einhard reports that the emperor loved to read Augustine's *City of God* and that he "zealously cultivated the liberal arts."[6] But he did not have to handle writing implements himself: he had scribes to whom he dictated his works. The English king Alfred also seems to have mastered writing only to a limited degree, yet this did not exclude him from

---

[4] Dhuoda, *Handbook for William,* trans. Neel, 5.
[5] Einhard, *Vita Karoli,* 25, ed. Pertz, 25. The English translation by Turner is available on the Internet, http://www.fordham.edu/halsall/basis/einhard.asp.
[6] Ibid., 24 and 25.

the benefits of a literate society.[7] Some form of literacy among the nobility of early medieval western Europe was the norm; as Rosamund McKitterick observes, "[t]he Carolingian laity, for a considerable way down the social scale, was a literate laity."[8] Among the peasant class, however, it was no doubt rare if not nonexistent.

In the twelfth century, literacy began to expand greatly, especially among the non-noble classes. The twelfth and thirteenth centuries saw enormous urban growth and an expansion of trade and manufacturing. This growth brought with it the rise of a new group of people, whose wealth and power were not based on landed propert, but on ready cash and investment capital. One of the effects of the growth of this merchant and manufacturing class was rising literacy. The growth of these literate urban classes created a new demand for devotional texts in the vernacular. Bibles, and Bible-related materials began to be produced in much greater quantities. However, as we will see the following, these societal changes also created a challenge to the Church, and when this challenge was not met, heresy sometimes resulted. The search for religious expression led some people outside the channels the official church provided.

VERNACULAR BIBLES OF THE EARLY MIDDLE AGES

The Latin Bible of the Middle Ages was, of course, itself a translation, intended to make the text of the Bible available for the average reader of the late Roman Empire. In antiquity, there seems to have been no hesitancy to translate the Bible into the language of the people, and the Latin translation was not the only one. There were translations into Syriac, Coptic, and Georgian. The Gothic Bible was the first translation into a Germanic language.

The Gothic Bible

In the fourth century, archbishop Ulfilas (ca. 310–ca. 383) translated the Greek Bible into Gothic. The Goths were a Germanic tribe living in the region now roughly defined as the Balkans, and Ulfilas was born of mixed Gothic-Greek parents. From 340 until 347, he worked as a missionary among the Goths until resistance to his work forced him into exile. The emperor, Constantius II, permitted him to settle within the Roman

---

[7] Asser, *Life of Alfred*, trans. Keynes and Lapidge, 93.
[8] McKitterick, *The Carolingians and the Written Word*, 270.

Empire, where he set out to translate the Bible. In time, the Goths accepted Christianity; however, the Arian Christianity they embraced was a form of the faith considered heretical in the western part of the Roman Empire at the time, although it was quite popular in the east. Arianism found its origin in the theology of Arius, a fourth-century priest from Alexandria, which had been rebutted by the council of Nicaea in 325. Many of the Germanic tribes, who by the end of the fourth century had won positions of power and influence at the expense of the crumbling Roman imperial government, adopted Arianism as their form of Christianity. It may have fostered their sense of political independence from the Roman elite. It was not until the sixth century that most of these new Gothic rulers started to integrate with the local landed and clerical elite and to convert to the orthodox faith.

Ulfilas's Gothic Bible is a fairly literal, word-by-word translation from the Greek. Ulfilas did more than just translate the Bible; he gave the Goths literacy in their own language. He composed an entirely new alphabet to render the Gothic sounds into a new writing system, based on Greek, Latin, and Futhark (also called runic) letters. According to his biographer Philostrogius, Ulfilas translated the entire text of the Bible, with the exception of the books of Samuel and Kings, which he deemed to be too violent to be edifying for the already war-prone tribe of the Goths.[9] It is hard to tell whether Philostrogius's claims are actually true: today, only fragments of the Gothic Bible survive, a little more than half of the New Testament and only small parts of the Old, and most of the fragments date from long after Ulfilas's lifetime. Its most famous copy, the Codex Argenteus (presently in the university library of Uppsala, Sweden, with one leaf on display in Speyer Cathedral in Germany), dates from the early sixth century, when the Ostrogoths (eastern Goths) had established themselves as rulers of a kingdom in Italy after the collapse of Roman rule there. The Codex Argenteus was a beautiful luxury copy, written (as the name "argenteus," silver, indicates) in silver ink on parchment that had been died purple, an imperial color.[10] It was commissioned by the most famous of the Gothic kings over Italy, Theoderic the Great (d. 523), who simultaneously commissioned a Latin Bible, the Codex Veronensis, of similar design. It was probably intended as a monument to the Gothic and Arian identity of

---

[9] Philostorgius, *Ecclesiastical History*, in *The Goths in the Fourth Century*, trans. Heather and Matthews, 134.

[10] It can be viewed online at the Web site of Uppsala University Library, *Codex Argenteus Online*: http://www.ub.uu.se/en/Collections/Manuscript-Collections/Silver-Bible/Codex-Argenteus-Online/.

his dynasty, and perhaps to snub the emperor in Constantinople.[11] Ironically, by the time the Codex Argenteus was written, Gothic was an almost "dead" language, as the Ostrogoths were commonly using a spoken form of Latin for their everyday communications. Some time after the death of Theoderic, Gothic rule over Italy collapsed in a series of wars with the eastern Roman Empire, and the last of the Gothic kings was killed in 553. Many of the Ostrogoths fled to their kinsmen in Spain. Visigothic rule over Spain would continue until the early eighth century, but the Spanish Visigoths, who converted from Arianism to orthodoxy in the late sixth century, would use Latin exclusively as their language of religion.

Bible Paraphrases in Old High German and Old English

Unlike the Arian Goths, and unlike the Slavic people of south-central Europe who converted in the ninth century to eastern Christianity and adopted a Scripture and liturgy in their own language, the "Roman" Christians in western Europe used the Latin Bible as their authoritative text and did not usually translate the Scriptures into the vernacular. The legacy of the Roman Empire here meant that there were two languages in use simultaneously; Latin became the language of learning, administration, and religion, whereas the vernacular Germanic and Romance languages were spoken in daily use. This presents a case of what Charles Ferguson termed *diglossia*, the use of two languages within one community, one an official, codified, literary standard, learned by formal education, and the other for daily and informal use.[12] The use of two languages does not mean that the clergy conversed only in Latin or that the laity only spoke and understood the vernacular. The choice between Latin and the vernacular was determined more by the context in which the language was used, rather than the question of who spoke it; many people, both laity and clergy, were probably conversant in both languages.

The medieval translations into the vernacular that do exist were made from the Latin Vulgate, which, as shown in Chapter 4, was the accepted authoritative version of the Bible in the west throughout the Middle Ages. Most of these vernacular translations did not contain the entire text of the Bible, but were limited to certain books or parts of the Bible only, such as

---

[11] Verona, Biblioteca capitolare, MS 6. I wish to thank Yitzhak Hen for drawing my attention to this manuscript. See also his forthcoming book, *Western Arianisms; Politics and Religious Culture in the Early Medieval West*.

[12] Ferguson, "Diglossia."

the Hexateuch, the Psalms, or the Gospels. Because "complete" bibles were rare even in Latin in the Early Middle Ages (as shown in Chapter 2), this should not really surprise us; however, as we will see later, the limitation to certain books and not others could also be dictated by theological reasons. Finally, some of the "translations" were not really literal translations; some were vernacular glosses added to a Latin text, and others were literary paraphrases of biblical texts. When studying this type of literature, we should be careful not to measure these medieval texts up against modern ideas about what constitutes a "translation."

The most common "translations" of the Bible in the Early Middle Ages were not literal translations, but were poetic reworkings of biblical materials. The vernacular was seen as an appropriate channel for epic poetry, and biblical materials were regarded a worthy subject matter for this genre. One of the most interesting examples of this biblical poetry is the Old Saxon *Heliand* (*The Savior*), a poetic rendering of the Gospel story that closely follows the text of the *Diatesseron,* composed in northern Germany some time in the early ninth century. As was said in Chapter 3, a copy of this *Diatesseron* was present in the monastery of Fulda in the mid-ninth century, and this text itself was translated into Old Saxon in a fairly literal rendering, with Latin and Old Saxon in parallel columns. It is quite likely that the *Heliand* was written by a monk at Fulda using the text of the *Diatesseron* as the base text. The text does reveal clerical learning; there is some evidence that the author made use of Hrabanus Maurus's commentary on Matthew, for example. The ninth-century Latin preface to the work describes the author as a notable Saxon poet, writing for a lay audience:

[Louis, the very pious emperor][13] ordered a certain man of the people of the Saxons, who was regarded as a rather well-known poet among his own, to translate the New Testament poetically into German, so that the sacred reading of holy commandments might be diffused not only among the literate, but even among the illiterate.[14]

The *Heliand* was clearly meant to appeal to an audience that was more fluent in Saxon than Latin and was more familiar with pre-Christian customs than Christian ones. G. Ronald Murphy, who rendered the text in modern

---

[13] Louis the Pious, ruled as emperor 813–840.

[14] *Heliand*, Praef., ed. Behaghel, 1. The newer edition, *Heliand*, ed. Cathey, does not include this preface.

English, pointed out that the author deliberately chose Saxon words, rather than borrowed words from the Latin for his translation; the word used to denote the Temple in Jerusalem, for instance, is never *tempal* (borrowed from the Latin *templum*), but rather the Germanic *uuiha*.[15] Christ was presented as a chieftain, rather than a rabbi, and the text takes great pains to explain some of the Jewish customs described in the Gospels.

The *Heliand* was written for a recently converted people whose allegiance to Christianity was still subject to question. The Saxons had only recently adopted Christianity. The new religion had first come to the Saxon lands in the mid-eighth century, brought by English monks and missionaries such as Boniface, who founded the monastery of Fulda in 743 (the same monastery where presumably the *Heliand* was written and where, later, Einhard would receive his education). In the last decades of the eighth century, the Carolingian rulers over the lands west of Saxony campaigned hard to gain overlordship of it; Christianization and military conquest thus went hand in hand. It was a long and (for Charlemagne) frustrating campaign, in which often freshly conquered peoples would relapse into rebellion against their Christian overlords. Charlemagne's biographer Einhard did not regard the Saxons with much sympathy. He considered them "fierce by nature, given to the worship of demons, and hostile to our religion, and they did not consider it dishonorable to violate and transgress all law, human and divine."[16] Finally, by the year 804, after a brutal campaign, which even raised the eyebrows of Charlemagne's own advisor Alcuin, who admonished the clergy to behave like "preachers, rather than predators," the Saxons were conquered:[17]

After the terms offered by the king were accepted by them, it was clear that the war that had waged for so many years was finished. They were to renounce the worship of demons and their other national religious customs and accept the sacraments of the Christian faith and religion, and be united with the Franks to form one people with them.[18]

By the time the *Heliand* was written, these bloody campaigns were probably still a fresh memory, and it is not inconceivable that, in the words of Murphy, the *Heliand* was "intended to bring the gospel home to the Saxons in a poetic environment in order to help the Saxons cease their

---

[15] Murphy, *The Saxon Savior*, xv.
[16] Einhard, *Vita Karoli*, 7, ed. Pertz, 8.
[17] Alcuin of York, *Epistolae*, 111, ed. Dümmler, MGH Epistolae, 4, 161.
[18] Einhard, *Vita Karoli*, 7, ed. Pertz, 9.

vacillation between their warrior-loyalty to the old gods and to the 'mighty Christ.'"[19]

Cultural conversion was not the only function of vernacular biblical poetry. Bible poetry was intended to delight as well as edify. In the ninth century, Otfrid of Weissenburg, a student of Hrabanus Maurus, composed a rhymed verse translation of the Gospels into Old Franconian. He dedicated the poem to the emperor Louis the Pious, but in his (Latin) preface, addressed to bishop Liutbert of Mainz, he tells us that he made his translation "at the request of some of his brethren" and especially the empress Judith, who were dismayed that there should be no worthy German equivalent to the works of pagans poets such as Vergil, Ovid and Lucan, or even Christian ones such as Juvencus, Arator, and Prudentius. "Sustained by their support," he

wrote a Gospel version, composed in Franconian, adding to it spiritual and moral words, so that those among them who might shudder at the difficulty of a foreign tongue, would get to know the holy words in their own language, and understand the law of God in this same language, and thus be mindful to become afraid to deviate even a little from it.[20]

Old Saxon was not the only language in which biblical poetry was written. The *Heliand* is preserved in two manuscripts and a number of manuscript fragments. One of the manuscripts also contains a fragment of a poetic paraphrase of Genesis in Old Saxon. This same text, translated into Old English, also appears in the manuscript Junius 11, a large collection of Old English biblical poetry, today preserved in the Bodleian Library in Oxford.[21] It is sometimes called the Caedmon manuscript, after the eight-century monk mentioned in Bede's *Church History of the English People*, who is the oldest English poet known by name. According to Bede, Caedmon "used to sing songs appropriate for religion and piety, in such a way that whatever he learned from divine scripture by way of interpreters, he could bring them forth with little effort and render them in his own, English tongue, in poetic words, composed with great sweetness and feeling."[22] Bede says that Caedmon was not taught by human skill, but by divine inspiration. One night, while he was still a layman and was guarding the stables, away

---

[19] Murphy, *The Saxon Savior*, xvi.
[20] Otfrid von Weissenburg, *Letter to Liutbert*, in *Das Evangelienbuch*, ed. Erdmann, 4. An edition is online at http://titus.uni-frankfurt.de/texte/etcs/germ/ahd/otfrid/otfri.htm.
[21] It can be viewed online: http://image.ox.ac.uk/show?collection=bodleian&manuscript=msjunius11.
[22] Bede, *Ecclesiastical History*, 4, 24, ed. Colgrave and Mynors, 414–16.

from the mead hall, where everyone was invited to recite in turn, he heard a voice

calling his name: "Caedmon!" It said, "sing me something." But he answered: "I do not know how to sing. This is why I have fled the hall and came here, since I cannot sing." But again, he who spoke to him said, "Still, I want you to sing me a song." "What shall I sing?" he said. And he said: "Sing me about the beginning of creation." And after that answer, [Caedmon] immediately started to sing a song of praise to God the Creator, which he had never heard before.[23]

Unlike the author of the Heliand, Caedmon thus seems to have been "illiterate," that is, not versed in Latin, because he needed to have the Scriptures read to him "by way of interpreters."

Even if the poet Caedmon did write several poems on religious themes, it is unlikely that any of the texts in the tenth-century Codex Junius 11 can be ascribed to him. It contains two versifications of Genesis (*Genesis A* and *Genesis B,* the latter being the version that also exists in Old Saxon), Exodus, and Daniel. Later scribes added a poem known as *Christ and Satan.* In addition to the texts in the Junius manuscript, there exist more biblical verse paraphrases in Old English, including a versified rendering of the book of Judith, a poem known as *Christ* (I, II, and III), and the *Dream of the Rood,* a vision that tells the story of Jesus' crucifixion as narrated by the cross. Richard Marsden points out that in contrast to the more literal prose translations, in the biblical poems "the narratives are re-imagined and rearranged to achieve a clear exegetical purpose."[24] These were not simply poems written to educate an illiterate and lay audience; they possessed a high level of exegetical sophistication, as well as literary quality. The materials from the Bible also are frequently supplemented with apocryphal materials. The Genesis story, for example, included a lengthy account of the rebellion of Lucifer, and other materials were taken from the *Life of Adam and Eve.* The poem *Christ and Satan* is based on the apocryphal Gospel of Nicodemus (all discussed in Chapter 3). As we will see, this fluency between biblical and apocryphal materials was quite common in vernacular translations. Even the manuscript of the prose Old English Hexateuch (discussed in the next subsection) had a translation of the apocryphal story of Joseph and Senath added to it at a later date. Because the vernacular translations were not regarded with the same authority as the Latin text, the boundaries of the canon were sometimes also less rigidly defined.

---

23 Ibid, 416.
24 Marsden, "The Bible in English," 219.

Vernacular Translations and the Old English Bible

Poetic paraphrases were not the only type of "translation" undertaken in the early Middle Ages. Other translations exist that seem to have been more clearly intended as aids in helping to comprehend the Latin text. One important category was interlinear glosses, which provided word-to-word renderings of each Latin word in the Bible text. Latin psalters were often glossed this way, even in later periods. The famous twelfth-century Eadwine Psalter, for instance, from Christ Church in Canterbury, had Old English glosses added to the Gallican Psalter and Old French glosses interlined with Jerome's version from the Hebrew (Photo 5). These were not translations in the strict sense, because one would have a difficult time reading the vernacular gloss by itself, but they were great aids for someone not entirely familiar with Latin. Glosses of this kind were not always conceived together with the original text. The Lindisfarne Gospels (Photo 7), dating from the early eighth century, had their Latin text glossed some time in the tenth century in Old English. Although it could be the case that glosses such as these were intended for the laity to understand the Latin text, it is more likely that they indicate a lack, or even loss, of Latin proficiency among the clergy.

In the ninth century, the knowledge of Latin was declining among the clergy in England. The very likely reason for this was the continuous attacks and plundering by Viking raiders, who caused a significant decline in the flourishing monastic culture that had existed in the century before. To make up for this decline in traditional learning, King Alfred (d. 899) made an effort to bolster learning at his court, and he decided to use English, rather than Latin, for this purpose. He ordered the translation of some key Christian texts into the vernacular: Gregory's *Pastoral Care*, and Boethius's *Consolation of Philosophy*. Some scholars also identify King Alfred as the author of a partial prose translation of the book of Psalms, preserved in an eleventh-century manuscript from Canterbury, now in Paris.[25] Alfred's attempt to establish a secular base for vernacular learning seems to have been an isolated experiment, but in the long run, it laid a foundation for a more significant vernacular Bible translation, the Bible in Old English.

The Old English Bible is often associated with the name of Ælfric of Eynsham (d.c. 1010), although his authorship is only certain for larger part of Genesis, Numbers, Joshua, and Judges. Ælfric was a priest and monk of Winchester and later Cerne Abbas. He later became abbot of the

---

[25] *King Alfred's Old English Prose Translation*, ed. O'Neill, 73–79.

monastery of Eynsham near Oxford. In the tenth century, with royal help, bishops Æthelwold and Oswald of Winchester and Saint Dunstan, abbot of Glastonbury attempted to revitalize monastic life in England. Their reform depended in many ways on the support of the laity. Many nobles in this period had strong ties to monastic communities; they acted as their benefactors, whereas these monasteries in turn acted as a spiritual guarantee for the benefactors' welfare in the world to come. Much of the monks' daily routine involved praying for the souls of their lay benefactors. As Ælfric's correspondence shows, these lay patrons often requested translations of Latin works into English for their own edification and education. In a letter to his lay patron and ealdorman Æðelwærd (d. 998), which was to become the preface to the Genesis translation, Ælfric tells us that Æðelwærd requested him to translate Genesis into Old English. He was initially reluctant to do this, even though he had regularly provided vernacular translations saints' lives and homilies for his friend and patron. However, Ælfric decided he might as well give in to the request, because "you told me that I only had to translate up to the story of Isaac, the son of Abraham, for some other person had translated it from Isaac to the end."[26] Ælfric hoped that, after this, his patron would not request any more translations of Scripture; otherwise, he might have to refuse. When the lay nobleman Sigeweard of Eastheolon had made a similar request, Ælfric had sent him not a translation of the Bible but, rather, an interpretive essay *about* the Bible (*The Book on the Old and New Testament; Libellus de veteri testamenti et novo*), as well as a translation of Alcuin's *Questions on Genesis*. He was concerned that it might be dangerous for untutored lay people to read the text of the Old Testament and draw their own conclusions from it:

if there is a foolish man who reads the book, or hears it read, he might fancy that he should live today under the new dispensation, just as the patriarchs lived in their own time before the old Law was established, or as men lived under Moses's law.[27]

Inexperienced lay readers, encouraged by "ungelæreden preostas" (illiterate priests) who ignored the distinction between the various dispensations (see Chapter 5) or who did not understand the allegorical meaning of certain passages, might end up believing that polygamy and incest were allowed by God. Stories such as the multiple marriages of the patriarch Jacob, or even Lot fathering offspring with his daughters, might lead them to think that

---

[26] Ælfric, *Preface to Genesis*, in *The Old English Heptateuch*, ed. Marsden, 3.
[27] Ibid., 3–4.

God sanctioned this kind of behavior, Ælfric feared. Precisely because the words of the Old Testament had a hidden and potentially spiritual meaning, translating it should be done with the utmost care. The word order, and even the words themselves, should be retained as much as possible. This is why Ælfric opted for a fairly literal, equivalent translation.[28] Ælfric's (and his anonymous coauthor's) Genesis translation eventually formed the basis for a translation of the first six books of the Bible, known as the "Old English Hexateuch" (or sometimes "Heptateuch," because one manuscript also includes a paraphrase of the book of Judges), which was completed by the beginning of the eleventh century.

The Old English Hexateuch was not used exclusively by a lay audience. One particular manuscript copy of it, the beautifully illuminated codex London, British Library, Cotton Claudius B.IV, was originally in the possession of Saint Augustine's Abbey in Canterbury. Some scholars have concluded that it was intended for use by literate laymen or uneducated monks.[29] But later users' marks suggest that it was also used by more learned monks. It was heavily annotated in the twelfth century, with excerpts from the *Historia scholastica* of Peter Comestor (see Chapter 6); some of the marginal notes were attributed to a certain "Normannus," presumably a local monk. These glosses are in both Latin and Old English. The use of the latter was probably an anachronism by the end of the twelfth century, when the glosses were written. Because of the Norman conquest in 1066, the dominant vernacular spoken in England among the ruling classes was no longer English but Anglo-Norman. Alger Duane and William Stoneman have suggested that the codex was deliberately glossed in Old English to boost the claims to antiquity of its possessor.[30]

The Hexateuch was not the only text translated into the vernacular in the eleventh century. A translation of the Gospels was also made, but there is hardly any evidence by whom, or for whom, this was done. Both the Old English Hexateuch and the West-Saxon Gospels became important documents in the time of the Reformation, when ecclesiastical dignitaries such as Matthew Parker, the sixteenth-century archbishop of Canterbury, used it to provide historical precedents for translating the Bible into the vernacular.

The use of the vernacular as a language of administration, education, and religion never became as widespread on the Continent as it was in England.

---

[28] Ibid., 4. See also Marsden, "Ælfric as Translator: The Old English Prose Genesis."
[29] Withers, "Present Patterns, Past Tense," 239–40.
[30] Doane and Stoneman, *Purloined Letters*, 356–60.

Still, there is plenty of evidence that vernacular Bible translations, intended for laity and clergy alike, were not uncommon here either. An Old Dutch translation of the Psalms, the Wachtendonk Psalms, dates from the tenth century, and fragments from Psalm translations also exist in Old High German dialects. As we will see in Chapter 8, the book of Psalms was used as a prayer book for clergy and laity alike. Around the middle of the eleventh century, an abbot of Ebersberg, Williram, translated the Song of Songs into Old High German. The work, which presented a parallel Latin and German text of the Song, was accompanied by a marginal commentary in two languages and was clearly intended for a monastic audience. The Song of Songs was not considered appropriate reading for a lay audience, and, as we saw in Chapter 6, even monks were advised not to study it until they had at least reached a mature age.

Thus, contrary to common perception, the Early Middle Ages saw a number of different Bible translations and the dispersion of biblical materials in the vernacular. Some of these translations, however, were not exactly what we today would call "translations," for rather than aiming for exact equivalence between the original text and the new text, they offered poetic paraphrases. Others were bilingual interlinear glosses. Some, indeed, such as the Old English Gospels and the Old English Hexateuch (especially the first books), were actual translations. Most were translations of individual books rather than the entire Bible. Their purpose was varied as well; some were intended to educate the laity, others the clergy; some were intended to entertain, others to edify, and some both. The questions about who wrote them and who used them are intricately connected to questions of lay literacy and the use of Latin in this period, and the answers can be complex. After the twelfth century, however, another factor started to play a role as well: the question of authority and orthodoxy.

VERNACULAR BIBLES BETWEEN HERESY AND ORTHODOXY

There is no evidence of any prohibition in the Early Middle Ages against Bible translation in the vernacular. However, the concern that Ælfric had voiced about his translation of Genesis would grow in the centuries to come. As we saw earlier, literacy, and with it book possession, increased in the twelfth and thirteenth centuries, and Bible translations in the vernacular became more common. Some of these translations were used among groups that found themselves in disagreement with the church hierarchy; as a result, not only these particular translations but by extension the very practice of translating Scripture itself sometimes also became tainted with the suspicion of heresy. The (sporadic and localized) attempts of the Church to curb or regulate these translations do not seem to have affected their popularity and wide circulation, however.

Heresy was relatively rare in the Middle Ages before 1100. To be sure, theological disputes could involve an accusation of heresy, and it was usually up to the local bishop or a church council to undertake action against the dissenters. These were matters of church discipline, and an aberrant monk or cleric might be confined to his monastery in silence. But by the end of the twelfth century, the Church was confronted with an increasing number of individuals and movements who defied ecclesiastical authority, criticized church practice, and faced ecclesiastical censure as a result. Medieval churchmen were apt to see all heresy as facets of one united enterprise to attack and destroy the Church, and they were convinced that this was all work of the devil. Modern historians can see more diverse origins for these various movements and recognize that some of the proliferation of heresy in this period is due at least in part to an increased concern about doctrinal orthodoxy on the part of the church hierarchy. Few heretics define themselves as dissenters by choice, but as the Church defined the parameters of orthodoxy more strictly, more people appeared to be outside the boundaries. Some of these heretical movements were urban protest movements that criticized the authority of bishops and clergy, and some gathered around a charismatic prophet. Others, such as the Albigensians or Cathars, popular especially in northern Italy and the south of France, had their own clergy and their own ascetic and dualist theology. Yet others, ironically, such as the Waldensians, may have been the result of the success of the reform movement of the twelfth century that had tried to popularize the preaching of orthodox devotion among the laity. In particular, the Waldensians would make Bible reading into one of their central tenets.

In 1180, in imitation of the life of the first apostles, Peter Waldes, founder of the Waldensians, decided to abandon his family and livelihood and seek a life of evangelical poverty. His ideals closely resemble those of many reformist preachers of the twelfth century and those of Francis of Assisi a few decades later. For Waldes, religious self-instruction and lay reading of the Bible were part of this apostolic ideal from the start, and as we saw, this was still quite an orthodox and common devotional practice in his time. Waldes and his followers read Gospel translations in the vernacular as well as Latin. When they asked for an approval for their movement at the Third Lateran Council in Rome in 1179, they presented some of these translations (including a glossed psalter) for examination.[31] It was not these translations that drew the disapproval of the council, but their request that as laypersons they should be allowed to preach. Although the pope was sympathetic to their movement, he instructed them to submit to the authority of their local bishop, who upheld a ban on their preaching. When they spurned this ban and continued to preach in defiance of the bishop, they were officially condemned as heretics, in 1184. Despite this condemnation, the Waldensian movement attracted a growing following, and they increasingly appealed to the Bible, rather than the Church's teaching, as justification for their beliefs and practices. These included a ban on all oaths, a rejection of the existence of purgatory, doubts about the validity of prayers for the dead, lay preaching, and the lay administration of the sacraments.

In his *Manual for the Inquisitor*, the Dominican inquisitor Bernard Gui (d. 1331) described the use of vernacular Scripture and preaching as common characteristic of Waldensian heretics. According to Bernard, a wide range of literacy could be found among the Waldensians:

They usually have the gospels and epistles in the vernacular and even in Latin, as some of them understand it. There are those among them who can read, and these at times read out their sermons from a book, but others preach without a book, especially those that cannot read but have learned their text by heart. They preach in their followers' houses, as we said above, or occasionally as they journey or in the street.[32]

Gui also mentions that the Cathars likewise made use of vernacular Scriptures, even though their beliefs were quite different from those of the Waldensians: "they read out passages from the gospels and epistles in the vernacular, applying and expounding these in their own favour and against the authority of the Roman Church."[33] The reading of the Bible in the vernacular in itself was not considered heretical. But when heretical groups used these translations to challenge ecclesiastical authority, it posed a dilemma for church authorities: should they impose a ban on such translations and discourage what was probably an act of genuine piety, or should they ignore what was probably a certain sign of heresy?

[31] Berger, *La Bible Française au Moyen Age*, 36–37.
[32] Bernard Gui, *Manuel de l'inquisiteur*, ed. Mollat and Drioux, 62. English translation in Bernard Gui, *The Inquisitor's Guide: A Medieval Manual on Heretics*, trans. Shirley 64.
[33] Bernard Gui, *The Inquisitor's Guide: A Medieval Manual on Heretics*, ed. Mollat and Drioux, 43; Bernard Gui, *Manuel de l'inquisiteur*, trans. Shirley, 26.

Pope Innocent III found himself in this dilemma when, in 1199, the bishop of Metz wrote to him about a group of laypersons, both men and women, whose behavior he found troubling:

They were drawn by the desire for Scripture, and had made translations of the Gospels, the letters of Paul, the Psalter and the *Moralia in Job* and several other books in French, and were studying this translation so freely (if not as prudently as one might wish), that they discussed these things openly in secret conventicles, and presumed to preach to each other.[34]

When some of the parish priests admonished them on this,

they resisted them openly, and brought up suitable reasons from Scripture that said that they should not be prohibited to do this. Some in their simplicity even scorned these priests, and when these priests expounded to them the word of salvation, they murmured in secret that they had it better in their books and could explain it better.[35]

Innocent answered the bishop that "the desire to understand sacred Scripture and the zeal to adhort according to them was not to be rebuked, but rather commended." However, he objected to their secret conventicles. Faithful and orthodox Christians should not have anything to hide, he thought. If these laypersons had complaints about certain priests, they should direct them to the local bishop, not openly scorn these priests. In a second letter, the pope advised the bishop to proceed cautiously; after all, it was the content of someone's teaching, and not the use of vernacular scriptures as such, that made him or her a heretic:

Inquire and find out the truth: who was the translator of that translation, what was the intention of the translator, what do its users believe, why do they teach, and do they uphold the apostolic see and the catholic faith? We will better be able to understand what must be done to track down the truth about these and others after we are instructed by your letters.[36]

A quarter century later, King Jaime I and the bishops of Aragon took a more rigorous course of action. The injunctions against heresy included a blanket prohibition:

No one should possess the books of the Old and New Testament in the Romance language. And if someone owns these, he should, within the time span of eight days after the publication of this edict, hand them over to the bishop in order to

---

[34] Innocent III, *Regesta sive epistolae* 141, PL 214, 695. Innocent's letters are available in an English translation on http://en.wikisource.org/wiki/Author:Innocent_III.

[35] Ibid.

[36] Innocent III, *Regesta sive epistolae* 142, PL 214, 699.

be burned. If he fails to do so, whether he be a lay person or a cleric, he will be held to be suspect of heresy, until he clears himself.[37]

Clearly, the concern for heresy here trumped the more prudent approach of Innocent III in 1199. Other provincial councils, in Toulouse in 1229 and Narbonne in 1246, made similar recommendations. It is not a coincidence that these restrictions were issued in regions where the influence of the Waldensian and Cathar heresies was most strongly felt.

BIBLES IN FRENCH

In the case of these conciliar restrictions, the main concern was clearly that the possession of these scriptures indicated heresy. There is ample manuscript evidence showing that vernacular prose translations of the Bible circulated elsewhere in the same period without any impediment, sometimes among the highest circles of nobility or royalty. There are twelfth-century translations into French of the books of Samuel, Kings, and Maccabees, with glosses and comments, fragments of a thirteenth-century translation of Revelation and the Gospels, and translations of the book of Psalms and glossed psalters.

By the middle of the thirteenth century, a completed translation of the Bible existed in French. A substantial number of copies of this text, called the *Old French Bible*, or *Bible française du XIIIe siecle* (*Thirteenth-Century French Bible*) still exist. Other Bible translations from this period are the so-called Acre Bible, now in the library of the Paris Arsenal, which contains most of the historical Old Testament books and was probably commissioned by King Louis IX, on his crusade to Egypt and Palestine in 1250–1254, and the *De Thou Bible*, named after its sixteenth-century owner, the historian Jacques Auguste de Thou (1553–1617). The latter contains the Gospels, the Psalter, Acts, and the Epistles, many of them with glosses from the *Glossa ordinaria*. No one doubted these bibles' orthodoxy or thought to prohibit their use. As Charles Robson concludes, "in the North of France, and in the French-speaking circles in England, the translation of Scripture was neither licensed nor prohibited by diocesan authority... It was a stationer's venture and encountered no official opposition or criticism."[38]

By the end of the thirteenth century, another popular Bible translation had appeared. It was the *Bible historiale* (*History Bible*), and its translator was Guyart Desmoulins, a canon of Saint Peter's church in Aire-sur-Lys

---

[37] *Sacrorum conciliorum,* ed. Mansi, vol. 23: 329.
[38] Robson, "The Vernacular Scriptures in France," 451.

in Northern France. It was a translation of the complete text of the historical books of the Bible, augmented with Peter Comestor's *Historia scholastica*.[39] In the fourteenth century, this text was augmented again, with materials from the thirteenth-century Bible translation. Scholars refer to this version as the *Bible historiale complétée* (*The Augmented History Bible*). The *Bible historiale* thus provided not just the Bible text but also commentary. This fact probably did much to assuage the concern that we already saw voiced by Ælfric, in his preface to Genesis, that the bare text without commentary might lead the laity into error. The *Bible historiale* also provided translations of those books of Scripture that Hugh of Saint Victor had deemed most apt to the literal understanding of Scripture, namely the historical books. It was a good "beginner's Bible," well suited for the untrained layperson. Desmoulins opted not to translate some of the more theologically difficult works, such as some of the Prophets, or the dialogues within the book of Job. In the words of Rosemarie McGerr, Desmoulins was thus successful in transforming the *Historia scholastica* from a scholastic textbook into a text that satisfied the desire for vernacular literature for lay edification.[40] More than 100 manuscripts of the *Bible historiale* exist today, which attests to its popularity. It was quite common for wealthy burghers, noblemen and -women, and even royalty to possess such a Bible. Nor was its influence restricted to France; the nobility of England was still Francophone, and its use was common there as well. Also, the concept was imitated in other regions of Europe. We find history bibles in languages as diverse as Dutch, German, Castilian, Czech, and even Old Norse.

Although ecclesiastical concerns about heresy thus could raise questions about the validity of vernacular translation, and did lead in some cases to injunctions against such translation, there was no universal, categorical objection to vernacular Bible translations in the Middle Ages. In general, Innocent's cautiously restrained attitude toward the use of vernacular bibles was followed in most parts of Europe. Because practice varied so much from place to place, it is difficult to generalize, but taking the Low Countries and England as examples, we can observe the spread of vernacular Bibles across northern Europe from the thirteenth to the sixteenth century, hampered and in some instances severely restricted, but never entirely suppressed, by sporadic prohibitions.

---

[39] A copy of the *Bible historiale*, in the Bibliothèque de Genève, can be viewed on-line thanks to the e-codices project: http://www.e-codices.unifr.ch/en/list/one/bge/fr0001–1.

[40] McGerr, "Guyart Desmoulins, the Vernacular Master of Histories," 213.

VERNACULAR TRANSLATIONS IN THE LOW COUNTRIES

The situation in the Low Countries (roughly the modern Netherlands and Belgium) was in many ways similar to that in France, in that concerns about heresy on occasion led to an official prohibition, which seems to have had little effect on the creation and circulation of vernacular translations, however. In 1369, Charles IV, king of Bohemia and Holy Emperor, issued a prohibition against the use of vernacular bibles. Although some scholars have wanted to see this as a general prohibition against the use of vernacular scriptures, the manuscript evidence for the spread of vernacular bibles indicates that its intent and effect were quite limited. In his bull, the emperor admonished the inquisitors Walter Kerling and Louis of Caliga to "diligently investigate the possession of sermons, treatises, and other writings in the vernacular, distributed among lay and semi-lay persons," and burn them if found heretical.[41] This was a matter of concern, the bull states, especially because laypersons, according to canonical sanctions, were not allowed to use "any vernacular books dealing with sacred scripture."[42] Although the bull evokes the decisions of the regional councils cited earlier, on closer inspection, it is not really a prohibition against all vernacular translation, but only those that were found heretical.

By the end of the fourteenth century, groups of devout laypersons, known as Beguines and Beghards, were quite common in the Low Countries. These were small conventicles of laypersons, mainly women, given to devotional practices, and, occasionally, Bible reading. At times, however, they could fall under the suspicion of heresy. In 1310, a laywoman associated with the Beguines, Marguerite Porete, author of a mystical work *Mirror of Divine Souls*, was burned at the stake in Paris for her allegedly antinomian beliefs, which rejected the necessity for moral laws. Three years later, the Council of Vienne also condemned certain antinomian doctrines held by Beguines and Beghards,[43] among them the tantalizing idea that, although kissing among unmarried people constituted an act of unchastity, sexual intercourse did not, because it was an act of nature, not of the will. When written in the first quarter if the fourteenth century Bernard Gui described the heresy of the Beguines in his *Manual for the Inquisitor*, he identified

---

[41] *Corpus documentorum*, ed. Fredericq, 214–17.

[42] *Corpus documentorum*, ed. Fredericq, 216.

[43] Beghards are sometimes mentioned as the male counterpart of the Beguines. Some medieval authors, such as Bernard Gui, apply the term *Beguine* to male and female religious alike. It is not clear whether the term *Beguines* meant the same throughout history, and throughout Europe. The "Beguines" of early fourteenth-century southern France seem to have little in common with the female religious of the Low Countries in the later Middle Ages.

them mainly as followers of the radical apocalyptic wing of the Franciscan movement, and readers of Peter John Olivi's *Postilla* on Revelation, which would be condemned posthumously by Pope John XXII in 1328. Although the Beguines in the Low Countries did not commonly espouse such beliefs, their name still was tainted with the suspicion of heresy. The use of vernacular scriptures was common among these Beguines, and it is likely that the legislation of 1369 was an admonition to investigate these groups more closely. However, it is unlikely that the act of translating the Bible in the Low Countries at the end of the Middle Ages was automatically seen as an act of heresy. Instead, there existed a flourishing culture of vernacular Bible translations and lay Bible reading by the end of the Middle Ages.

One of the earliest Bible translations that circulated in the Netherlands was a Gospel harmony, or *Diatesseron*, copied around 1280 at the abbey of Saint Tronde near Liège in Limburg. The Dutch scholar Cebus Cornelis de Bruin hypothesizes that its translator may have been the abbot of that abbey, William of Afflighem (d. 1277), and that he intended this translation for a group of devout women, not too different from the Beguines. Some scholars have argued that the text of the Liège *Diatesseron* was representative not of the Vulgate *Diatesseron* tradition as represented by the Codex Fuldensis (see Chapter 3) but, instead, of an Old Latin text that was directly translated from the second-century Syriac version of Tatian's *Diatesseron*, the original of which is now lost. Most recently, this hypothesis has been discredited, as other scholars pointed out that many of these "variant readings" in fact found their source in the twelfth-century commentary of the *Glossa ordinaria* (see also Chapter 6).[44] The Liège *Diatesseron* stands out as a piece of great literature. The Middle Dutch has a high literary quality, characterized by, for instance, frequent alliterations, in contrast to most medieval translations, which usually followed the original language very closely.

A translation of the Old Testament in Middle Dutch was written a century later, around 1360. Its author, until recently only known summarily as "the Bible translator of 1360" can be identified as Petrus Naghel, a Carthusian monk from Herne near Brussels and a proliferate translator of several Latin works, such as Jacob of Varazzo's *Golden Legend*, a medieval collection of saints' lives. Naghel worked for a lay patron from Brussels, who is mentioned in the foreword. His Bible was a translation of the

---

[44] The hypothesis was stated by De Bruin, *De statenbijbel*, 28. It was discredited by Den Hollander and Schmid, "The Gospel of Barnabas." I wish to thank Suzan Folkerts for drawing my attention to this article.

historical books of the Old Testament, interspersed with glosses taken from Peter Comestor's *Historia scholastica*. Although Naghel's translation was modeled after Desmoulins's *Bible historiale*, the translation was made fresh from the Latin, and not from Desmoulins's work. A verse paraphrase of Comestor's work already existed in Dutch; it was made by the end of the thirteenth century by Jacob van Maerlant, and it proved to be immensely popular. The first version of Naghel's History Bible contained a translation of the historical biblical books of the Old Testament only, but, in successive stages, more and more books were added, including a Gospel harmony, the book of Acts, and excerpts from the first-century Jewish-Roman author Josephus's *Antiquities* and *Jewish Wars*, dealing with historical materials between the Old and New Testaments and the destruction of the Temple in Jerusalem by the Romans in 70 A.D. By the 1370s, almost the entire Bible was translated into Middle Dutch. In the preface, Naghel expresses the hope that this translation will profit "many a blessed man, who is not taught by the clergy," and he expects that reading it will keep the laity from spending their time in idle pursuits. He also warned readers, however, of the dangers of unguided reading:

One should know and understand, since the Bible is many places is too obscure to understand, that I will at those places where it is advantageous and proper take parts of the *Historia scholastica,* and put it side by side with the text, distinguishing them with red ink.[45]

Thus, like Desmoulins, Naghel used Comestor's glosses as a way to make sure that his Bible translation was embedded in a tradition of commentary, lest it be "too obscure" for the laity. Also like Desmoulins, Naghel was reluctant to extend his translation to the more difficult-to-understand parts of the Old Testament.[46]

One of the biblical books that was separately translated was the book of Psalms, which was, of course, the main prayer book for the medieval laity. It was translated many times, most prominently by Geert Groote toward the end of the fourteenth century, as part of his Middle Dutch translation of the Book of Hours. Geert (or Gerard) Groote is best known for his role in the late medieval devotional movement of the *Devotio moderna*, the reform movement that was prominent in the Low Countries and Germany during the later Middle Ages. His zeal for reform eventually inspired the formation of the Brethren of the Common Life, a community that chose a way of life between the cloister and the world, guided by the Augustinian Rule. Book

---

[45] *Vetus Testamentum,* ed. De Bruin, 4.
[46] Folkerts, "The 'duncker' voor leken?"

production was an essential element in the life of the *Devotio moderna's* members; as was pointed out in Chapter 2, their houses often provided some income for themselves by copying books for lay patrons, especially prayer books. They also produced a large array of devotional literature for their own use, including a vernacular translation of all four Gospels, in a fairly literal, word-by-word translation. The author of the latter was Johann Scutken (d. 1423). This Gospel translation was accompanied by a translation of selections from Old Testament passages that were read in the liturgy. This seems to indicate that the primary use of these texts was to enable the worshipper to follow the Mass when attending church.

By the end of the fifteenth century, bibles in Middle Dutch also started to appear in print. In 1477, a complete vernacular translation of the Old Testament was printed in Delft, by Jacob Jacobszoon and Maurice Iemandtszoon ("somebody's son") of Middelburgh. The text was that of Naghel's Bible, but without the glosses, and the editors had taken care to correct the translation against the text of the Vulgate. Thus, the entire Old Testament was now available in Dutch in one printed volume, "to the honor and glory of his great name, and for the edification of his people,"[47] as the preface stated. This Delft Bible, as it was called, did not include the New Testament or the Psalms, but two years later, a complete Bible translation, including the Apocrypha, was printed in Cologne. It was a translation of the Latin Vulgate into a Nether-Rhenish dialect, and because of the negligible language differences among Dutch and Low-German dialects, this Bible became widely disseminated in the Low Countries (just as the Dutch translations mentioned above often spread into the Rhineland). This Cologne Bible offered a fairly literal word-by-word translation of the printed Vulgate, and on occasion, the translation included glosses and comments taken from Nicholas of Lyra's *Postilla litteralis*. In sum, there is little or no evidence that the bull of 1369 in any way hindered the spread of vernacular bibles in the Low Countries, or indeed the practice of lay Bible reading.

THE WYCLIFFITE BIBLE

Things did not go as smoothly in England, however, where the use of the vernacular Bible was much more restricted in the fifteenth century, as a result of fears about heresy. The heretical sect of the Lollards, who appeared around the end of the fourteenth century, emphasized lay preaching and

---

[47] *De Delfise Bijbel van 1477*, p. 2. The bible is also available online at www.bijbelsdigitaal.nl/view/? bible=db1477.

Bible reading in small conventicles, and defied ecclesiastical authority in their insistence that the Bible had a higher authority than priestly teaching. They commonly referred to the Bible as "Goddis lawe."[48] The movement was also seen as politically dangerous; it inspired a revolt against the crown in 1413. To justify their theology, the Lollards often invoked the teaching of John Wycliffe (1328–1384), who was not only a controversial theologian but also the most energetic advocate of vernacular Bible translation in Middle English.

What today we know as the "Wycliffe Bible" actually exists in two versions; the first is a fairly literal word-by-word translation, probably dating from around 1382, and the second is a freer revision of this translation made around in 1390. Neither translation is likely the work of John Wycliffe himself, although he is likely the one who initiated or at least inspired the project. The only scholar who is identified by name as a translator in one of the manuscripts is a Nicholas of Hereford. Other manuscripts mention a "master N." (probably the same Nicholas of Hereford) as a translator, and for the second half a "master J. and other men." There are several candidates for the identification of this "J." It is possible, but unlikely, that it is John Wycliffe himself, who died in 1384. Scholars have mentioned Wycliffe's friend from Oxford John of Trevisa (d. 1402) or possibly John Purvey as possible candidates, but there is scant evidence for this, especially in case of the latter.[49] In his preface to the translation, the translator described himself as a "symple creature of God," whose purpose it was to "saue [save] alle men in our rewme which God wole haue saued." This was all the more necessary because in the universities, the Bible was not taught until after many years of study. "Þis semeþ vtterli þe deuelis purpose, þat fewe men or noone shulen lerne and kunne Goddis lawe."[50] He describes how he first consulted "many elde biblis," the works of many Church fathers, and glosses, and especially Nicholas of Lyra, before undertaking his translation. In particular, in the Psalter, he took care to note the divergence of the Latin with the Hebrew:

And where þe Ebreu, bi witnesse of Ierom and of Lire and oþere expositours, discordiþ from oure Latyn bookis, I haue set in þe margyn bi the maner of a glose what þe Ebreu haþ, and hou it is vnderstonden in sum place . . . [51]

---

[48] See below, n50.
[49] Dove, *The First English Bible*, 68–81.
[50] Dove, *Earliest Advocates*, 84 and 71.
[51] "And where the Hebrew, by witness of Jerome and Lyra and other exegetes, disagrees with our Latin books, I have put in the margin by means of a gloss what the Hebrew has, and how it is understood in that place." Dove, *Earliest Advocates*, 82.

The author did not hide his Lollard sympathies; he compared unworthy priests to the idols of ancient Israel, and likened the rulers of England to King Manasseh, who with his support of idolatry provoked the wrath of God (2 Kings 21). By contrast, people who "speke onour of God and of his lawe" were slaundered, and called "lollardis, eretikis and reisers of debate and of tresoun agenus þe king."[52] It was this defence of heretics and attack on the established clergy that raised the ire of the authorities.

In 1408, the archbishop of Canterbury, Thomas Arundel, issued an edict to ban the translation of the Bible into the English vernacular. The edict, which was part of a larger set of legislation known as the *Constitutions of Arundel*, was as much aimed against the Lollards as against the teachings of John Wycliff. After an admonition against lay preaching, and a condemnation of the writings of John Wycliff, Arundel warned the reader:

It is a dangerous matter, as Jerome says, to translate the text of sacred Scripture from one language into another, because in these translations the same meaning is not always easily retained in all matters, as Jerome, even though he was inspired, confesses that he often erred in this. We therefore state and ordain that from henceforth no one by his own authority shall translate the text of Sacred Scripture in the English language, or any other language, by way of book, pamphlet or treatise. Nor may anyone read such a book, pamphlet or treatise, whether written recently by said John Wycliff, or to be written henceforth, either in part or as a whole, publicly or in secret, under threat of major excommunication, unless this translation be approved by the Diocesan council, or, as the case might require, by a provincal council. Whosoever acts to the contrary, shall be punished as a protector of heresy and error.[53]

Arundel's constitutions followed a lively debate, mainly at the University of Oxford, on the question whether vernacular translation was desirable, or even possible. The more outspoken adversaries of translation argued that the Bible was too difficult even to understand in its literal sense; the laity should be content with the clergy explaining the main points of Christian doctrine to them rather than wishing to read the Bible for themselves. But even some of the more outspoken anti-Lollard spokesmen, such as Richard Ullerston, admitted that it was legitimate to translate Scripture into the vernacular, because Jerome himself had done the very same thing.

This type of debate was not confined to England. In the Low Countries, within the movement of the *Devotio moderna*, there also was a lively discussion on whether it was appropriate to make Sacred Scripture available

---

[52] Dove, *Earliest Advocates*, 52.
[53] *Concilia Magnae Britanniae et Hiberniae*, ed. Wilkins, 316–17.

to lay people. In his work *On Books in Dutch* (*De libris teutonicalibus*), for instance, Gerhard Zerbolt of Zutphen (1367–1398) argues that there are no good reasons to prohibit the use of vernacular translations of Scripture, since Jerome himself translated Scripture into Latin for the use of both clergy and laity. At the same time, he had some reservations when it came to translating the more "obscure parts of Scripture," which laypeople needed help interpreting.

It is very likely that Archbishop Arundel wanted to quell the Bible debate and by doing so deal a simultaneous blow to the Lollard sect; he was successful in neither. A close friend of the king, the nobleman John Oldcastle, led a Lollard revolt in 1413, and was executed in 1417. Lollardy came to be regarded as a dangerous subversive sect and was persecuted for much of the fifteenth century. The debate over Bible translation continued until far into the sixteenth century, when the few remaining Lollards were absorbed into the nascent Protestant movement.

To what extent was Arundel's prohibition enforced, or effective? There are a large number of manuscripts of Wycliffite Bibles still extant today; some 250 are scattered in English libraries. That is three times as many as there are manuscripts of Chaucer's *Canterbury Tales*. Most of these are translations of the New Testament only, but about twenty complete Bibles are still extant. Were these copies made with the approval of the church authorities or copies that escaped their notice? Many of them were owned by prominent nobility, even royalty, and there is no evidence that they incurred their owners the suspicion of heresy. Richard Ullerston pointed out that Thomas Arundel himself praised the late queen Anne, first wife of Richard II, at her burial in 1394 because "sche hadde on Engliche al þe foure gospeleris wiþ þe doctvris vpon him."[54] It was not the possession of a vernacular Bible, as such, but who owned it and whether they were associated with heretical movements that irked the church authorities; Bible possession had become a political issue in fifteenth-century England.

To quote Margaret Deanesly, "[t]he attitude of the mediaeval Church to biblical translations has thus been seen to have been one of toleration in principle, and distrust in practice."[55] The Church did not object to translations, as long as the authority of the Vulgate text as the center of theological discourse was not challenged and as long as the understanding of the text was vested in an interpretation that was sanctioned by the Church, such as the work of Comestor, the *Glossa ordinaria*, and of Nicholas of

---

Lyra. But when the translations became a basis for theological assumptions that contradicted ecclesiastical doctrine, a heated (and sometimes mortal) debate on the legitimacy of these translations could ensue.

VERNACULAR BIBLE AND CHURCH AUTHORITY

The picture of the spread of the Bible in the vernacular after the twelfth century is thus somewhat paradoxical. On one hand, there are a number of edicts and injunctions against the translating of the Bible into the vernacular, and against the use of such Bibles. On the other hand, no text was more widespread and popular than the Bible in its many vernacular versions, and many of these do not seem to have raised an eyebrow from the ecclesiastical authorities. Historians studying this period must thus acknowledge a wide range of opinions and practices that were not always consistent with each other. In order to make sense of this complex medieval situation, several points bear reemphasizing.

First, the injunctions against Bible translation should be studied against the background of the history of medieval heresy. Contrary to popular perception, there was no blanket prohibition against biblical translation in the vernacular in the Middle Ages. However, a number of provincial councils issued edicts and injunctions against vernacular translations. They seem to have been more concerned with the spread of heresy than with the vernacular Bible as such. There was a large corpus of medieval vernacular translations and paraphrases of biblical texts, and there were no objections against their use, as long as these texts and their users avoided association with heretical groups.

Second, the history of the medieval vernacular Bible is closely connected to that of medieval literacy and the status of Latin. The situation in the Early Middle Ages was quite different from that of the later Middle Ages. Whether the laity had access to bibles, and whether they read them in Latin or in the vernacular, depended on a variety of factors: the level of literacy of the user, the societal and economic status of the reader, and, finally, the status of Latin as what Ferguson has called the "H language" (the language of formal education) of the Middle Ages.[56] This status itself was subject to change throughout the period studied in this book. We can see a gradual increase of biblical literacy and Bible possession among the laity, especially the rising burgher class, which by the later Middle Ages had acquired a prolific taste for devotional literature. Bishops and priests

---

[56] Ferguson, "Diglossia," 234.

encouraged the laity to read and meditate on the biblical text, although certain parts of the Bible were not considered appropriate material for lay people to consider. In general, we may agree with Andrew Gow's challenge to the "Protestant paradigm" and conclude that Bible translations before the time of the Reformation were indeed frequent and that they laid the groundwork for the Reformers who would make biblical literacy into a hallmark of true Christianity.

Third, what constituted a "bible" in the Middle Ages does not always correspond to the modern concepts of what a bible is. Depending on one's definition of a "Bible translation," one may see either a plethora of Bible translations or none at all while looking at the same set of texts. When considering the evidence of the Dutch vernacular translations, for instance, we notice that Gospel harmonies were more popular than were Gospel texts themselves. Of course, Gospel harmonies contained the entire Gospel text, but they generally did not present the interpretive problems that the Gospel readings by themselves posed, of contradicting Bible passages. Of the Old Testament texts, translations of the historical books abound, but we also see a greater reluctance to translate the theologically more difficult books, such as the Prophets, Job, or some of the books of Solomon. Many of these translations were interspersed with glosses that aimed to explain some of the more obscure passages to the reader, glosses that were taken either from the *Glossa ordinaria*, Peter Comestor's *Historia scholastica*, or Nicholas of Lyra's *Postilla litteralis*.

Furthermore, the zone between paraphrase and translation was fairly fluid. Was the Old English Genesis a Bible translation or a piece of poetry inspired by the Bible? Is the *Rijmbijbel* (*Rhyming Bible*) of Jacob van Maerlant, a free narrative account in rhyming verses and based on Peter Comestor's *Historia scholastica*, a bible, or is it not? Petrus Riga's *Aurora* was widely translated in the vernacular; although it no doubt presented the biblical story and helped to advance biblical literacy, it seems a stretch to call it a bible, strictly speaking. Were interlinear glossed psalters translations or aids to understanding the Latin Psalms? One should avoid lumping these texts together as translations, and one should not judge them by modern standards. Instead, the discussion about the vernacular Bible in the Middle Ages should be embedded in a wider investigation of what constitutes biblical literacy and how people achieved it.

Perhaps the most important distinction between medieval and modern vernacular translations is the degree of authority that these texts had. For the most part, medieval Bible translations were not accorded the same degree of authority as the Latin Vulgate. For most late medieval theologians, *the* authoritative Bible remained the Vulgate text. To be sure, vernacular texts could teach biblical history and even moral concepts, but for a further, deeper understanding, the "naked" text of the Bible, in whatever language it was read, needed to be surrounded by a protective hedge of interpretation. When certain heretical groups claimed that such an interpretive fence was not necessary, or indeed detrimental to the true understanding of God's word, vernacular translations could become the subject of controversy.

On both of these last points – paraphrase *versus* translation and biblical authority – perhaps a modern parallel can be drawn to the status of the Qur'an in Islam. It is a dogma that this holy book of Islam is untranslatable.[57] Although many translations into modern languages are available, usually, these texts are referred to as "interpretations" rather than translations, and they do not have the same status as the Arabic original. Similarly, many late medieval theologians thought the Latin Bible to be untranslatable for the purpose of authoritative teaching and theology. However, it was perfectly acceptable to render it in the vernacular in order to edify oneself in the primary sense of Scripture, as long as the translation was clearly marked as a translation and not regarded as God's authoritative word itself.

Finally, the medieval debate about vernacular translations and Scriptural authority continued into the Reformation era. Luther's translation was a novel step, for it was not a translation of the Vulgate, as the earlier translations we have just considered. Luther claimed, rather, to be translating from the "original" Hebrew and Greek texts, which in Luther's time were newly available in printed editions. Not everyone agreed with Luther on the necessity of returning to the Hebrew and Greek original; even in Alcalá, some of the scholars working on the Complutensian Polyglot argued that the Greek New Testament should be corrected by comparing it to the Vulgate, not the reverse, as Erasmus had done.[58] This early Reformation-era discussion, which reflected many of the concerns that were central to the late medieval Bible debate, was by no means over or decided by the time Luther completed his *Bibel auf Deutsch* (*Bible in German*) in 1534.

RESOURCES FOR FURTHER STUDY

It is impossible to mention all the various medieval vernacular Bible traditions in this short chapter. However, the *New Cambridge History of the*

---

[57] Ruthven, *Islam in the World*, 90.
[58] Bentley, *Humanists and Holy Writ*.

Bible has excellent chapters on Bibles in most European languages and Arabic. In addition, *The Practice of the Bible in the Western Middle Ages* contains good introductions to the Bible in English (Richard Marsden), French (Clive Sneddon), and Castilian (Emily Francomano). Study of the Wycliffe Bible should start with Dove's book. Many translations mentioned in the text, including Wycliffe's, are available in modern editions; the bibliography in the back of this book lists a number of them. Links to a great number of digitized manuscripts with French vernacular biblical materials can be found at the Web site http://www.utm.edu/staff/bobp/vlibrary/bible.shtml. For Old English, there is Morrell's *Manual*; for Middle English, Morey offers an excellent introduction. A European Research Council grant "Holy Writ and Lay Readers" sponsors a large project of research into medieval vernacular translations at the University of Groningen: http://www.rug.nl/research/de-samenleving-en-de-kunsten/researchgroups/holyandlay/. Finally, Thompson, McKitterick, and Liuzza address the wider issues of lay literacy and biblical literacy in the Middle Ages.

SUGGESTIONS FOR FURTHER READING

La Bibbia in Italiano tra medioevo e Rinascimento: Atti del convegno internazionale, Firenze, Certosa del Galluzzo, 8–9 novembre 1996. Edited by Lino Leonardi. Firenze: SISMEL, 1998.

Biller, Peter. "The Cathars of Languedoc and Written Materials." In *Heresy and Literacy, 1000–1530*, edited by Peter Biller and Anne Hudson. Cambridge Studies in Medieval Literature, 23, 61–82. Cambridge: Cambridge University Press, 1994.

Bogaert, Pierre-Maurice, and Christian Cannuyer, eds. *Les Bibles en Français. Histoire illustrée du moyen âge à nos jours.* Turnhout: Brepols, 1991.

Boyle, Leonard E. "Innocent III and Vernacular Versions of Scripture." In *The Bible in the Medieval World. Essays in Honour of Beryl Smalley*, edited by Katherine Walsh and Diana Wood. Studies in Church History, Subsidia 4, 97–107. Oxford: Blackwell, 1985.

Deutsche Bibelübersetzungen des Mittelalters. Beiträge eines Kolloquiums im Deutschen Bibel-Archiv. Edited by Heimo Reinitzer and Nikolaus Henkel. Vestigiae Bibliae, Jahrbuch des Deutschen Bibel-Archivs Hamburg, 9/10. Bern: Peter Lang, 1987/1988.

Dove, Mary. *The First English Bible: The Text and Context of the Wycliffite Versions.* Cambridge Studies in Medieval Literature, 66. Cambridge: Cambridge University Press, 2007.

Fowler, David C. *The Bible in Early English Literature.* Seattle: University of Washington Press, 1976.

Gow, Andrew. "Challenging the Protestant Paradigm: Bible Reading in Lay and Urban Contexts of the Later Middle Ages." In *Scripture and Pluralism: Reading the Bible in the Religiously Plural Worlds of the Middle Ages and Renaissance*, edited by Thomas. J. Heffernan and Thomas E. Burman. Studies in the History of Christian Traditions, 123, 161–91. Leiden: E. J. Brill, 2005.

———. "The Bible in Germanic." In *The New Cambridge History of the Bible*. 198–216.

Hargreaves, Henry. "From Bede to Wyclif: Medieval English Bible Translations." *Bulletin of the John Rylands Library* 48 (1965): 118–40.

Infant Milk or Hardy Nourishment? The Bible for Lay People and Theologians in the Early Modern Period. Edited by W. François and August A. Den Hollander. Bibliotheca Ephemeridum Theologicarum Lovaniensium, 221. Leuven: Peeters, 2009.

Liuzza, Roy M. "Who Read the Gospels in Old English?" In *Words and Works: Essays for Fred C. Robinson.* Edited by P. S. Baker and N. Howe. Toronto: University of Toronto Press, 1998.

Marsden, Richard. "Ælfric as Translator: The Old English Prose Genesis." *Anglia* 109 (1991): 317–58.

———. "The Bible in English." In *The New Cambridge History of the Bible*. 217–38.

McGerr, Rosemarie Potz. "Guyart Desmoulins, the Vernacular Master of Histories, and His 'Bible Historiale.'" *Viator. Medieval and Renaissance Studies* 14 (1983): 211–44.

McKitterick, Rosamond. *The Carolingians and the Written Word.* Cambridge: Cambridge University Press, 1989.

Middelnederlandse bijbelvertalingen. Edited by August A. Den Hollander, Erik Kwakkel, and Wybren Scheepsma. Hilversum: Verloren, 2007.

Morey, James H. *Book and Verse: A Guide to Middle English Biblical Literature.* Illinois Medieval Studies. Urbana: University of Illinois Press, 2000.

Morrell, Minnie Cate. *A Manual of Old English Biblical Materials.* Knoxville: University of Tennessee Press, 1965.

Robson, C. A. "The Vernacular Scriptures in France." In *The Cambridge History of the Bible*. 436–52

Stanton, Robert. *The Culture of Translation in Anglo-Saxon England.* Cambridge: D.S. Brewer, 2002.

The Bible in Its Ancient and English Versions. Edited by Henry Wheeler Robinson. Oxford: Clarendon Press, 1954.

Thompson, James Westfall. *The Literacy of the Laity in the Middle Ages.* Burt Franklin Research and Source Works Series, 2. New York: B. Franklin, 1960.

CHAPTER 8

The Bible in Worship and Preaching

Most medieval Christians came to know the Bible not by reading, but by hearing it. It was read aloud in the liturgy of the Church, during Mass and in the prayers of the divine office (the daily liturgical prayer), and during meal times in the monastic refectory. Scripture was also read in prayer, both privately and collectively. Medieval authors quoted the Bible more often from hearing than from a written source, suggesting that medieval Christians, especially monks, had a large memory store of Scripture that resulted from the hours they spent each week reading it aloud. The sources for the liturgical uses of the Bible in the Middle Ages are legion, and they include lectionaries (books that contained selected Bible readings for Mass arranged according to the liturgical calendar) and breviaries (books that contained the text of the daily liturgical prayers of the divine office, for the use of bishops, priests, and deacons who could not always attend the communal prayer). Although collective prayer as a communal practice is well documented from the earliest centuries of Christianity, the sources for private prayer, which included reciting psalms and other Bible readings, are much less forthcoming, at least for the Early Middle Ages. We may suppose that at least some lay people imitated monastic practice by reading Psalms as part of their private devotions. By the thirteenth century, prayer books called Books of Hours had become common among the laity; they elaborated on the "little office of the Virgin Mary," a number of psalms, canticles, and prayers dedicated to the Virgin Mary, to be prayed at particular times of the day. This "little office" started as a monastic devotion, but it became the daily lay devotion par excellence. People also heard the Bible, at least heard about its contents and stories, through preaching. Both prayer and preaching contributed to the huge resonance that biblical stories and ideas had in medieval society.

THE BIBLE IN LITURGY AND PRAYER

Medieval liturgy was not uniform throughout the Middle Ages, even within the western Church. What was read in the Church's worship was determined by a tradition called the rite, and these rites could vary from region to region. Rome had its Roman Rite, Milan the Ambrosian Rite, and Christians in Spain under Muslim rulers followed their own liturgy, the Mozarabic Rite, which dated in part back to the time that Spain had been ruled by the Visigothic kings in the seventh century. Large parts of Europe celebrated the liturgy according to the Gallican Rite, which originated in France in the fifth century, whereas in England the Sarum Rite (established in the eleventh century) was common. In all these rites, however, two kinds of worship services could be distinguished: the celebration of the Eucharist (the Mass), and the ritual of daily prayer (the office).

The liturgy of the Mass began with preparatory prayers (such as the *Kyrie*, "Lord have mercy"), followed by readings from the Scriptures, usually followed by a homily or sermon. Then came the celebration of the Lord's Supper, or the Eucharist. In the ancient Church, non-baptized members of the community (the *catechumens*) were not allowed to attend this part of the Mass and would be led out of the sanctuary just before the celebration of this sacred ritual. But they were certainly allowed to attend the part of the liturgy that was intended for their instruction into the Christian faith, the service of the word. Depending on the rite, there could be two (in the Roman Rite) or three (in, for instance, the Ambrosian and Gallican Rites) Bible readings, and these normally included readings from the Old Testament, the Epistles, and the Gospel, often alternating with a sung Psalm. It is hard to tell how frequently the laity in the Middle Ages attended Mass. At the Fourth Lateran Council of 1215, Pope Innocent III admonished the laity to take communion at least once annually,[1] and to prepare for this by going to confession, but it is impossible to tell whether this frequency was anywhere near what was normal Mass attendance. It was quite common, for instance, to attend Mass without actually partaking in the communion.

In the early Church, the Scripture readings during Mass were initially "continuous readings," which means that one entire book was read from beginning to end over successive Sundays. Since at least the fourth century, it was the custom to have the Bible books relate to the liturgical season.

---

[1] Lateran Council IV (1215), 21, in *Conciliorum oecumenicorum decreta*, ed. Alberigo et al., 245.

The custom seems to have been pioneered in Jerusalem, by Bishop Cyril of Jerusalem (313–386). When, in the late fourth century, the Spanish nun Egeria travelled to Palestine and reported back to her sisters at home about her travels, the appropriateness of the readings to the liturgical time was one of the aspects of the liturgy that struck her most:

What I admire and value most is that all the hymns and antiphons and readings they have, and all the prayers the bishop says, are always relevant to the day which is being observed and to the place in which they are used. They never fail to be appropriate.[2]

The custom was to become common throughout Christendom. The *Ordines romani* (*Roman Liturgical Instructions*), describing the liturgical customs in sixth- and seventh-century Rome, for instance, give detailed information about what was to be read during what season:

In springtime – that is from seven days before the beginning of Lent until the eighth day before Easter – the five books of Moses are read, along with Joshua and Judges. For the seven days before Easter until the Passion of Christ, the Book of Isaiah and the Lamentations of Jeremiah. From Easter Day until Pentecost, the Epistles of the Apostles and Acts.[3] From summertime until the middle of Fall (that is the fifteenth of the kalends of November), Kings, Chronicles. After that, the Books of Solomon, and the Book of Women,[4] Maccabees, and the Book of Tobit, until the calends of December. Then from before Nativity of Our Lord until Epiphany, Isaiah, Jeremiah, and Daniel. Afterwards Ezekiel and the Minor Prophets and Job, until the ides of February. Psalms and the Gospel at all times, and the Apostles. The treatises of Jerome and Ambrose and of the other Fathers[5] are read according to the demands of the season.[6]

Thus, the liturgical readings in Rome cycled through almost the entire canon of Scripture in the course of the liturgical year, with special attention to the prophetic books in the seasons of Lent and Advent. It is not clear, however, whether these readings covered these entire Bible books or only selections from them. In any case, beginning in the twelfth century the selections tended to be shortened; these shorter bible readings are called pericopes. These readings could be done from a bible or from a partial bible, or from a lectionary, a book that contained only the liturgical readings, sometimes in shortened form. The earliest lectionaries date from the sixth

---

[2] Egeria, *Egeria's Travels*, trans. Wilkinson, 46.
[3] As noted in Chapter 3, this was the usual order in which medieval Bibles contained these books in the New Testament.
[4] Esther, Judith, and possibly Ruth. See Bogaert, "La Bible latine," 283–84.
[5] Some manuscripts add here the line "the Passions of the Saints and the Lives of the Catholic Fathers."
[6] *Ordo* XIV, in *Les Ordines Romani*, ed. Andrieu, 24, 39–41.

century. Many medieval Bible manuscripts have indications in the margin for what pericope needed to be read on what date, showing that they were indeed used for reading aloud during the service. The division of the text into *cola et commata*, as was done in the Codex Amiatinus, discussed in Chapter 2, was also clearly a device to help the reading aloud of these bibles. In a poem in praise of scribes, Northumbrian scholar Alcuin prayed that they might

distinguish the proper meaning by *cola* and *commata*, and put each point in the place where it belongs, so that the lector makes no mistakes nor suddenly happens to fall silent when reading before the pious brothers in church.[7]

Liturgical readings were intoned (sung on a single tone) or chanted (sung on a melody). The Old Testament and Epistle readings were usually done from a lectern in the front of the church, whereas the Gospel was carried to the middle of the Church in a more solemn procession and read there. As was pointed out in the last chapter, some of the vernacular translations of the later Middle Ages, such as some copies of the Wycliffite Bible or the Bible translation of the *Devotio moderna*, were probably intended primarily to make it easier for the laity to follow along with the Latin readings.

As is apparent from the *Ordines romani*, these Bible readings were alternated with the reading (or rather singing) of psalms. According to the collection of papal biographies called the *Book of the Popes* (*Liber pontificalis*), the singing of psalms as a liturgical custom was introduced by Pope Celestine in the fifth century, who "appointed that the 150 psalms of David should be chanted antiphonally before the sacrifice by everyone; this was not done previously, but only the epistle of blessed Paul, the apostle, was read, and the holy Gospel."[8] The attribution is probably apocryphal, and the tradition is almost certainly much older than that. Psalm verses were also the basis of many of the other liturgical chants that were sung during the rest of the liturgy: the introit, the graduale, the alleluia, and communion, for instance. For the singing of Psalms, the text of the Gallican Psalter was commonly used throughout western Europe, although the Roman Psalter remained in use in Rome until the thirteenth century. Jerome's Psalms translation made directly from the Hebrew, the so-called Hebrew Psalter, never really caught on for liturgical use.

Psalms were also read and heard in the cycle of daily prayer, the divine office; this practice is known mostly from its use in medieval monasteries,

---

[7] Godman, *Poetry of the Carolingian Renaissance*, 138.
[8] *The Book of the Popes (Liber pontificalis) I*, trans. Loomis, 92.

where monks would convene for daily prayer at eight fixed times throughout the night and day: matins and lauds (typically combined into a single nocturnal office called vigils), prime, terce, sext, nones, vespers, and compline. On the recommendation of the leading sixth-century monastic rule, the Rule of Benedict, all 150 Psalms were prayed during the course of a week.[9] This became the custom in most monasteries in western Europe. Daily prayers were also said in the cathedral churches twice daily. Although Psalms were at the heart of the office prayers in both monasteries and cathedrals, the office prayers also included other biblical readings. The night vigil in monasteries was reserved for reading large parts of the Old and New Testaments, as well as the writings of the fathers. For the nightly vigil, the Rule of Benedict, the leading monastic rule in medieval western Europe, prescribed the reading (or rather chanting) of Psalm 4 (an evening prayer), Psalm 95, a hymn, and six other Psalms with their antiphons (refrains), according to the order of the week. After these, three readings "from the book on the lectern" followed. These readings thus did not follow the liturgical season, but were continuous throughout the year. The Rule says: "Let the divinely inspired books, of both the Old and the New Testament, be read at the night office, and also the commentaries upon them written by the most renowned, orthodox, and Catholic fathers."[10]

Monks were not the only ones to use the Psalter regularly for prayer. As was said previously, in cathedral churches, the Psalms were prayed at regular hours of the day, usually in the morning and in the evening. The use of the Psalter as a personal prayer book is well documented, as early as the Carolingian period. The noblewomen Dhuoda, for instance (mentioned in the previous chapter), advises her son to "say the proper prayers for the respective hours."[11] In addition, she tells him which psalm to recite for what specific moods and occasion. She sees the recitation of psalms as a good way to focus the attention of the mind on specific devotion:

The singing of Psalms, when it is done with the heart's concentration, prepares for our omnipotent God a way to enter us, infusing those who intently meditate with the mystery of prophecy or the grace of compunction . . . Thus the path to Jesus is shown in the sacrifice of divine praise, for when we pour forth compunction in the singing of Psalms, we prepare in our hearts the road by which we come to Jesus. . . . There is nothing in this mortal life by which we can fasten ourselves to God more closely than by the divine praise of Psalm singing.[12]

---

9 Benedict of Nursia, *Regula*, 29, ed. Neufville and trans. De Vogüé, SC 181, 529–35.
10 Benedict of Nursia, *Regula*, 9, ed. Neufville and trans. De Vogüé, SC 181, 512.
11 Dhuoda, *Handbook for William*, trans. Neel, 20.
12 Ibid., 103.

There are psalms for doing penance, for praying for deliverance from evil, for giving thanks, and for praising God, she tells her son. The so-called Golden Psalter, a small but beautifully executed manuscript, which contains all psalms and canticles, may actually be such a psalter intended for personal devotion. (See Chapter 2.)

The daily private reading of the psalms as a devotional practice became even more popular and widespread after the twelfth century. One of the books most commonly found in the possession of laypersons was the Book of Hours, the prayer book for the laity par excellence. The evolution of psalm reading from liturgical and communal to a more personal devotion, read privately from a book, had already started much earlier, with the admonition that monks who could not attend the daily office should read the psalms in private, from a breviary (*breviarium*, meaning "brief compendium"). This eventually became a personal prayer book, not just for monks but also for the laity. Unlike the breviary, a Book of Hours did not contain the entire divine office. It focused instead on a devotional prayer cycle that was thought to be specifically appropriate for the laity, namely, the hours of the Virgin. The psalms of the hours of the Virgin gave the reader the occasion throughout the day to commemorate moments from the Virgin's life, such as the annunciation of Christ's birth, the visitation of Elizabeth, and the Nativity. In addition, the Books of Hours contained the seven penitential psalms (Pss. 6, 32 [Vulg. 31], 38 [Vulg. 37], 51 [Vulg. 50], 102 [Vulg. 101], 130 [Vulg. 129], and 143 [Vulg. 142]), the litany of the saints (a long intercessionary prayer, addressing a large number of saints), and the office of the dead (prayers for the deceased). A calendar at the beginning of the book indicated what prayers were appropriate for which liturgical season or feastdays. Books of Hours could also included short Gospel lessons, called sequences, which focused on the birth and passion of Christ. Some also contained a variety of personal prayers for use at certain occasions, which carried indulgences (papal guarantees of forgiveness of sins), varying from a few days' release from the fire of purgatory to complete forgiveness of sins. One such prayer, in the richly illustrated Bolton Hours, now in the library of York Minster, stated, for instance, "Say this kneland befor the crucifix ilk day anse, and ye sal se the gates of heven opyne in the owre of thi dyinge."[13]

The Franciscans and Dominicans popularized this kind of piety among the laity. Some of the Books of Hours with their lavishly executed illustrations were clearly intended for the very rich, and probably meant to

---

[13] "Say this kneeling before the crucifix every day hence, and you shall see the gates of heaven open in the hour of your dying." York Minster, MS Add. 2, fol. 177r.

showcase the owner's economic status as much as his or her piety. But more modest prayer books were also owned by pious men and women (often beguines) of more humble means. Many of these Books of Hours were made for women (a telltale sign is the female grammatical forms in many of the Latin prayers); interestingly, most of them were completely in Latin, challenging somewhat the notion that educated laypersons did not read Latin. However, as was pointed out in the previous chapter, Geert Groote (d. 1384) also translated the Book of Hours into Dutch in the fourteenth century.

THE BIBLE PREACHED

Bible reading, the celebration of Mass, and personal prayer were not the only acts of worship of the medieval Church. Preaching was one of the most widespread, frequent, and well-attended activities of the medieval church, especially during the later Middle Ages. It also left the most copious written records, in the form of innumerable sermons. Sermons were known by a variety of Latin terms, including *homiliae, tractationes, collationes, sermones, expositiones,* and sometimes even *sententiae.* To an extent, these terms reflect the variety within the genre itself: early medieval sermons were often very dependent on patristic material; monastic sermons could be more expository explanations of the Bible text; academic sermons could be more philosophical and theological in character; and popular sermons could be stirring discourses intended to provoke listeners to conversion and penitence and focused on Christian virtues and vices. Some sermons were purely catechetical in character, in that they intended to teach basic Christian doctrine. Others were dependent on the sequence of the liturgical year, and some were more continuous expositions on parts of Scripture or on particular themes. The number of medieval sermons that has been preserved is quite staggering. In his repertory of medieval sermons, Jean Baptiste Schneyer enumerates some 140,000 sermons alone for the period he covers, 1150 to 1350. This does not even include sermons written in languages other than Latin or the much larger number of sermons written in the later Middle Ages. Most of this material is available only in manuscript form and still waits its first printed edition.

The question, "What is a sermon?" is harder to answer than it seems. The French scholar Jean Longère has defined *sermon* as "a public discourse, founded on some divine revelation, which aims at the instruction or edification of the audience."[14] This definition makes clear how difficult it is to

---

[14] Longère, *La prédication médiévale,* 12.

encompass all medieval sermons with one common denominator. First, the sermon was a "public discourse." Most sermons were delivered in churches, of course, during the worship service. They were preached throughout the year on Sundays and saints' feast days; in Latin, these are called, respectively, *sermones per annum* (also *de tempore*) and *sermones de sanctis*. The first usually take a reading for that particular Sunday as their theme, whereas the latter usually expounded the virtues that were embodied in the life of the particular saint whose feast was celebrated. But sermons could also be preached on special occasions, and outside churches. One of the most famous examples is sermon of Pope Urban II calling for the first Crusade, which was preached in the open air at the closing of the Council of Clermont in 1095, to a group of clergy and laity. The audience for a sermon could vary greatly as well. Some were preached by wandering preachers and were aimed at raising religious enthusiasm among large crowds at revivalist meetings. Others were specifically preached for learned audiences; preaching was one of the regular scholarly activities at medieval universities, and students were required to attend. University sermons were preached on the occasion of the opening of the academic year and on Sundays and feast days during the academic year. Sermons were also preached to monks during the time after dinner, which was set apart for reflection and learning. Usually sermons of this type were called *collationes*. Bernard of Clairvaux's sermons on the Song of Songs are an example of this. Most medieval sermons do not inform us about their intended audience, but some were collected with a special audience in mind (such as cathedral clergy, or married women). These are called, in Latin, *sermones ad status*.

Medieval sermons were, in Longère's words, "founded on some divine revelation." This could mean a variety of things. Most were based on Scripture, and were intended to explain Scripture or to communicate scriptural content to their audience. "Scripture" should be defined loosely in this context, however. Medieval preaching could also be based on a hymn, a phrase from the liturgy, or an episode from the lives of the saints. Later medieval sermons (sometimes called the "scholastic" sermons) took as their beginning a Bible verse (*thema*), sometimes complemented by a second, closely related Bible verse (*prothema*), but in the rest of the sermon, the preacher was free to touch on a wide variety of other Bible passages and verses, as we will see. Finally, sermons aimed "at the instruction or edification of the audience." This implies a wide range of possibilities. Some were exegetical in nature, and followed a biblical passage fairly closely, to explain it verse by verse. Others intended to give moral instruction and elaborated on the virtues and vices. Yet other sermons, especially those intended for the laity, were not so much exegetical (expounding scripture) as catechetical (teaching doctrine). They explained basic points of Christian doctrine and were often based on the Lord's Prayer or the Creed, two texts that laypeople were supposed to know by heart as a minimum token of Christian education.

Thus, the label "sermon" covers a wide variety of texts. The study of these texts offers a wealth of insight, not just about exegetical practice but also about the worldview and mentality of the medieval believer. However, sermons in their written form do not always tell us everything we would like to know about the actual practice of preaching. There were no sound recordings in the Middle Ages, nor has a medieval sermon been preserved in exactly the way it was preached, as we will see.

Since early Christian times, preaching was one of the duties of the bishop. The sermons of Caesarius, the sixth-century bishop of Arles, constitute a very lively example of episcopal preaching. More than 200 sermons survive by this prolific preacher, whom contemporaries said could even be heard preaching in his sleep.[15] It is not entirely clear whether ordinary priests were also permitted to preach in this period, but Caesarius of Arles himself argued forcefully that they should not only be allowed but even encouraged to preach as well. He also defended the right of deacons to preach, although in practice this probably meant reading from sermons by the church fathers during the church service.[16] Lay preaching required episcopal permission, even in the later Middle Ages, when bishops no longer held a monopoly on preaching and parochial preaching had become common. The movements of the Waldensians and Lollards, for instance, as we have seen in the previous chapter, incurred the accusation of heresy because they promoted lay preaching without official episcopal consent.

A BRIEF HISTORY OF SERMONS

The Early Middle Ages

For the Early Middle Ages, the main sources we have are sermon collections, called homiliaries. These homiliaries contained short model sermons, which for the most part were abbreviations of patristic sermons. Caesarius's sermons, for instance, were frequently used for this purpose, and so were sermons by Gregory the Great and Augustine. The Venerable Bede wrote one in the early eighth century, whereas that of Paul the Deacon, compiled

---

[15] Kienzle and D'Avray, "Sermons," 661.
[16] Caesarius of Arles, *Césaire d'Arles, Sermons au peuple*, ed. Delage, SC 175, 58.

a century later, was also widely used. Several of the biblical commentators who worked in the school of Auxerre, such as Haimo and Heiric, also compiled homiliaries, and Haimo's was subsequently translated into Old French. Ælfric of Eynsham wrote one in Old English, also chiefly excerpted from Haimo of Auxerre. These homiliaries were meant to provide the clergy with sermon materials on which they could draw for their own preaching. It is also quite possible that less experienced preachers simply read the scripted sermon aloud. Paul the Deacon's homiliary was excerpted "from the treatises and sermons of several Catholic fathers," and presented to the bishops "to be read in the churches of Christ."[17] Ælfric intended for his homilies to be "read in their entirety by the ministers of God in church." In his (Latin) preface, addressed to Archbishop Sigeric, he says,

I have set the matter which I have turned into two books, because I thought that it were less tedious to hear, if the one book were read in the course of one year, and the other in the year following.[18]

The Third Council of Tours, in 813, seems to recommend a somewhat freer use of the sermon material:

Every bishop should have homilies, containing the necessary admonitions, by which the flock should be educated on the Catholic faith, in as far as they can understand it, on the perpetual reward for the good, and the eternal damnation of the bad, the future resurrection of the dead, and the last judgement, and with which works one might deserve eternal life, and with which one might be excluded from it. And everyone should zealously translate these homilies into the Romance or German language, so that all may more easily understand what is said.[19]

Homiliaries could also be used for personal devotional reading. Hrabanus Maurus, for instance, compiled a collection of sermons for Emperor Lothar, in order "so that you might have something which could be read in your presence, if it pleases you, at the appropriate times during spring and summer."[20]

Preaching was high on the agenda of the Carolingian reform movement. The homiliary of Paul the Deacon was composed at the request of Charlemagne himself, to replace the deficient homiliaries that were in use for the

[17] Charlemagne, *Preface to Paulus Diaconus' Homiliarius*, PL 95, 955–56 .
[18] Ælfric, *Sermones Catholici*, ed. Thorpe, 3.
[19] *Concilium Turonense* (813), in *Concilia aevi Karolini*, ed. Werminghoff, MGH Concilia, 2.1, 288.
[20] Hrabanus Maurus, *Epistola* 49, ed. Dümmler, MGH Epistolae, 5, 509. Mayke de Jong has pointed out that Hrabanus refers here to mealtime reading, rather than reading in Church; De Jong, "The Empire as *Ecclesia*: Hrabanus Maurus and Biblical *Historia* for Rulers," 191n.

nocturnal office.[21] Several councils and chapters in the eighth and ninth centuries warned the bishops and the clergy not to neglect preaching in their churches. The Council of Pavia of 845–50, for instance, complained that "the teaching and preaching for the people is not being administered as it should, through the negligence of in part the priests and other bishops, and partly the people; the negligence of priests can never be excused."[22] This has led some church historians to conclude that "by the end of the eighth century, preaching was not regularly heard except in cathedral churches, and not always there."[23] To them, the abundance of homiliaries suggested that "preaching at the dawn of the Carolingian Age was often not much more than the reading of a sermon from the homiliary."[24] It is hard, however, to draw any conclusions on the actual state of preaching in the Carolingian Empire based on church legislation, and it is impossible to say whether these homiliaries were indeed always preached as "canned" sermons. Ælfric, cited earlier, anticipated a certain ennui on the part of his audience and thought that alternating the cycle of sermons every year was sufficient to stave it off. But it is impossible to tell in how far preachers may have extemporized on the materials they found in these homiliaries. The manuscripts of the homiliaries, as opposed to their neat printed form, suggest that they were often used as a preacher's notes rather than scripted sermons. The relationship between the written form of the sermons and the actual preaching is more complicated than it seems at first sight.

The Carolingian abbot Hrabanus Maurus, for instance, was the author of two series of sermons, one for major feast days and one for the liturgical year (per annum), on readings from the Gospels and the Letters of Paul. The first series is dedicated to Archbishop Haistulf of Mainz and was explicitly written at the latter's request to "preach to the people," to educate them on the virtues and vices and "everything else that was necessary" for them to reach salvation.[25] Most of the content of these sermons was catechetical. In Hrabanus's words, they touched on

the various kinds of virtues, that is, faith, hope, and love, chastity, continence, and other kinds of virtues, and how by striving for them and guarding them they can please God, and receive eternal life in heaven with the holy angels. After that, we

21 Charlemagne, *Preface to Paulus Diaconus' Homiliarius*, PL 95, 955–56.
22 Council of Pavia, 845–850, c. 3, in *Die Konzilien der karolingischen Teilreiche*, ed. Hartmann, MGH Concilia, 3, 211.
23 Old, *The Reading and Preaching of the Scriptures*, 190.
24 Ibid., 192.
25 Hrabanus Maurus, *Epistola* 6, ed. Dümmler, MGH Epistolae, 5, 391.

add some words on the various errors and seductions of vices by which the ancient enemy deludes and deceives the human race, that is, bad pride and arrogance, anger, envy, fraud, avarice, gluttony and fornication, and similar things, so that the sheep of Christ know how to evade the bites of the ferocious wolf and savage dragon, and, being forewarned, take heed of them.[26]

Hrabanus makes liberal use of patristic sources, which may sometimes deceive the reader when he addresses the audience in the first person. Such is the case, for instance, in the sermon where Hrabanus preaches against the (in his eyes, pagan) custom of "howling at the moon":

When I remained some days quietly at home, and was pondering for your benefit how I could enlarge your progress in the Lord, suddenly, there ensued such a clamor of the people on that day, in the evening tide and around nightfall, that its irreligiosity reached to Heaven. And when I inquired what the meaning of this clamor was, they told me that this howling of yours was aiding the waning moon, and it sought to prevent its fading with this effort.[27]

Although Hrabanus appears to be relating a firsthand experience here, the entire passage is actually a citation from a sermon by the fifth-century bishop of Turin, Maximus. This raises the question of how recognizable Maximus's experience of a howling fifth-century Italian mob would have been to a ninth-century German audience. It is hard to tell, and we will never know for sure how exactly this particular sermon was used and reused. In the assessment of the preaching practice in the Early Middle Ages, one needs to take into account the tensions between orality and written culture and the question of to what extent the surviving written records reflect actual homiletic practice. The proliferation of homiliaries in this period, however, suggests that they were, in some form, seen as useful tools for the exegetical and catechetical instruction of the laity.

The Twelfth Century

The form and content of medieval sermons, the context in which they were preached, and the manner in which they were committed to writing changed considerably in the twelfth century. Scholars have identified a veritable "sermon revolution" occurring in the century between 1150 and 1250, because of the huge rise in the number of sermons preserved in

---

26 Ibid.
27 Hrabanus, *Homiliae de Festis*, PL 110, 9–135; *Homiliae in Evangelia et Epistulas*, PL 110, 135–467. The sermon "against those who howl at the moon" is on col. 78–79.

written form. One of the factors that may have contributed to this is the rise of the Dominican and Franciscan orders, two religious orders founded in the early thirteenth century, which specifically made preaching to the laity their main vocation. But the rise in the number of sermons began several decades before the appearance of these orders. It may be rooted in the changes in the character of medieval education and the growth of literacy in the twelfth century. Schools, and later universities, took great care to make preaching into one of their educational goals, and, with the expansion of literacy, especially among the middle classes in society, the demand for written sermons grew. The change was not just a matter of quantity. The character of the medieval sermon also changed.

Some sermons recorded in writing in this period were preached by monks for the edification and instruction of their fellow monks. The Cistercian order in particular placed great importance on preaching; Bernard of Clairvaux produced an impressive cycle of over eighty sermons on the Song of Songs, covering only the first few chapters of this Bible book. As we saw in Chapter 6, the boundary between sermon and commentary is sometimes hard to draw. These monastic "collationes" were written for monks to hear in the hour set apart for meditation on the *lectio divina*. As Bernard told his fellow brothers in his first sermon, these were more advanced than the sermons addressed to less mature lay audiences: "The preacher who desires to follow Saint Paul's method of teaching will give [the laity] milk, rather than solid food." However, for his monastic audience, Bernard prescribes three "loaves of bread": the book of Ecclesiastes, which warns against the love of the world; the book of Proverbs, which warns against the excessive love of oneself; and the final bread, the Song of Songs, teaches the love of God.[28] Cistercians such as Geoffrey of Auxerre and John of Ford preached very similar sermon cycles.

After the twelfth century, however, sermons were increasingly preached by itinerant preachers to the laity at large. Ironically, this type of popular preaching seems to have been pioneered by people who were deemed heretics, such as Waldensians and Cathars; the only way the Church could fight these heresies was by meeting them on equal terms, by preaching to the laity. At the Fourth Lateran Council of 1215, Innocent III exhorted the bishops to appoint special preachers to "minister the Word of God to the people," especially when they themselves were unable to attend to these

---

[28] Bernard of Clairvaux, *In Cant.*, 1, 1, in Bernard of Clairvaux, *Sancti Bernardi Opera*, ed. Leclercq, Rochais, and Talbot, 1: 1. An online translation is available at http://archive.org/details/StBernardsCommentaryOnTheSongOfSongs.

duties.[29] Perhaps the earliest examples of exhortative preaching by itinerant preachers were in connection with the Crusades. The word about the first Crusade was spread by preachers such as Peter the Hermit, who raised a huge popular following with his stirring message. Unfortunately, this kind of preaching also led to excesses, such as violence against the local Jewish communities. Despite condemnations by the official church authorities, several Jewish settlements in the Rhineland were attacked by marauding crusading mobs, inspired by a mistaken notion of waging war against those whom they took to be the enemies of God.

Bernard of Clairvaux also preached for larger audiences outside the monastery. He seems to have been well aware that this brought him into conflict with his monastic vow of *stabilitas*, to stay in one place and not venture outside his monastery. He called himself the "chimaera of his age, neither cleric nor layman; I have laid down the life of a monk, but not its habit."[30] His monastic vocation did not stop him from traveling wide and far. In 1146, at the request of Pope Eugenius III, he traveled to preach the Second Crusade. After a very successful sermon at Vezelay in France in the presence of the king of France, Bernard went to Germany to deliver the message there. On these trips, he was probably accompanied by someone who provided simultaneous translations into German. Contrary to Peter the Hermit, however, a large part of Bernard's message was aimed at protecting the Jews from overzealous crusaders.

Preaching was thus increasingly seen as an important pastoral duty of the clergy towards the laity. The prominent Paris theologian Peter the Chanter, as we saw in Chapter 6, listed the activities of the educated cleric as reading, disputation, and preaching. He emphasized that all intellectual activity at the schools should be subordinated to the latter.[31] The sermon collections of Maurice of Sully, bishop of Paris in the mid-twelfth century, attest to this spirit. Many of these were written, and probably delivered, in the vernacular. Maurice had close connections to the abbey of Saint Victor, which was not only an influential center of biblical and theological studies, as we saw in Chapter 5, but also an important center of preaching, both for its own community of canons and for outsiders. It was no coincidence that in the second half of the twelfth century, the abbey of Saint Victor

[29] Lateran Council IV (1215), 10, in *Conciliorum oecumenicorum decreta*, ed. Alberigo *et al.*, 239–40. On-line translation provided by the Global Catholic Network, at http://www.ewtn.com/library/councils/lateran4.htm.
[30] Bernard of Clairvaux, *Epistola* 250, 4, in Bernard of Clairvaux, *Sancti Bernardi Opera*, ed. Leclercq, Rochais, and Talbot, 8:147.
[31] Peter the Chanter, *Verbum Adbreviatum*, 1, 1, ed. Boutry, CCCM 196, 9.

assumed pastoral responsibility over the student population of Paris and the canons served as its main confessors. Preaching was part of this pastoral responsibility. We know of sermon collections by a number of Victorine canons, especially Achard, Geoffrey, and Richard of Saint Victor. About 100 of Richard's sermons have been preserved; most of these were intended for saints' feast days and other occasions of the liturgical calendar, but others carry more generic titles, such as "On the fear of the Lord" or "On spiritual health." It seems that, unlike the sermons of Maurice of Sully, which were intended for the "people," Richard's intended audience was the narrower circle of the canons at Saint Victor.

Mendicant Preaching

If the great turning point in the history of popular preaching was the rise of schools and universities in the twelfth century, the coming of two new religious orders, the Franciscans (founded 1209) and the Dominicans (founded 1215), did much to intensify this development. These orders defined the following of Christ not primarily as a life of ascetic seclusion but as the apostolic life, that is, the life of a wandering preacher who was dedicated to evangelical poverty. Francis of Assisi, for instance, took his inspiration from the verse in Matthew 10:8–10: "As you go, proclaim the message: 'The Kingdom of Heaven is upon you'. Provide no gold, silver, or copper to fill your purse, no pack for the road, no second coat, no shoes, no stick; the worker earns his keep." Both the Franciscans and the Dominicans trained their members to be effective preachers and to assist the clergy in their duty of instructing the laity. More often and more accurately, however, they took over this task from the secular clergy because, in their view, the latter were not doing it very well. Needless to say, this sometimes led to tensions between the two groups. Still, the new orders could count on the strong support of the pope, Innocent III, and his successors and were given many privileges, among them the right to preach without specific license from the local bishop.[32] By the middle of the thirteenth century, the wandering preacher had become a prominent feature of medieval society.

Some of these Franciscans and Dominicans were celebrities similar to today's pop stars. Preachers such as John of Viterbo, Berthold of Regensburg and Bernardino of Siena, for instance, provoked great outbursts of enthusiasm in their audiences. John of Viterbo's preaching led to the popular "Alleluia" movement, named after the alleluias that its followers chanted,

---

[32] Martin IV, *Ad fructus uberes*, in *Bullarium Franciscanum*, ed. Eubel, 3, 480.

in mid-thirteenth-century Italy; this gave a great deal of political power to the revered Dominican. Some of the most colorful late medieval mendicant preachers, such as Bernardino of Siena, were connected to the late medieval mendicant reform known as the Observance. Bernardino was such a popular preacher that the medieval chronicler Salimbene de Adam reported that he was followed by a great number of men and women, sometimes for "sixty or a hundred miles around." Especially effective were his sermons on the Antichrist and the Last Judgment; when he preached these, his audience "all trembled like a reed in the water."[33] After one sermon by Bernardino de Siena, the crowd was known to have shouted "Jesus, Jesus, Jesus," for three hours. Some charismatic preachers were even known to perform miracles.[34] Although this kind of spectacle probably did not accompany most weekly sermons, dynamic preaching had become frequent in the later Middle Ages, even to the extent that some Church authorities worried that there might be too much of it. In 1508, at the request of clergy and citizens, the bishop of Breslau sought to limit the number of sermons preached in the city, one of many such prohibitions.[35]

WRITTEN SOURCES AND THE SPOKEN WORD

We know a great deal more about medieval sermons than we know about the actual practice of medieval preaching. A sermon is a written source, while preaching is an oral performance. Sermons, in their written form, can reflect various forms of the live performance. They can be a report on an actual sermon that was delivered, by someone in the audience who took notes; we call this a *reportatio*. Many sermons by popular preachers were recorded in this fashion and were made into sermon collections afterward. The risk here was that the recorder might misunderstand the preacher and misrepresent his words, even though it was common practice for a preacher to correct a *reportatio* before the written form was circulated. Sermons could also be written down by the preacher himself, either for use by private readers or for others to use as a model sermon. Of course, this type of written sermon is also to a certain extent an "ideal" form and does not necessarily reflect the way it was delivered. Some sermons intended to be models were extremely abbreviated and often consisted of no more than a sketch or a truncated form. Some collections of "notes" or "sentences" of

[33] Salimbene de Adam, *Chronicle*, trans Baird, Baglivi, and Kane, 566.
[34] Hanska, "Reconstructing the Mental Calendar of Medieval Preaching," 294.
[35] McLaughlin, "The Word Eclipsed," 77.

Hugh of Saint Victor, for instance, were small sermon sketches, intended to be extemporized upon, either by the author or by whoever used the material for his own sermons. It is not uncommon to have sermons by medieval preachers in various forms, one by *reportatio* and another being the author's own version. If a sermon was used as a model, it is also difficult to tell how it was used by subsequent preachers, unless by chance we find the same sermon among the work of another preacher.

Medieval sermons, especially in the twelfth century, were often attributed to several different authors. Richard of Saint Victor, for instance, was the author of a series of seven sermons "On the Lord's Prayer," which presumably originated as a series of "collationes" for the brethren at the abbey of Saint Victor. The same set has also been attributed to Hugh of Saint Victor, Maurice of Sully, Peter Comestor, and even Peter Abelard. This shows that the authorship of sermons was often considered secondary to their utility; sermons could circulate without an author's attribution and be freely reused by other preachers.

All this means that the language of the written sermon is not necessarily the language in which it was delivered. A sermon delivered in the vernacular may have been translated into Latin by the reporter, and sermons written in Latin in a model sermon collection may have been intended to be translated ad hoc in the pulpit. The admonition of the Council at Tours, cited earlier, gives a clear indication that sermons in Latin homiliaries were intended to be preached in the vernacular, for instance. It is difficult to imagine that an audience would have been addressed in a language they did not understand. A few sermons have also been preserved in the vernacular. In the eleventh century, Wulfstan, the archbishop of York, wrote a number of sermons in Old English. Of particular importance is his *Sermon of the Wolf to the English* (a pun on Wulfstan's name), about the coming of Antichrist, in which he argued that the persecutions suffered by the English at the hands of the Vikings were God's punishment for their own sins.[36] The manuscript of this sermon, attached to the so-called York Gospels, is of particular interest because it may have been corrected by the author himself before wider distribution. In the twelfth century, Maurice of Sully's sermons were written in both French and Latin; sometimes we even find the same sermon in both languages. This all suggests that preaching in the vernacular, at least to the common people, was the norm, despite the fact that many of these sermons in their written form exist in Latin

---

[36] Wulfstan of York, *Sermo Lupi ad Anglos*, ed. Whitelock. An electronic edition with translation by Melissa Bernstein Ser is available at http://english3.fsu.edu/~wulfstan/.

only. Preaching in Latin was probably the norm only for a more learned audience, such a monastic or university community. A considerable group of sermons, the so-called macaronic sermons, mix both languages, and some scholars even have suggested that bilingual preaching was a common practice.[37] It certainly seems to have been common practice to cite Scripture first in Latin, before translating it into the vernacular, even in vernacular sermons. It could also be the case that the "mixing" was done by the scribe who wrote down the sermon.

Although some preachers may have preached from notes or books, it is very likely that the best sermons were delivered by more experienced preachers without the written source at hand. Pope Innocent III, according to Salimbene, was accustomed to preach with a book open before him, which raised some questions among his chaplains as to why a man as experienced a preacher as he needed that. "I do it for your benefit, as an example to you, because you are ignorant and yet you are ashamed to learn," the pope answered.[38]

Some reports on actual medieval preaching exist, but these often report on exceptional performances by celebrity preachers, and thus may not be very representative. Most sermons were preached from a pulpit, and some medieval village churches still preserve beautiful examples of this type of church furniture. They were sometimes decorated with carved scenes from the Bible. A sounding board was often attached above the pulpit, to improve acoustics. A sixteenth-century print by Pieter Breughel the Elder, entitled "Faith," shows such a medieval pulpit, where a preacher delivers his sermon to a captive audience (see Photo 9). Sermons by itinerant friars were often preached outdoors, with the preacher standing on a raised platform. The church of Santa Maria Nuova in Viterbo still has an eleventh-century stone pulpit on the outside of the church, to facilitate public preaching in the town square. It is popularly known as "the chair of Thomas Aquinas," who is said to have preached here in 1266.[39] Berthold of Regensburg preached his sermons from a small wooden structure that looked like a bell tower, with a wind vane atop, so that his audience could use the wind direction to determine the best place to sit.[40]

Some preachers were known to use props during the sermon. One fifteenth-century Franciscan preacher, it is told, hid a human skull under his robe, which he would show the audience suddenly, with great dramatic

---

[37] Constable, "The Language of Preaching in the Twelfth Century."
[38] Salimbene de Adam, *Chronicle*, trans. Baird, Baglivi, and Kane, 5.
[39] Spiazzi, *San Tommaso d'Aquino*, 103.
[40] Salimbene de Adam, *Chronicle*, trans. Baird, Baglivi, and Kane, 566.

FIDES   MAXIME A NOBIS CONSERVANDA EST PRAECIPVE IN RELIGIONEM,
QVIA DEVS PRIOR ET POTENTIOR EST QVAM HOMO.

Photo 9. Allegory of Faith. The figure of *Ecclesia* (Church) is surrounded by the instruments of Christ's passion. Several sacraments are depicted (eucharist, baptism, confession, and marriage) but the largest part of the print shows a preacher on a pulpit addressing his audience. Philippe Galle, engraving after Pieter Breughel the Elder, *The World of Seven Virtues: Faith*. Photo (c) The Metropolitan Museum of Art, New York. Image source: Art Resource, New York.

effect, to remind them of the brevity of human life.[41] Another preacher, a certain Brother Gerard of Modena, would cover his head with his hood, pause in the midst of his sermon, and keep the people waiting in suspense.[42] Some of the best sermons received intermittent applause, whereas some of the more boring sermons may have been interrupted by chatter in the audience. When a Franciscan preacher in late medieval England rebuked a lady for speaking during the sermon, she responded in kind: "Marry, sir, I beshrew [curse] his heart that babbleth most of us both! For I do but whisper a word with my neighbour here, and thou babblest there all this hour."[43] In more extreme cases, the audience might walk out. Caesarius of Arles, in the fifth century, admonished his deacons to close the doors

[41] Owst, *Preaching in Medieval England*, 351.
[42] Salimbene de Adam, *Chronicle*, trans. Baird, Baglivi, and Kane, 54.
[43] Owst, *Preaching in Medieval England*, 188.

of the church, so that the faithful would not stray during the sermon.[44] Salimbene relates as a sign of Fra Berthold's preaching skill that no one ever got up and walked away before the sermon was ended. The alleged soporific effect of sermons was clearly the brunt of as many jokes in the Middle Ages as it is today.

Preaching in the Middle Ages was not confined to bishops, parish priests, monks, and mendicants. Laymen were also known to preach, with episcopal permission. Robert of Anjou (king of Naples 1309–1343) preached on numerous occasions, even addressing the papal court in Avignon. Despite the prohibition against it, lay preaching was commonly practiced in the circles of Waldensians and Lollards, as we have seen in the previous chapter. One satirical poem of the fifteenth century mocked Sir John Oldcastle for his desire to "bable the Bibel day and night," a behavior regarded as very "unkyndly (unbecoming) for a knight."[45] This kind of "Bible babble," as lay preaching was mockingly called, probably occurred within the intimate circles of house churches. Cathars likewise spread their religious beliefs through the private preaching of the "perfecti," the inner circle of initiates of this heretical sect. To church officials, however, such as Alain of Lille (discussed later), secret preaching seemed a telltale sign of heresy.[46] As Carolyn Muessig has pointed out, in an oral world, religious ideas were most often communicated and transmitted through speech. The same is true for heretical ideals, and this is why lay preaching was regarded with just as much suspicion by the church authorities as the spread of the Bible in the vernacular.[47]

Women were not generally permitted to preach in public. Paul's warning that "women are to remain quiet in church since they have no permission to speak" (1 Cor. 14:34) was seen as a binding injunction against female preaching. By contrast, preaching by women to women, within the more enclosed circle of the cloistered community, was quite common in religious communities, often despite (or simply out of sight of) the church authorities. However, there are several exceptions to the rule, especially if the female preacher had an untainted reputation for saintliness. The German abbess Hildegard of Bingen (1098–1179), for instance, went on several preaching tours around Germany, after obtaining papal permission. Due to her saintly reputation, this was not considered problematic. Rose of

[44] Caesarius of Arles, *Life, Testament, Letters*, trans. Klingshirn, 22.
[45] Wright, *The Political Poems and Songs Relating to English History*, 244.
[46] Alain of Lille, *Summa de arte praedicandi*, PL 210, 111D.
[47] Muessig, "Sermon, Preacher, and Society in the Middle Ages," 83.

Viterbo, a laywomen, and Catherine of Siena, a Dominican tertiary, likewise preached sermons in the public sphere. The early-sixteenth-century Spanish abbess Juana Vásquez Gutiérrez's fame for preaching was such that even Cardinal Cisneros and King Charles V could occasionally be found among her audience. She was even known to speak out critically about the use of indulgences and other contentious topics.[48]

Preaching was not an exclusively Christian religious practice either. Sermons were preached within the Jewish community, both in the house and in the synagogue, with the same fervor as they were within the Christian Church. The Hebrew word for sermon is *derashah*, which is related to *derash* and *midrash* (see also Chapter 5). The Torah scroll was read from every Sabbath in synagogue worship, and also preached on, but sermons could also be delivered on special occasions: marriage, circumcision, or death, at private homes.

TOOLS FOR THE MEDIEVAL PREACHER

As we saw earlier, by the end of the twelfth century, preaching had come to be seen as the most important goal of clerical education at the schools in Paris. One of the challenges was how to connect the Scripture from the lectionary to the catechetical and moral instruction seen as the main purpose of preaching to the people. Of course, the medieval exegetical scheme of the threefold sense, literal, allegorical, and moral, already offered a basic form for delivering a sermon, covering the exegetical, doctrinal, and ethical dimensions of the text. For a modern reader of medieval sermons, it seems that in many medieval sermons, the exegetical aspect took second seat to the allegory and moral instruction, however. The later medieval or "scholastic" sermon could be rather free in its treatment of the biblical passage it took as its starting point, and it was likely to fan out in all directions. The sound advice that modern preachers often receive, to stick to one point for the whole sermon, hardly applied to medieval sermons. Instead, many medieval sermons were built on numbered lists, because numbers were great rhetorical and mnemonic devices. Sermons could be held on the four cardinal virtues, the four Last Things (death, judgment, heaven, and hell), the seven deadly sins, the seven petitions of the Lord's Prayer, the seven gifts of the Holy Spirit, the Ten Commandments, or the twelve articles of faith (also known as the Apostle's Creed).

---

[48] Roest, "Female Preaching in the Late Medieval Franciscan Tradition," 150–51.

A number of scholarly tools existed to help the clergy construct an effective sermon, and to help them make the transition from exegesis to sermon. The most prominent of these were the *Artes praedicandi* (*The Arts of Preaching*), but concordances and *distinctiones* also helped the preacher to find the right texts, and to expound on the multiple meaning of single words, whereas exempla collections helped him find appropriate stories to illustrate his theological or moral points. These tools can give us great insight into how medieval preachers constructed their sermons.

The Artes praedicandi

An *Ars praedicandi*, the "art of preaching," was essentially a preachers' handbook for rhetoric, applying the classical rules of rhetoric, as taught in the schools following the guidelines of Quintilian and Cicero, to the making of sermons. The first such guide for preachers on how to compose a sermon was written by Alain of Lille in the twelfth century. In his preface, Alain stated that, although there were how-to guides written for confession, prayer, and exegesis,

because few things have yet been written about preaching, of what kind it needs to be, by whom and to whom it should be offered, and about what, and how, and when, and where it should be, at present we consider it a worthy matter to write a short treatise about this, for the use of our peers.[49]

Alain's preface starts out with the allegory of Jacob's vision of the ladder to heaven, on which angels ascended and descended (Gen. 28:12). There are seven steps leading to perfection, Alain says. The first is confession of one's sins; the second, prayer; the third, thanksgiving. After this comes the reading of Scripture, learning the interpretation of Scripture, and teaching the interpretation of Scripture. But the final and highest step of this ladder is preaching, "when one teaches in public that what one has learned from Scripture."[50] Just as the angels ascend and descend this ladder, Alain points out that in preaching there is both a movement of man towards God and a movement of God towards man: the first is theological, and the second moral instruction.

According to Alain, every sermon should take a "theological authority" as its beginning, "as its foundation, especially from the Gospels, Psalms, Epistles of Paul, or the books of Solomon. For in these especially resounds

---

[49] Alain of Lille, *Summa de arte predicandi*, PL 210, 111BC.
[50] Ibid., 111B.

moral instruction."[51] Alain's instruction reflected the practice of the scholastic sermons, which usually started out with a biblical verse, called *thema*. Although the *thema* was normally dictated by a reading from the lectionary, a preacher was free to choose the second verse, called the *prothema*. After the *thema* came the *captatio benevolentiae*. A good preacher needs to capture the benevolence of the listener by his own humility, and by pointing to the usefulness of his words, by saying,

that in these things, he is preaching the word of God, so that it may bear fruits in their minds. He is not doing this to gather earthly riches, but for their advancement and spiritual profit; not in order to be excited by shouts of the audience, to be flattered by sweet compliments, or mollified by theatrical applause, but in order to instruct their souls, and that they should not consider who is speaking, but what is said.[52]

Alain next discusses chapter by chapter the various virtues and vices the preacher might chose to preach upon (gluttony, lust, avarice, laziness, envy; against joy, hope, obedience, perseverance, etc.), and he presents various Bible verses that such a sermon might take as its authority. The second part of his treatise includes a description of the qualities a good preacher should possess, and the possible audience he might address (university masters, clergy, knights, princes and judges, religious women, widows, and married laity), along with a list of moral topics that are especially appropriate for people in that particular walk of life. Alain here essentially presents a number of mini-sermons, which could be used and adapted by the readers of his treatise.

Lexicography

In addition to the *artes*, there were a number of more specialized lexicographical tools, which allowed scholars either to quickly find a Bible verse that could be used as a proof text or illustration or to find an appropriate story to illustrate a moral or theological point, or elaborate on the meaning of a particular word in the Bible text. These were, strictly speaking, exegetical tools, adapted specifically for the making of sermons.

The most popular of these genres was perhaps the so-called *distinctions* (*distinctiones*), lists of biblical key words that listed for each word three or

---

[51] Ibid., 113C.
[52] Ibid., 113D.

more allegorical and moral applications, with the relevant biblical verse. An example from Alain's *distinctiones* collection illustrates its potential use in sermons:

Wormwood:

- properly speaking, the name for the devil, on account of its bitterness, because his teaching is bitter. Hence it says in Revelation: "The name of the star is Wormwood," (Rev. 8:11) that is, the devil.
- also: bitter doctrine. Hence, in the same place: "And the third part of the waters was made into wormwood," that is, bitter doctrine.
- also: punishment. Hence in Jeremiah: "Wormwood and gall, etc." (Lam. 3:19)[53]

Thus, if a preacher encountered the word *wormwood* in his text, he could find the appropriate word associations, preach on their various meanings, and lace his sermon with corresponding Bible texts. He could build an entire sermon just on the various uses of one word.

Concordances facilitated the quick lookup of biblical passages, by placing the key words in alphabetical order, and giving the chapter and verse for each occurrence. The first concordances were authored by Dominicans from Saint Jacques in Paris in the thirteenth century; they used the standardized chapter division for the Vulgate text that came into place by the late twelfth century. The Dominican scholars divided these chapters into even shorter sections designated by letters (see Chapter 4).

There was more than one way to organize a concordance, however. Even more useful for the preacher than an alphabetical list were topical concordances, which listed appropriate bible texts by topic. One such concordance can be found today in the collection of Chicago's Newberry Library. It starts out,

Here begins the concordance of the Bible, organized in five books. The first book deals with the topics pertaining to the deprivation of the first Man, and their opposites. There are four parts to it: first, sin and its effects. Second, the principle vices and their rubrics. Third, the vices of the mouth and their rubrics, and their opposites, and the five senses. The fourth part consists of the previously mentioned vices in combination, and their opposites.[54]

---

[53] Alain of Lille, *Liber in distinctionibus dictionum theologicalium*, PL 210: 687–1012. Unfortunately, the layout of the medieval manuscript was not followed in this edition, which as a result sometimes rendered the highly visually structured text completely incomprehensible.

[54] Newberry Library, MS Case 19.1, fol. 1r.

The concordance itself gives appropriate Bible verses for each topic. A preaching chosing to preach on "sin and its effects," for instance, could find the following verses to start his sermons: "His hand pierced the winding serpent (Job 26:13)," or: "Let destruction tread upon him like a king (Job 18:14)," or "Evil pursueth sinners (Prov. 13:21)."[55]

Previously, Bible reading was done discursively, slowly digesting the text from beginning to end. But after the twelfth century, the use of these lexical tools enabled the preacher to jump immediately to the place in the text he needed for his particular purpose. These tools revolutionized not only preaching but also the way in which texts were read, not unlike the way digitized books and electronic search tools have changed the use of today's library collections.

Bestiaria, Lapidaria, *and Exempla*

To draw more allegorical meaning from a certain text, a preacher could also use so-called bestiaries and lapidaries, books that provided an allegorical meaning of, respectively, animals and stones. The widely popular *Physiologus* was one such bestiary. It taught, for instance, that a lion signifies Christ, because it sleeps with its eyes open, a symbol for immortality. The pelican, so the story went, sacrificed itself to feed it own offspring with its own blood; it was a symbol for Christ, who sacrificed himself, so that his spiritual offspring, the Church, might live.[56] Medieval preachers could also spice up their sermons with funny stories and moralistic tales (called *exempla*) found in special exempla collections. One of the best-known collections was *On Various Preachable Materials*, written by Stephan of Bourbon. According to his own words, he collected his edifying stories from a variety of historical authors, such as Josephus, Hegesippus (also known as Pseudo-Josephus), Eusebius, Paulus Orosius, Bede, Gregory of Tours, Pseudo-Turpin, and a range of other historical and pseudo-historical sources. Stephan's anecdotes offer fascinating and lively insight into medieval lore and folklore, as his stories hope to incite the listeners to "refrain from sin and pursue good," because "eternal, incorporeal and invisible wisdom" can be better understood if it is associated with "stories, miracles, and examples." He cites Dionysius the Areopagite to justify his use of stories in sermons: "Wise philosophers dress up their words with parables and examples. A concrete word is more easily transferred from the sense to the imagination,

---

[55] Ibid., fol. 3r.
[56] *Physiologus*, trans. Curley, 9.

and from the imagination into memory."[57] The great thirteenth-century preacher Jacob of Varazzo (d. 1296) agreed:

A preacher must present a simple and clear doctrine to the ignorant lay folk, to edify them better, by concrete and recognizable examples, such as they know by their own experience, and not only to edify them, but also to wake them up when they start to doze off, tired and bored as they are.[58]

Some preachers, however, expressed skepticism about those preachers who added so many jokes and anecdotes that the message of the sermon got lost. The Cistercian Caesarius of Heisterbach (d. 1240) tells of one preacher who in the middle of a sermon included a sentence, "Once upon a time, there lived a king named Arthur . . . " Suddenly his audience was all ears. But the preacher went on to scold his audience that they were more willing to pay attention to stories about King Arthur than to the Gospel being preached.[59] Ironically, Caesarius's *Dialogue of Miracles*, where we find the story, is one of the best-known exempla collections of the Middle Ages, containing some 746 miraculous anecdotes. Alain of Lille, too, expressed his disapproval of preachers who inserted stories, gratuitous jokes, and even songs into their sermons and compared them to the Pharisees whom Jesus criticized for wearing long robes and ostentatious phylacteries (prayer boxes).[60]

Even without these colorful stories, the late medieval sermon was full of associations, allegory, and figurative language. Scholar David D'Avray has observed that the medieval art of sermonizing sometimes had more in common with the genre of poetry than that of prose.[61]

THE BIBLE IN MEDIEVAL SERMONS

Sermons allowed medieval people to become acquainted with biblical content. Late medieval sermons, thick with biblical imagery, exposed their listeners to what D'Avray has called the "drip-drip method of inculcating medieval beliefs" and, we might add, biblical materials, albeit filtered through medieval church doctrine and moral teaching.[62] Clearly, the claim of nineteenth-century historian Philip Schaff that "it was not until the

---

[57] Stephan of Bourbon, *Tractatus de diversis materiis prædicabilibus*, ed. Lecoy de la Marche, 4–5.

[58] Cited in Menache and Horowitz, *L'humour en chaire: le rire dans l'église médiévale*, 67.

[59] Caesarius of Heisterbach, *Dialogus miracolurum*, 4.36. Cited in Menache and Horowitz, *L'humour en chaire: le rire dans l'église médiévale*, 111.

[60] Alain of Lille, *Summa de arte praedicandi*, PL 210, 112. Citing Matt. 23:5.

[61] D'Avray, *The Preaching of the Friars*, 9.

[62] D'Avray, "Method in the Study of Medieval Sermons," 9.

Reformation of the sixteenth century that the sermon and the didactic element were restored and fully recognized in their dignity and important and essential parts of public worship" is untenable.[63]

However, the medieval sermon was a florid discourse, rich in images, illustrations, symbols, and stories. In such a thick wilderness, it was sometimes hard to see the forest for the trees. Some critics maintain that as a result, the Bible was communicated only "in bits and pieces, reduced to banal fragments; . . . a Bible glossed or condensed; a Bible whose simple and immediate meaning is lost."[64] Martin Luther voiced such sentiments when he called for a more Christ-centered preaching and a return to "the naked Gospel." The exegetical tools that late medieval preachers used to build their sermons, Luther summarily dismissed as "Eselsmist" (donkey excrement).[65] The body of late medieval sermons is too large and varied to allow such a one-sided judgment, however. The quality of medieval preaching varied dramatically from place to place. Exegetical preaching, in addition to the more catechetical discourse on virtues and vices, was alive and well in Luther's time; many Bible commentaries of the later Middle Ages were, in fact, sermon collections. They were called *Postillae*. Just as the verse-by-verse Bible commentaries of the great mendicant commentators such as Nicholas of Lyra, the late medieval Latin term for this exegetical preaching, was *postillare*, and it is evident that Luther did appreciate, and indeed make use of, the late medieval commentary tradition of the *Postillae*. Although Luther might thus disagree with the late medieval friars on how to preach, and even what to preach (whereas most medieval sermons would preach redemption through penitence, Luther's theology stressed grace through faith), they did not disagree on the effectiveness and importance of the sermon as a vehicle for Christian theology and the biblical message.

RESOURCES FOR FURTHER STUDY

Comprehensive narrative histories of preaching exist in German (Schneyer) and French (Longère), but regrettably not in English. Partial histories, however, can be found in D'Avray, Gatch, and even Owst (still a good read, despite its age). Muessig's "Sermon, Preacher, and Society" offers

---

[63] Schaff, *History of the Christian Church. Vol. 4: Medieval Christianity, AD 590–1073*, 402.
[64] Martin, *Le métier de prédicateur en France*, 268 and 625. Cited in Wenzel, "The Use of the Bible in Preaching," 690.
[65] Cited in Berger, *La Bible au XVIe siècle*, 22.

an excellent introduction to the study of sermons, and Kienzle's *The Sermon* a good starting point for scholarly study. Sermon-repertoria exist for Latin sermons, by Schneyer, *Repertorium der lateinischen Sermones*, and for Middle English, by O'Mara and Paul, *Repertorium of Middle English Prose Sermons*. There is a good bibliographical section on sermons in Kaske, Groos, and Twomey, *Medieval Christian Literary Imagery*. The International Medieval Sermon Studies Society is a research group dedicated entirely to the study of medieval sermons: http://imsss.net/. A website with resources for the study of medieval liturgy is offered at http://medievalliturgy.com/medievalliturgy.htm. A good resource for the study of liturgy, not just medieval, is *The Study of Liturgy*, edited by Jones, Wainwright, and Bradshaw. For those interested specifically in Books of Hours, the entire text of the Book of Hours is online in Latin and in English translation: http://medievalist.net/hourstxt/home.htm.

SUGGESTIONS FOR FURTHER READING

Amos, Thomas L., Eugene A. Green, and Beverly Mayne Kienzle, eds. *De ore Domini: Preacher and Word in the Middle Ages*. Studies in Medieval Culture, 27. Kalamazoo, MI: Medieval Institute Publications, 1989.

Boynton, Susan. "The Bible and the Liturgy." In *The Practice of the Bible*. 10–33.

D'Avray, David. *The Preaching of the Friars: Sermons Diffused from Paris before 1300*. Oxford: Clarendon Press, 1985.

Daniélou, Jean. *The Bible and the Liturgy*. Liturgical Studies, 3. Notre Dame, IN: University of Notre Dame Press, 1956.

Fassler, Margot E., and Rebecca A. Baltzer. *The Divine Office in the Latin Middle Ages: Methodology and Source Studies, Regional Developments, Hagiography*. Oxford: Oxford University Press, 2000.

Gatch, Milton McG. *Preaching and Theology in Anglo-Saxon England: Aelfric and Wulfstan*. Toronto: University of Toronto Press, 1977.

Harthan, John. *Books of Hours and Their Owners*. London: Thames & Hudson, 1977.

Illich, Ivan. "'Lectio divina'." In *Schriftlichkeit im frühen Mittelalter*, edited by Ursula Schaefer. ScriptOralia, 53, 19–35. Tübingen: Narr, 1993.

Jungmann, Joseph A. *The Mass of the Roman Rite: Its Origins and Development (Missarum sollemnia)*. Translated by Francis A. Brunner. New York: Benziger, 1951–55.

Kienzle, Beverly Mayne, and David L. D'Avray. "Sermons." In *Medieval Latin: An Introduction and Bibliographical Guide*, edited by Frank A.C. Mantello and A.G. Rigg, 659–69. Washington, DC: Catholic University of America Press, 1996.

The Liturgy of the Medieval Church. 2nd ed. Edited by Thomas J. Heffernan and E. Ann Matter. Kalamazoo, MI: Medieval Institute Publications, 2005.

Longère, Jean. *La prédication médiévale*. Paris: Études augustiniennes, 1983.

Maier, Christoph T. *Preaching the Crusades: Mendicant Friars and the Cross in the Thirteenth Century*. Cambridge Studies in Medieval Life and Thought, vol. 28. Cambridge: Cambridge University Press, 1994.

McLaughlin, Emmet. "The Word Eclipsed? Preaching in the early Middle Ages." *Tradition. Studies in Ancient and Medieval History* 46 (1991): 77–122.

Medieval Sermons and Society: Cloister, City, University. Edited by Jacqueline Hamesse, Beverly Mayne Kienzle, Debra L. Stoudt, and Anne T. Thayer. Louvain-la-Neuve: FIDEM, 1998.

Muessig, Carolyn, ed. *Medieval Monastic Preaching*. Brill's Studies in Intellectual History, 90. Leiden: E. J. Brill, 1998.

Muessig, Carolyn. "Sermon, Preacher, and Society in the Middle Ages." *Journal of Medieval History* 28 (2002): 73–91.

The Old English Homily and Its Background. Edited by Bernard F. Huppé and Paul Szarmach. Albany: SUNY Press, 1978.

Owst, Gerald Robert. *Preaching in Medieval England; an Introduction to Sermon Manuscripts of the Period c. 1350–1450*. Cambridge Studies in Medieval Life and Thought. Cambridge: Cambridge University Press, 1926.

Schneyer, Johann Baptist. *Geschichte der katholischen Predigt*. Freiburg: Seelsorge Verlag, 1969.

The Sermon. Edited by Beverly Mayne Kienzle. Typologie des sources du moyen âge occidental, 81–83. Turnhout: Brepols, 2000.

Stock, Brian. *The Implications of Literacy. Written Language and Models of Interpretation in the Eleventh and Twelfth Centuries*. Princeton: Princeton University Press, 1983.

Taft, Robert. *The Liturgy of the Hours in East and West: The Origins of the Divine Office and Its Meaning for Today*. Collegeville, MN: Liturgical Press, 1986.

Vogel, Cyrille. *Medieval Liturgy. An Introduction to the Sources*. Translated by William Storey and Niels Rasmussen. NPM Studies in Church Music and Liturgy. Washington, DC: The Pastoral Press, 1986.

Wenzel, Siegfried. "The Use of the Bible in Preaching." In *The New Cambridge History of the Bible*. 680–92.

Zink, Michel. *La prédication en langue romane: avant 1300*. Nouvelle bibliothèque du Moyen Age. Paris: H. Champion, 1976.

CHAPTER 9

The Bible of the Poor?

When Benedict Biscop traveled to Rome in the late seventh century (as told in the introduction to Bede's *Lives of the Abbots*; see Chapter 1), books were not all that he brought back for the fledgling church in Northumbria. Another necessity for the foundation of a vibrant Christian church in pagan northern England was "sacred images." On his return from Rome, Bede tells us, Benedict

brought with him pictures of sacred images, to adorn the church of St. Peter, which he had built; namely, an image of the blessed mother of God and always Virgin Mary and of the twelve Apostles, with which he intended to adorn the central nave, on boards placed from one wall to the other; and also figures from ecclesiastical history to decorate the south wall of the church, and images from the Revelation of St. John similarly for the north wall; so that all who entered the church, even if they could not read, wherever they turned their eyes, might always contemplate the amiable countenance of Christ and His saints, even if only in image, and thus either, with more watchful minds, might be reminded of the benefits of our Lord's incarnation, or, having before their eyes the perils of the Last Judgement, might be reminded to examine themselves more strictly on that account.[1]

Regrettably, none of these art works has survived, but Bede's story does remind us that art is an integral part of the story of the Bible in the Middle Ages. Depictions of biblical stories adorned houses of worship, as well as liturgical objects such as altars, Gospel books, and lectionaries. Alongside preaching, art and theatre (much like film and television today) allowed biblical content and Christian teaching to permeate the medieval mentality. This last chapter explores some of the contexts where art and the Bible intersected in the Middle Ages.

---

[1] Bede, *Historia Abbatum*, 6, ed. Plummer, 369–70. The translation by Giles, which I modified here, is available online at http://www.fordham.edu/halsall/basis/bede-jarrow.asp.

237

The widespread Reformation attacks on images that began in the 1520s and destroyed countless works of religious art in places such as Germany, England and the Low Countries were not entirely unprecedented. The use of images was also contested in the Early Middle Ages. It seemed to contradict the biblical command against "graven images" in the Decalogue (Ex. 20:4). Medieval churchmen, starting with Gregory the Great, usually stressed that sacred images were meant to educate, not to be worshipped. For Gregory, images were the "book of the illiterate." This theme was picked up by some of the pioneers of the study of medieval art in the nineteenth century, such as Emile Mâle, who explained the rich influence of biblical imagery on medieval art by arguing that medieval art was intended as a "bible of the poor," teaching the Word of God to those who could not read or write.[2] This is how Bede suggests Benedict Biscop wanted these sacred images to function: those who could not read could gain familiarity with "the benefits of the Lord's incarnation" and the "perils of the Last Judgement" by looking at the images. As we will see, however, the relation between art, Bible, and literacy was more complicated than Bede and Gregory (or, indeed, Emile Mâle) suggested.

THE USE AND THE DEFENSE OF IMAGES

Gregory's defense of images, cited by Bede, was articulated in a polemical context. Around the year 600, Bishop Serenus of Marseilles had started to destroy images of the saints out of concern that his flock was worshipping them in defiance of the Second Commandment. Serenus's policies were not isolated incidents. The eighth and ninth centuries saw a violent conflict in the eastern Churches on whether images could be used in worship, and similar doubts were sometimes raised in the west as well. In his response to Serenus, Gregory insisted that the use of images was permitted as a didactic tool. Gregory rejected the adoration of these images, but, he said, "it was one thing to adore these picture, another to learn by them what to adore."[3] As modern scholars have pointed out, Gregory's notion that the illiterate "read" these images like a book is problematic.[4] If images had a

---

[2] Mâle, *The Gothic Image*, vii. Mâle derived his term "bible of the poor" from the picture bible described later.

[3] Gregory, *Epistolae*, IX, 209 and XI, 10, in *Registrum Epistolarum*, ed. Norberg, CCSL 140A, 768 and 874.

[4] See Duggan, "Was Art Really the 'Book of the Illiterate'?"; and Chazelle, "Pictures, Books, and the Illiterate".

didactic function at all, it is more likely that they reinforced, rather than instructed, and helped to visualize stories that were already known, or were being taught in other ways. Even those who could not read (which was not exactly synonymous with being "poor," as we saw in Chapter 7) would probably not have to rely on images for their religious instruction; they would have heard Bible stories and pastoral exegesis through sermons, as we saw in the previous chapter. But the polemic context of Gregory's letter caused him to emphasize the didactic and to downplay the devotional role that images played in medieval society.

Painted images were not the only art to be found in medieval churches. When one observes the abundance of sculpture in late medieval churches, it is sometimes hard to imagine that before the tenth century the medieval attitude towards sculpture was quite restrained. Several Carolingian churchmen, among them the biblical scholar Theodulf of Orleans, forcefully objected to sacred sculpture, arguing that such images (which, after all, were objects as much as illustrations) were no longer didactic, but had become objects of worship. An even more energetic iconoclast was his contemporary, bishop Claudius of Turin, who reports that he "found all the churches filled, in defiance of the precept of Truth, with those sluttish abominations – images. Since everyone was worshipping them, I undertook singlehandedly to destroy them."[5]

After the tenth century, however, the use of sculpted art became quite widespread in western Christendom, although doubts about its legitimacy lingered. The twelfth-century Jew Herman of Cologne, for instance, recalls that before his conversion to Christianity, he once entered a Christian church, and saw a crucifix, which he considered a "monstrous idol," of the kind that "by a many-formed delusive error paganism normally dictated for itself."[6] Herman here very likely describes the magnificent Gero crucifix, dating from the tenth century, which can still be seen in Cologne cathedral today. It was not just one of the earliest monumental sculpted crucifixes but also one of the first images showing Christ on the cross as dead, rather than as a regal figure who triumphs over death. Contemporary crucifixes often showed Jesus standing upright in front of the cross, robed in red, and with his eyes wide open. The Gero crucifix, in contrast, showed him stripped naked, eyes closed, and hanging down from the cross. Not only Jews like Herman voiced doubts about the propriety of plastic art. In the

---

[5] Claudius of Turin, "Defense and Reply to Abbot Theodemir," cited in Diebold, *Word and Image*, 110. See also Noble, *Images, Iconoclasm, and the Carolingians*.

[6] Morrison, *Conversion and Text*, 80.

twelfth century the classically educated cleric Bernard of Angers, when first confronted with a gilded statue of Saint Gerald, initially thought it "quite contrary to Christian Law" and a "very old, incorrect practice and the ineradicable and innate custom of simple people."[7] By contrast, he did not think the use of "insubstantial images depicted on painted walls" problematic in the same way. Bernard was also more lenient when it came to the use of a crucifix, "because it arouses our affective piety in the commemoration of Our Lord's Passion."[8]

Other thinkers in the west were more open to the use of art in a devotional context, however. They could draw upon a tradition in eastern Christianity that had defended the devotional use of images against much more stringent opposition in the eighth and ninth centuries. Saint John of Damascus, for instance, in the eighth century, defended the use of sacred images in the Eastern Orthodox Church, by likening them to the Incarnation of Christ. Just as Christ had assumed human flesh, so the materiality of images was an acceptable way to access the immaterial divine reality represented by these images.[9] We can see his influence in the use of images at the abbey of Cluny. Although the magnificent eleventh-century sculpture from the abbey survives only in fragments today, having been destroyed in 1790 during the French Revolution, its influence radiated out to much of Burgundy, southern France, and northern Spain. For the monks of Cluny, art and beauty were an essential part of worship; they heightened the sense that the onlookers were part of the divine mystery they were observing. Other philosophies went even further. The sixth-century Neoplatonic philosopher Dionysius the Areopagite had argued that all earthly matter, and specifically visual and plastic art, was a visible sign for an invisible truth. His influence came to permeate western thinking through the philosophy of twelfth-century Victorine scholars such as Hugh and Richard of Saint Victor. It was also used by Suger of Saint Denis, the abbot of Saint Denis. Suger described his newly built church of Saint Denis and its ornamentation as a sacred space, permeated with a sense of the divine, which eventually transport the onlooker to the contemplation of God.[10] Saint Denis functioned as a model for Gothic church building in France and beyond and not only helped to bring about the birth of Gothic art, but also provided theologians in the west with a new rationale for the use of art in churches.

7 *The Book of Sainte Foy*, trans. Sheingorn, 77.
8 Ibid.
9 John of Damascus, *Three Treatises on the Divine Images*.
10 Suger of Saint Denis, *De rebus in administatione sua gestis*, 27, trans. Panofsky, 46–47.

Art in the medieval Church was thus much more than a "book for the illiterate." Art helped believers to visualize biblical stories and impress theological ideas on the minds of spectators in a way that hearing could not achieve. Later medieval authors agreed that visual art could provoke a stronger emotional response than words alone. Thus, the thirteenth-century Franciscan theologian Bonaventure of Bonareggio observed that

our devotion shall be excited by what we see, rather than what we hear. Wherefore Horace: "The mind is stirred less vividly by what passes through the ears than by what is brought before the trusty eyes, and what the spectator can see for himself."[11]

His contemporary, the Dominican Thomas Aquinas, agreed. He named three reasons for permitting images: education, recall, and affect. In his *Commentary on the Sentences*, Thomas stated,

There were three reasons for the institution of images in churches. First, for the instruction of simple people, because they are instructed by them as if by books. Second, so that the mystery of the Incarnation and the examples of the saints may be the more active in our memory through being represented daily to our eyes. Third, to excite feelings of devotion, these being aroused more effectively by things seen than by things heard.[12]

Judging from the abundant use of art in medieval churches and in manuscripts, the latter reason was perhaps the most important one.

READING MEDIEVAL ART

Although the Bible and its interpretation did provide the subject matter of medieval art, without a previous knowledge of the Bible, one could not have discerned many of the meanings conveyed by medieval painting and sculpture. The process of deciphering the pictorial conventions of an image, recognizing what is represented, often through association with written sources, is called iconographic analysis. Through it, we can start to discover the meanings that artists intended to convey with images. A solid familiarity with the contents of the Bible is essential for the iconographic analysis of medieval art, as much for modern students as for medieval viewers.

---

[11] Bonaventure, *Commentary on Sentences*, in Bonaventure, *Opera Omnia*, 3, 203. Cited in Brown, *The Holkham Bible Picture Book. A Facsimile*, 1–2.

[12] Thomas Aquinas, *In IV Libros Sententiarum*, III, ds. 9, q. 1, art 2b, sol., ra3, in Thomas Aquians, *Opera Omnia*, ed. Busa, 1, 294. Cited in Duggan, "Was Art Really the 'Book of the Illiterate'?" 232.

The example of medieval depictions of Adam and Eve in the Garden of Eden may illustrate that this "reading of images" is not always a self-evident process, and that it must be guided by a careful consideration of both artistic conventions and written texts. Recognizing what the images depict already assumes a certain familiarity with the biblical narrative. An uninitiated spectator would obviously not infer the story of the fall of humankind from the image of a nude couple with a snake in a garden under a fruit tree. A reading of Genesis 3, however, and its medieval interpretation, can put the image in its proper context. So can knowledge of an important medieval artistic convention, such as the custom of depicting several sequential scenes in one image. For instance, the Carolingian Moutier-Grandval Bible (Photo 10) offered a large illuminated page to illustrate the first chapters of Genesis. Their style is very reminiscent of some of the famous late antique Vergil manuscripts, illustrating the classicizing tendency of the Carolingian renaissance. The images on the top row show the creation of Adam and Eve, and in the second row, we can see Christ introducing Adam to Eve[13] and instructing them not to eat the forbidden fruit. In the next row, we see Eve simultaneously eating the fruit and offering it to Adam; it is clear from the text, however, that these scenes happened in succession. The next scene we can see Christ rebuking Adam and Eve; in the bottom row, Adam and Eve are driven out of the garden, and to the right, we see Adam tilling the soil and Eve nursing a child.[14]

However, not all elements of the image can be explained either by the reading of Genesis 3 or by artistic convention. Many medieval depictions of the expulsion from Paradise, for instance, depict the serpent as having hands, and the face of a woman.[15] The Bible text simply describes this serpent as "more crafty than any other wild animal that the Lord God had made" (Gen. 3:1). But a hint at an explanation for appearance of the serpent can be found in the *Historia scholastica* by Peter Comestor, who states that Satan, to seduce Eve, took possession of one particular kind of snake, which possessed a very "maiden-like appearance," so that Eve would be more likely to listen to her, because, as Comestor says, women are more likely to take advice from women.[16] The serpent has hands, because,

[13] Following John 1:3, medieval theology commonly identified the second person of the Trinity as the creator. The inscription (XPS, an abbreviation for "Christus") accompanying the image confirms this identification.

[14] London, BL, MS Add. 10,546, dated 840. See photo 10. *Die Bibel von Moutier-Grandval.*

[15] One example is the late medieval Book of Hours known as the *Tres riches heures du Duc de Berry*, http://www.wikipaintings.org/en/limbourg-brothers/the-fall-and-the-expulsion-from-paradise.

[16] Peter Comestor, *Historia scholastica*, 22, ed. Sylwan, CCCM 191, 40.

Photo 10. Illuminated page illustrating Genesis 3, in the Moutier-Grandval Bible. The images show, respectively, Christ creating Adam, the creation of Eve, Christ leading Adam to Eve, Christ forbidding the tree, Adam and Eve eating from the tree, Christ's rebuke, the expulsion from paradise, and Eve nursing while Adam works the soil. London, British Library, MS Add. 10546, f.5v. Photo (c) The British Library Board.

according to Comestor, serpents did not lose their limbs until they were cursed by God, with the words "On your belly you will crawl, and dust you will eat." (Gen. 3:14).

In considering the meaning of this image, we also have to consider its position in context. In medieval theology, rooted in Augustine's exegesis of this Bible passage, the story of Genesis 3 is one about the origin of human sin. On the doors of Hildesheim Cathedral, cast in bronze in the tenth century by Bishop Bernward, we find the same story of Genesis depicted on the left door.[17] The door adjacent to it depicts the story of Christ's crucifixion and resurrection. The juxtaposition of the two is meant to signify that, although sin came into the world through Adam and Eve, its redemption was achieved by Christ's sacrifice on the cross, an idea expressed in Paul's Epistle to the Romans, 5:12.

The principle of typology often underlay the theological juxtaposition of images in medieval art, as discussed in Chapter 5. It was quite common to depict scenes from the New Testament with corresponding scenes from the Old Testament. The images that Ceolfrid brought back from Rome, for instance, were organized according to this theological principle. On the return from the fifth voyage to Rome, Bede tells us, Benedict

brought with him pictures out of our Lord's history, which he hung round the chapel of Our Lady which he had made in the larger monastery; and others to adorn St. Paul's church and monastery, ably describing the connexion of the Old and New Testament; for instance, the images of Isaac bearing the wood for his own sacrifice, and Christ carrying the cross on which he was about to suffer, were placed side by side. Again, the serpent raised up by Moses in the desert was adjoined to the Son of Man exalted on the cross.[18]

Again, Ceolfrid's images have not been preserved, but we may recognize the themes in other works of medieval art. The magnificent altar retable of Klosterneuburg in Austria by Nicholas of Verdun (1181), for instance, shows seventeen scenes from the life of Christ depicted in a middle row of enamel images, while the images in the top and bottom row show the corresponding Old Testament events, from the time before and after Noah, respectively. The Last Supper of Christ and his disciples is linked to the sacrifice of Melkisedek (Gen. 14:17–20) and the finding of the manna (Ex. 16:1–36), respectively. The crucifixion is juxtaposed with the sacrifice of Isaac (Gen. 22:10–11) and the carrying of the grapes from the Promised Land by the spies (Num. 13:21–23). The laying of Christ into the tomb

---

[17] Mende, *Die Bronzetüren des Mittelalters, 800–1200*, plates 20–27.
[18] Bede, *Historia Abbatum 9*, ed. Plummer, 373.

shows Joseph's brothers throwing him into a well (Gen. 37:22–24) and the boatmen throwing Jonah overboard where he is swallowed by a fish (Jon. 2:1). These typological connections were derived from patristic exegetical writings and could be found in the *Glossa ordinaria* as well. Inscriptions in Latin surrounding the enamels identify each individual scene.[19]

Another example of the use of typology we find in Church windows, such as the so-called typological window of Bourges Cathedral. Here one can see a depiction of Christ carrying the cross surrounded by images of Isaac carrying wood for the sacrifice, Abraham sacrificing Isaac, the widow of Zarephath carrying wood for Elijah (1 Kings 17:10), and the Jews marking their doors with the blood of the lamb on the eve of the Exodus (Ex. 12:21–27). The crucified Christ is flanked by an image of Moses' brazen serpent (Num. 21:6–9), and Moses bringing forth water from the rock (Num. 20:11, typologically linked to the water that flowed from Jesus' side, John 19:34). The resurrection is surrounded by Elijah reviving the son of the widow of Zarephath (1 Kings 17:17–24), and Jonah and the fish. We find the same typological imagery in instructional picture books such as the *Biblia Pauperum* (*Bible of the Poor*), discussed later in this chapter. In addition, the window shows a pelican and a lion. The latter two images, the first a symbol of sacrifice, and the other a symbol of eternal life, were derived from the so-called *Physiologus*, a medieval bestiary.[20] As we saw in Chapter 8, the book was also often used by preachers.

Reading art thus required an intricate process of visual interpretation. The art described above was intended to be viewed and understood by people with a literate background. Only a previous knowledge of the contents of the Bible would allow viewers to appreciate the many layers of artistic meaning. Rather than serving simply as a "book for the illiterate," medieval art drew on the Bible and its exegesis to express it some of its deepest mysteries in visual form.

THE ART OF ILLUMINATION

Not all medieval art adorned churches. Some of the most impressive and beautiful medieval art can be found in the illustration and illumination of books, especially bibles, psalters, and prayer books. In this context the book itself became an art object, and image and text worked together to

---

[19] Buschhausen and Kunst, *Der Verduner Altar.*
[20] Martin and Cahier, *Monographie de la Cathédrale de Bourges; Physiologus,* trans. Curley, 9 and 1 (see also earlier discussion and Chapter 8).

convey the sacred message. Art could enhance the beauty and value of a book, as it did in some of the most luxurious books of the Middle Ages, such as the *Très riches heures* (*The Very Rich Book of Hours*) of the duke of Berry, or the Luttrell Psalter, now in the London British Library. Or, in the case of the medieval illuminated large bibles, they could inspire the reader to meditate on that what was beyond the text. Starting in the thirteenth century, illustrated books were increasingly used as a visual tool to teach biblical content.

Illuminated Bibles as Visual Exegesis

The Bible of Moutier-Grandval, whose miniature of Adam and Eve was discussed earlier, contained several large illuminated pages. There is the page illustrating Genesis; other illuminated pages accompanied the beginning of the Gospels and the book of the Apocalypse. William Diebold has pointed out that early medieval bible illustrators were usually reluctant to depict biblical scenes directly; they more often presented the art of writing itself, by providing portraits of the evangelists, or even the translator Jerome, at work, or, as we have seen in the case of the Codex Amiatinus, the guardian of the biblical library, whether this was understood to be Ezra, or, as some have suggested (see Chapter 1 and the earlier discussion in this chapter), Cassiodorus.[21] Later, Romanesque, bibles seem to have abandoned this reluctance. The monumental bibles of the eleventh century were often lavishly illustrated. Art historian Walter Cahn has identified no fewer than 150 such beautifully illuminated large bibles for the period from 1050 to 1200 alone.[22] Unlike monumental art, this art was not meant to convey a message to a wide audience; the number of viewers who glimpsed these works of art must have been limited, and it is unlikely that they were illiterate. More in line with Pseudo-Dionysius' philosophy, cited earlier, these illustrations were intended not to substitute for the written word but to help raise the reader's mind to a higher truth. Or, as the title of a picture of Christ in glory in the eleventh-century Hidta Codex expressed it, "[t]his visible image represents the invisible truth/whose splendor penetrates the world."[23] And in some cases, they could provide a rich pictorial commentary on Scripture.

---

[21] Diebold, *Word and Image*, 107.
[22] Cahn, *Romanesque Bible Illumination*.
[23] Hidta codex, cited in Diebold, *Word and Image*, 126.

One device that allowed the illuminator to comment on the text was historiated initials (initials that have a story scene depicted in them, as opposed to non-figurative ornaments, such as flowers, or abstract art). Some good examples can be found in medieval psalters, where the initials often hint at the allegorical (or, as medieval theology would call it, prophetic) meaning of the psalm. For instance, Psalm 97, "The Lord has made known his salvation," would typically have a depiction of the angel announcing the shepherds the birth of Christ, whereas Psalm 68, "Save me, O God, for the waters are come even unto my soul," usually had an illuminated initial depicting the Prophet Jonah.[24] The images often provided a pictorial commentary that made visible the unspoken and unwritten theological interpretation that the bare text of Scripture lacked.

Early medieval psalters, however, more rarely used illustration as a form of exegesis. Diebold suggests that the "superiority of word to image" that the Carolingian artists professed is noticeable in the illustrations of the so-called Utrecht Psalter, which provided very "literal" illustrations to the text of the Psalms. Byzantine psalters of the period use the same technique of exegetical illustration. The twenty-third Psalm, for instance (Vulg. Ps. 22) illustrated the line "The Lord is my shepherd" with an abundance of sheep grazing in a field; the "still waters" of verse 2 are depicted as a running stream; an angel offers the psalmist a staff (vs. 4), and anoints his head with oil while he holds a cup (vs. 5). The prepared table of verse five is prominent in the middle of the image, whereas the "house of the Lord" (vs. 6) is depicted at the left. Without the text, the images would make little sense.[25] (See Photo 5.) Not all pictorial exegesis of the Utrecht Psalter, however, was as literal-minded as the above-cited example. In its illustration of Psalm 51 (Vulg. Ps. 50), for instance, the artist chose to illustrate not single elements from the psalm's text, but instead the story the prophet Nathan told David, when he rebuked him for his adultery with Bathsheba (2 Sam. 11). Thus, it takes the first verse as its point of departure: "A Psalm of David, when the prophet Nathan came to him because he had been with Bathseba." In some cases, the pictorial commentary could be Christological in character. Its depiction of Psalm 16:10, "You will not abandon my soul to the pit/nor allow the one you love to see the pit," for instance, has an image of the three women on Easter morning visiting

---

[24] Panayotova, "The Illustrated Psalter: Luxury and Practical Use," 253–54.
[25] Images of the Utrecht Psalter can be viewed online at http://bc.library.uu.nl/node/599.

the sepulchre (depicted as a small rotunda) where Christ was buried, while an angel sitting in front of it announces his resurrection. The illustration program of the Utrecht Psalter was copied several times, among others in the Eadwine Psalter discussed in Chapter 2.

Exegetical Picture Bibles

In the late twelfth century, some books began to represent parts of the biblical story in more extensive pictorial form, with more emphasis on image than on text. One could call these books "picture bibles," although the ones discussed here were not bibles in the strict sense of the word. The *Bible moralisée* (French for "moralized Bible") was an illustrated partial Bible (featuring the historical books) with commentary, whereas the *Biblia pauperum* was an extended typological meditation on the life of Christ. The former emphasized a practical and moral understanding of the text, and the latter, a more mystical understanding. Neither book was intended for illiterate patrons, the poor even less so, although the latter title did inspire Emile Mâle to call all medieval art a "bible of the poor." What these books do show, however, is that from the thirteenth century, there was a more positive attitude toward the use of images in conveying the biblical message, whether for didactic or devotional purposes.

The *Bibles moralisées* (*Moralized Bibles*) consisted of an illustrated biblical story, with an emphasis on the historical books of the Bible: the Pentateuch (minus the more legalistic parts), Joshua, Judges, Samuel and Kings, Maccabees, the Gospels, Acts, and Revelation. In this sense, they followed the narrative of the *Bible historiale*, described in Chapter 7. Each narrative scene was represented in an illuminated medallion, four per page, with a brief caption. Each story was accompanied by a moral or allegorical interpretation in a medallion underneath it, also with a brief caption. Thus, each page of this lavishly illustrated Bible had eight medallions, with the first and third rows following the biblical narrative, and the second and fourth rows offering moral-allegorical interpretations (see Photo 11). The theology of these moral interpretations corresponded very closely to some of the late twelfth-century commentaries written in the schools in Paris. About a dozen of these picture bibles have been preserved, dating from as early as the thirteenth century, some in one volume and some in three volumes; the two oldest copies are now in Vienna, National Library MS 1179 and 2554. These volumes seem to have been made for members of the thirteenth-century Capetian royal family, the latter possibly under the

Photo 11. *Bible moralisée* ("Bible de Saint Louis"), showing scenes from the Apocalypse (starting at Rev. 19:17) and their moral applications. New York, Pierpont Morgan Library M.240, fol. 1v. Photo: (c) Morgan Library and Museum, Courtesy of the Index of Christian Art.

patronage of Blanche of Castile, the wife of Louis VIII of France. Another copy, called the Bible de Saint Louis, now in Toledo, Spain, and in the Pierpont Morgan Library in New York, was given by the young Louis IX of France as a present to Alphonso X of Castile. Its title page depicts King Louis IX and his mother, Blanche, on the title page. Under these royal portraits, a team is shown at work in the production of this same book. A cleric gives instructions to a lay scribe, who is writing what can be identified as a page of the *Bible moralisée*. It is quite possible that these Bibles were intended as biblical mirrors for princes, royal picture Bibles providing a biblical foundation for the royal exercise of power.

Whereas the *Bibles moralisées* were guidebooks for moral and political conduct, and intended for a noble, even royal audience, the *Biblia pauperum* was a guide for personal meditation and devotion toward the passion of Christ. Its audience was probably wealthy middle class laity. It was essentially an illustrated life of Christ, in which the main scene from Christ's life was surrounded with two corresponding allegorical types, as well as four texts from the prophetic books of the Bible (see Photo 12). Many of the typologies were commonplace; they are not all that different from those on the Altar of Klosterneuburg or the windows in Bourges, discussed earlier. The illustration showing Christ's crucifixion, for instance, was flanked by an image of the sacrifice of Isaac and one of the brazen serpent that Moses held up in the desert. The entombment of Christ was flanked by an image of Joseph thrown into the well and Jonah swallowed by the fish. Each scene was surrounded by four prophetic figures carrying scrolls with Bible texts that were seen as predictions of the events from the life of Christ shown on the page. Captions (some books were in Latin, some in German, and others in both) on the bottom of the page explained the entire scene. It seems evident that the purpose of this book was not so much to narrate Christ's passion as it was to offer an extended meditation on its mystical and spiritual dimension. With all the Old Testament events and prophesies pointing to that passion, the viewer becomes intensely aware of its cosmic significance.

The first "bibles of the poor" were produced in the late thirteenth or early fourteenth century in Bavaria, and the genre was most widely diffused in German-speaking lands. It became increasingly common after the advent of wood-block printing in the fifteenth century. The technique of the woodcut, which arose in response to the growing demand for mass-produced illustrated books arose among the more literate laity, transformed the character of medieval book illustration. Even a mass-produced book of this kind would still be a considerable financial investment for people of

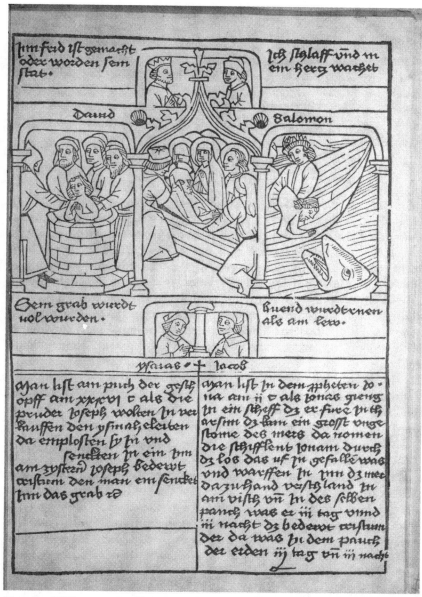

Photo 12. *Biblia pauperum:* Christ in the tomb, flanked by Joseph in the well and Jonah in the fish. Prophetic texts by David, Solomon, Isaiah, and Jacob elucidate the event. Hans Sporer: Nuremberg, 1471. Scheide Collection, Princeton, NJ. Photo courtesy of William H. Scheide.

modest means, although the title suggests that it was marketed as a more affordable bible. It is quite possible, of course, that the word *poor* refers neither to the unlettered (as Emile Mâle interpreted the title) nor to those of modest means, but to the poor Christ mentions in Matthew 5:3: "Blessed are the poor in spirit; theirs is the kingdom of heaven." But perhaps one should not attach too much weight to the title of the book. The title *Biblia pauperum* only occurs on two of the many medieval manuscripts of this work. According to Avril Henry, the title is a "misnomer, . . . approved by mere usage."[26]

Picture Bibles as Didactic Art

Alongside the *Bibles moralisées* and the *Biblia pauperum*, the later Middle Ages also saw the production of books of Bible stories consisting almost entirely of pictures. These "bibles" offered a more straightforward illustrated narrative, with captions often in the vernacular. This type of book seems to have become more common in the later Middle Ages, fed by growing demand from a wealthy lay middle class. The Holkham Bible is an excellent example. Today in the British Library, it is a picture bible from the first half of the fourteenth century, containing stories from Genesis, the Gospels, and the book of Revelation, depicted in more than 200 images, with captions in Anglo-Norman French. It was probably commissioned by a layperson with strong ties to the Dominican convent in London, because a Dominican friar is prominently displayed on the title page.[27] Although the Holkham Bible stands out for the quality of its illumination, similar picture bibles, often with vernacular captions, circulated throughout Europe, and they probably filled a need for a devotional reading and meditation on the biblical narrative in a manner way similar to that of the *Biblia pauperum*.[28]

These picture bibles were not always strictly following the biblical text. More correctly characterized as illustrated "lives of Jesus," they depict not only elements from the Gospel stories but also extra-biblical materials from the life of Mary found in the apocryphal proto-Gospel of James, as well as scenes from the childhood of Christ derived from the apocryphal "infancy Gospels." Such illustrated bibles often drew on the "Life of Christ"

---

26 Henry, *Biblia Pauperum. A Facsimile and Edition*, 3.
27 *The Holkham Bible Picture Book. A Facsimile*, ed. Brown, 10.
28 See, for instance, the facsimile edition of MSS Freiburg U.L. 334 and New York, Pierpont Morgan 719–20, in *Picture Bible* [sic] *of the Late Middle Ages. Deutsche Bilderbibel aus dem späten Mittelalter.*

tradition exemplified in the *Meditations on the Life of Christ* (*Meditationes vitae Christi*), a work falsely attributed to Saint Bonaventure, which in turn influenced the even more popular *Life of Christ* by the fourteenth-century Carthusian Ludolf of Saxony. Both works drew not only on the Gospel narratives but also on apocryphal traditions and exegetical works, mainly the *Historia scholastica* of Peter Comestor and Jacob of Varazzo's *Golden Legend*.

Images and Devotional Practice in the Books of Hours

A similar devotional use of images is attested in the illuminations of the Books of Hours, discussed in Chapter 8. Many of these books were lavishly illustrated, and, as was said above, their beauty was often a statement about the wealth of their owners. The calendar, which listed the specific ecclesiastical feast days, was often illustrated with scenes depicting the work that was performed during the specific months of the year: pruning in March, harvesting in July, threshing in August, and hunting and winemaking in October. These Books of Hours, intended for lay use, are among the most beautifully executed manuscripts that the Middle Ages have produced. Some of the illuminations may have served the purpose of ostentation as much as devotion. But many clearly did have a devotional purpose. The illustrations that accompanied the Hours of the Virgin, for instance, depicting the Annunciation, Visitation, Nativity, Adoration of the Shepherds, the Magi, the Presentation in the Temple, the Flight into Egypt, and the Coronation of the Virgin, were intended to intensify the focus of the Psalm prayer on these specific events in the life of Mary. The scenes depicting the passion of Christ, or portraits of patron saints were also clearly intended to provoke the reader to devotion towards either Christ or the saints. Some of the less lavishly illuminated Books of Hours could have devotional images added to them later. The so-called Pavement Hours, now in York Minster Library, for instance, had devotional images from other prayer books stitched in at several places, including a printed devotional image of the so-called "arms of Christ." It depicts the instruments with which Christ was tortured during his passion, such as the scourge, hammer and nails, spear, and cross. The accompanying text promised an indulgence to "wersumever devotedly beholdeth thes armys of Christe."[29] The viewing of the image itself had become an act of prayer.

[29] York Minster MS XVI.K.6, fol. 44/45. The practice of rewarding the viewing of images with an indulgence was not uncommon. Cf. Swanson, *Indulgences in Late Medieval England*, 258–59.

THE BIBLE ON STAGE

Liturgical Reenactment

The plastic arts were not the only medium in which the biblical story could be visualized. Drama also brought the Word to life for medieval Christians. The first staged performances of biblical stories were closely connected to the liturgy. In a way, of course, the Mass itself was a staged drama, a reenactment of God's salvational work in human history. But other parts of the liturgy lent themselves to being enhanced with additional dramatic performance. Egeria, the fourth-century nun mentioned in the previous chapter, reported to her sisters that in Jerusalem, it was common to celebrate Palm Sunday in Jerusalem with a procession carrying palm branches from the Mount of Olives to the church of the Holy Sepulche.[30] Similar processions were probably also commonplace in western Europe; several extant full-sized statues of Jesus on a donkey, which could be pulled along on wheels, probably served as centerpieces in such processions.

A more dramatic example of liturgical reenactment is the *Quem quaeritis* (*Whom Do You Seek?*), a short play about the events of Easter morning, which grew out of the monastic reform movement in late-tenth-century England. The Customary for Monasteries, drawn up in Winchester in an attempt to regularize the customs of all monasteries in England, gives a description of how this liturgical drama could have been performed in a monastic setting. On Easter morning, some of the sung liturgical sequences were accompanied by a dramatic reenactment of the three women coming to the empty tomb seeking the buried Christ. An angel announces to them that Christ is not there:

Four of the brethren shall vest, one of whom, wearing an alb as though for some different purpose, shall enter and go stealthily to the place of the 'sepulchre' and sit there quietly, holding a palm in his hand. Then . . . the three other brethren, vested in copes and holding thuribles in their hands, shall enter in their turn and go to the place of the "sepulchre," step by step, as though searching for something. Now these things are done in imitation of the angel seated on the tomb and of the women coming with perfumes to anoint the body of Jesus. When, therefore, he that is seated shall see these three draw nigh, wandering about as it were and seeking something, he shall begin to sing softly and sweetly, *Whom do you seek?* As soon as this has been sung right through, the three shall answer together, *Jesus of Nazareth.* Then he that is seated hall say He is not here. *He has risen, as he foretold.*

---

[30] Egeria, *Egeria's Travels*, trans. Wilkinson, 133.

Go, and announce that he has risen from the dead. At this command the three shall turn to the choir, saying *Alleluia. The Lord has risen.*[31]

England was probably not the only place where this kind of liturgical drama was performed. In some churches in medieval Europe, such as Gernrode, in Germany's Harz Mountains, we can still see the "sepulchre" where this play was performed: a small square stone building in the nave of the church, presumably the location of a staging similar to the one described above.

Dramatic Exegesis

Not all medieval biblical drama was liturgical; some theater plays inspired by biblical stories were not intended as part of worship services but were performed outside the churches, usually outdoors. The earliest surviving examples date to the eleventh century. The Beauvais *Play of Daniel*, a lively theatrical production in Latin that depicts the life of Daniel, probably intended to be performed around Christmas or Advent (it ends with the prediction of the birth of Christ), was written by "the young people" of the city, presumably students:

To your glory, O Christ / is this play of Daniel.
It was written in Beauvais / and the young people wrote it.[32]

These non-liturgical dramas, whether in Latin or the vernacular, often added dramatic details and developed characters that were only marginally important in the biblical narrative. In the *Play of Noah*, for instance, as it was performed in the English town of Chester, the wife of Noah, whose role is not highlighted in the Bible, becomes a comic character, reluctant to accept her husband's claim that God commanded him to build the ark. She scolds and disobeys her husband, rejecting his sound advice and refusing to go on board. Such marital disputes, and the farcical violence that accompanied them, would have been regarded as highly comical by the medieval audience. But Noah's wife also embodied a moral lesson, albeit a misogynistic one; her disobedience served as a foil to her husband's godly obedience, and Noah's eventual triumph over his foolish spouse could be read as a lesson about obedience both to God and to male domestic authority.

---

[31] Æthelwold, *Regularis Concordia*, ed. and trans. Symons, 49–50. For the benefit of the reader, I have translated the Latin phrases into English, while retaining Symons's translation.
[32] Dronke, *Nine Medieval Latin Plays*, 120.

Vernacular biblical drama in the later Middle Ages was often sponsored by the cities' guilds. On the feast of Corpus Christi, which fell on the Thursday after the feast of Trinity (the Sunday after Pentecost), usually in June, medieval cities customarily staged a procession in which the sacrament was carried reverentially through town. In several cities, these processions were expanded into a procession of acted-out biblical scenes. Specially made wagons functioned as portable theaters, on which the guilds of the town staged consecutive plays, aiming to depict the entire biblical narrative of creation, fall, and redemption. Such biblical plays are called "mystery plays," possibly after the guilds or "misteries," that produced them.[33] Series of mystery plays, called cycles, normally consisting of several dozen plays to be performed in a specific order (beginning with Genesis and ending with Revelation) are preserved from a number of cities throughout Europe. One of the fullest preserved and most expansive examples comes from York, England. The tradition of performing these mystery plays began some time in the early fourteenth century, and was banned in 1569 during the reign of Elizabeth I. (It was revived in 1951 and continues today.) The text of the entire cycle (which probably grew over time) is recorded in a single manuscript, now in the British Library in London. The 47 plays, containing some 14,000 lines of text and more than 300 speaking parts were performed on wagons that were drawn in a procession along twelve stations on a route through the city of York. The procession started just after dawn, which in June was before 4:00 A.M., and lasted until well after midnight. Each guild was responsible for one particular play, and often, the play was thematically related to the craft of each guild: the shipwrights traditionally performed the play about the building of Noah's Ark; the vintners performed the wedding of Cana, where water was changed into wine; and the bakers' guild was responsible for the Last Supper play.

The choice of the stories in the York cycle starkly emphasizes original sin and redemption. The Old Testament plays are few in comparison to those from the New Testament, with all but one taken from the book of Genesis and one from Exodus. Although the stories of Creation and the Fall can be seen as a prologue to the story of redemption, other materials were chosen for typological relevance; the sacrifice of Abraham, for instance, looked forward to the sacrifice of Christ on Golgotha. The main narrative is centered around the birth, death, and resurrection of Christ, with relatively

---

[33] Thus the Online Etymological Dictionary (http://www.etymonline.com/index.php?term=mystery). The *Oxford English Dictionary*, however, suggests that the term is nineteenth-century, not medieval.

little on the ministry of Christ. The play of the Last Judgment closes off the entire cycle, which thus encompasses the entire span from creation to the end of times. We see in the staging of these stories not just some artistic liberties (the invention of marginal characters, burlesque humor, and lively dialogue), but also a sizeable influence of apocryphal traditions. The fall of Angels, for instance, a story originating in the apocryphal Enoch tradition, is given elaborate attention. The harrowing of hell, where Christ descends into hell and liberates Adam and the Old Testament patriarchs and prophets, is staged in great detail; its narrative is derived from the Gospel of Nicodemus. Plays such as these were probably not intended as didactic tools for teaching the Bible; their main purpose was to showcase the piety of the guilds that produced them. Nevertheless, they give a good impression of the extent of biblical literacy of the laity in the Late Middle Ages, and they no doubt contributed to shaping that literacy among the large public that witnessed and performed them.

THE BIBLE, IMAGINATION, AND ART

We have seen that art in the Middle Ages was rarely used intentionally as a didactic tool; it did not serve as a bible of the poor in the sense that Emile Mâle imputed to it. But it did help believers to visualize biblical content, and enrich their imagination. The "biblical" images depicted in medieval art were not derived from the Bible alone, but also from the thick theological, devotional, and exegetical discourse that surrounded the Bible at the time. Apocryphal and exegetical traditions determined the way that artists imagined biblical content. A good example of how an exegetical tradition could influence an artistic interpretation can be found in the York cycle play of the Nativity. When Joseph approaches the place where Mary has just given birth to Christ, he remarks,

Ah, Lord, God, what light is this
That comes shining thus suddenly?
I cannot say, as have I bliss . . .

And when he beholds Mary, with Jesus on her knee, he says,

Me marvels mickle of this light
That thusgates shines in this place
Foorsooth, it is a selcouth [marvellous] sight.[34]

---

[34] *York Mystery Plays*, ed. Beadle and King, 62.

A light pouring forth from the place where Christ is born is also mentioned in one of the early apocryphal sources on the birth of Christ, although not in any of the canonical Gospels.[35] It also features prominently in the mystical writings of Bridget of Sweden, a visionary who lived in the beginning of the fourteenth century. In one vision, Bridget saw herself transported to the place of the nativity and describes the scene thus:

And while she was thus in prayer, I saw the One lying in her womb then move; and then and there, in a moment and the twinkling of an eye, she gave birth to a Son, from whom there went out such great and ineffable light and splendor that the sun could not be compared to it. Nor did that candle that the old man had put in place give light at all, because that divine splendor totally annihilated the material splendor of the candle.[36]

Although we cannot be sure what written sources influenced the writers of the York mystery plays when they envisioned the light surrounding the infant Jesus' cradle, it is clear that some such extra-biblical sources were shaping their imagination. Visionary writings influenced the way medieval playwrights and medieval painters imagined biblical scenes. When one considers, for instance, the paintings of the Nativity of fourteenth- and fifteenth-century Flemish painters such as Hugo van der Goes, Petrus Christus, or Geertgen tot Sint Jans, one notices a shift in the way that the Nativity is depicted. Instead of the traditional image of Mary lying on a bed while Christ lies in the manger and Joseph sits in the background, these late medieval painters depicted Mary and Joseph adoring the Christ child, who lies on the ground in the middle of the stable, radiating a mystical light. A similar influence may be seen in the play of the Nativity in the York cycle. This kind of influence is not unique to the Middle Ages. In the 2004 film *The Passion of Christ*, director Mel Gibson insisted that he followed the biblical narrative very literally, but it has been shown that much of the graphic imagery in his depiction of Christ's suffering borrowed heavily from the nineteenth-century mystical visions by the nun Anne Catherine Emmerich.[37]

Medieval art thus hardly ever offered a straightforward illustration of the biblical narrative; its presentation was dictated by a range of theological and exegetical assumptions. The media of sculpture, painting, illustration, and drama allowed for an almost infinite symbolic layering of the subject, and medieval artists used these possibilities to the fullest. Medieval art

[35] *De infantia salvatoris*, 73, in *The Apocryphal New Testament*, ed. Elliott, 110.
[36] Birgitta of Sweden, *Life and Selected Revelations*, trans. Kezel, 203.
[37] Emmerich, *The Dolorous Passion of Our Lord Jesus Christ*, trans. Brentano.

rarely served as the bible of the poor, but the Bible and its interpretation provided an almost limitless pool of resources for the artistic imagination of the Middle Ages.

RESOURCES FOR FURTHER STUDY

Again, the articles in the *New Cambridge History of the Bible* are the best starting point for further study. Many facsimile editions of the works mentioned in this chapter exist and are listed in the bibliography, and some of them can even be viewed online, such as the Princeton copy of the Biblia Pauperum: http://pudl.princeton.edu/objects/ht24wj49c. The British Library maintains a catalogue of illuminated Bible manuscripts, with images: http://www.bl.uk/catalogues/illuminatedmanuscripts/Tour BibGen.asp. An interactive online edition of the *Biblia pauperum*, by Tamara Manning, can be viewed at http://amasis.com/biblia/.

An interactive CD-ROM with a trove of medieval images is *Images of Salvation: the Story of the Bible through Medieval Art*, edited by Dee Dyas, of the Center for the Study of Christianity and Culture at York University (http://www.christianityandculture.org.uk/). Two important subscription-only databases of medieval religious images, searchable by iconographic themes, are invaluable resources: the Index of Christian Art, http://ica.princeton.edu/, and the Warburg Institute Iconographic Database, http://warburg.sas.ac.uk/vpc/VPC_search/main_page.php. The latter contains subcategories and images for the terms *bible moralisées*, *biblia pauperum*, and *picture bibles*.

SUGGESTIONS FOR FURTHER READING

The Bible in the Middle Ages: Its Influence on Literature and Art. Edited by Bernard S. Levy. Medieval and Renaissance Texts and Studies, 89. Tempe: Arizona Center for Medieval and Renaissance Studies, 2003. Originally published Binghamton, 1992.

Cahn, Walter. *Romanesque Bible Illumination.* Ithaca, NY: Cornell University Press, 1982.

Caviness, Madeline H. "Biblical Stories in Windows: Were They Bibles for the Poor?" In *The Bible in the Middle Ages.* 103–47.

Chazelle, Celia M. "Pictures, Books, and the Illiterate: Pope Gregory I's Letters to Selenus of Marseilles." *Word and Image* 6 (1990): 138–53.

Diebold, William J. *Word and image: An Introduction to Early Medieval Art.* Boulder, CO: Westview Press, 2000.

Duffy, Eaton. *Marking the Hours: English People and Their Prayers, 1240–1570.* New Haven, CT: Yale University Press, 2006.

Duggan, Lawrence G. "Was Art Really the 'Book of the Illiterate'?" *Word and Image* 5 (1989): 227–51.

Hartman, John. *Books of Hours and Their Owners*. London: Thames & Hudson, 1977.

Hearn, M. F. *Romanesque Sculpture. The Revival of Monumental Stone Sculpture in the Eleventh and Twelfth Centuries*. Ithaca, NY: Cornell University Press, 1985.

Hughes, Christopher G. "Art and Exegesis." In *A Companion to Medieval Art*. Ch. 8.

Kaufmann, C. M. "The Bible in Public Art, 1050–1450." In *The New Cambridge History of the Bible*. 785–820.

Kessler, Herbert L. "Gregory the Great and Image Theory in Northern Europe during the Twelfth and Thirteenth Centuries." In *A Companion to Medieval Art*. Ch. 7.

Lowden, John. *The Making of the Bibles Moralisées*. University Park: Pennsylvania State University Press, 2000.

Mâle, Emile. *The Gothic Image: Religious Art in France of the Thirteenth Century*. Translated by Dora Nosey. New York: E. P. Dutton & Co., 1913.

Mende, Ursula. *Die Bronzetüren des Mittelalters, 800–1200*. Irmgard Ernstmeier-Hirmer and Albert Hirmer, photographers. München: Hirmer, 1983.

Mitchell, John. "The Bible in Public Art, 600–1050." In *The New Cambridge History of the Bible*. 755–784.

Muir, Lynette R. *The Biblical Drama of Medieval Europe*. Cambridge: Cambridge University Press, 1995.

Noble, Thomas X. *Images, Iconoclasm, and the Carolingians*. The Middle Ages Series. Philadelphia: University of Pennsylvania Press, 2009.

Panayotova, Stella. "The Illustrated Psalter: Luxury and Practical Use." In *The Practice of the Bible in the Western Middle Ages*. 247–71.

Williams, John. *Imaging the Early Medieval Bible*. The Penn State Series in the History of the Book. University Park: Pennsylvania State University Press, 2002. Paperback version of the 1999 edition.

Young, Karl. *The Drama of the Medieval Church*. Oxford: The Clarendon Press, 1957–67.

Afterword

The sixteenth century marked a watershed in the history of the Bible. The invention of the printing press in the previous century had profoundly altered notions of just what constituted a "text" and a "book." Renaissance scholars no longer studied Hebrew and Greek as a way to correct the Latin Bible text as medieval scholars had done, but as a way to uncover the "original" Bible. The reformers challenged the authority of the Church to interpret this Bible and denied the validity of the medieval tradition of interpretation. Extra-biblical traditions, apocryphal texts, and mystical commentaries, once seen as essential to the understanding of the sacred text, came to be regarded as "monkish lore" and were dismissed as irrelevant. Although, of course, the achievements of the Renaissance and Reformation brought genuine improvements to the understanding of the Bible, one may ask whether they did not also obscure some essential elements of its history. This book has tried to recover some of this "lost" history of the Bible. I hope that it has provided students of medieval culture some insight into the peculiarities of the Bible as a sacred text and has shed some light on its place in medieval culture. But I also hope that it has done something to challenge the notion that the Middle Ages contributed little to our own understanding of the Bible.

The "lost" history of the medieval Bible may be closer to our daily lives than we realize. Today, few people are familiar with apocryphal texts such as the Gospel of Nicodemus, the book of Enoch, or the Infancy Gospels. Yet the notions of Christ's descent into hell and the fall of the angels are common, even if many are unaware of their sources. Nativity scenes and Christmas cards display an ox and a donkey at the scene of Christ's birth, but few people will realize the non-canonical origins of these images. The study of the formation of the medieval biblical canon may help to clarify these religious traditions. At the same time, assessing the popularity of these books in their medieval context may help to dispel sensationalist myths (propagated especially in recent popular fiction) about

261

"lost books of the Bible." On an even more fundamental level, it should now be clear that the notion of the Bible as a single book, and the tradition of lay Bible reading, both promoted by the Reformation and still valued in Protestant circles today as a devotional practice, had deep roots in medieval practice.

Although, in some cases, studying the medieval approach to the Bible may help to explain modern beliefs and practices, in other cases, it is the "otherness" of medieval practice that draws our attention and invites reflection. The medieval interpretation of Scripture is often quite counter-intuitive for modern readers. We have been trained to reconstruct an author's intention by textual and historical analysis. This method was of course not alien to medieval interpreters, who called it "literal" or "histori-cal" exegesis. But for most of the Middle Ages, it compared unfavorably to the "spiritual" interpretation of Scripture, because "the letter kills, but the Spirit gives life" (2 Cor. 3:6). The study of medieval exegesis can make the reader aware that texts, and especially sacred texts, rarely say "just what they mean," because even their most fundamental meanings are embedded in a tradition of interpretation. The exploration of a tradition so wholly alien to one's own may sometimes lead to a renewed perception and a critical examination of one's own criteria of interpretation. At the same time, it has been argued here that early modern biblical interpretation (Catholic and Protestant alike) owes a huge debt to the tradition of literal exegesis and textual scholarship that developed in the later Middle Ages.

In trying to outline the ways that the Bible influenced medieval culture, this book has challenged three kinds of accepted notions about the Middle Ages. Each one of these notions involves a form of reductionism: dismissing the period as the benighted Dark Ages, idealizing it as an "age of faith," and reducing it to a mere prelude to what came afterward, whether the Renais-sance or the Reformation. The dangers of first notion must be obvious to anyone who has read this book. The second notion, the idealization of the Middle Ages as a glorious "age of faith," is less crude but no less dangerous in its own way. It is a stance often taken by Roman Catholic scholars, who have seen the Middle Ages as a golden age of the *Roman* Catholic Church. This stance can lead not only to an appropriation of history that excludes other groups of believers (Protestants also profess their belief in a catholic Christian Church, which includes the medieval church), but sometimes to an overly defensive and apologetic stance in scholarship as well. Protestant scholars have been more likely to embrace the third notion, that is, the fallacy of interpreting the distant past as inevitably leading up to the events of a more recent past. As we have seen in the case of the history of the vernacular Bible, this often led to a selective reading of the sources and a distortion of historical evidence. For example, when the Dutch Protestant scholar Cebus Cornelis de Bruin prepared an edition of the text of the medieval Dutch Old Testament,[1] he chose to print them without their marginal glosses and commentaries, as he did not regard these extraneous materials as part of the Bible. However, for their medieval authors, these glosses were essential to the text, and an edition without them created a text that would have been very unfamiliar to medieval readers (at least before 1477).

Freed from these fallacies, the study of the medieval Bible can be a rich source for the appreciation of medieval culture, as several decades of recent scholarship have proved. Sermons, for instance, were long considered a second-rate source for intellectual history and theology, and modern discussion on medieval sermons long centered on questions about whether medieval preaching was "biblical" or not (i.e., measuring up to the nineteenth-century Protestant definition of that concept). Then, in the 1970s and 1980s, sermons were rediscovered as a rich source for the "history of mentalities" and as a way to uncover the collective psychology of the medieval mind.[2] Through their understanding of the Bible, communicated in the sermons, medieval authors provided a glimpse of how medieval people understood themselves and the world around them. A similar revolution in the field is currently occurring in the study of the vernacular Bible, which is turning away from its entrenchment along confessional lines and evolving into a social study of the late medieval culture of lay devotional literacy. The history of the Bible as a book offers great insight in the history of literacy and use of the written word in medieval society.

Today, a "Society for the Study of the Bible in the Middle Ages" at the International Congress on Medieval Studies in Kalamazoo sees Protestants, Catholics, and Jews collaborating fruitfully in a spirit of ecumenism and interreligious dialogue. This cooperation has opened up several valuable new approaches. The field of Jewish-Christian relations in medieval exegesis has been a growing subject in the last decades, for instance. In the coming decades, this field promises to expand to include Islamic attitudes to biblical and sacred texts as well.[3] In this project, students and scholars alike have more resources at their fingertips than generations before them could have dreamed of. The digitization of sources has revolutionized the field.

---

[1] *Vetus Testamentum. Pars prima*, ed. De Bruin.

[2] For the term "history of mentalities," see Chartier, *Cultural History*, 19–52.

[3] One initiative to enable such a study is the monograph series *Commentaria: Sacred Texts and Their Commentaries: Jewish, Christian, and Islamic*, founded by Grover A. Zinn, Jr.

Broad access to such sources is not in fact as new as it may seem. For the last 150 year, scholars studying the history of biblical interpretation and sermons have made grateful use of Jean-Paul Migne's *Patrologia latina*, a comprehensive printed edition of Latin patristic and medieval church writers. The goal of Abbé Migne was to put the rich heritage of patristic and medieval Christian writing within the financial reach of even the common priest and small seminary library. Migne would have been delighted to see this tool now available in electronic form and searchable for students of the Latin Christian tradition. The Patrologia Latina Database has its problems: users should be aware that the larger part of these volumes are reprints of sometimes defective editions of the seventeenth and eighteenth centuries and that they often include spurious materials. Also, the *Patrologia latina* does not include materials *post* 1215.[4] Since 1953, the *Corpus Christianorum*, the monumental edition series of patristic and medieval Christian authors, has aimed to replace Migne's opus with solid, critical editions, and expand the range and number of medieval works available in print.[5] Both offer a rich wealth of source materials to the modern researcher, especially in their digitized forms.

The digitization revolution has transformed medieval studies in more ways than can be sketched here. The digitization of library materials (such as Google Books and the Open Library Project) brings the early modern editions of medieval sources (which are, in some cases, the only editions available) within reach of modern scholars, and scholars studying medieval manuscripts now have medieval bibles from Paris, London, or Saint Gall easily available at a touch of the mouse. Rare reference works, such as Stegmüller's *Repertorium Biblicum*, are now available online. Given this wealth of resources and source materials, it seems more important than ever to have a basic introduction that enables future researchers to understand these source materials in their historical context. It is hoped that this book has been of some use toward that end.

---

[4] Bloch, *God's Plagiarist*.
[5] *Corpus Christianorum 1953–2003. Xenium Natalicum*, ed. Leemans and Jocqué.

A Comparative Canon Chart

The following chart will clarify the canon and book order of the Hebrew Bible (according to the tenth-century Aleppo Codex and Codex Leningradensis), the early-eighth-century Amiatnus, a thirteenth-century northern French Bible, and the post-Trent modern Christian Bible, respectively. Apocryphal books in the Protestant canon of the modern Christian Bible are in parenthesis.

OLD TESTAMENT

Hebrew Bible	Amiatinus	Late Medieval	Modern Christian Bible
Torah	**Old Testament**	**Pentateuch**	**Pentateuch**
Genesis	Genesis	Genesis	Genesis
Exodus	Exodus	Exodus	Exodus
Leviticus	Leviticus	Leviticus	Leviticus
Numbers	Numbers	Numbers	Numbers
Deuteronomy	Deuteronomy	Deuteronomy	Deuteronomy
Former Prophets		**Historical Books**	**Historical Books**
Joshua	Joshua	Joshua	Joshua
Judges	Judges	Judges	Judges
	Ruth	Ruth	Ruth
1 Samuel	1 Samuel	1 Kings = 1 Samuel	1 Samuel
2 Samuel	2 Samuel	2 Kings = 2 Samuel	2 Samuel
1 Kings	1 Kings	3 Kings = 1 Kings	1 Kings
2 Kings	2 Kings	4 Kings = 2 Kings	2 Kings
	1 Chronicles	1 Chronicles	1 Chronicles
	2 Chronicles	2 Chronicles	2 Chronicles
		+ Prayer of Manasseh	

(continued)

(*continued*)

Hebrew Bible	Amiatinus	Late Medieval	Modern Christian Bible
		1 Ezra	Ezra
		2 Ezra / Nehemiah	Nehemiah
		3 Ezra / 2 Ezra	
		4 Ezra*	
		Tobit	Tobit
		Judith	Judith
		Esther	Esther
		+ additions to Esther	(+ additions to Esther)
			(1 Maccabees)
			(2 Maccabees)
		Wisdom Books	**Wisdom Books**
		Job	Job
	Psalms	Psalms	Psalms
		+ Ps. 151**	
	Proverbs	Proverbs	Proverbs
	Ecclesiastes	Ecclesiastes	Ecclesiastes
	Song of Songs	Song of Songs	Song of Songs
	Wisdom	Wisdom	(Wisdom)
	Ecclesiasticus	Ecclesiasticus	(Ecclesiasticus)
		+ Prayer of Solomon	
Latter Prophets		**Prophets**	**Prophets**
Isaiah	Isaiah	Isaiah	Isaiah
Jeremiah	Jeremiah	Jeremiah	Jeremiah
	Lamentations #	Lamentations	Lamentations
		Baruch	(Baruch)
		+ Letter of Jeremiah ##	(+ Letter of Jeremiah)
Ezechiel	Ezechiel	Ezechiel	Ezechiel
	Daniel	Daniel	Daniel
	+ additions to Daniel	+ additions to Daniel	(+ additions to Daniel)
Hosea	Hosea	Hosea	Hosea
Joel	Joel	Joel	Joel
Amos	Amos	Amos	Amos
Obadiah	Obadiah	Obadiah	Obadiah
Jonah	Jonah	Jonah	Jonah
Micha	Micha	Micha	Micha

Nahum	Nahum	Nahum	Nahum
Habakkuk	Habakkuk	Habakkuk	Habakkuk
Zephaniah	Zephaniah	Zephaniah	Zephaniah
Haggai	Haggai	Haggai	Haggai
Zechariah	Zechariah	Zechariah	Zechariah
Malachi	Malachi	Malachi	Malachi
Writings			
Psalms			
Job	Job		
	Tobit		
	Judith		
Proverbs			
Ruth			
Song of Songs			
Ecclesiastes			
Lamentations			
Esther	Esther		
	+ additions to Esther		
Daniel			
Ezra	1 Ezra		
Nehemiah	2 Ezra = Nehemiah		
1 Chronicles			
2 Chronicles			
	1 Maccabees	1 Maccabees	
	2 Maccabees	2 Maccabees	
		3 Maccabees**	
		4 Maccabees**	

(. . .) Considered apocryphal.
+ Addition to the previous book.
# Included under the title Jeremiah.
In some Bibles included after Baruch.
* Omitted in some Bibles.
** Added in some Bibles.

NEW TESTAMENT

Amiatinus	Late Medieval	Modern New Testament
New Testament	**Gospels**	**Gospels**
Matthew	Matthew	Matthew
Mark	Mark	Mark
Luke	Luke	Luke
John	John	John
Acts of the Apostles		Acts of the Apostles
	Letters of St. Paul	**Letters of St. Paul**
Romans	Romans	Romans
1 Corinthians	1 Corinthians	1 Corinthians
2 Corinthians	2 Corinthians	2 Corinthians
Galatians	Galatians	Galatians
Ephesians	Ephesians	Ephesians
Philippians	Philippians	Philippians
Colossians	Colossians	Colossians
1 Thessalonians	1 Thessalonians	1 Thessalonians
2 Thessalonians	2 Thessalonians	2 Thessalonians
	Laodicenses**	
1 Timothy	1 Timothy	1 Timothy
2 Timothy	2 Timothy	2 Timothy
Titus	Titus	Titus
Philemon	Philemon	Philemon
Hebrews	Hebrews	Hebrews
	Acts of the Apostles	
	Catholic Letters	**Catholic Letters**
James	James	James
1 Peter	1 Peter	1 Peter
2 Peter	2 Peter	2 Peter
1 John	1 John	1 John
2 John	2 John	2 John
3 John	3 John	3 John
Jude	Jude	Jude
	(Acts of the Apostles)***	
Revelation	Revelation	Revelation

** Added in some Bibles.
*** Acts is placed between Letters and Revelation in many medieval Bibles.

APPENDIX B

Names for Biblical Books

BOOKS OF THE BIBLE KNOWN BY
DIFFERENT NAMES

1–2 Samuel	1–2 Kings	1–2 Kingdoms	
1–2 Kings	3–4 Kings	3–4 Kingdoms	Malachim
Chronicles	Paralipomenon	Verba dierum	
Ecclesiasticus	Jesus Sirach		
Wisdom	Wisdom of Solomon		
Song of Songs	Canticle of Canticles	Song of Solomon	
Tobit	Tobias		
Ezra	1 Ezra		
Nehemiah	2 Ezra		
3 Ezra	1 Esdras		
4 Ezra	2 Esdras		
Revelation	Apocalypse		

NAMES FOR GROUPS OF BIBLICAL BOOKS
(SEE ALSO APPENDIX A)

Pentateuch (Torah in the Hebrew Bible): Genesis, Exodus, Leviticus, Numbers, Deuteronomy

Hexateuch: Pentateuch (see preceding listing) plus Joshua

Heptateuch: Pentateuch (see preceding listing) plus Joshua and Judges

Former Prophets (Hebrew Bible): Joshua, Judges, 1–2 Samuel, 1–2 Kings

Latter Prophets (Hebrew Bible): Isaiah, Jeremiah, Ezechiel, Minor Prophets (see subsequent listing)

Minor Prophets: Hosea, Joel, Amos, Obadiah, Jonah, Micah, Nahum, Habacuc, Zephaniah, Haggai, Zachariah, Malachi.

Book of Women (rare): Esther, Judith, possibly Ruth

Books of Solomon: Proverbs, Ecclesiastes, Song of Songs

269

Wisdom Books: Proverbs, Ecclesiastes, Song of Songs, Wisdom, Ecclesiasticus

Gospels: Matthew, Mark, Luke, John

Pauline Epistles: Romans, 1–2 Corinthians, Galatians, Ephesians, Philippians, Colossians, 1–2 Thessalonians, 1–2 Timothy, Titus, Philemon, Hebrews

Catholic Epistles: James, 1–2 Peter, 1–3 John, Jude

PSALMS IN THE VULGATE AND MODERN BIBLES

Modern Bibles (following the Hebrew canon)	Vulgate
Ps. 1–8	= Ps. 1–8
Ps. 9–10	= Ps. 9*
Ps. 11–146	= Ps. 10–145
Ps. 147[†]	= Ps. 146–147
Ps. 148–150	= Ps. 148–150
	Ps. 151[‡]

* Modern Ps. 10 begins at verse 20 of the Vulgate Ps. 9.

[†] Vulgate Ps. 147 starts at verse 12 of the modern Ps. 147.

[‡] Apocryphal; only in some manuscripts.

A Schematic Genealogy of Old Testament Translations

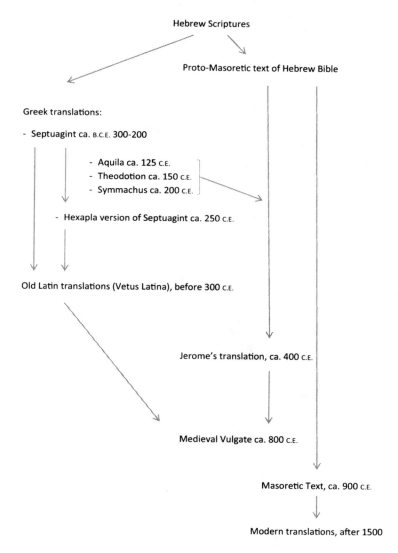

Hebrew Scriptures

Proto-Masoretic text of Hebrew Bible

Greek translations:

- Septuagint ca. B.C.E. 300-200

  - Aquila ca. 125 C.E.
  - Theodotion ca. 150 C.E.
  - Symmachus ca. 200 C.E.

  - Hexapla version of Septuagint ca. 250 C.E.

Old Latin translations (Vetus Latina), before 300 C.E.

Jerome's translation, ca. 400 C.E.

Medieval Vulgate ca. 800 C.E.

Masoretic Text, ca. 900 C.E.

Modern translations, after 1500

271

Bibliography

SERIES, ABBREVIATIONS

BL   British Library

CCCM   *Corpus Christianorum, Continuatio Mediaeualis* (Turnhout: Brepols, 1967–).

CCSL   *Corpus Christianorum. Series Latina* (Turnhout: Brepols, 1954–).

CCT   *Corpus Christianorum in Translation* (Turnhout: Brepols, 2009–).

MGH   *Monumenta Germaniae Historica* (Berlin: Weidmann; Hannover: Hahnsche Buchhandlung, 1819–)

PL   *Patrologiae cursus completus sive bibliotheca universalis, integra, uniformis, commoda, oeconomica, omnium ss. Patrum, doctorum scriptorumque ecclesiasticorum qui ab aevo apostolico ad Innocentii III tempora floruerunt, . . . series Latina*, ed. J.-P. Migne, 221 vols. (Paris: Migne, 1844–64).

SC   *Sources Chrétiennes* (Paris: Cerf, 1942–).

Vat.   Biblioteca Apostolica Vaticana

Vulg.   Vulgate

FACSIMILES

Bible moralisée. Codex Vindobonensis 2554, Vienna, Österreichische Nationalbibliothek. With an introduction by Gerald B. Guest. Manuscripts in Miniature, 2. London: Harvey Miller Publishers, 1995.

Bible moralisée. Faks.-Ausg. im Originalformat des Codex Vindobonensis 2554 der Österr. Nationalbibliothek. Edited by Reiner Haussherr. Codices selecti phototypice impressi. Graz: Akadem. Druck-u. Verlagsanst., 1973.

The Bible of the Poor = Biblia Pauperum: A Facsimile Edition of the British Library Blockbook C.9 d.2. Edited by Albert C. Labriola and John W. Smeltz. Pittsburgh: Duquesne University Press, 1990.

Biblia: das ist die gantze Heilige Schrifft. Translated by Martin Luther, with an introduction by Stephan Füssel. Köln: Taschen, 2003. Facsimile reproduction of 1534 original.

Biblia de San Luis. Barcelona: M. Moleiro, 2000–02.

The Biblia Pauperum. A Facsimile and Edition. Edited by Avril Henry. Aldershot: Scolar Press, 1987.

The Book of Durrow. Evangeliorum quattuor Codex Durmachensis: Auctoritate Collegii Sacrosanctae et Individuae Trinitatis juxta Dublin totius codicis similitudinem accuratissime depicti exprimendam curavit. Edited by Arthur Aston Luce. With an introduction by George Otto Simms, Petrus Meyer, and Ludwig Bieler. Olten, Lausanne, and Freiburg-im-Breisgau: Urs Graf-Verlag, 1960.

The Book of Kells: Fine Art Facsimile Edition. With an introduction by Peter Fox. Luzern: Faksimile Verlag Luzern, 1990.

The Codex Alexandrinus (Royal MS. 1.D.V-VIII) in Reduced Photographic Facsimile. London: British Museum, 1909–57.

Codex Amiatinus. Bibbia Amiatina: Ms. Laurenziano Amiatino 1: Biblioteca Medicea Laurenziana di Firenze. Firenze: La Meta Editore, 2003.

Codex Caesareus Upsaliensis: A Facsimile Edition of an Echternach Gospel-Book of the Eleventh Century [Published in 1971 for the 350th Anniversary of the University Library of Uppsala]. With an introduction by Carl Adam Johan Nordenfalk. Stockholm: Almqvist & Wiksell, 1971.

Die Bibel von Moutier-Grandval: British Museum Add. Ms. 10546. Edited by Johannes Duft. In collaboration with Bonifatius Fischer, Albert Bruckner, Ellen J. Beer, Alfred A. Schmid, and Eva Irblich. Bern: Verein Schweizerischer Lithographiebesitzer, 1971.

Biblia latina cum Glossa ordinaria. Facsimile reprint of the editio princeps (Adolph Rusch of Strassburg, c. 1480/1). Edited by Karlfried Froehlich and Margaret T. Gibson. Turnhout: Brepols, 1992.

De Delftse Bijbel van 1477: Facsimile van de oorspronkelijke druk. With an introduction by Cebus Cornelis De Bruin. Amsterdam: Buijten & Schipperheijn, 1977.

The Eadwine Psalter: Text, Image, and Monastic Culture in Twelfth-century Canterbury. Margaret T. Gibson, T.A. Heslop, and Richard William Pfaff. London: Modern Humanities Research Association, 1992.

Der Goldene Psalter, "Dagulf-Psalter": Vollständige faksimile Ausgabe im Originalformat von Codex 1861 der Österreichischen Nationalbibliothek. With an introduction by Kurt Holter. Codices selecti phototypice impressi, 69. Graz: Akademische Druck- u. Verlagsanstalt, 1980.

The Golden Gospels of Echternach, Codex aureus Epternacensis. Edited by Peter Metz. New York: Praeger, 1957.

The Gutenberg Bible: A New Facsimile Edition of the Famous Keystone of Western Printing Presented in its Original Size with the Illuminations Reproduced in Full Color and Gold. Edited by John S. Blay. Paterson, NJ: Pageant Books, 1960.

The Holkham Bible Picture Book. A Facsimile. Edited by Michelle P. Brown. London: The British Library, 2007.

The Luttrell Psalter: A Facsimile. Commentary by Michelle P. Brown. London: The British Library, 2006.

The Old English Illustrated Hexateuch. Edited by C.A. Dodwell and Peter A. M. Clemoes. Early English Manuscripts in Facsimile, 18. London and Copenhagen: Rosenkilde and Bagger, 1974.

Picture Bible [sic] of the Late Middle Ages. Deutsche Bilderbibel aus dem späten Mittelalter. Edited by Josef Hermann Beckmann and Ingeborg Schroth. Konstanz: Jan Thorbecke Verlag, 1960.

The Vespasian Psalter: British Museum, Cotton Vespasian A.1. Edited by David Herndon Wright. Contribution by Alistair Campbell. Early English manuscripts in facsimile, 14. Copenhagen: Rosenkilde and Bagger, 1967.

Wycliffe, John, and John Purvey, trans. *The New Testament in English.* Sexcentenary facsimile edition edited by Donald L. Brake. Portland, OR: International Bible Publications, 1986.

PRIMARY SOURCES

Abelard, Peter. *The Letters of Abelard and Heloise.* Translated by Betty Radice, revised by Michael T. Clanchy. Penguin Classics. London: Penguin Books, 2003.

Aquinas, Thomas. See Thomas Aquinas

Alain of Lille. *Summa de arte praedicandi.* PL 210, 109–198

————. *Liber in distinctionibus dictionum theologicalium.* PL 210, 687–1012.

Alberic of Troisfontaines. *Chronica.* Edited by Georg Heinrich Pertz. MGH Scriptores, 23. Hannover: Hahnsche Buchhandlung, 1874.

Alcuin of York. Epistolae." In *Epistolae Karolini Aevi, II.* Edited by Ernest Dümmler. MGH Epistolae, 4. Berlin: Weidmann, 1895. Available online at http://www.dMGH.de.

Alfred, King. *King Alfred's Old English Prose Translation of the First Fifty Psalms.* Edited by Patrick Paul O'Neill. Medieval Academy Books, 104. Cambridge, MA, 2001. Available online at http://www.medievalacademy.org/resource/resmgr/maa_books_online/oneill_0104.htm.

Andrew of Saint Victor. *Expositio hystorica in librum Regum.* Edited by Frans A. van Liere. CCCM 53A. Turnhout: Brepols, 1996.

————. *De concordia annorum regum Israel et Iuda.* Edited by Frans A. van Liere. CCCM 53A. Turnhout: Brepols, 1996.

————. *Commentary on Samuel and Kings.* Translated by Frans A. van Liere. CCT 3. Turnhout: Brepols, 2009.

Anglo-Saxon Riddles. Translated by John Porter. Hockwold-cum-Wilton: Anglo-Saxon Books, 1995.

Anonymous, *Vita abbatum.* See Bede, Venerable. *Historia Ecclesiastica.*

The Apocryphal New Testament: A Collection of Apocryphal Christian Literature in an English Translation. Edited by James Keith Elliott. Oxford: Clarendon Press, 1993.

The Apocryphal New Testament, Being All the Gospels, Epistles, and Other Pieces Now Extant, Attributed to the First Four Centuries to Jesus Christ, his Apostles, and Their Companions, and not Included in the New Testament by its Compilers. Translated by Jeremiah Jones and William Wake. London: Printed for William Hone, 1820. Reprinted as *The Lost Books of the Bible.* Mineola, NY: Dover Publications, 2005.

Asser. *Alfred the Great. Asser's Life of Alfred and Other Contemporary Sources.* Translated by Simon Keynes and Michael Lapidge. Penguin Classics. London: Penguin Books, 1983.

Augustine of Denmark. "Augustinus de Dacia. Rotulus Pugillaris." Edited by A. Waltz. *Angelicum* 6 (1929): 253–78.

Augustine of Hippo. *De doctrina christiana.* Edited by K. D. Daur and J. Martin. CCSL 32. Turnhout: Brepols, 1962.

———. *Confessionum libri XIII.* Edited by Lucas Verheijen and Martin Skutella. CCSL 27. Turnhout: Brepols, 1981.

———. *Epistolae.* PL 33.

———. *Quaestionum in Heptateuchum libri VII.* Edited by I. Fraipont. CCSL 33. Turnhout: Brepols, 1958.

———. *Saint Augustine. On Christian Teaching.* Translated by R. P. H. Green. The World's Classics. Oxford: Oxford University Press, 1997.

———. *St. Augustine's Confessions.* Edited by P. Knöll. Translated by William Watts. The Loeb Classical Library. Cambridge, MA: Harvard University Press; London: Heinemann, 1989.

Ælfric. *Sermones Catholici. Homilies of the Anglo-Saxon Church. The First Part, Containing the Sermones Catholici, or Homilies of Ælfric.* Edited by Benjamin Thorpe. London: Printed for the Ælfric Society, 1844–46.

———. *Prefatio to Genesis.* In *The Old English Heptateuch.* Ed. Marsden. 3–7

———. *Libellus de ueteri testament et nouo.* In *The Old English Heptateuch.* Ed. Marsden. 201ff.

Æthelwold. *Regularis Concordia. The Monastic Agreement of the Monks and Nuns of the English Nation.* Edited by Thomas Symons. Medieval Classics. London: Thomas Nelson and Sons Ltd., 1953.

The Babylonian Talmud. Translated into English with Notes, Glossary and Indices. Translated by I. Epstein. London, Jerusalem, New York: The Soncino Press, 1935–52.

Bacon, Roger. *Opera quaedam hactenus inedita. Vol. 1, containing: I. Opus tertium; II. Opus minus; III. Compendium philosophiae.* Edited by John Sherren Brewer. Rerum Britannicarum Medii Aevi Scriptores, 15. London: Longman, Green, Longman, and Roberts, 1859.

Bede, Venerable. *Historia ecclesiastica gentis Anglorum; Historia abbatum; Epistola ad Ecgberctum; una cum Historia abbatum auctore anonymo.* Edited by Charles Plummer. Oxford: Clarendon, 1896.

———. *Ecclesiastical History of the English People (Historia ecclesiastica gentis anglorum).* Edited by B. Colgrave and Roger Aubrey Mynors. Oxford Medieval Texts. Oxford, 1969.

———. *Ecclesiastical History of the English Nation.* Translated by J.A. Giles. Everyman's Library, 479. New York: Dutton, 1910. Online at http://www.fordham.edu/halsall/basis/bede-jarrow.asp.

———. *Opera exegetica, pars II, 1: Libri quatuor in principium Genesis.* Edited by C. W. Jones. CCSL 118A. Turnhout: Brepols, 1967.

————. *Opera exegetica, Pars II, 2: In primam partem Samuhelis libri IIII, In Regum librum XXX quaestiones*. Edited by D. Hurst. CCSL 119. Turnhout: Brepols, 1962.

————. *Opera exegetica II.3: In Lucae evangelium expositio; In Marci evangelium expositio*. Edited by D. Hurst. CCSL 120. Turnhout: Brepols, 1960.

————. *Opera didascalica VI.2: De temporum ratione liber*. C. W. Jones. CCSL 123B. Turnhout: Brepols, 1957.

————. *The Reckoning of Time*. Translated by Faith Wallis. Translated Texts for Historians, 29. Liverpool: Liverpool University Press, 1999.

Benedict of Nursia. *Regula*. In *La règle de Saint Benoît*. Edited by Jean Neufville. Translated by Adalbert de Vogüé. Série des textes monastiques d'Occident, no. 34–35. SC 181–182. Paris: Éditions du Cerf, 1971–7.

Bernard of Clairvaux. *Sancti Bernardi Opera*. Edited by Jean Leclercq, Henri-Marie Rochais, and Charles H. Talbot. Roma, 1957–77.

————. *Bernard de Clairvaux. Sermons sur le Cantique*. Edited by Jean Leclercq, H. Rochais, and C.H. Talbot. Translated by Paul Verdeyen and Raffaele Fassetta. SC 414, 431, 452, 472, 511. Paris: Les éditions du Cerf, 1996.

Bernard Gui. *Manuel de l'inquisiteur*. Edited by Guillaume Mollat and G. Drioux. Les classiques de l'histoire de France au Moyen Âge. Paris: Les Belles Lettres, 2006.

————. *The Inquisitor's Guide: A Medieval Manual on Heretics*. Translated by Janet Shirley. Welwyn Garden City: Ravenhall Books, 2006.

Bibelwerk. See *Reference Bible*

La Bible française du XIIIe siècle. Édition critique de la Genèse. Edited by Michel Quereuil. Genève: Droz, 1988.

Biblia maxima versionum ex linguis orientalibus... collectarum; earumque concordia cum vulgata et eius expositione litterali, cum annotationibus Nicolai de Lyra... etc. Edited by Joannes De La Haye. Paris: Sumptibus D. Bechet & L. Billaine, Antonii Bertier, Simeonis Piget, 1660.

Biblia Sacra iuxta Latinam Vulgatam Versionem, ad codicum fidem iussu Pii PP. XII. Cura et studio Monachum Abbatiae Sancti Hieronymi in urbe O.S.B. Roma: Ex typis polyglottis Vaticanis, 1926–95. 18 vols.

Biblia sacra iuxta vulgatam versionem. Edited by Robert Weber, Bonifatius Fischer, Jean Gribomont, H. F. D. Sparks, and W. Thiele. Stuttgart: Deutsche Bibelgesellschaft, 1969. 2 vols. Fourth edition 1994.

Bibliorum Sacrorum Latinae Versiones Antiquae, seu Vetus Italica. Edited by Petrus Sabatier. Reims, 1743–51. 3 vols.

Bibliorum sacrorum cum glossa ordinaria... et Postilla Nicolai Lyrani, additionibus Pauli Burgensis ad ipsi Lyranum ac ad easdem Matthiae Thoringi replicis. Venice: Giunta, 1603.

Birgitta of Sweden. *Life and Selected Revelations*. Edited by Marguerite Tjader Harris. Translated by Albert Ryle Kezel, with an introduction by Tore Nyberg. Classics of Western Spirituality. New York/Mahwah, NJ: Paulist Press, 1990.

Bischoff, Bernhard, and Michael Lapidge, eds. *Biblical Commentaries from the Canterbury School of Theodore and Hadrian.* Cambridge Studies in Anglo-Saxon England, 10. Cambridge: Cambridge University Press, 1994.

Bonaventure, Saint. *Doctoris Seraphici S. Bonaventurae. Opera Omnia.* Cura et studio pp. collegii S. Bonaventurae. Quaracchi, 1882–1902.

The Book of Sainte Foy. Translated by Pamela Sheingorn, in collaboration with Robert L.A. Clark. Middle Ages Series. Philadelphia: University of Pennsylvania Press, 1995.

The Book of the Popes (Liber pontificalis) I. Translated by Louise Ropes Loomis. Records of Civilization: Sources and Studies. New York: Columbia University Press, 1916.

Bullarium Franciscanum, sive romanorum pontificium constitutiones, epistolae, diplomata tribus ordinibus Minorum. Edited by Konrad Eubel. Roma: E Typis Vaticanis, 1898–1904.

Caesarius of Arles. *Life, Testament, Letters.* Translated by William E. Klingshirn. Translated Texts for Historians, 19. Liverpool: Liverpool University Press, 1994.

————. *Césaire d'Arles. Sermons au peuple.* Edited and translated by Marie-José Delage. SC 175. Paris: Éditions du Cerf, 1971.

Canons and Decrees of the Council of Trent. English Translation. Translated by H. J. Schroeder. Rockford, Ill.: Tan Book, 1978.

Capitularia regum Francorum. Edited by Alfred Boretius. MGH, Leges, 2. Hannover: Hahnsche Buchhandlung, 1883. Available online at http://www.dMGH.de.

Cassian. *Conferences.* Translated by Edgar C. S. Gibson. A Select Library of Nicene and Post-Nicene Fathers of the Christian Church, 11. Grand Rapids: Wm. B. Eerdmans Publishing Co., 1973. Reprint, New York 1894.

Cassiodorus. *Institutiones.* Edited by Roger Aubrey Baskerville Mynors. Oxford: Clarendon Press, 1937.

————. *Institutions of Divine and Secular Learning and On the Soul.* Translated by James W. Halporn and Mark Vessey. Translated Texts for Historians, 42. Liverpool: Liverpool University Press, 2004.

Chartularium Universitatis Parisiensis. Edited by Henricus Suso Denifle and Aemilius Chatelain. Paris, 1889–97. 2 vols.

Charlemagne. Preface to Paulus Diaconus' *Homiliarius.* PL 95, 955–56.

Codex Fuldensis: Novum Testamentum Latinum interprete Hieronymo. Edited by Ernest Ranke. Marburg: N. G. Elwert, 1868.

Comestor, Peter. See Peter Comestor.

Concilia aevi Karolini. Edited by Albert Werminghoff. MGH Legum sectio III, Concilia, 2.1. Hannover and Leipzig: Hahnsche Buchhandlung, 1906. Available online at http://www.dMGH.de.

Concilia Magnae Britanniae et Hiberniae. Vol. 3: Ab anno MCCCL ad annum MDXLV. Edited by David Wilkins. London: Gosling, Giles, Woodward, and Davis, 1737.

Conciliorum oecumenicorum generaliumque decreta, editio critica. Vol. 3: The Oecumenical Councils of the Roman Catholic Church from Trent to Vatican II (1545–1965). Edited by Klaus Ganzer, Giuseppe Alberigo, and Alberto Melloni. Turnhout: Brepols, 2010.

Conciliorum oecumenicorum decreta. Edited by Giuseppe Alberigo, Giuseppe Dossetti, Claudio Leonardi, and Paulo Prodi. In collaboration with Hubert Jedin. Bologna: Istituto per le scienze religiose, 1973.

The Complete Jewish Bible with Rashi Commentary. Translated by A. J. Rosenberg. New York: Judaica Press, n.d. Online at http://www.chabad.org/library/bible_cdo/aid/63255/jewish/The-Bible-with-Rashi.htm.

Corpus documentorum inquisitionis Neerlandicae. Vol 1: Tot aan de herinrichting der Inquisitie onder keizer Karel V (1025–1520). Edited by Paul Fredericq. Gent: J. Vuylsteke; 's Gravenhage: Martinus Nijhoff, 1889.

Das Decretum Gelasianum de libris recipiendis in kritischem Text herausgegeben und untersucht. Edited by Ernst von Dobschütz. Untersuchungen zur Geschichte der altchristlichen Literatur, 3. Reihe, 8:4. Leipzig: Hinrichs'sche Buchhandlung, 1912.

Dhuoda. *Handbook for William. A Carolingian Woman's Counsel for Her Son.* Translated by Carol Neel. Medieval Texts in Translation. Washington: The Catholic University of America Press, 1999.

Dove, Mary, ed. *The Earliest Advocates of the English Bible: The Texts of the Medieval Debate.* Exeter: Exeter University Press, 2010.

Dronke, Peter, trans. and ed. *Nine Medieval Latin Plays.* Cambridge Medieval Classics. Cambridge: Cambridge University Press, 1994.

Egeria. *Egeria's Travels: Newly Translated (from the Latin) with Supporting Documents and Notes.* Translated by John Wilkinson. London: S.P.C.K., 1971.

Einhard. *Vita Karoli Magni.* Edited by Georg Heinrich Pertz. MGH Scriptores rerum gemanicarum 2. Hannover: Hahnsche Buchhandlung, 1863. Available online at http://www.dMGH.de.

————. *The Life of Charlemagne.* Translated by Samuel Epes Turner, with an introduction by Sidney Painter. Ann Arbor Paperbacks. Ann Arbor: University of Michigan Press, 1960.

Enchiridion symbolorum, definitionum et declarationum de rebus fidei et morum. 3rd ed. Edited by Henricus Denzinger and Adolfus Schönmetzer. Barcelona: Herder, 1976.

Emmerich, Anne Catherine. *The Dolorous Passion of Our Lord Jesus Christ.* Translated by Clemens Brentano. Charlotte: TAN Press, 1994.

Erasmus. *The Correspondence of Erasmus.* Translated by and edited by Roger Aubrey Baskerville Mynors, Douglas Ferqus Scott Thomson, and Wallace Klippert Ferguson. Collected Works of Erasmus, 3. Toronto and Buffalo: University of Toronto Press, 1976.

Eusebius of Pamphilia. *Church History.* Translated by Arthur Cushman McGiffert. A Select Library of Nicene and Post-Nicene Fathers of the Christian Church, 1. Grand Rapids: Wm. B. Eerdmans Publishing Co., 1976. Reprint.

_____. *Life of Constantine*. Translated by Averil Cameron and Stuart G. Hall. Clarendon ancient history series. Oxford: Clarendon Press, 1999.

The Exeter Book Riddles. Translated by Kevin Crossley-Holland. London: Enitharmon Press, 2008.

Gilbert Foliot. *Expositio in Cantica Canticorum*. PL 202, 1147–1304.

Ginzberg, Louis. *The Legends of the Jews*. Translated by Henrietta Szold, with a foreword by James L. Kugel. Baltimore and London: The Johns Hopkins University Press, 1998. Originally published: Philadelphia: Jewish Publication Society of America, 1909, 1937.

Glossa ordinaria. See *Biblia latina*, under Facsimiles, earlier.

The Goths in the Fourth Century. Translated by Peter Heather and John Matthews. Translated Texts for Historians, vol. 11. Liverpool: Liverpool University Press, 1991.

Gregory the Great. *Sancti Gregorii Magni Moralia in Iob*. Edited by Marcus Adriaen. CCSL 143–143B. Turnhout: Brepols, 1979–85.

_____. *Registrum Epistolarum, Libri VIII–XIV*. Edited by Dag Norberg. CCCM 140A. Turnhout: Brepols, 1982.

Godman, Peter, ed. *Poetry of the Carolingian Renaissance*. Duckworth Classical, Medieval, and Renaissance Editions. London: Duckworth, 1985.

Haimo of Auxerre, *Enarratio in Jonam Prophetam*. PL 118, 127–138.

_____. *Commentary on the Book of Jonah*. Translated by Deborah Everhart. TEAMS Commentary Series. Kalamazoo: Medieval Institute Publications, 1993.

Heliand. Edited by Otto Behaghel. Altdeutsche Textbibliothek, no. 4. Halle: M. Niemeyer, 1882.

Heliand: Text and Commentary. Edited by James E. Cathey. Morgantown: West Virginia University Press, 2002.

The Heliand: The Saxon Gospel. Translated by G. Ronald Murphy. New York and Oxford: Oxford University Press, 1992.

Hildebert of Lavardin. *De mysterio missae*. PL 171, 1177–1194.

Historical Creeds and Confessions, edited by Rick Brannan. Grand Rapids: Christian Classics Ethereal Library, 1998. E-book http://www.ccel.org/ccel/brannan/hstcrcon.

Honorius Augustudonensis. *In Canticum Canticorum*. PL 172, 347–496.

Hrabanus Maurus. *Epistolae*. In *Epistolae Karolini Aevi, III*, edited by Ernest Dümmler. MGH Epistolae, 5. Berlin: Weidmann, 1899. Available online at http://www.dMGH.de.

_____. *Homiliae de Festis*, PL 110, 9–135.

_____. *Homiliae in Evangelia et Epistulas*. PL 110, 135–467.

Hugh of Saint Victor. *Didascalicon de Studio Legendi. A Critical Text*. Edited by Charles Henry Buttimer. The Catholic University of America Studies in Medieval and Renaissance Latin, 10. Washington: Catholic University of America Press, 1939.

_____. *Didascalicon*. In *Interpretation of Scripture: Theory*. 81–202.

_____. *The Diligent Examiner*. In *Interpretation of Scripture: Theory*. 231–52.

————. *Hugh of St. Victor. Selected Spiritual Writings.* With an introduction by Aelred Squire, translated by a Religious of C.S.M.V. London: Harper & Row, Publishers, 1962.

————. "Hugh of Saint Victor. De Tribus Maximis Circumstantiis Gestorum." Edited by William M. Green. *Speculum* 18 (1943): 484–93.

————. *On Sacred Scripture and Its Authors.* In *Interpretation of Scripture: Theory.* 213–230.

Hugh of Saint Cher. *Hugonis de Sancto Charo Opera omnia in uniuersum Vetus & Nouum Testamentum. Editio vltima prae caeteris recognita et emendata.* Lyon: Ioannes Antonius Huguetan & Guillelmus Barbier, 1669.

Innocent III, *Regesta sive epistolae.* PL 214

Interpretation of Scripture: Theory. Edited by Franklin T. Harkins and Frans A. van Liere. Victorine Texts in Translation, 3. Turnhout: Brepols, 2012.

Interpretation of Scripture: Practice. Edited by Franklin T. Harkins and Frans A. van Liere. Victorine Texts in Translation, 6. Turnhout: Brepols, forthcoming.

Isidore of Seville. *De veteri et novo testamento quaestiones.* PL 83, 200–208.

————. *The Etymologies of Isidore of Seville.* Translated by Stephen A. Barney, W.J. Lewis, J.A. Beach, and Oliver Berghof. Cambridge: Cambridge University Press, 2006.

————. *Quaestiones in Vetus Testamentum.* PL 83, 208–433.

Jerome. *Epistolae.* PL 22. 325–1191.

————. *Liber Hebraicorum nominum.* PL 23, 771–858.

————. *Prologus in epistulis Pauli,* in *Biblia sacra,* ed. Weber, 1748–49.

————. *Prologus Hiezechielis Prophetae,* in *Biblia sacra,* ed. Weber, 1266–67.

————. *Prologus in Isaia, Biblia sacra,* ed. Weber, 1096.

————. *Prologus in libro Ezrae,* in *Biblia sacra,* ed. Weber, 638–39.

————. *Prologus in libro Iosue,* in *Biblia sacra,* ed. Weber, 285–86.

————. *Prologus in libris Solomonis,* in *Biblia sacra,* ed. Weber, 957.

————. *Prologus in libris Regum,* in *Biblia sacra,* ed. Weber, 364–65.

————. *Prologus in libro Paralipomenon,* in *Biblia sacra,* ed. Weber, 546–47.

————. *Prologus in Pentateucho,* in *Biblia sacra,* ed. Weber, 3–4.

John of Damascus, St. *Three Treatises on the Divine Images.* Translation and introduction by Andrew Louth. Popular Patristics Series. Crestwood, N.Y.: St. Vladimir's Seminary Press, 2003.

Josephus, Flavius. *Contra Apionem.* Edited and translated by H. S. J. Thackeray. Loeb Classical Series. Cambridge, MA: Harvard University Press, 1961.

Die Konzilien der karolingischen Teilreiche 843–859. Edited by Wilfried Hartmann. MGH Concilia, 3. Hannover: Hannsche Buchhandlung, 1984. Available online at http://www.dMGH.de.

Lettre d'Aristée à Philocrate. Edited by André Pelletier. SC 89. Paris: Éditions du Cerf, 1962.

Medieval Literary Theory and Criticism, c.1000–c.1375. The Commentary Tradition. Edited by Alastair J. Minnis and A.B. Scott. Oxford: Oxford University Press, 1988.

Mikra'ot gedolot. Genesis: a New English translation. Translated by A.J. Rosenberg. New York: Judaica Press, 1993.

Milo Crispin. *Vita Lanfranci.* PL 150, 29–58.

The Mishnah. Translated by Herbert Danby. Oxford: Oxford University Press, 1933.

Nicholas of Lyra. *Biblia sacra cum glossis, interlineari et ordinaria, Nicolai Lyrani Postilla et moralitatibus, Burgensis additionibus, et Thoringi replicis.* Lyon: [s.n], 1545.

————. *Bibliorum sacrorum cum glossa ordinaria... et Postilla Nicolai Lyrani, additionibus Pauli Burgensis ad ipsi Lyranum ac ad easdem Matthiae Thoringi replicis.* Venice: Giunta, 1603.

Notker of Saint Gall, *Charlemagne.* In *Einhard and Notker. Two Lives of Charlemagne.* Translated by Lewis Thorpe. Penguin Classics. London and Harmondsworth: Penguin Books, 1969.

The Old English Heptateuch, and Ælfric's Libellus de Veteri Testamento et Novo. Edited by Richard Marsden. Early English Text Society, no. 330. Oxford: Oxford University Press for the Early English Text Society, 2008.

The Old English Riddles of the Exeter Book. Edited by Craig Williamson. Chapel Hill: University of North Carolina Press, 1977.

The Old English Version of the Gospels. Vol. 1: Text and Introduction. Edited by Roy M. Liuzza. Early English Text Society, Original Series, 304. Oxford: Oxford University Press, 1994.

Olivi, Petrus Iohannis. *Peter of John Olivi on the Bible: Principia Quinque in Sacram Scripturam; Postilla in Isaiam et in I ad Corinthios.* Edited by David Flood and Gedeon Gál. Franciscan Institute Publications. St. Bonaventure: Franciscan Institute, 1997.

Les Ordines romani du haut Moyen Age. Edited by Michel Andrieu. Spicilegium sacrum lovaniense. Études et documents, 11, 23, 24, 28, 29. Louvain, 1930–56.

Otfrid von Weissenburg. *Das Evangelienbuch.* Edited by Oskar Erdmann. Altdeutsche Textbibliothek. Tübingen: M. Niemeyer, 1957.

Peter Abelard. See Abelard, Peter.

Peter the Chanter. *Verbum Adbreviatum. Textus conflatus.* Edited by Monique Boutry. CCCM 196. Turnhout: Brepols, 2004.

Peter Comestor. *Scholastica historia, liber Genesis.* Edited by Agneta Sylwan. CCCM 191. Turnhout: Brepols, 2005.

————. *Historia scholastica.* PL 198, 1045–1721.

Petrus Aureoli. *Compendium sensus litteralis totius divinae Scripturae.* Edited by Philibertus Seeboeck. Quaracchi: Collegium S. Bonaventurae, 1896.

Petrus Iohannis Olivi. See Olivi, Petrus Iohannis.

Petrus Riga. *Aurora, Petri Rigae Biblia Versificata. A Verse Commentary on the Bible.* Edited by Paul E. Beichner. Publications in Medieval Studies, 19. Notre Dame: Notre Dame University Press, 1965.

Petrus Venerabilis. *Adversus Iudaeorum inveteratam duritiem.* Edited by Yvonne Friedman. CCCM 58. Turnhout: Brepols, 1985.

Physiologus. Translated by Michael J. Curley. Chicago: University of Chicago Press, 1979.

The Prose Solomon and Saturn and Adrian and Ritheus. Edited by James E. Cross and Thomas D. Hill. McMaster Old English Studies and Texts, 1. Toronto and Buffalo: University of Toronto Press, 1982.

Le Psautier Romain et les autres anciens psautiers latins. Edited by Robert Weber. Collectanea Biblica Latina, vol. 10. Roma: Abbaye Saint-Jérôme, 1953.

Pseudo-Jerome. *Quaestiones on the Book of Samuel.* Edited by Avrom Saltman. Studia Post-Biblica, 26. Leiden, 1975.

The Reference Bible. Das Bibelwerk. Inter pauca problesmata de enigmatibus ex tomis canonicis nunc prompta sunt Praefatio et libri de Pentateucho Moysi. Edited by Gerard MacGinty. CCCM 173. Turnhout: Brepols, 2000.

Richard of Saint Victor. *De concordantia temporum,* PL 196, 255–265. Translation forthcoming in *Interpretation of Scripture: Practice.*

————. *De emmanuele,* PL 196, 601–665. Translation forthcoming in *Interpretation of Scripture: Practice.*

————. *Explicatio in Cantica Canticorum.* PL 196, 405–523.

The Riddles of the Exeter Book. Translated by Frederick Tupper. Boston: Ginn, 1910.

Robert of Melun. *Sentences.* In *Interpretation of Scripture: Theory,* 445–478.

Roger Bacon. See Bacon, Roger.

Rupert of Deutz. *De Sancta Trinitate et operibus eius.* PL 167, 197–1570.

Sacrorum conciliorum nova et amplissima collectio. Edited by Joannes Dominicus Mansi, 330–31. Venezia: Zatta, 1779.

Salimbene of Adam. *The Chronicle of Salimbene de Adam.* Translated by Joseph L. Baird, Giuseppe Baglivi, and John Robert Kane. Medieval & Renaissance Texts & Studies, vol. 40. Binghamton, NY: Center for Medieval and Early Renaissance Studies, 1986.

Senensis, Sixtus. *Bibliotheca sancta.* Edited by Johannes Hayo. Paris: Rolini Theodorici, 1610. First edition 1566.

Septuaginta, id est Vetus Testamentum graece iuxta LXX interpretes. Edited by Alfred Ralphs. Stuttgart: Deutsche Bibelstiftung, 1935.

————. *A new English translation of the Septuagint.* Translated by Albert Pietersma and Benjamin G. Wright. New York: Oxford University Press, 2000.

Sigebert of Gembloux. *Gesta abbatium Gemblacensium.* PL 160, 625B.

Spinoza, Benedictus de. *Works: Tractatus theologico-politicus.* Translated from the Latin with an introduction by R. H. M. Elwes. New York: Dover, 1951. Reprint, London: G. Bell, 1883.

Stephan of Bourbon. *Tractatus de diversis materiis prædicabilibus.* Edited by Albert Lecoy de La Marche. Société de l'histoire de France. Publications in octavo. 185. Paris: Librairie Renouard, H. Loones, successeur, 1877.

Stephen of Cîteaux, *Censura de aliquot locis bibliorum,* PL 166, 1373–1376.

Suger, Abbot of Saint Denis. *De rebus in administatione sua gestis.* In *Abbot Suger on the Abbey Church of St.-Denis and Its Art Treasures.* Translated by Erwin Panofsky. Princeton: Princeton University Press, 1946.

Thomas Aquinas. *S. Thomae Aquinatis Opera omnia*. Edited by Roberto Busa. Stuttgart/Bad Cannstadt: Frommann-Holzboog, 1980.

———. *Catena Aurea: Commentary on the Four Gospels Collected out of the Works of the Fathers*. Translated by John Henry Newman. London: Baronius Press, 2009.

Vetus Latina: Die Reste der Altlatinischen Bibel, nach Petrus Sabatier neu gesammelt und herausgegeben von der Erzabtei Beuron. Gen. ed. Bonifatius Fischer. Freiburg: Herder, 1949–

Vetus Testamentum. Pars prima: Genesis-IV Regum. Het Oude Testament. Eerste stuk, Genesis-II Koningen. Edited by Cebus Cornelis De Bruin. Corpus Sacrae Scripturae Neerlandicae Medii Aevi, series maior, 1. Leiden: Brill, 1977.

Wolbero of St Pantaleon. *Commentaria in Canticum Canticorum*. PL 195, 1001–1278.

Wulfstan of York. *Sermo Lupi ad Anglos*. Edited by Dorothy Whitelock. Exeter Medieval English texts. London: Methuen, 1963.

Wyclif, John. *On the Truth of Holy Scripture*. Translated by Ian Christopher Levy. TEAMS Commentary Series. Kalamazoo: Medieval Institute Publications, 2001.

The Wycliffe New Testament (1388): An Edition in Modern Spelling, with an Introduction, the Original Prologues and the Epistle to the Laodiceans. Edited by W. R. Cooper. London: British Library, 2002.

The York Play: A Facsimile of British Library MS Additional 35290; together with a Facsimile of the Ordo Paginarum section of the A. Edited by Richard Beadle and Peter Meredith. Leeds Texts and Monographs. Leeds: The University of Leeds, School of English, 1983.

York Mystery Plays: A Selection in Modern Spelling. Edited by Richard Beadle and Pamela M. King. Oxford: Oxford University Press, 1984.

SECONDARY SOURCES

Adkin, Neil. "A Note on Jerome's Knowledge of Hebrew." *Euphrosyne. Revista de filologia clássica*, N.S. 23 (1995): 243–45.

Amos, Thomas L., Eugene A. Green, and Beverly Mayne Kienzle, eds. *De ore Domini: preacher and Word in the Middle Ages*. Studies in Medieval Culture, 27. Kalamazoo: Medieval Institute Publications, 1989.

Archambault, Paul. "The Ages of Man and the Ages of the World: A Study of Two Traditions." *Revue des études augustiniennes* 11 (1966): 193–228.

Aune, David E. "On the Origins of the 'Council of Javneh' Myth." *Journal of Biblical Literature* 110 (1991): 491–93.

Backhouse, Janet. *Medieval Rural Life in the Luttrell Psalter*. Toronto and Buffalo: University of Toronto Press, 2000.

Bagnall, Roger S. *Early Christian Books in Egypt*. Princeton: Princeton University Press, 2009.

Banitt, Menahem. "The La'azim of Rashi and the French Biblical Glossaries." In *World History of the Jewish People: Second Series: Medieval Period. Vol. 2: The*

Dark Ages. Jews in Christian Europe 711–1096, edited by Cecil Roth and I.H. Levine, 291–96. Tel Aviv: Massadah Publishing, 1966.

Barre, Henri. *Les homéliaires carolingiens de l'école d'Auxerre; authenticité, inventaire, tableaux comparatifs, initia.* Studi e testi, 225. Città del Vaticano: Biblioteca Apostolica Vaticana, 1962.

Bataillon, Louis-Jacques. "Intermédiaires entre les traités de morale pratique et les sermons: les 'distinctiones' bibliques alphabétiques." In *Les genres littéraires dans les sources théologiques et philosophiques médiévales: définition, critique et exploitation. Actes du Colloque international de Louvain-la-Neuve, 25–27 mai 1981.* Publications de l'Institut d'études médiévales, 2me série, 5, 213–26. Louvain-la-Neuve, 1982.

Bayless, Martha. "The *Collectanea* and Medieval Dialogues and Riddles." In *Collectanea pseudo-Bedae*, edited by Martha Bayless and Michael Lapidge, contributor Debby Banham. Scriptores Latini Hiberniae, vol. 14, 13–41. Dublin: School of Celtic Studies, Dublin Institute for Advanced Studies, 1998.

Bentley, Jerry H. *Humanists and Holy Writ: New Testament Scholarship in the Renaissance.* Princeton: Princeton University Press, 1983.

Berger, Samuel. *Histoire de la Vulgate pendant les premiers siècles du moyen âge.* Paris: Hachette, 1893. Reprint Hildesheim and New York: Georg Olms Verlag, 1976.

———. *La Bible Française au Moyen Age. Étude sur les plus anciennes versions de la Bible écrits en langue d'oïl.* Paris: Imprimerie nationale, 1884. Reprint: Genève: Slatkine, 1967.

———. *La Bible au XVIe siècle. Étude sur les origines de la critique biblique.* Paris, 1879. Reprint: Genève: Slatkine, 1969.

Berndt, Rainer. "Gehören die Kirchenväter zur heiligen Schrift? Zur Kanontheorie des Hugo von St Viktor." In *Zum Problem des biblischen Kanons*, edited by Ingo Baldermann, 191–99. Neukirchen-Vluyn: Neukirchener Verlag, 1988.

La Bibbia nel Medioevo. Edited by Giuseppe Cremascoli and Claudio Leonardi. La Bibbia nella Storia, 17. Bologna: Edizioni Dehoniane, 1996.

La Bibbia nel XIII secolo. Storia del testo, storia dell'esegesi. Atti del Convegno della Società Internazionale per lo Studio del Medioevo Latino (SISMEL). Firenze, 1–2 giugno 2001. Edited by Giuseppe Cremascoli and Francesco Santi. Millenio Medievale 49. Atti di convegni 14. Firenze: Edizione del Galluzzo, 2004.

La Bibbia "Vulgata" dalle origini ai nostri giorni: Atti del Simposio internazionale in onore di Sisto V, Grottamare, 29–31 Agosto 1985. Edited by Tarcisio Stramare. Collectanea Biblica Latina, 16. Roma: Abbazia S. Girolamo, 1987.

Le Bibbie Atlantiche, il libro delle Scritture tra monumentalità e rappresentazione. Edited by Marilena Maniaci and Giulia Orofino. Milano/Roma: Centro Tibaldi, 2000.

The Bible as Book. The Manuscript Tradition. Edited by John L. Sharpe and Kimberly Van Kampen. London/New Castle: British Library/Oak Knoll Press, 1998.

The Bible in Its Ancient and English Versions. Edited by Henry Wheeler Robinson. Oxford: Clarendon Press, 1954.

The Bible in the Middle Ages: Its Influence on Literature and Art. Edited by Bernard S. Levy. Medieval and Renaissance Texts and Studies, 89. Tempe: Arizona Center for Medieval and Renaissance Studies, 2003. Originally published Binghamton, NY, 1992.

Biller, Peter. "The Cathars of Languedoc and Written Materials." In *Heresy and Literacy, 1000–1530*, edited by Peter Biller and Anne Hudson. Cambridge Studies in Medieval Literature, 23, 61–82. Cambridge: Cambridge University Press, 1994.

Bischoff, Bernhard. "Das griechische Element in der abendländischen Bildung." In *Mittelalterliche Studien. Ausgewählte Aufsätze zur Schriftkunde und Literaturgeschichte. Vol. 2*, 246–75. Stuttgart: Hiersemann, 1966.

―――――. "Wendepunkte in der Geschichte der lateinischen Exegese im Mittelalter." *Sacris erudiri* 6 (1954): 189–281. Also in *Mittelalterliche Studien. Ausgewählte Aufsätze zur Schriftkunde und Literaturgeschichte. Vol. 1*, 205–73. Stuttgart: Hiersemann, 1967.

Bloch, R. Howard. *God's Plagiarist: Being an Account of the Fabulous Industry and Irregular Commerce of the Abbé Migne.* Chicago: University of Chicago Press, 1994.

Blondheim, David Simon. *Les parlers judéo-romans et la Vetus latina: étude sur les rapports entre les traductions bibliques en langue romane de juifs au moyen âge et les anciennes versions.* Paris: É. Champion, 1925.

Bogaert, Pierre-Maurice. "La Bible latine des origines au moyen âge. Aperçu historique, état des questions." *Revue théologique de Louvain* 19 (1988): 137–59, 276–314.

―――――, and Christian Cannuyer, eds. *Les Bibles en Français. Histoire illustrée du moyen âge à nos jours.* Turnhout: Brepols, 1991.

Bori, Pier Cesare. *L'interpretation infinie. L'herméneutique chrétienne ancienne et ses transformations.* Translated by F. Vial. Passages. Paris: Éditions du Cerf, 1991.

Boyle, Leonard E. "Innocent III and Vernacular Versions of Scripture." In *The Bible in the Medieval World. Essays in Honour of Beryl Smalley*, edited by Katherine Walsh and Diana Wood. Studies in Church History, Subsidia 4, 97–107. Oxford: Blackwell, 1985.

Boynton, Susan. "The Bible and the Liturgy." In *The Practice of the Bible*, 10–33.

Brisson, Luc. *How Philosophers Saved Myths: Allegorical Interpretation and Classical Mythology.* Translated by Catherine Tinanyi. Chicago: The University of Chicago Press, 2004.

Brown, Michelle P. *The Lindisfarne Gospels. Society, Spirituality, and the Scribe.* British Library Studies in Medieval Culture. London: British Library, 2003.

―――――. *The Holkham Bible Picture Book. A Facsimile.* London: British Library, 2007.

Brown, Peter. *The Rise of Western Christendom: Triumph and Diversity, A.D. 200–1000.* The Making of Europe. Oxford: Blackwell Publishers, 2003. Second edition, 1996.

Bullough, Donald A. *Alcuin: Achievement and Reputation.* Education and Society in the Middle Ages and Renaissance, 16. Leiden: E. J. Brill, 2004.

Burstein, Eitan. "La compétence de Jérôme en hébreu: explication de certaines erreurs." *Revue des études augustiniennes* 21 (1975): 3–12.

Buschhausen, Helmut, and Österreichisches Museum für angewandte Kunst. *Der Verduner Altar: Das Emailwerk des Nikolaus von Verdun im Stift Klosterneuburg.* Wien: Tusch, 1980.

Cahn, Walter. *Romanesque Bible Illumination.* Ithaca, NY: Cornell University Press, 1982.

The Cambridge History of the Bible. Vol. 2: The West from the Fathers to the Reformation. Edited by G. W. H. Lampe. Cambridge: Cambridge University Press, 1969.

The Canon Debate: On the Origins and Formation of the Bible. Edited by Lee Martin McDonald and James A. Sanders. Peabody, MA: Hendrickson, 2002.

Carruthers, Mary J. *The Book of Memory: A Study of Memory in Medieval Culture.* Cambridge, 1993.

Cauwe, Matthieu. "Le Bible d'Étienne Harding." *Revue Bénédictine* 103 (1993): 414–44.

Caviness, Madeline H. "Biblical Stories in Windows: Were They Bibles for the Poor?" In *The Bible in the Middle Ages.* 103–47.

Chartier, Roger. *Cultural History: Between Practices and Representations.* Translated by Lydia G. Cochrane. Ithaca, NY: Cornell University Press, 1988.

———. *The Order of Books. Readers, Authors, and Libraries in Europe between the Fourteenth and the Eighteenth Centuries.* Translated by Lydia Cochrane. Stanford, CA: Stanford University Press, 1994.

Chazelle, Celia. "Ceolfrid's gift to St Peter: the first quire of the *Codex Amiatinus* and the evidence of its Roman destination." *Early Medieval Europe* 12 (2003): 129–57.

———. "Pictures, Books, and the Illiterate: Pope Gregory I's Letters to Selenus of Marseilles." *Word and Image* 6 (1990): 138–53.

———. "Romanness in Early Medieval Culture: The Codex Amiatinus Portrait of Ezra." In *Paradigms, Methods, and Periodization: Rethinking Early Medieval Studies in Twenty-First Century America,* 81–98. New York: Palgrave Macmillan, 2007.

Chenu, Marie-Dominique. "Les deux âges de l'allegorisme scripturaire au moyen âge." *Recherches de théologie ancienne et médiévale* 18 (1951): 19–28.

Chevalier-Royet, Caroline. "Les révisions bibliques de Théodulf d'Orléans et la question de leur utilisation par l'exégèse carolingienne." In *Études d'exégèse carolingienne: Études autour d'Haymon d'Auxerre. Atelier de recherches, 25–26 avril 2005, Centre d'Études médiévales d'Auxerre,* edited by Sumi Shimahara. Collection Haut Moyen Âge, 4, 237–56. Turnhout: Brepols, 2007.

Cimosa, Mario, and Carlo Buzzetti. *Guida allo studio della Bibbia Latina, dalla Vetus Latina, alla Vulgata, alla Nova Vulgata.* Sussidi Patristici, 14. Roma: Istituto Patristico "Augustinianum", 2008.

Clavis apocryphorum Novi Testamenti. Edited by Maurice Geerard. Turnhout: Brepols, 1992.

Clavis apocryphorum Veteris Testamenti. Edited by Jean-Claude Haelewyck. Turnhout: Brepols, 1998.

Coates, Alan. *English Medieval Books: The Reading Abbey Collections from Foundation to Dispersal.* Oxford Historical Monographs. Oxford: Clarendon Press, 1999.

Cohen, Jeremy. *Living Letters of the Law: Ideas of the Jew in Medieval Christianity.* The Mark S. Taper Foundation Imprint in Jewish Studies. Berkeley and Los Angeles: University of California Press, 1999.

Collins, Ann. *Teacher in Faith and Virtue. Lanfranc of Bec's Commentary on Saint Paul.* Commentaria. Sacred Texts and Their Commentaries: Jewish, Christian, and Islamic, 1. Leiden: Brill, 2007.

A Companion to Medieval Art, edited by Conrad Rudolph. Oxford: Blackwell, 2006. Available online at http://www.blackwellreference.com/public/book?id=g9781405102865_9781405102865.

Constable, Giles. "The Language of Preaching in the Twelfth Century." *Viator. Medieval and Renaissance Studies* 25 (1994): 131–52.

Corpus Christianorum 1953–2003. Xenium Natalicum. Fifty Years of Scholarly Editing. Edited by Johan Leemans and Luc Jocqué. Turnhout: Brepols, 2003.

D'Avray, David. *The Preaching of the Friars: Sermons Diffused from Paris before 1300.* Oxford: Clarendon Press, 1985.

————. "Method in the Study of Medieval Sermons." In *Modern Questions about Medieval Sermons: Essays on Marriage, Death, History and Sanctity*, Nicole Bériou, David L. D'Avray, with P. Cole, J. Riley-Smith, and M. Tausche. Biblioteca di "Medioevo latino" / Società internazionale per lo studio del Medioevo latino, 3–29. Spoleto: Centro italiano di studi sull'Alto medioevo, 1994.

D'Esneval, Amaury. "Les quatre sens de l'écriture à l'époque de Pierre le Mangeur et de Hugues de Saint Cher." In *Medievalia Christiana XIe-XIIIe siècles: hommage à Raymonde Foreville*, edited by C.E. Viola, 355–69. Tournai: Editions universitaires, 1989.

Dahan, Gilbert. *Lire la Bible au moyen âge: Essais d'herméneutique médiévale.* Titre courant, 38. Genève: Droz, 2009.

————. *L'exégèse chrétienne de la Bible en occident médiéval, XIIe–XIVe siècle,* Patrimoines. Christianisme. Paris: Éditions du Cerf, 1999.

————. "La connaissance de l'hébreu dans les correctoires de la Bible du XIIIe siècle." *Revue théologique de Louvain* 23 (1992): 178–90.

————. "Juifs et Chrétiens en occident médiéval. La rencontre autour de la Bible (XIIe-XIVe siècle)." *Revue de synthèse, 4 série* 110 (1989): 3–31.

Daniélou, Jean. *Essai sur le mystère de l'histoire.* Paris: Éditions du Seuil, 1953.

————. *Sacramentum futuri; études sur les origines de la typologie biblique.* Etudes de théologie historique. Paris: Beauchesne, 1950.

————. *The Bible and the Liturgy.* Liturgical Studies, 3. Notre Dame, IN: University of Notre Dame Press, 1956.

De Bruin, Cebus Cornelis. *De statenbijbel en zijn voorgangers.* Leiden: A.W. Sijthof, 1937. Online at http://www.dbnl.org/tekst/brui007stat01_01/.

De Bruyne, Donatien. "Études sur les origines de notre texte de saint Paul." *Revue Biblique* 24 (N.S. 12) (1915): 358–92.

De Hamel, Christopher F. R. *The Book. A History of the Bible.* London: Phaidon, 2001.

————. *Glossed Books of the Bible and the Origins of the Paris Booktrade*. Woodbridge/Dover: D. S. Brewer, 1984.

De Jong, Mayke. "The Empire as *Ecclesia*: Hrabanus Maurus and Biblical *Historia* for Rulers." In *The Uses of the Past in the Early Middle Ages*, edited by Yitzhak Hen and Matthew Innes, 191–226. Cambridge: Cambridge University Press, 2000.

De l'homelie au sermon: Histoire de la prédication médiévale. Actes du colloque international de Louvain-la-Neuve (9–11 Juillet 1992). Edited by Jacqueline Hamesse and Xavier Hermand. Université Catholique de Louvain. Institut d'Études Médiévales. Textes, Études, Congrès, 14. Louvain-la-Neuve: FIDEM, 1993.

De Lubac, Henri. *Exégèse médiévale. Les quatre sens de l'Écriture*. Théologie. 41 études publiées sous la direction de la Faculté de théologie S.J. de Lyon-Fourvière, 42. Paris: Aubier, 1959–64. English translation: *Medieval exegesis*. Translated by Mark Sebanc. Grand Rapids, MI: Eerdmans; Edinburgh: T&T Clark, 1998.

Deanesly, Margaret. *The Lollard Bible and Other Medieval Biblical Versions*. Cambridge: Cambridge University Press, 1920.

Den Hollander, August A., and Ulrich Schmid. "The *Gospel of Barnabas*, the Diatesseron, and Method." *Vigiliae Christianae* 61 (2007): 1–20.

Derolez, Albert. *Les catalogues de bibliothèques*. Typologie des sources du moyen âge occidental, 31. Turnhout: Brepols, 1979.

Deutsche Bibelübersetzungen des Mittelalters. Beiträge eines Kolloquiums im Deutschen Bibel-Archiv. Edited by Heimo Reinitzer and Nikolaus Henkel. Vestigiae Bibliae, Jahrbuch des Deutschen Bibel-Archivs Hamburg, 9/10. Bern: Peter Lang, 1987/1988.

Diebold, William J. *Word and Image: An Introduction to Early Medieval Art*. Boulder, CO: Westview Press, 2000.

Dinkova-Bruun, G. "The Verse Bible as Aide-mémoire." In *The Making of Memory in the Middle Ages*, edited by Lucie Doležalová. Later Medieval Europe, vol. 4, 113–32. Leiden and Boston: Brill, 2010.

Doane, A. N., and William P. Stoneman. *Purloined Letters: The Twelfth-Century Reception of the Anglo-Saxon Illustrated Hexateuch (British library, Cotton Claudius B. IV)*. Medieval and Renaissance Texts and Studies, vol. 395. Tempe: Arizona Center for Medieval and Renaissance Studies, 2011.

Doležalová, Lucie. "« Mémoriser la Bible au bas Moyen Âge ? Le Summarium Biblicum aux frontières de l'intelligibilité »." In *Les usages sociaux de la Bible, XIe-XVe siècles*. Cahiers électroniques d'histoire textuelle, 3, 1–45. Paris: Laboratoire de Médiévistique Occidental de Paris, 2010.

Dove, Mary. *The First English Bible: The Text and Context of the Wycliffite Versions*. Cambridge Studies in Medieval Literature, 66. Cambridge: Cambridge University Press, 2007.

Duffy, Eamon. *Marking the Hours: English People and Their Prayers*, 1240–1570. New Haven, CT: Yale University Press, 2006.

Duggan, Lawrence G. "Was Art Really the 'Book of the Illiterate'?" *Word and Image* 5 (1989): 227–51.

L'école carolingienne d'Auxerre: de Murethach à Rémi, 830–908 : entretiens d'Auxerre 1989. Edited by Dominique Iogna-Prat, Colette Jeudy, and Guy Lobrichon. L'Histoire dans l'actualité. Paris: Beauchesne, 1991.

The Early Medieval Bible. Its Production, Decoration, and Use. Edited by Richard Gameson. Cambridge Studies in Palaeography and Codicology. Cambridge: Cambridge University Press, 1994.

Encyclopedia of the Bible and Its Reception. Edited by Dale C. Allison, Hans-Josef Klauck, Volker Leppin, Choon-Leong Seow, Hermann Spieckermann, Barry D. Walfish, and Eric Ziolkowski, eds. Berlin and New York: Walter de Gruyter, 2010–

Étaix, Raymond. "Les homéliaires carolingiens de l'école d'Auxerre." In *L'école carolingienne d'Auxerre: de Murethach à Rémi, 830–908 : Entretiens d'Auxerre 1989,* edited by Dominique Iogna-Prat, Colette Jeudy, and Guy Lobrichon. L'Histoire dans l'actualité, 243–52. Paris: Beauchesne, 1991.

——. "L'homéliaire composé par Hraban Maur pour l'empereur Lothaire." *Recherches Augustiniennes et patristiques* 19 (1984): 211–40.

——. "Le recueil de sermons composé par Raban Maur pour Haistulfe de Mayence." *Revue des études augustiniennes* 32 (1986): 124–37.

Études d'exégèse carolingienne: Études autour d'Haymon d'Auxerre. Atelier de recherches, 25–26 avril 2005, Centre d'Études médiévales d'Auxerre. Edited by Sumi Shimahara. Collection Haut Moyen Âge, 4. Turnhout: Brepols, 2007.

Evans, Gillian R. *The Language and Logic of the Bible. The Earlier Middle Ages.* Cambridge: Cambridge UP, 1984.

Fabricius, Johann. *Codex pseudepigraphus Veteris Testamenti.* Hamburg: C. Liebezeit, 1713.

Fassler, Margot E., and Rebecca A. Baltzer. *The Divine Office in the Latin Middle Ages: Methodology and Source Studies, Regional Developments, Hagiography.* Oxford: Oxford University Press, 2000.

Ferguson, Charles A. "Diglossia." In *Language and Social Context: Selected Readings,* edited by Pier Paolo Giglioli, 232–51. Harmondsworth: Penguin, 1972.

Fernández Marcos, Natalio. *Scribes and Translators. Septuagint and Old Latin in the Books of Kings.* Supplements to Vetus Testamentum, 54. Leiden, 1994.

Filson, Floyd V. *Which Books Belong in the Bible? A Study of the Canon.* Philadelphia: Westminster Press, 1956.

Fischer, Bonifatius. *Lateinische Bibelhandschriften im frühen Mittelalter.* Vetus Latina: Die Reste der altlateinischen Bibel. Aus der Geschichte der lateinischen Bibel, 11. Freiburg i. Br.: Herder, 1985.

Folkerts, Suzan. "The 'duncker' voor leken? Middelnederlandse bijbelvertalingen vanuit het perspectief van de gebruikers." *Jaarboek voor de Nederlandse boekgeschiedenis* 18 (2011): 155–70.

Forme e modelli della tradizione manoscritta della Bibbia. Edited by Paolo Cherubini. Littera Antiqua, 13. Città del Vaticano: Scuola vaticana di paleografia, diplomatica e archivistica, 2005.

Fowler, David C. *The Bible in Early English Literature.* Seattle: University of Washington Press, 1976.

Frei, Hans W. *The Eclipse of Biblical Narrative; A Study in Eighteenth and Nineteenth Century Hermeneutics*. New Haven, CT: Yale University Press, 1974.

Froehlich, Karlfried. "An Extraordinary Achievement: The Glossa Ordinaria in Print." In *The Bible as Book*, 15–21.

———. "The Fate of the Glossa Ordinaria in the Sixteenth Century." In *Die Patristik in der Bibelexegese des 16. Jahrhunderts*, edited by David C. Steinmetz, Wolfenbütteler Forschungen, 85. Wiesbaden: Harrassowitz, 1999.

———. "Christian Interpretation of the Old Testament in the High Middle Ages." In *Hebrew Bible / Old Testament*. 496–558.

Frymire, John M. *The Primacy of the Postils: Catholics, Protestants, and the Dissemination of Ideas in Early Modern Germany*. Studies in Medieval and Reformation Traditions, 147. Leiden: Brill, 2010.

Gamble, Harry Y. *Books and Readers in the Early Church: A History of Early Christian Texts*. New Haven, CT: Yale University Press, 1995.

Ganz, David. "Carolingian Bibles." In *The New Cambridge History of the Bible*. 325–37.

———. "Mass Production of Early Medieval Manuscripts: The Carolingian Bibles from Tours." In *The Early Medieval Bible*. 53–62.

Gatch, Milton McG. *Preaching and Theology in Anglo-Saxon England: Aelfric and Wulfstan*. Toronto: University of Toronto Press, 1977.

Gibson, Margaret T. *The Bible in the Latin West*. The Medieval Book, 5, 1. Notre Dame, IN: University of Notre Dame Press, 1993.

———. "Carolingian Glossed Psalters." In *The Early Medieval Bible*, 78–100.

———. "The Twelfth-Century Glossed Bible." In *Papers presented to the Tenth International Conference on Patristic Studies held in Oxford 1987*, edited by Elizabeth A. Livingstone. Studia Patristica, 232–44. Leuven, 1989.

Glunz, Hans Hermann. *History of the Vulgate in England from Alcuin to Roger Bacon, Being an Inquiry into the Text of some English Manuscripts of the Vulgate Gospels*. Cambridge: Cambridge University Press, 1933.

Goez, Werner. *Translatio imperii; ein Beitrag zur Geschichte des Geschichtsdenkens und der politischen Theorien im Mittelalter und in der frühen Neuzeit*. Tübingen: Mohr, 1958.

Goodwin, Deborah L. "Take Hold of the Robe of a Jew". *Herbert of Bosham's Christian Hebraism*. Studies in the History of Christian Traditions, 126. Leiden: E. J. Brill, 2006.

Gorman, Michael Murray. "Manuscript Books at Monte Amiata in the Eleventh Century." *Scriptorium* 56 (2002): 225–93.

———. "The Myth of Hiberno-Latin Exegesis." *Revue Bénédictine* 110 (2000): 42–85.

Gow, Andrew. "Challenging the Protestant Paradigm: Bible Reading in Lay and Urban Contexts of the Later Middle Ages." In *Scripture and Pluralism: Reading the Bible in the Religiously Plural Worlds of the Middle Ages and Renaissance*, edited by Thomas. J. Heffernan and Thomas E. Burman. Studies in the History of Christian Traditions, 123, 161–91. Leiden: E. J. Brill, 2005.

———. "The Bible in Germanic." In *The New Cambridge History of the Bible*. 198–216.

Gribomont, Jean. "La Bible de Saint-Paul." In *La Bibbia "Vulgata" dalle origini ai nostri giorni: Atti del Simposio internazionale in onore di Sisto V, Grottamare, 29–31 Agosto 1985*, edited by Tarcisio Stramare. Collectanea Biblica Latina, 16, 30–39. Roma: Abbazia S. Girolamo, 1987.

Hanska, Jussi. "Reconstructing the Mental Calendar of Medieval Preaching: A Method and Its Limits: An Analysis of Sunday Sermons." In *Preacher, Sermon and Audience in the Middle Ages*, edited by Carolyn Muessig, 293–315. Leiden: E. J. Brill, 2002.

Hargreaves, Henry. "From Bede to Wyclif: Medieval English Bible Translations." *Bulletin of the John Rylands Library* 48 (1965): 118–40.

Harris, Jennifer. "The Bible and the Meaning of History in the Middle Ages." In *The Practice of the Bible*, 84–104.

Harthan, John. *Books of Hours and Their Owners*. London: Thames & Hudson, 1977.

Häring, Nikolaus M. "Commentary and Hermeneutics." In *Renaissance and Renewal in the Twelfth Century*, edited by Robert L. Benson and Giles Constable, 173–200. Cambridge, MA: Medieval Academy of America, 1982.

Hearn, M. F. *Romanesque Sculpture. The Revival of Monumental Stone Sculpture in the Eleventh and Twelfth Centuries*. Ithaca, NY: Cornell University Press, 1985.

Hebrew Bible / Old Testament. The History of Its Interpretation. Vol 1: From the Beginning to the Middle Ages (Until 1300). Part 1: Antiquity. Edited by Magne Sæbø, Chris Brekelmans, and Menaham Haran. Göttingen: Vandenhoeck & Ruprecht, 1996.

Hebrew Bible / Old Testament. The History of Its Interpretation. Vol 1: From the Beginning to the Middle Ages (Until 1300). Part 2: The Middle Ages. Edited by Magne Sæbø, Chris Brekelmans, and Menaham Haran. Göttingen: Vandenhoeck & Ruprecht, 2000.

Heil, Johannes. *Kompilation oder Konstruktion? Die Juden in den Pauluskommentaren des 9. Jahrhunderts*. Forschungen zur Geschichte der Juden. A. Abhandlungen. Hannover: Hahnsche Buchhandlung, 1998.

Henry, Avril, ed. *Biblia Pauperum. A Facsimile and Edition*. Aldershot: Scolar Press, 1987.

Hilpert, Hans-Eberhard. "Geistliche Bildung und Laienbildung: Zur Überlieferung der Schulschrift Compendium historiale in genealogia Christi (Compendium veteris testamenti) des Petrus von Poitiers (1205)." *Journal of Medieval History* 11 (1985): 315–29.

Huck, Johannes Chrysostomus. *Joachim von Floris und die Joachitische Literatur*. Freiburg im Breisgau: Herder & Co. Verlagsbuchhandlung, 1938.

Hughes, Christopher G. "Art and Exegesis." In *A Companion to Medieval Art*. 173–192.

Hugues de Saint-Cher († 1263), bibliste et théologien. Edited by Louis-Jacques Bataillon, Gilbert Dahan, and Pierre-Marie Gy. Bibliothèque d'histoire culturelle du moyen âge, 1. Turnhout: Brepols, 2004.

Illich, Ivan. "'Lectio divina'." In *Schriftlichkeit im frühen Mittelalter*, edited by Ursula Schaefer. ScriptOralia, 53, 19–35. Tübingen: Narr, 1993.

Infant Milk or Hardy Nourishment? The Bible for Lay People and Theologians in the Early Modern Period. Edited by W. François and August A. Den Hollander. Bibliotheca Ephemeridum Theologicarum Lovaniensium, 221. Leuven: Peeters, 2009.

The Jewish Study Bible. Edited by Adele Berlin, Marc Zvi Brettler, and Michael Fishbane. Oxford: Oxford University Press, 1999.

Jobes, Karen H., and Silva Moisés. *Invitation to the Septuagint.* Grand Rapids, MI: Baker Academic, 2000.

Jungmann, Joseph A. *The Mass of the Roman Rite: Its Origins and Development (Missarum sollemnia).* Translated by Francis A. Brunner. New York: Benziger, 1951–55.

Kamin, Sarah. *Jews and Christians Interpret the Bible.* Jerusalem: Magnes Press, 1991.

Kaske, R.E., Artur Groos, and Michael W. Twomey, eds. *Medieval Christian Literary Imagery: A Guide to Interpretation.* Toronto Medieval Bibliographies. Toronto and Buffalo: University of Toronto Press, 1988.

Kaufmann, C. M. "The Bible in Public Art, 1050–1450." In *The New Cambridge History of the Bible.* 785–820.

Kenyon, Frederic G. *Recent Developments in the Textual Criticism of the Greek Bible.* The Schweich Lectures on Biblical Archaeology, 1932. London: British Academy, 1933.

Kessler, Herbert L. "Gregory the Great and Image Theory in Northern Europe during the Twelfth and Thirteenth Centuries." In *A Companion to Medieval Art.* 151–172.

Ker, Neil Ripley. *Medieval Libraries of Great Britain; a List of Surviving Books.* Royal Historical Society. Guides and Handbooks, 3. London: Offices of the Royal Historical Society, 1964.

Kienzle, Beverly Mayne, and David L. D'Avray. "Sermons." In *Medieval Latin: An Introduction and Bibliographical Guide*, edited by Frank A.C. Mantello and A.G. Rigg, 659–69. Washington: The Catholic University of America Press, 1996.

Klepper, Deeana Copeland. *The Insight of Unbelievers: Nicholas of Lyra and Christian Reading of Jewish Text in the Later Middle Ages.* Philadelphia: University of Pennsylvania Press, 2007.

Kors, Mikel. *De Bijbel voor leken: Studies over Petrus Naghel en de Historiebijbel van 1361.* With an introduction by Geert H. M. Claasens. Encyclopédie Bénédictine. Turnhout: Brepols, 2007.

Kroesen, Justin E. A., and Regnerus Steensma. *The Interior of the Medieval Village Church: Het Middeleeuwse Dorpskerkinterieur.* Louvain and Dudley: Peeters, 2004.

Kugel, James L. *Traditions of the Bible. A Guide to the Bible As It Was at the Start of the Common Era.* Cambridge, MA: Harvard University Press, 1998.

————. *How to Read the Bible: A Guide to Scripture, Then and Now.* New York: Free Press, 2007.

Laistner, M. L. W. "Antiochene Exegesis in Western Europe during the Middle Ages." *Harvard Theological Review* 40 (1947): 19–31.

Lambert, Malcolm D. *Medieval Heresy. Popular Movements from the Gregorian Reform to the Reformation.* 2nd ed. Oxford: Blackwell Publishing, 1992.

Lapidge, Michael. *The Anglo-Saxon Library.* Oxford: Oxford University Press, 2006.

Leff, Gordon. *Heresy in the Later Middle Ages: The Relation of Heterodoxy to Dissent, c. 1250–c. 1450.* Manchester: Manchester University Press, 1967.

Levy, Ian Christopher. *Holy Scripture and the Quest for Authority at the End of the Middle Ages.* Notre Dame, IN: Notre Dame University Press, 2012.

Light, Laura. "French Bibles c. 1200–30: A New Look at the Origins of the Paris Bible." In *The Early Medieval Bible.* 155–76.

———. "Roger Bacon and the Origin of the Paris Bible." *Revue Bénédictine* 111 (2001): 483–507.

———. "The Bible and the Individual." In *The Practice of the Bible.* 228–46.

———. "The Thirteenth Century and the Paris Bible." In *The New Cambridge History of the Bible.* 380–91.

The Liturgy of the Medieval Church. 2nd ed. Edited by Thomas. J. Heffernan and E. Ann Matter. Kalamazoo, MI: Medieval Institute Publications, 2005.

Liuzza, Roy M. "Who Read the Gospels in Old English?" In *Words and Works: Essays for Fred C. Robinson.* Edited by P. S. Baker and N. Howe. Toronto: University of Toronto Press, 1998.

Livesey, Benjamin. *The Life of John Wiclif, Morning Star of the Reformation.* London: Hamilton, Adams and Co. and Barclay, 1831.

Lobrichon, Guy. "Gli usi della Bibbia." In *Lo spazio letterario del medioevo, I. Il medioevo latino, 1. La produzione del testo,* vol. 1, edited by Guglielmo Cavallo, Claudio Leonardi, and Enrico Menestó, 523–62. Roma, 1992.

———. "Le Bibbie ad immagini, secoli XII–XV." In *Forme e modelli della tradizione manoscritta della Bibbia.* 423–58.

Longère, Jean. *La prédication médiévale.* Paris: Études augustiniennes, 1983.

Louth, Andrew. *Discerning the Mystery: An Essay on the Nature of Theology.* Oxford: Clarendon Press, 1983.

Lowden, John. *The Making of the Bibles Moralisées.* University Park: Pennsylvania State University Press, 2000.

Magennis, Hugh, and Mary Swan, eds. *A Companion to Ælfric.* Brill's Companions to the Christian Tradition, vol. 18. Leiden: Brill, 2009.

Maier, Christoph T. *Preaching the Crusades: mendicant friars and the Cross in the Thirteenth Century.* Cambridge Studies in Medieval Life and Thought, 28. Cambridge: Cambridge University Press, 1994.

Marsden, Richard. "Anglo-Saxon Biblical Manuscripts." In *The Cambridge History of the Book in Britain.* Edited by Richard Gameson. 1: 406–35 Cambridge: Cambridge University Press, 2011.

————. *The Text of the Old Testament in Anglo-Saxon England*. Cambridge Studies in Anglo-Saxon England, 15. Cambridge: Cambridge University Press, 1995.

————. "Ælfric as Translator: The Old English Prose Genesis." *Anglia* 109 (1991): 317–58.

————. "The Bible in English." In *The New Cambridge History of the Bible*. 217–38.

Martin, Arthur, and Charles Cahier. *Monographie de la cathédrale de Bourges. Première partie. Vitraux du XIIIe siècle*. Paris: Poussielgue-Rusand, 1841–44.

Martin, Hervé. *Le métier de prédicateur en France septentrionale à la fin du Moyen Age (1350–1520)*. Histoire. Paris: Éditions du Cerf, 1988.

Matter, E. Ann. *The Voice of My Beloved: The Song of Songs in Western Medieval Christianity*. Philadelphia: University of Pennsylvania Press, 1990.

Mâle, Émile. *The Gothic Image: Religious Art in France of the Thirteenth Century*. Translated by Dora Nussey. New York: E. P. Dutton & Co., 1913.

McClymond, Michael J. "Through a Gloss Darkly: Biblical Annotations and Theological Interpretation in Modern Catholic and Protestant English-Language Bibles." *Theological Studies* 67 (2006): 477–97.

McDonald, Lee Martin. *The Biblical Canon. Its Origin, Transmission, and Authority*. 2nd ed. Peabody, MA: Hendrickson, 2007.

McGerr, Rosemarie Potz. "Guyart Desmoulins, the Vernacular Master of Histories, and His 'Bible Historiale'." *Viator. Medieval and Renaissance Studies* 14 (1983): 211–44.

McKane, William. *Selected Christian Hebraists*. Cambridge: Cambridge University Press, 1989.

McKitterick, Rosamond. "Nuns' Scriptoria in England and Francia in the Eighth Century." In *Books, Scribes, and Learning in the Frankish Kingdoms, 6th-9th Centuries*. Collected Studies Series, VII.1–35. Aldershot and Brookfield, VT: Variorum, 1994.

————. *The Carolingians and the Written Word*. Cambridge: Cambridge University Press, 1989.

————. *Charlemagne: The Formation of a European Identity*. Cambridge: Cambridge University Press, 2008.

McLaughlin, Emmet. "The Word Eclipsed? Preaching in the Early Middle Ages." *Traditio. Studies in Ancient and Medieval History* 46 (1991): 77–122.

Medieval Sermons and Society: Cloister, City, University. Edited by Jacqueline Hamesse, Beverly Mayne Kienzle, Debra L. Stoudt, and Anne T. Thayer. Louvain-la-Neuve: FIDEM, 1998.

Menache, Sophia, and Jeannine Horowitz. *L'humour en chaire: le rire dans l'église médiévale*. Histoire et société, no. 28. Genève: Labor et Fides, 1994.

Mende, Ursula. *Die Bronzetüren des Mittelalters, 800–1200*. Irmgard Ernstmeier-Hirmer and Albert Hirmer, photographers. München: Hirmer, 1983.

Metzger, Bruce M. *The Text of the New Testament. Its Transmission, Corruption, and Restoration*. 3rd enlarged ed. Oxford: Oxford University Press, 1992.

Bibliography

Meyer, Paul. "Notice sur les 'Corrogationes Promethei' d'Alexandre Neckam." *Notices et extraits des manuscrits de la Bibliothèque Nationale et autres bibliothèques* 35 (1896): 641–82.

Meyvaert, Paul. "Bede, Cassiodorus, and the Codex Amiatinus." *Speculum* 71 (1996): 827–83.

Middelnederlandse bijbelvertalingen. Edited by August A. Den Hollander, Erik Kwakkel, and Wybren Scheepsma. Hilversum: Verloren, 2007.

Minnis, Alastair J. *Medieval Theory of Authorship. Scholastic Literary Attitudes in the Later Middle Ages.* The Middle Ages Series. Philadelphia: University of Pennsylvania Press, 1984.

Mitchell, John. "The Bible in Public Art, 600–1050." In *The New Cambridge History of the Bible.* 755–784.

Mohrmann, Christine. *Études sur le latin des chrétiens. Vol. 1: Le latin des chrétiens.* Storia e letteratura, 65. Roma: Edizioni di storia e letteratura, 1961.

_____. *Études sur le latin des chrétiens. Vol. 3: Latin chrétien et liturgique.* Storia e letteratura, 103. Roma: Edizioni di storia e letteratura, 1965.

Morey, James H. *Book and Verse: A Guide to Middle English Biblical Literature.* Illinois Medieval Studies. Urbana: University of Illimois Press, 2000.

Morrell, Minnie Cate. *A Manual of Old English Biblical Materials.* Knoxville: University of Tennessee Press, 1965.

Morrison, Karl F. *Conversion and Text. The Cases of Augustine of Hippo, Herman-Judah, and Constantine Tsatsos.* Charlottesville: University Press of Virginia, 1992.

Muessig, Carolyn, ed. *Medieval Monastic Preaching.* Brill's Studies in Intellectual History, 90. Leiden: E. J. Brill, 1998.

_____. "Sermon, Preacher, and Society in the Middle Ages." *Journal of Medieval History* 28 (2002): 73–91.

Muir, Lynette R. *The Biblical Drama of Medieval Europe.* Cambridge: Cambridge University Press, 1995.

Murdoch, Brian. *The Medieval Popular Bible. Expansions of Genesis in the Middle Ages.* Cambridge: D.S. Brewer, 2003.

Murphy, G. Ronald. *The Saxon Savior: The Germanic Transformation of the Gospel in the Ninth-Century Heliand.* New York and Oxford: Oxford University Press, 1989.

Murphy, Michael. "Antiquary to Academic: the Progress of Anglo-Saxon Scholarship." In *Anglo-Saxon Scholarship: The First Three Centuries,* edited by Carl T. Berkhout, and Milton McC. Gatch, 1–18. Boston: G. K. Hall, 1982.

Nestle, Eberhardt. "Lesefrüchte." *Jahrbuch für deutsche Theologie* 22 (1877): 668–70.

Neue Richtungen in der hoch- und spätmittelalterlichen Bibelexegese. Edited by Robert E. Lerner and Elisabeth Müller-Luckner. Schriften des Historischen Kollegs, Kolloquien 32. München: R. Oldenbourg Verlag, 1996.

Neusner, Jacob. *Introduction to rabbinic literature.* The Anchor Bible Reference Library. New York: Doubleday, 1994.

Newman, Robert C. "Council of Jamnia and the Old Testament canon." *Westminster Theological Journal* 38 (1976): 319–49.

The New Cambridge History of the Bible. Vol. 2: From 600 to 1450, edited by Richard Marsden and E. Ann Matter. Cambridge: Cambridge University Press, 2012.

Nicholas of Lyra. The Senses of Scripture. Edited by Philip D. W. Krey and Lesley Smith. Studies in the History of Christian Thought, 90. Leiden: E. J. Brill, 2000.

Nicolas de Lyre, franciscain du XIV siècle: exégète et théologien. Edited by Gilbert Dahan. Collection des Études Augustiniennes. Série Moyen-Age et temps modernes, 48. Paris: Institut d'Études Augustiniennes, 2011.

Noble, Thomas X. *Images, Iconoclasm, and the Carolingians*. The Middle Ages Series. Philadelphia: University of Pennsylvania Press, 2009.

Nothaft, C. Philipp E. *Dating the Passion: The Life of Jesus and the Emergence of Scientific Chronology (200–1600)*. Time, Astronomy, and Calendars, 1. Leiden: E. J. Brill, 2012.

O Cróinín, Dáibhí. "Bischoff's Wendepunkte Fifty Years On." *Revue Bénédictine* 110 (2000): 204–37.

Ocker, Christopher. *Biblical Poetics before Humanism and Reformation*. Cambridge: Cambridge University Press, 2002.

The Old English Homily and its Background. Edited by Bernard F. Huppé and Paul Szarmach. Albany: State University of New York Press, 1978.

Old, Hughes Oliphant. *The Reading and Preaching of the Scriptures in the Worship of the Christian Church. Vol. 3: The Medieval Church*. Grand Rapids, MI: Wm. B. Eerdmans Publishing Co., 1998.

Olszowy-Schlanger, Judith. "The Knowledge and Practice of Hebrew Grammar among Christian Scholars in Pre-Expulsion England: The Evidence of 'Bilingual' Hebrew-Latin Manuscripts." In *Hebrew Scholarship in the Medieval World*, edited by Nicholas De Lange, 107–30. Cambridge: Cambridge University Press, 2001.

Owst, Gerald Robert. *Preaching in Medieval England; an Introduction to Sermon Manuscripts of the Period c. 1350–1450*. Cambridge Studies in Medieval Life and Thought. Cambridge: Cambridge University Press, 1926.

Panayotova, Stella. "The Illustrated Psalter: Luxury and Practical Use." In *The Practice of the Bible*, 247–71.

Parkes, Malcolm Beckwith. *Pause and Effect. Punctuation in the West*. Berkeley and Los Angeles: University of California Press, 1993.

Peri, Vittorio. "'Correctores immo corruptores', un saggio di critica testuale nella Roma del XII secolo." *Italia medioevale e umanistica* 20 (1977): 19–125.

Petrucci, Armando. *Writers and Readers in Medieval Italy: Studies in the History of Written Culture*. Edited and translated by Charles M. Radding. New Haven, CT: Yale University Press, 1995.

Pépin, Jean. *Mythe et allégorie: les origines grecques et les contestations judéo-chrétiennes*. Philosophie de l'Esprit. Paris: Aubier, 1958.

The Place of the Psalms in the Intellectual Culture of the Middle Ages. Edited by Nancy Van Deusen. SUNY Series in Medieval Studies. Albany: State University of New York Press, 1999.

Poirel, Dominique. "Un manuel de l'exégèse spirituelle au service des prédicateurs: les Allegoriae d'Isidore de Séville." *Recherches Augustiniennes* 33 (2003): 95–107.

The Practice of the Bible in the Western Middle Ages. Production, Reception, and Performance in Western Christianity. Edited by Susan Boynton and Diane J. Reilly. New York: Columbia University Press, 2011.

Predicazione e società nel medioevo: riflessione etica, valori e modelli di comportamento. Proceedings of the XII Medieval Sermon Studies Symposium. Padova, 14–18 luglio 2000. Edited by Riccardo Quinto and Laura Gaffuri. Padova: Centro Studi Antoniani, 2002.

Pryds, Darleen N. *The King Embodies the Word: Robert d'Anjou and the politics of Preaching.* Studies in the history of Christian thought, 93. Leiden: Brill, 2000.

Saltman, Avrom, *Pseudo Jerome. Quaestiones on the Book of Samuel.* Studia Post-Biblica, 26. Leiden, 1975.

Quentin, Henri. *Mémoire sur l'établissement du texte de la Vulgate. Ière partie: Octateuque.* Collectanea Biblica Latina, 6. Roma: Desclée & Cie., 1922.

Reeves, Marjorie. *Joachim of Fiore and the Prophetic Future: A Medieval Study in Historial Thinking.* London: S.P.C.K., 1976.

Reisch, Gregorius. *Margarita philosophica.* Freiburg: Johann Schott, 1504.

Repertorium of Middle English Prose Sermons. Edited by Veronica O'Mara and Suzanne Paul. Sermo: Studies on Patristic, Medieval, and Reformation Sermons and Preaching, 1. Turnhout: Brepols, 2007.

Reventlow, Henning. *History of Biblical Interpretation. Volume 2: From Late Antiquity to the End of the Middle Ages.* Translated by James O. Duke. SBL – Resources for Biblical Study, 61. Atlanta: Society of Biblical Literature, 2009.

Riché, Pierre. *Education and Culture in the Barbarian West: From the Sixth through the Eighth Century.* Translated by John J. Contreni. Columbia: University of South Carolina Press, 1976.

Roberts, Colin Henderson. *The Birth of the Codex.* In collaboration with Theodore Cressy Skeat. London: Published for The British Academy by Oxford University Press, 1987. Originally published 1983.

Roberts, Phyllis Barzillay. "Sermons and Preaching in/and the Medieval University." In *Medieval Education,* edited by Ronald B. Begley and Joseph W. Koterski. Fordham Series in Medieval Studies, no. 4, 83–98. New York: Fordham University Press, 2005.

Robinson, Benedict Scott. "'Darke Speech': Matthew Parker and the Reforming of History." *Sixteenth Century Journal* 29 (1998): 1061–83.

Robson, C. A. "The Vernacular Scriptures in France." In *The Cambridge History of the Bible.* 436–52.

Rodriguez, C. Marano. *Glosas marginales de Vetus Latina en las biblias vulgatas españolas. 1–2 Samuel.* Textos y estudios "Cardinal Cisneros" de la Biblia poliglota matritense, 48. Madrid: Consejo Superior de Investigaciones Científicas, Instituto de filología, 1989.

Roest, Bert. "Female Preaching in the Late Medieval Franciscan Tradition." *Franciscan Studies* 62 (2004): 119–54.

————. "Mendicant School Exegesis." In *The Practice of the Bible*. 179–204.

————. "Franciscan Commentaries on the Apocalypse." *Studies in Church History, Subsidia* 10 (1994): 29–37.

Rosier, James L. "Four Old English Psalter Glosses." *Philologica Pragensia* 21 (1978): 44–45.

Rost, Hans. *Die Bibel im Mittelalter. Beiträge zur Geschichte und Bibliographie der Bibel*. Augsburg: Kommissions-Verlag M. Seitz, 1939.

Rouse, Richard H., and Mary A. Rouse. *Manuscripts and their Makers. Commercial Book Producers in Medieval Paris, 1200–1500*. Turnhout: Brepols, 2000.

Ruthven, Malise. *Islam in the World*. Oxford: Oxford University Press, 2006. Third edition, 1984.

Saenger, Paul. *Space between Words. The Origins of Silent Reading*. Stanford, CA: Stanford University Press, 1997.

————. "The Anglo-Hebraic Origins of the Modern Chapter Division of the Latin Bible." In *La fractura historiografica: Edad Media y Renacimento desde el tercer milenio*, edited by Francesco Javier Burguillo and Laura Meier, 177–202. Salamanca: Seminario de Estudios Medievales y Renacentistas, 2008.

Saperstein, Marc. "The Medieval Jewish Sermons." In *The Sermon*, 175–201.

Schaff, Philip. *History of the Christian Church. Vol. 4: Medieval Christianity, AD 590–1073*. New York: Scribner, 1891.

Schneyer, Johann Baptist. *Repertorium der lateinischen Sermones des Mittelalters: für die Zeit von 1150–1350*. Beiträge zur Geschichte der Philosophie und Theologie des Mittelalters, Texte und Untersuchungen, 43. Münster, 1969–90.

————. *Geschichte der katholischen Predigt*. Freiburg: Seelsorge Verlag, 1969.

Schreckenberg, Heinz. *Die Flavius-Josephus-Tradition in Antike und Mittelalter*. Arbeiten zur Literatur und Geschichte des hellenistischen Judentums, 5. Leiden: E. J. Brill, 1972.

Schulz-Flügel, Eva. "The Latin Old Testament Tradition." In *Hebrew Bible/Old Testament*. 642–62.

Selden, John. *The Historie of Tithes; That Is, the Practice of Payment of Them, the Positiue Laws Made for Them, the Opinions Touching the Right of Them; a Review of It Is Also Annext, Which Both Confirmes It and Directs in the Vse of It*. London: n.p., 1618.

The Sermon. Edited by Beverly Mayne Kienzle. Typologie des sources du moyen âge occidental, 81–83. Turnhout: Brepols, 2000.

Shepherd, Geoffrey. "English Versions of the Scriptures before Wyclif." In *The Cambridge History of the Bible*. 362–86.

Sheppard, Jennifer M. *The Buildwas Books: Book Production, Acquisition and Use at an English Cistercian Monastery, 1165–c.1400*. Oxford Bibliographical Society Publications, 3rd series, 2. Oxford: Oxford Bibliographical Society, Bodleian Library, 1997.

Smalley, Beryl. *The Study of the Bible in the Middle Ages*. Oxford: Blackwell Publishing, 1952. Third edition, 1983.

——. "The Bible in the Medieval Schools." In *Cambridge History of the Bible. Vol. 2: The West from the Fathers to the Reformation*, edited by G.W.H. Lampe, 197–220. Cambridge: Cambridge University Press, 1969.

——. "Gilbertus Universalis, Bishop of London (1128–34), and the Problem of the 'Glossa Ordinaria'." *Recherches de Théologie ancienne et médiévale* 7 (1935): 235–62. and 8 (1936): 24–60.

Smith, Lesley. *The* Glossa ordinaria: *The Making of a Medieval Bible Commentary*. Commentaria. Sacred Texts and Their Commentaries: Jewish, Christian, and Islamic, 3. Leiden: Brill, 2009.

——. "Robert Amiclas and the Glossed Bible." In *From Knowledge to Beatitude. St. Victor, Twelfth-Century Scholars, and Beyond. Essays in Honor of Grover A. Zinn, Jr.*, edited by E. Ann Matter and Lesley Smith, 131–52. Notre Dame, IN: University of Notre Dame Press, 2012.

Spiazzi, Raimondo. *San Tommaso d'Aquino. Biografia documentata di un uomo buono, intelligente, veramente grande*. Bologna: Edizioni studio Domenicano, 1995.

Spicq, Ceslas. *Esquisse d'une histoire de l'exégèse latine au Moyen Âge*. Bibliothèque thomiste, 26. Paris: J. Vrin, 1944.

Stanton, Robert. *The Culture of Translation in Anglo-Saxon England*. Cambridge: D.S. Brewer, 2002.

Stegmüller, Friedrich. *Repertorium Biblicum Medii Aevi*. Madrid: Consejo Superior de Investigaciones Científicas, Instituto Francisco Suárez, 1950–80. Online at http://gepc189.uni-trier.de/rebi/cgi-bin/index.php.

Steinmetz, David C. "The Superiority of Pre-Critical Exegesis." *Theology Today* 37 (1980): 27–38.

Stock, Brian. *The Implications of Literacy. Written Language and Models of Interpretation in the Eleventh and Twelfth Centuries*. Princeton: Princeton University Press, 1983.

Stocking, Rachel L. *Bishops, Councils, and Consensus in the Visigothic Kingdom, 589–633*. History, Languages, and Cultures of the Spanish and Portuguese Worlds. Ann Arbor: University of Michigan Press, 2000.

The Study of Liturgy. Rev. ed. Edited by Cheslyn Jones, Edward Yarnold Wainwright, and Paul Bradshaw. London: S.P.C.K., 1992. First published 1978.

Stummer, Friedrich. *Einführung in die lateinische Bibel. Ein Handbuch für Vorlesungen und Selbstunterricht*. Paderborn: F. Schöningh, 1928.

Sutcliffe, E. "The Name 'Vulgate.'" *Biblica* 29 (1984): 345–52.

Swanson, R.N. *Indulgences in Late Medieval England: Passports to Paradise?* Cambridge: Cambridge University Press, 2007.

Synan, Edward A. "The Four 'Senses' and Four Exegetes." In *With Reverence for the Word. Medieval Scriptural Exegesis in Judaism, Christianity, and Islam*, edited by Jane Dammen McAuliffe, Barry D. Walfish, and Joseph W. Goering, 225–36. Oxford: Oxford University Press, 2003.

Synave, Paul. "La doctrine de Saint Thomas d'Aquin sur le sens littéral des Écritures." *Revue Biblique* 35 (1926): 40–65.

Taft, Robert. *The Liturgy of the Hours in East and West: The Origins of the Divine Office and Its Meaning for Today.* Collegeville, MN: Liturgical Press, 1986.

The Theological Interpretation of Scripture: Classic and Contemporary Readings. Edited by Stephen E. Fowl. Blackwell Readings in Modern Theology. Cambridge, MA: Blackwell, 1997.

Thesaurus proverbiorum medii aevi = Lexikon der Sprichwörter des romanisch-germanischen Mittelalters. Berlin and New York: De Gruyter, 2001.

Thompson, Augustine. *Revival Preachers and Politics in Thirteenth-Century Italy. The Great Devotion of 1233.* Oxford: Oxford University Press, 1992.

Thompson, James Westfall. *The Literacy of the Laity in the Middle Ages.* Burt Franklin Research and Source Works Series, 2. New York: B. Franklin, 1960.

Thomson, Rodney M. "Robert Amiclas: A Twelfth-Century Parisian Master and His Books." *Scriptorium* 49 (1995): 238–43.

Tov, Emanuel. *Textual Criticism of the Hebrew Bible.* 2nd rev. ed. Minneapolis: Augsburg Fortress Publishers, 2001.

University of Texas. *Gothic and Renaissance Illuminated Manuscripts from Texas Collections. 23 April–23 June 1971.* With a foreword by June Moll. Austin: Miriam Lutcher Stark Library, University of Texas, 1971.

Val, Barry. "The Bible in the Middle Ages." Online at suite101.com/article/the-bible-in-the-middle-ages-a112611.

Van Engen, John H. *Sisters and Brothers of the Common Life: The Devotio Moderna and the World of the Later Middle Ages.* The Middle Ages Series. Philadelphia: University of Pennsylvania Press, 2008.

Van Liere, Frans A. "The Latin Bible, c. 900 to the Council of Trent, 1546." In *The New Cambridge History of the Bible.* 93–109.

———. "Andrew of Saint Victor and His Franciscan Critics." In *The Multiple Meaning of Scripture,* edited by Ineke Van 't Spijker. Commentaria. Sacred Texts and their Commentaries: Jewish, Christian, and Islamic, 2, 291–309. Leiden: Brill, 2008.

———. "Andrew of St Victor and the Gloss on Samuel and Kings." In *Media Latinitas. A Collection of Essays to Mark the Occasion of the Retirement of L.J. Engels,* edited by Renée I. A. Nip and Hans van Dijk. Instrumenta Patristica, 28, 249–53. Steenbrugge and Turnhout: Brepols, 1995.

———. "Tools for Fools: Marchesinus of Reggio and his Mammotrectus." *Medieval Perspectives* 18 (2003): 192–206.

Vernet, André. *La Bible au Moyen Age, Bibliographie.* Paris: Éditions du C.N.R.S., 1989.

Vogel, Cyrille. *Medieval Liturgy. An Introduction to the Sources.* Translated by William Storey and Niels Rasmussen. NPM Studies in Church Music and Liturgy. Washington, DC: The Pastoral Press, 1986.

Von Campenhausen, Hans. *Die Entstehung der christlichen Bibel.* Beiträge zur historischen Theologie, 39. Tübingen: J. C. B. Mohr (Paul Siebeck), 1968.

Watkin, Aelred, ed. *Archdeanery of Norwich: Inventory of Church Goods, temp. Edward III.* Norfolk Record Society, 19:1. Norwich: Norfolk Record Society, 1947.

Weber, Robert. "Les interpolations du livre de Samuel dans les manuscrits de la Vulgate." In *Miscellanea Giovanni Mercati, vol. 1, Bibbia-Letteratura Cristiana Antica.* Studi e testi, 121, 19–39. Città del Vaticano: Biblioteca Apostolica Vaticana, 1946.

Wenzel, Siegfried. "The Use of the Bible in Preaching." In *The New Cambridge History of the Bible.* 680–92.

West, Martin L. *Textual Criticism and Editorial Technique, Applicable to Greek and Latin texts.* Teubner Studienbücher. Philologie. Stuttgart: B. G. Teubner, 1973.

Williams, John. *Imaging the Early Medieval Bible.* The Penn State Series in the History of the Book. University Park: Pennsylvania State University Press, 2002. Paperback version of the 1999 edition.

Williams, Megan Hale. *The Monk and the Book. Jerome and the Making of Christian Scholarship.* Chicago: The University of Chicago Press, 2006.

Withers, Benjamin Carl. "Present Patterns, Past Tense: Structuring History, Law and Society in London, British Library Cotton Claudius B.iv." Dissertation, The University of Chicago, 1994.

Wright, Thomas, ed. *The Political Poems and Songs Relating to English History.* Rerum Britannicarum Medii Aevi Scriptores, 14. London: Longman, Green, Longman, and Roberts, 1861.

Würthwein, Ernst. *The Text of the Old Testament.* 2nd ed. Translated by Erroll F. Rhodes. Grand Rapids: Wm. B. Eerdmans Publishing Co., 1995.

Wüstefeld, W.C.M. *De boeken van de grote of Sint Bavokerk: een bijdrage tot de geschiedenis van het middeleeuwse boek in Haarlem.* Hilversum: Verloren, 1989.

Yawn-Bonghi, Lila Elizabeth. "The Italian Giant Bible, Lay Patronage and Professional Workmanship (11th and 12th Centuries)." In *Les usages sociaux de la Bible, XIe-XVe siècles.* Cahiers électroniques d'histoire textuelle, 3, 161–255. Paris: Laboratoire de Médiévistique Occidental de Paris, 2010. Online at http://lamop.univ-paris1.fr/IMG/pdf/Lila_Yawn.pdf.

Young, Frances M. *Biblical Exegesis and the Formation of Christian Culture.* Cambridge: Cambridge University Press, 1997.

————. "Typology." In *Crossing the Boundaries. Essays in Biblical Interpretation in Honour of Michael D. Goulder,* edited by Stanley E. Porter, Paul Joyce, and David. E Orton, 29–48. Leiden: E. J. Brill, 1994.

Young, Karl. *The Drama of the Medieval Church.* Oxford: Clarendon Press, 1957–67.

Zier, Mark A. "Preaching by Distinction; Peter Comestor and the Communication of the Gospel." *Ephemerides liturgicae* 105 (1991): 301–29.

Zink, Michel. *La prédication en langue romane: Avant 1300.* Nouvelle bibliothèque du Moyen Age. Paris: H. Champion, 1976.

Index of Manuscripts Cited

Cambridge, Trinity College
R.17.1: 32

Chicago, Newberry Library
Case 19.1: 231
Case 203: 25

Florence, Biblioteca Medicea Laurenziana
Amiatinus 1: 5–7, 9, 12, 21, 25–27, 41, 54, 64, 72, 94, 211, 246

Freiburg, University Library
MS 334: 252n

London, British Library
Add. 10,546: 35–36, 95, 242–243
Add. 15,253: 33
Add. 24,142: 73, 94
Add. 43,725: 24
Add. 37,777: 9, 46
Add. 40,006: 47–48
Add. 45,025: 9, 24, 46
Cotton Nero D. IV: 107, 189
Egerton 3031: 47
Harley 2805: 35
Royal 1.B.X: 24, 47, 169
Royal 1.D.V-VIII: 24

New York, Pierpont Morgan Library
M.240: 249
M.719-720: 252n
M.962: 154

Oxford, Bodleian Library
Auct. D.4.10: 106, 169
Junius 11: 185–186

Paris, Bibliothèque Nationale
Lat. 9380: 35
Lat. 11,937: 94

Saint Gall, Stiftsbibliothek
MS 913, fol. 148ff.: 151

Stuttgart, Württembergische Landesbibliothek
HB.II.16: 94

Vatican Library
Vat. gr. 1209: 24
Vat. lat. 1027: 170

Verona, Biblioteca capitolare
MS 6: 91

Vienna, Österreichische Nationalbibliothek
MS 1179: 248
MS 2554: 248

York, Minster Library
Add. 2: 213
XVI.D.13: 47
XVI.K.6: 253
XVI.N.6: 97
XVI.Q.3: 97, 105

Index of Biblical References

Subject and Author Index

Mary, Blessed Virgin, 133, 208, 213, 237, 252–253, 257–258
Mary, Queen I, 177
Masorah, 86, 104–105
Masoretes, 43, 86, 104. *See also* Ben Asher family
Masoretic text, 61, 63, 102–103; vocalization, 104–105. *See also* Aleppo Codex; Codex Leningradensis; Hebrew Bible; Hebrew language
Mass / Eucharist, 209–211, 254
Mathematics, 156–157
Matthew, gospel of, 44, 68, 183
Maurice Iemantszoon, 199
Maurice of Sully, bishop of Paris, 221–222, 224
Maximus of Turin, bishop, 219
McDonald, Lee Martin, 78
McGerr, Rosemary, 195
McKane, William, 132
McKitterick, Rosamund, 180, 206
Meditation, 125–127
Meditations on the Life of Christ, 253
Melanchton, Philip, 173–174
Melkisedek, 119, 244
Memorization, Bible, 127, 158–159, 162, 169
Merovingian period, 34
Metaphor, 112, 114, 127; allegory and, 120; Bible as, 112–113; building, 164; of Christ, 136–138; Jonah story as, 114; zither as, 122
Metz, bishop of, 193
Michelangelo, 89
Michigan, University of, 22
Middle Ages, definition, 4
Midrash Rabbah, 123
Midrash, midrashim, 123
Migne, Jean-Paul, 1, 264
Milan, 209
Milton, John, 66
Minnis, Alastair, 139
Mishnah, 59, 123
Monasticism, 143–144, 149–150, 160–162, 211–212, 254; dramas, 254–255; English reform, 188, 254; sermons, 220
Moral, action, 159; exhortation, 123; instruction, 121, 163, 165, 215, 228; interpretation, 248
Moralia in Job, 91
Morey, James, 206
Moriah, 124
Morrell, Minnie Cate, 206
Moses ben Gerson Soncino, 50
Moses, 119, 160, 245; horns/radiance of, 88–89; as Pentateuch author, 54, 75; Tabernacle of, 161
Mount of Olives, 254
Moutier-Grandval Bible, 242–244, 246
Muessig, Carolyn, 227, 234
Muretach of Auxerre, 149

Murphy, G. Ronald, 183–184
Mystery plays, 256–257

Nag Hammadi, 67
"Naked" text, 205
Nathan, prophet, 106, 247
Nativity, 213, 255, 257–258, 261
Nebuchadnezzar, king, 63
Nehemiah, book of, 47, 55, 60, 63, 75, 146
Neoplatonism, 116–117, 240
Nevi'im, 58, 101. *See also* Prophets
New Cambridge History of the Bible, 2, 17, 18, 50, 108, 205, 259
Newberry Library, Chicago, 231
Nicaea, Council of. *See* Council of Nicaea
Nicene Creed, 29, 216
Nicholas Maniacoria, 98, 99
Nicholas of Hereford, 200
Nicholas of Lyra, 166–167, 199, 200; double-literal sense, 136–137; Jewish commentary use, 101; *Postilla*, 49, 173–174
Nicholas of Verdun, 244
Nicodemus, 70
Nineveh, 113–116
Noah, 145, 244; ark, 127, 256; wife of, 255
Nonnenwerth, monastery, 162
Norman conquest, 189
Normandy, 155, 166
Normannus, 189
Northumbria, 94, 145, 237
Norwich, archdeanery, 45
Notker of St. Gall, 146–147
Notre Dame, Cathedral, Paris, 126, 164, 169
Numbers, book of, 46
Numerology, 114–115, 116

Observance, the, 223
Octateuch, 54, 87, 151
Office, Divine. *See* Divine Office
Olbert of Gembloux, abbot, 95
Old English Bible, 187–188, 204
Old English Hexateuch (Heptateuch), 66, 186, 189, 190
Old French, 130–131
Old French Bible, 194
Old Latin bibles, 64, 73, 197. *See also* Vetus Latina
Olivi, Peter John. *See* Peter John Olivi
Open Library Project, 264
Oral Torah, 123
Order (*ordo*), 129
Ordines romani, 210–211
Origen, 33–34, 76, 83–84, 87, 142, 143
Orleans, 35, 73, 93–94
Ostrogothic kingdom, 26, 91